1915 · 100 YEARS · 2015

Washington's Revolution

Washington's Revolution

THE MAKING OF
AMERICA'S FIRST LEADER

Robert Middlekauff

Alfred A. Knopf
NEW YORK
2015

THIS IS A BORZOI BOOK
PUBLISHED BY ALFRED A. KNOPF

www.aaknopf.com

Knopf, Borzoi Books, and the colophon are registered trademarks of Random House LLC.

Library of Congress Cataloging-in-Publication Data
Middlekauff, Robert.
Washington's revolution : the making of America's first leader /
Robert Middlekauff.
pages   cm
Includes bibliographical references.
ISBN 978-1-101-87423-3 (hardcover)   978-1-101-87424-0 (eBook)
1. Washington, George, 1732–1799.   2. Generals—United
States—Biography.   3. United States—History—Revolution,
1775–1783—Biography.   4. United States—History—Revolution,
1775–1783—Campaigns.   I. Title.
E312.25.M54 2015   973.3'4092—dc23   [B]   2014020087

Front-of-jacket image: *Washington Crossing the Delaware River,
25th December 1776* (detail) by Emanuel Gottlieb Leutze, 1851.
Copy of an original painted in 1848. Metropolitan Museum of Art,
New York, U.S.A. / Bridgeman Images
Jacket design by Carol Devine Carson
Maps by Mapping Specialists

Manufactured in the United States of America
First Edition

For my son, Sam; my daughter, Holly;
And my grandchildren, Ben Katz, Haley Katz, and Cole Katz

Contents

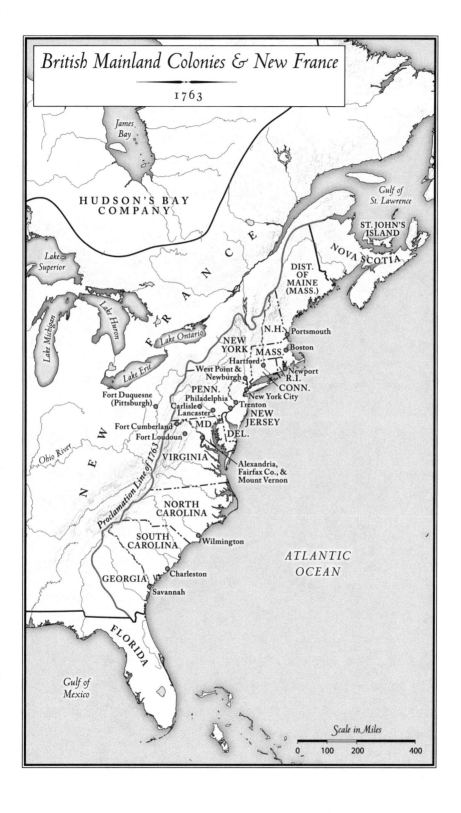

British Mainland Colonies & New France

1763

James Bay

HUDSON'S BAY COMPANY

Gulf of St. Lawrence

ST. JOHN'S ISLAND

NOVA SCOTIA

Lake Superior

NEW FRANCE

Lake Michigan

Lake Huron

Lake Ontario

Lake Erie

DIST. OF MAINE (MASS.)

N.H.   Portsmouth

NEW YORK   MASS.   Boston

Hartford

West Point & Newburgh

Newport

R.I.

CONN.

PENN.

Fort Duquesne (Pittsburgh)

Philadelphia   New York City

Carlisle   Trenton

Lancaster   NEW JERSEY

Fort Cumberland   MD.   DEL.

Fort Loudoun

Ohio River

VIRGINIA

Alexandria, Fairfax Co., & Mount Vernon

NEW FRANCE

Proclamation Line of 1763

NORTH CAROLINA

SOUTH CAROLINA   Wilmington

GEORGIA   Charleston

Savannah

ATLANTIC OCEAN

FLORIDA

Gulf of Mexico

Scale in Miles

0   100   200   400

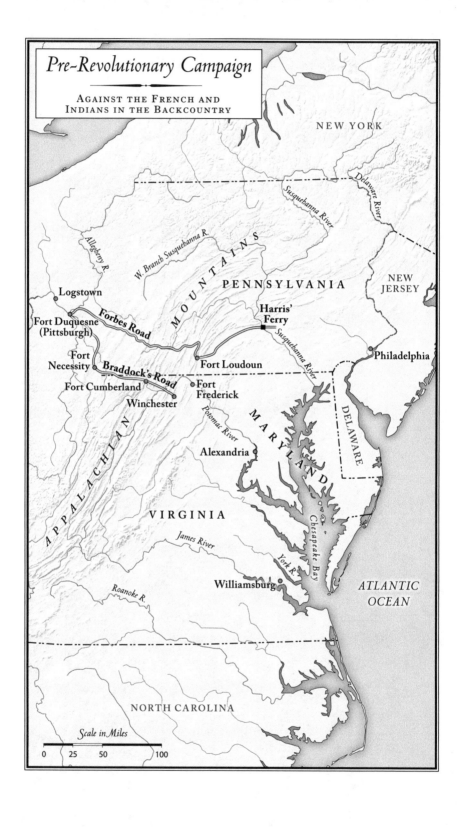

Pre-Revolutionary Campaign

AGAINST THE FRENCH AND
INDIANS IN THE BACKCOUNTRY

NEW YORK

Delaware River

Susquehanna River

Allegheny R.

W. Branch Susquehanna R.

PENNSYLVANIA

NEW
JERSEY

Logstown

M O U N T A I N S

Harris'
Ferry

Forbes Road

Fort Duquesne
(Pittsburgh)

Susquehanna River

Philadelphia

Fort
Necessity

Braddock's Road

Fort Loudoun

Fort Cumberland

Fort
Frederick

DELAWARE

Winchester

Potomac River

M A R Y L A N D

A P P A L A C H I A N

Alexandria

VIRGINIA

James River

Chesapeake Bay

York R.

Roanoke R.

Williamsburg

ATLANTIC
OCEAN

NORTH CAROLINA

Scale in Miles

0   25   50   100

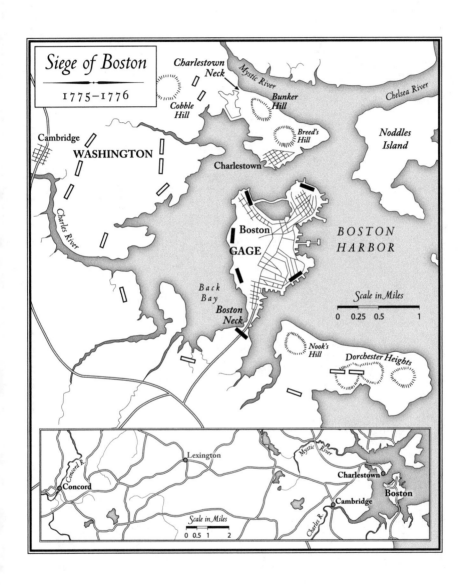

Siege of Boston

1775-1776

Charlestown Neck

Mystic River

Chelsea River

Cobble Hill

Bunker Hill

Breed's Hill

Noddles Island

Cambridge

WASHINGTON

Charlestown

Charles River

Boston

GAGE

BOSTON HARBOR

Back Bay

Boston Neck

Scale in Miles

0   0.25   0.5   1

Nook's Hill

Dorchester Heights

Lexington

Mystic River

Concord R.

Concord

Charlestown

Boston

Cambridge

Charles R.

Scale in Miles

0 0.5 1   2

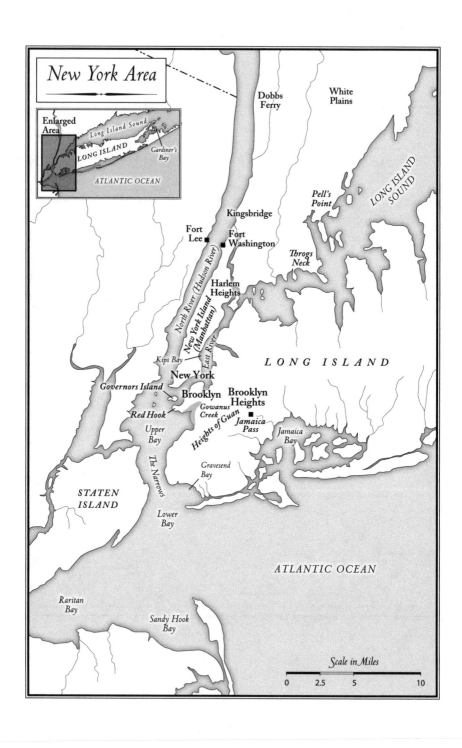

New York Area

Enlarged
Area

Long Island Sound

LONG ISLAND

Gardiner's
Bay

ATLANTIC OCEAN

Dobbs
Ferry

White
Plains

Pell's
Point

LONG ISLAND
SOUND

Kingsbridge

Fort
Lee ■

Fort
■ Washington

Throgs
Neck

North River (Hudson River)

Harlem
Heights

New York Island (Manhattan)

East River

LONG ISLAND

Kips Bay

New York

Governors Island

Brooklyn

Brooklyn
Heights

Gowanus
Creek

Heights of Guan

Jamaica
Pass

Red Hook

Jamaica
Bay

Upper
Bay

The Narrows

Gravesend
Bay

STATEN
ISLAND

Lower
Bay

ATLANTIC OCEAN

Raritan
Bay

Sandy Hook
Bay

Scale in Miles

0   2.5   5   10

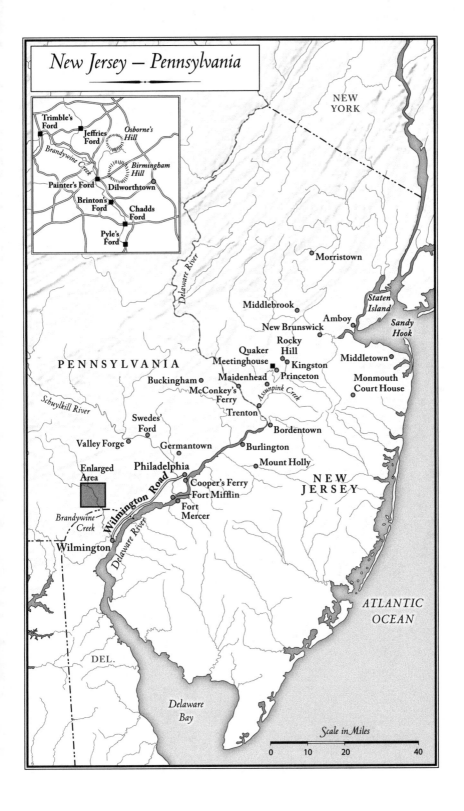

New Jersey — Pennsylvania

Trimble's
Ford
Jeffries
Ford
Osborne's
Hill
Brandywine Creek
Birmingham
Hill
Painter's Ford
Brinton's
Ford
Dilworthtown
Chadds
Ford
Pyle's
Ford

NEW
YORK

Morristown

Middlebrook

Staten
Island

Amboy

Sandy
Hook

New Brunswick

Rocky
Hill

Quaker
Meetinghouse

Kingston

Middletown

PENNSYLVANIA

Maidenhead

Princeton

Monmouth
Court House

Buckingham

McConkey's
Ferry

Assunpink Creek

Schuylkill River

Trenton

Swedes'
Ford

Bordentown

Valley Forge

Germantown

Burlington

Mount Holly

Enlarged
Area

Philadelphia

NEW
JERSEY

Wilmington Road

Brandywine
Creek

Cooper's Ferry
Fort Mifflin
Fort
Mercer

Delaware River

Wilmington

DEL.

ATLANTIC
OCEAN

Delaware
Bay

Scale in Miles

0   10   20   40

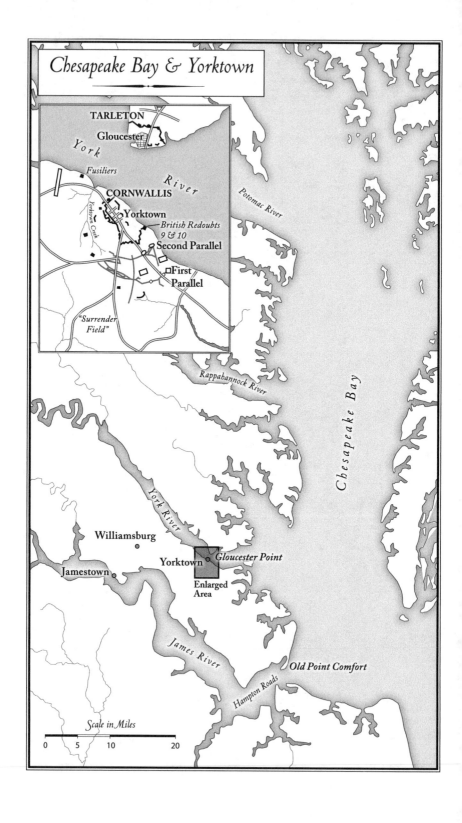

Chesapeake Bay & Yorktown

TARLETON

Gloucester

York

Fusiliers

River

CORNWALLIS

Yorktown

British Redoubts 9 & 10

Second Parallel

Yorktown Creek

First Parallel

"Surrender Field"

Potomac River

Rappahannock River

Chesapeake Bay

York River

Williamsburg

Yorktown Gloucester Point

Jamestown

Enlarged Area

James River

Old Point Comfort

Hampton Roads

Scale in Miles

0   5   10   20

Preface

This book might have been entitled *Washington and the Revolution,* for it deals with both the man and the Revolution. But since Washington's part was so critical to the way the Revolution was fought, I have given it a title that emphasizes his enormous importance to its course and outcome. There was no one on the British side who played a comparable role. The king and his chief minister, Lord North, were political figures who gave much of their time in the years of the war to other matters; and their military leaders in America—Admiral Lord Richard Howe and his brother General William Howe, along with Henry Clinton and Guy Carleton, generals who commanded the army in America, all men of high professional standards—did not impress peers or their enemies in America and France as genuine leaders. In any case, they sought to preserve an empire; Washington overturned it, in a struggle with immeasurable implications for the world ever since.

To tell Washington's story, I have resorted to both history and biography, with the assumption that the two fields reinforce each other. The life Washington led before and through the Revolution requires a careful look at historical circumstances of several sorts, and the ways his action affected the history of this period are matters that cannot be understood without knowledge of his life. He felt the underlying conditions of his time and his life and responded to them in a struggle that affected the Revolution deeply. Washington was always a self-conscious man. He grew during the revolutionary years, but he never lost his self-awareness. Like many Americans of the time, he began as a provincial and became a nationalist, without however shedding all of his provincial skin. A Virginian when he took over the Continental Army, he found himself transformed into an American by the demands of many British measures before 1775. By the middle years of the war, he, an American, had become something more. As the war had changed, so had he; and as he changed, so also did the war and his conception of it. How he mastered himself and the Revolutionary War provides the focus of this book.

PART ONE

Virginian

Prologue

The Young Washington's World

L ong before George Washington's death, Americans began writing about him in terms resembling the descriptions the New England Puritans had used to describe God. The Puritans never claimed ultimate insight into God's essence—God, no matter how thoroughly studied, no matter how lovingly worshipped, remained unknown and unknowable. He could be approached, in a manner of speaking, by listing his attributes—his power and justice, for example—but the list could never be more than a beginning, certainly not a full understanding. George Washington, a mere man, was called godlike while still alive—meaning that he had been chosen by Providence to do great things; he was the being created to take the leading role, indeed the essential part, in leading his country out of the British Empire and into the new world of republics.[1]

The world in which he was born—the British colony of Virginia— was hardly one of republics. On the surface, at the time of Washington's birth, Virginia appeared to conform to the understanding of many in Parliament of what a royal colony should be. The Crown appointed the governor, who almost always was of high social standing in England, and there was a bicameral legislature composed of a Governor's Council, appointed by the Crown, and a House of Burgesses, a lower chamber, elected by and from property owners. There was also a general court, the councilors sitting in a judicial capacity. The republican element in this structure, if indeed it could be called that, was the House of Burgesses.

At the time of Washington's boyhood, the Virginia gentry increasingly controlled the government and much else in the colony. Since the late seventeenth century, the Crown and its local agent, the governor, had struggled to maintain royal authority. They did not exactly lose the struggle, but as the years passed they had to concede that their power had slipped gradually into the hands of men who considered themselves an elite, a group that had amassed land and slaves and in the process set the tone of society.

Compared with Virginian society of the previous century, that of the eighteenth was stable. It was stratified, with a landed group providing most of the government and fashioning a society indebted in several ways to English institutions and attitudes. It was also a slave-owning society, with Africans providing the bottom of the social order and almost all of the manual labor.

There were no conflicts within white society that led to large-scale violence during the years of Washington's youth, but there were fears of a slave uprising. Many plantation masters may have recognized the injustice of holding men in slavery, but few felt guilt, and almost none felt compelled to explain their conduct. Indeed, they seemed to feel little uneasiness in resorting to whipping and chaining their slaves when discipline was called for.

Despite the lack of open conflict, there was a latent tension in the social system, which owed only a part of its nature to slavery. It arose from the system of plantation agriculture itself. One of the assumptions of planters held that the social order in Virginia should remain unchanged, because it expressed the natural order of things. The planter class owned the land and the labor force, and it welcomed new members to its number only if they met well-understood rules and conduct. Standards of behavior and life were to be found in the preferences of this class. The economy underlying this system centered on tobacco.

Growing tobacco had implications that went unrecognized during much of Washington's early years. Seemingly a simple agrarian activity, managing a plantation and producing a crop (later, grains and other commodities began to supplant tobacco) led to activity not ordinarily associated with agrarianism or pastoralism: The crops had to be sold abroad, both in England and on the European continent, involving arrangements with British firms—no small matter when the market lay across the Atlantic Ocean and when no currency was readily available. Then there were the local problems, the management of a slave labor force, and replacing lands quickly worn out by the destructive force of tobacco. To sustain such a system was not a small affair for a class sometimes pictured as a leisured group.

Behind such a system, there had to be a propelling force, and there was—an ethic that valued leisure but also demanded effort and saving. It was a commitment primarily to acquisition and work—in a real sense the Protestant ethic. Planters sometimes fancied that their plantations were simply large families governed by a patriarch, but in fact the life of the average planter was often made up of transactions, not of the contemplation of flocks grazing on green fields. Indeed, there was much hurly-burly in a planter's daily existence.

Their dealings with British merchants brought home to planters that their rights—indeed, their welfare—depended in part on circumstances far removed from the province. In this broad setting—Virginia and western Europe—they learned of their vulnerability, an awakening not always welcomed. In a sense, their business dealings taught them what it meant to live in an empire. Much of the time, that awareness provided reassurance as they saw British power used in ways that served their interests. But at times the lessons of imperial life were different—as they discovered in the 1760s.

The plantation system had taken firm hold of the colony when Washington was young. He took to it almost instinctively, though in his twenties he looked to a career in the British army—not in the cultivation of tobacco. The French and the Indians were the enemies of these years, and he made his early reputation fighting both. Because he was a younger son in a second-level family, he could not find the clear passage to wealth and power that lay before sons of great planters. He was born on the margins of planting society, and if he was not quite an outsider, he was far from the center of the elite.

Two qualities seem decisive in Washington's character—neither had emerged fully in his youth, but both were well developed by the time of his marriage. They were his will and his judgment. Whatever their deepest sources, they remained firm throughout his life. They have to be seen together to be understood; only a few men have them in the proportions found in Washington. His will was an independent force, a compound of energy and hardness. He was not aggressive in a violent way, but he possessed a desire, a forceful impulse, to force action and not give way when resisted. In many men, such a will is often violent, at least in verbal expression and sometimes in physical aggression. Countering, or holding down, even controlling, Washington's will was a sense of restraint—a brake on unrestrained impulse that could yield destructive or self-defeating action. For much of his life his temperament was peaceful—he was not an angry man, and he seldom if ever gave way to uncontrolled passion. He did occasionally seem reckless in battle, and even to lose control, but these were moments only, and they passed in a minute or two as far as we can tell. (A battle at Kips Bay, New York, in 1776 marked one such episode, but it quickly yielded to the self-mastery that distinguished Washington's behavior at virtually every critical moment in the combat of the Revolution.)

Such shifts in conduct may have revealed a glimpse of the passions within him. What comes through in both his inner life and the life visible to others is a prevailing steadiness. He gave no evidence, under almost any circumstances, of deep mood swings. Rather, he seems always to have been given to implacable constancy. The people around him near the end of the French and Indian War, when it seems he gave up all hope of further military service, thought of him in rather romantic terms. He had apparently been a dashing soldier in the war and had shrugged off the dangers of fighting both the French and the Indians. He had in print declared that "I heard Bullets whistle and believe me there was something charming in the sound."

Washington had reached his twenty-second year when he wrote these words. He had wanted to find acceptance in the British army as a commissioned officer, and, failing that, he turned to the traditional role of Virginian planter. He had little idea where such a calling would carry him. At this moment he was a conventional Virginia provincial—not a man who knew the wide world well, but one who had got a taste of it while serving in the wilderness.

The Revolution would offer much more. At its beginning he was a provincial, and during its course he became an American. But he was a most unusual American by war's end: He was an established citizen of the world. This membership in the European world pleased him. It owed much to the French, in particular to the French he had come to know in the Revolutionary War, men of the Enlightenment. He was proud of the connection, just as he was proud to be a Virginian and an American. His feeling was fully justified, for there was substance behind it, a commitment clear in his service to enlightenment and liberty.

Young Washington

Boys in George Washington's Virginia grew up fast. If they were black, they were slaves and had little choice; they were meant for work, and work they did or they perished. At an early age they went to the fields, most commonly tobacco fields, where they helped put in the crop and then helped tend it, pulling the suckers off plants, weeding, and eventually harvesting it. Most boys with black skin could look forward to an existence that revolved around tobacco, and those few who did not go to tobacco fields performed tasks connected to the needs of its cultivation. These boys might learn a craft—black craftsmen shoed horses, others made hogsheads or manhandled them when they were full of tobacco. Some planters, eager to diversify the economy of their plantation, occasionally turned to small-scale manufacturing. A few young blacks learned to make things with their hands—for example on Thomas Jefferson's plantation, Monticello, where he had set up a nailery.

There were many tasks to be done on tobacco plantations. Boys like George Washington recognized that they had to be done, but of course George Washington and his kind did not do them. Boys of Washington's status—he was the son of a tobacco planter—were usually destined to become estate managers. Running a plantation came down to managing land and slaves. By 1732, the year of Washington's birth, tobacco cultivation had been carried on for more than a hundred years, and as a boy he almost instinctively began preparing himself to take his place in the long line of planters. His father, Augustine Washington, who owned land and slaves, was securely in this line, and young Washington hoped he would be.

In fact, Augustine Washington had several fields of interest in speculation and business. Born in Virginia, he had been taken to England for schooling when he was three years old; after a few years he was taken back to Virginia, where he grew up. Augustine Washington's father, Lawrence, had been an attorney who did business in Virginia with English merchants, and Augustine inherited his father's estate. As an adult, he bought and sold land on his own; among his holdings was a section that contained iron. To develop it, he entered into a partnership with Principio Company, an English firm. His relations with Principio proved troublesome to both sides, with disputes carried out across the Atlantic.[1]

In 1729, hoping to resolve the problems with the company, Augustine Washington went to England, leaving behind a wife and three children: Lawrence, Augustine Jr., and Jane. When he returned a few months later, he was a widower, and not long after that his youngest child, Jane, died. Planters widowed did not usually remain without a wife for long, and Augustine followed conventional practice by marrying again. This time he chose Mary Ball, a woman of twenty-three and of a good but not distinguished family. George Washington was her first child, born February 22, 1732, on a plantation sometimes called Pope's Creek, the name taken from a stream that fed into the Potomac River.

Augustine Washington moved often in his son's first years. His family grew as he looked to improve his fortunes, with five more children coming after George—two girls and three boys. The younger girl, Mildred, died, still a baby, in 1740. Augustine was on the move looking for wealth in these years, and though he did not get it, he did not fall into poverty. We cannot tell how he might have fared, for he lived only a little more than eleven years after George's birth, dying in 1743.

Washington's education departed from the usual model preferred by Virginia planters who thought of themselves as gentlemen and hoped that their offspring would prove equal to their examples. What these planters had in mind for their sons was a grammar school education—learning in Latin and Greek and a certain style that demonstrated their promise as leaders in government and polite society. They would also learn, outside of their formal training in school, to manage land and slaves. Displaying comfort and skill in the larger world of politics and society, including overseas commerce, was essential.[2]

Augustine's death removed the possibility that his son would follow his example and attend a grammar school, or board with a tutor who taught the classical languages in either England or America. George's mother, Mary Ball Washington, did not have genteel status, nor did she seem to hold such aspirations for her son. Virtually all of the great founders from Virginia, most notably Jefferson, Madison, and George Mason, were better educated, according to the usual standards, than George Washington. But almost all of these men came from families of greater distinction than the Washingtons.

George Washington was, in his early years, on the fringe of genteel society and to some extent an outsider. As far as one can tell, matters of status did not interest him in the first twelve to fifteen years of his life. Nor did his temperament set him apart, and as a boy and adolescent he resembled in most ways his peers in Virginia. He probably was a quiet youth, perhaps quieter than most of his age. If he wanted to rise in status, it must have seemed that he would have to do it on his own. His father had been a minor planter looking for the main chance; no great forebears could be summoned up to elevate his status, and there was little wealth in the family and no impressive achievements in politics or society.

He seems to have realized that little would come easily to him, and he responded, as he grew older, with effort and resolution. Knowledge of surveying was valuable in a land-rich society, and he mastered its requirements well before he entered manhood. But there was much more to be learned if he was to make his way into gentry society. Washington was an awkward youth and aware of the fact. His size had something to do with his self-consciousness about his appearance. He had large hands and feet, encumbrances in the polite company of any society. Everyone has seen adolescents who seem to act only under duress when they are with their elders and betters. Washington, for a time at least, conformed to this type. Not surprisingly, he turned to a book for help, a guide called *Rules of Civility & Decent Behaviour in Company and Conversation,* whose purpose was to advise boys and young men on how to "keep to the usual Customs," rules instructing readers on, among other things, when and when not to pull off their hats. Besides the specific instances of behavior to avoid or emulate— "bedew no mans face with your Spittle" when you speak, kill no fleas "in the sight of others," "keep alive in your Breast that Little Spark of Celestial fire called Conscience"—the rules conveyed a sense of social status and its importance. The planter class from which Washington sprang needed no instruction concerning its own importance, but the rules provided it anyway, and Washington transcribed some of this teaching into his copybook.[3]

A much better teacher began to affect Washington's life shortly before his father's death. That "teacher" was Lawrence Washington, his older brother, now a veteran of the War of Jenkins' Ear, returned from military duty after serving in a major expedition that captured Cartagena, on the northern coast of South America. He was a dashing figure who had held an officer's commission in the Virginia Regiment that was so important in defeating the Spanish. He arrived back in Virginia in 1742 or early 1743 and almost immediately received appointment as adjutant general of the colony. A few months later he married Ann Fairfax, daughter of Colonel William Fairfax, who had recently built a handsome house at Belvoir, the family estate. Belvoir was about four miles from Lawrence's plantation, which he had named Mount Vernon, after Admiral Edward Vernon, the commander of the expedition against Cartagena.

Lawrence was fourteen years older than George. As a matter of law and practice, the oldest son, having received the bulk of a planter's estate, was expected to care for it and all the family living there. Lawrence followed this practice willingly—and without opposition from his brothers or anyone else. He was an excellent model, thoughtful and modest in style, but leaving no doubt who was in charge.

Lawrence had made a brilliant marriage—he had joined one of the greatest landholding families in Virginia. The head of the Fairfax family was Thomas, Lord Fairfax, the proprietor (in rough parlance, the owner) of the Northern Neck Proprietary, some six million acres lying between the Potomac and Rappahannock Rivers and extending in the West to the Shenandoah Valley. Lord Fairfax did not manage this immense holding; rather, he chose his kinsman Colonel William Fairfax as his agent with full powers to run the business. With this responsibility came Belvoir and informal agreement that the colonel would head the family. William Fairfax thereby became one of the big men in Virginia.

Mount Vernon's proximity to Belvoir undoubtedly had played a part in bringing Ann Fairfax and Lawrence together, and the marriage changed their lives, but in a sense it did far more for George Washington than for Lawrence and Ann. He, a fatherless boy with little wealth and limited prospects, was now a part of a great Virginia family. His tie to the Fairfaxes was soon made stronger, when he became the friend of George William Fairfax, the son of the family's head. Colonel Fairfax clearly approved; indeed, he seems to have taken a liking to Washington almost from their first meeting.

One consequence of these affectionate associations was participation with the colonel and his son in a surveying expedition to locate Fairfax lands in the West. Surveying land was in most respects a simple affair: A survey party mounted its horses and got to work. Washington's initial experience in such a venture had occurred in March 1748, with George William Fairfax and men chosen by his father. Their trip was made primarily on horseback and carried the Fairfax party over the Blue Ridge and down the Shenandoah Valley. William Fairfax claimed significant amounts of land in the valley, and in order to lease it to settlers he had to have it surveyed, with individual lots laid out. George Washington increased his skill as a surveyor on this trip and, more important, got a feel for landownership.

The expedition itself proved to be demanding, as the distances traversed were great, the weather frequently bad, and the accommodations for travelers sparse or nonexistent. Young Washington's responses to the roughness that greeted the expedition were high-spirited at best and rueful at worst. On the fourth night of the journey, he stripped off his clothes in going to bed in primitive quarters on straw that, to his surprise, was covered by only one "Thread Bear blanket." In the middle of the night he discovered why his companions had chosen to sleep under the stars. The blanket proved to house "double its Weight" in fleas and lice.[4]

Washington's eyes were opened to more sights than the "game" that had infested his body during that night. Although he did not remark on the beauty of the sugar trees that he encountered more than once, he was clearly taken by them. The "richness" of the land impressed him even more, and he studied it as he and the others laid out lots along the valley. He also found interesting the Indians the party met. He watched one Indian dance around a large fire and recorded the details of the "comicle" running and jumping that constituted the dance, both actions performed while drums were played and gourd rattles shaken.[5]

The next year, the Fairfaxes lent their weight to a proposal to appoint Washington, their young friend, surveyor for Culpeper County. In this post he continued to survey Fairfax lands in the Shenandoah Valley. While he was serving the Fairfaxes he was also serving himself. An obvious benefit to surveying lands was an opportunity to buy some for himself, and in 1750 he purchased almost fifteen hundred acres.

During this period Lawrence Washington came to his aid in a different manner: He invited his younger brother to live with him at Mount Vernon. Lawrence in these years was not in good health, perhaps having contracted tuberculosis on the Cartagena expedition. By 1751 his sickness had become so serious that he turned to travel abroad for a cure. Late in that year he took George with him to Barbados in search of better health. He did not find a cure, and his young brother caught smallpox, a disease dreaded by all in the eighteenth century. Contracting smallpox proved to be a fortunate event in his life, for he recovered and was from that time immune to fresh exposures. Lawrence avoided the disease but died about six months later after a second, futile voyage to Bermuda.[6]

George had loved his brother and felt grief at his death, but in keeping with a gentleman's code, he kept his feelings to himself. He was one of those people fortunate in his friends, and in Virginia friends may have been important in helping him in his sadness. Years after Lawrence's death, the Fairfax connection proved useful to Washington, leading to his appointment by the Council of Virginia as adjutant of militia for the southern military district of the colony. The Council bestowed the rank of major on him at the same time. He was twenty years old, young for the rank.

Although Washington was a young man, he was not without qualifications for this military post. He was physically imposing—at least six feet in height—strong, and already a splendid horseman. He had shown that he could handle himself in the surveying expeditions across the Blue Ridge for the Fairfaxes and others. He also knew something about the West, and everyone knew that if war or violence came, the most likely action would occur in the wilderness or in the thinly settled areas of the Piedmont and beyond. There the French made claims to the land that Virginians believed threatened their own. Recognition of his talents came the next year, when Governor Robert Dinwiddie sent him off to confront the French in the Ohio Valley, territory claimed by Virginia since the colonies' founding. Governor Dinwiddie did not know Washington well, and chose him for the mission only after talking with William Fairfax. As governor, Dinwiddie had invested heavily in the Ohio Company, recently chartered and granted a half million acres by King George II in the old Northwest. He also carried the responsibilities of protecting the Crown's interests in Virginia. Fairfax, a member of the colony's Council, was also an investor and, of course, a friend of the young Washington. Dinwiddie consulted the Council but not the House of Burgesses and undoubtedly received a report from Fairfax and men like him that Washington, with his background of surveying the West, would do very nicely.[7]

The French presence rested on royal claims first made in the seventeenth century. New France, as Canada was called, had followed a course of development far different from the English colonies to the south, and had attracted few immigrants. While it lacked population and wealth, New France was valued by the French Crown, which nourished hopes of extending its power in North America. Four years before the crisis that led to a great war for empire, the French sought to solidify their claim to the immense area drained by the Ohio River. Explorers sent out by the government in Canada in 1749 made their way on the rivers in the Ohio Country, burying lead plates claiming millions of acres in the valleys and hills. The Indians who had the only legitimate rights to the land were to be shoved aside in treaties that forced them to yield. Indeed, the French and English saw these native peoples as an obstacle except when they could be persuaded to act as allies against the other European power.

When Washington, accompanied by a handful of Virginians and Delawares, arrived in December 1753 at the French headquarters— Fort Le Boeuf, near the south shore of Lake Erie—he presented Dinwiddie's letter, with its demand that the French evacuate the Ohio Country. Although we do not know exactly what the French commander, Captain Jacques Legardeur de Saint-Pierre, thought when he regarded the young officer standing in front of him, we may be certain that it was not fear. He knew that Washington had stopped at Logstown to recruit Indian support for English claims. That only a few Indians joined Washington suggested that the English had little force behind them. The recent history of Indian-white relations, in which the French received Iroquois support against the British, reassured the French about their own backing in the contest for the Ohio Country.[8]

Nothing overly unpleasant occurred in this meeting—Legardeur explained his position firmly but courteously. Washington was, as always, a little stiff, but he behaved with tact and according to form. The French force, he was given to understand, would remain where it was. Larger matters of policy, as far as Legardeur was concerned, would be left to his superiors in Canada.

Four days after this meeting, Washington began the ride back to Williamsburg, arriving in mid-January 1754. He had not wasted his time on this expedition. He had gained experience in dealing with the French and the Indians, and he had learned something about the Ohio Country. More than that, he had used his opportunity well at the French post, for example by examining the fort and counting the number of canoes along the river to get a sense of the French force that might sail down against the English in the spring. One other consequence of this meeting with the French was the lift it gave to his reputation as a man of force and energy. Dinwiddie wanted news of the French presence spread as widely as possible and therefore asked Washington to write an account of the affair. Washington complied, with the *Journey to the French Commandant,* which was published in Virginia and reprinted in Maryland and Massachusetts newspapers and shortly afterwards in London as a pamphlet. It was not an essay of distinction either as literature or as analysis, but it served its purpose.

Hardly back home in Virginia, Washington was commissioned lieutenant colonel of militia, made adjutant of the Northern Department, and then was sent off in April to hold the Forks of the Ohio, at what would become the city of Pittsburgh. He could not have had full knowledge of what he had been sent to do. He knew of course that Britain and France were at peace. In the British government there was concern, however, about French intentions in the Ohio Country, with successive secretaries of the Southern Department, which was responsible for relations with France (and France in the New World), increasingly fearful of French expansionism. These fears were not self-generated, though war with the French in the recent past had disposed British officials to think the worst of their old enemy. Such dispositions in London were strengthened by colonial officials in America, especially the governors of Virginia, Pennsylvania, and New York, who painted the French as aggressors bent on dominating the Ohio Country and threatening their colonies. None was more insistent in conveying such an impression than Governor Dinwiddie. Dinwiddie now dispatched Washington, who himself had no favorable opinion of the French and may have been eager to test his military skill against them.

Besides sending Washington on this second mission, the governor hired men to construct forts and supply houses to oppose French troops and their Indian allies thought to be moving deeper into disputed lands. These men were not trained in the use of arms, or as militia, and they quickly gave way as the French moved down from Lake Erie with the intention of gaining control of the Ohio Country.

The French commander at the Forks, Captain Claude-Pierre Pécaudy, sieur de Contrecoeur, had no orders to attack Washington's Virginians; he could defend himself, but he was not to initiate hostilities. Uncertain of Washington's intentions, he sent Ensign Joseph Coulon de Villiers de Jumonville, with thirty-five French soldiers and instructions to seek out Washington, discover his purposes, and order him out of territory claimed by the French, if Washington had advanced that far. Jumonville's mission was diplomatic, and he had no expectation that his meeting with the British might end in fighting.[9]

Washington, of course, knew none of this, and when on May 27 a small force of his own, made up of militia and Iroquois led by Tanaghrisson, collided with the French soldiers, he gave the French no opportunity to explain themselves. The collision indeed was more of an ambush, in which Tanaghrisson and the Iroquois slaughtered French soldiers attempting to surrender. Washington had given the order to fire into the French after his men had surrounded the French encampment. The French, wholly surprised, put up little resistance and in fact attempted to throw themselves on the Virginians' mercy after the Indians began killing men who were wounded. Washington's description of the affair has the French firing first, the English responding with volleys that killed ten of the enemy and wounded one, and the remaining twenty-one French attempting to surrender. Testimony of witnesses suggests great confusion in the skirmish, with Jumonville being either shot by an Indian or murdered by Tanaghrisson while he tried to read his "summons" explaining his mission and to call a ceasefire. Washington later reported that the Indians, without orders, had scalped and killed the wounded French soldiers. Whatever the truth, Washington appears not as a leader in control of his forces, but as one who allowed control to slip away—if he ever really had it. His famous remark in a letter to his brother John, to the effect that "I heard bullets whistle and believe me there was something charming in the sound," was empty bravado from an officer who recognized something had gone wrong in this encounter with the French.[10]

The clash with the French had one unanticipated effect: It softened the antagonism Washington and Governor Dinwiddie had begun to feel for each other. Frenchmen had died in the confrontation of May 28, an encounter that confused observers then and long afterwards. The entire affair surely was unnecessary, but killing Frenchmen pleased Englishmen in these years, whatever the circumstances surrounding their deaths. Dinwiddie was delighted.

Neither Washington nor Dinwiddie ever acknowledged their feeling about each other, but just a few days before the firefight with the French, Washington complained bitterly to Dinwiddie that neither he nor his officers were paid enough. What he meant was that they were not paid as much as the soldiers in British regiments were, and they resented the disparity. In this complaint he was speaking for himself as well as for his officers and troops; indeed, his own feelings drove his anger as much as anything his troops said. To his credit, he did not scant the interests of common soldiers, though the demands of his officers moved him even more. He knew that common soldiers on enlisting asked immediately who their paymaster was. It was a question with an edge, because the answer was ordinarily the colonel of the regiment. In March, Washington had accepted that responsibility when the appointee Joshua Fry, the officer to whom he was to report, died, and the command with the rank of lieutenant colonel—with the responsibility of paymaster—was given to him by Dinwiddie.[11]

Washington answered his soldiers' discontent with assurances that things would improve once the legislature acted to provide the financial underpinnings of military action. Dinwiddie had worried not that ordinary soldiers might leave the service, but that the officers in the Virginia Regiment and their immediate commander, George Washington, would. The disagreements between the two men had begun before the firefight with the French. Washington had first opened up the question of pay earlier in May. Dinwiddie reacted with bluntness, saying that Washington's complaints were "ill timed" and not "founded in such real Cause as I am sorry to find You think they are. . . . The first objection to pay," he wrote, "should have been made before engaging in the Service." To this Washington replied, "I could not object to the Pay before I knew it," and then reviewed for Dinwiddie's benefit the history of their earlier discussions of pay and why what was offered to a Virginian officer was less than what a member of the British Army in America received.[12] The intricacies of this exchange included references to compensation for certain "necessaries" an officer received or did not receive—the leading example being his "regimentals" (uniforms). Irrelevance soon made its way into the argument, with back-and-forth over pay allowed officers in the 1746 expedition to Canada. Washington also remarked unfavorably on the quality of the rations provided to officers in camp.

At some point in the fray Washington threatened to resign. It was a thought that grew far more from his conception and feeling about military service than from a simple desire to have more pay. He wrote Dinwiddie at this time that the complaints from the officers were "not frivolous," but "are founded on strict Reason: for my own part, it is a matter almost indifferent whether I serve for full pay, or as a generous volunteer; indeed, did my circumstances correspond with my Inclinations, I should not hesitate a moment to prefer the latter: for the motives that lead me here were pure and Noble; I had no view of acquisition but that of Honour, by serving faithfully my King and Country."[13]

There is in this declaration the beginnings of an idea of disinterested service that would grow and lead to action in the Revolution. For now it would carry him into a full-scale attempt to win a commission in the British army. He was surrounded by men who held such commissions, and he would soon serve with them. At this moment, just before he fought an important battle in the Ohio, he felt undervalued, even though he commanded a force of considerable size against an old enemy. The resentments evoked by his situation were not to leave him for years, though they subsided somewhat after the Jumonville affair.

In the two weeks that followed the battle with the French, Washington received supplies and reinforcements from Virginia until his command numbered around four hundred men. Among the supplies were weapons: light artillery, nine guns capable of firing small shells. He also began the construction of a fort at Great Meadows, Pennsylvania, a low palisade of logs enclosing an area that conceivably could hold seventy men. He called it Fort Necessity, but what the fort was for is not entirely clear: It could house supplies, including ammunition, but it was dominated by high ground and was unsuitable for serious defense.[14]

Washington soon revealed that he did not have defense in mind. He had little knowledge of French numbers at Fort Duquesne, at the Forks, but he was determined to drive them out, and in mid-June he began his advance toward them. The French meanwhile had received heavy reinforcements and could soon count a thousand soldiers, more than twice Washington's number. Washington had about fifty miles of rough terrain to cover to get at them and soon found that making his way through heavy woods and hills that seemed like tall mountains would yield little besides many dead horses, broken wagons, and exhausted troops. Near the end of June, he learned that his enemy possessed a much greater force than his own and was on the way to attack. Turning around was humiliating, but he nonetheless retreated to Fort Necessity.

Fort Necessity was not a fort, though it was called one by the English forces. It resembled nothing so much as a circle made by a palisade of recently cut wood, no more than seven feet in height. It was located in a large meadow, surrounded by high ground. The circle—or palisade—was about 53 feet in diameter; its perimeter measured 168 feet. An entrance of about 3.5 feet was cut on the southwest side of the fort. Washington raised Fort Necessity quickly, and claimed that, with it, "I shall not fear the attack of 500 Men."[15] Inside, he had a small, rickety storehouse built—the roof of which leaked, as he was to discover when rain began to fall—and there he stored the small stock of powder and lead he had carried forward. Since the fort could not accommodate all of his troops, he ordered outworks dug—trenches, not redoubts. The soil was soft, almost a marsh, and a few days after the trenches were completed, they filled up with water.

By the time his soldiers reached Great Meadows, in near flight, many were in bad shape. At least one hundred suffered from sicknesses of various sorts, probably induced by bad diet and the unsanitary conditions often found in American camps. Fort Necessity hardly afforded the care that might have readied them for battle.

The Indians were nominally under the leadership of Tanaghrisson, customarily referred to as the Half King in the letters of Washington, who chose this moment to detach himself from the English at Great Meadows. He had expressed skepticism about the effectiveness of the palisade that passed as the fort; he had, after all, seen the powerful structures the French had built and were building at Fort Duquesne. The English fort would not stop anyone of force, he said.[16]

A few days before Washington bottled himself up at Great Meadows, they had listened to him proclaiming the desire of the English to protect Indian interests. Washington had declared in the conference with the Indians that it was the purpose of the governor of Virginia to defend Indian lands that presumably were being threatened by the French. It does not take much thought to imagine how the Indians regarded such assurance. The history that they all knew held scenes of Virginians advancing into the West, pushing the Indians aside when they did not kill them, while converting woods, groves, and meadows into farms and hamlets. If no such remembrances entered into Indian consciousness, the knowledge of French infantry advancing up the river removed any possibility that Indian warriors would throw their lives away defending a circular fence against overwhelming power.

On July 2, Washington received warning that the French were only a few miles away. When he discovered the next day that they were almost upon him, he reacted as if he were encountering the French army in Europe. His first impulse was to march his troops out in a formation designed to array armies against one another in the open. Bravery, honor, and tradition were served in battles fought in such circumstances. There were surely brave and honorable men on both sides in the battle that followed, but the French took the hills that dominated the fort and proceeded to pick off the men crouching behind the palisade and in the outworks. The French looked downward from concealment behind trees and bushes, while the Virginians, exposed in their positions, looked upward and saw few of their enemy. After taking casualties, the Virginians, some of whom had broken into the supply of rum, were willing to surrender. The French offered terms—among them that after surrendering the enemy soldiers would give their word not to return to the Ohio Country for a year, free the French

prisoners they had taken earlier, and supply two hostages, both officers, to secure their agreement to the surrender. Once such terms were
agreed to, the French would allow the defeated to march off with their
arms, colors, and personal property. The terms required Washington's
signature, which he gave in the dim light of candles, unaware that he
was signing a document in French that carried the admission that he
was responsible for the "assassination" in June of Jumonville, a confession of guilt that he did not feel and had no intention of agreeing to.
But his name on this hastily composed document was there and would
be used against him for years afterwards by the French enemy.[17]

It was a costly defeat. Not only had Washington made a damaging
concession to the French version of the struggle for the Ohio Country;
he had suffered one hundred killed and wounded. The day following,
he led his tattered three hundred back to Wills Creek, where many of
them began deserting. They were a broken force; he, though not broken in body or spirit, was badly bruised.

He may not even have thought much about his part in the surrender
of Fort Necessity, but others had, and their judgments soon affected
his own. One in particular, Governor Robert Dinwiddie, seems surprising, for in the weeks immediately following the defeat, the governor concealed his disappointment in Washington. He did not upbraid
him for action that appeared rash or at best poorly planned. Nor did
many others, at least not in public. The House of Burgesses, which like
all legislative bodies was filled with military experts, said little but,
later in September, passed a resolution of thanks to Washington and
his officers "for their late gallant and brave Behavior in the Defense of
their Country in the battle at Fort Necessity." William Fairfax, by now
almost a surrogate father of Washington, wrote a thoughtful and kind
letter of reassurance, comparing the battle at Fort Necessity to "Marl-
boro's Campaigns" as examples of "many wise Retreats performed
that were not called Flights." Comparison to Marlborough would
have pleased any British commander, but whatever good effect Colonel Fairfax hoped to achieve slipped in September when he referred
to the encounter at Fort Necessity as a "rout." Still, the blunt phrasing
did not offend, for Fairfax indicated that he had not lost confidence in
Washington's leadership.[18]

Washington had hardly begun to think through the meaning of his failure at the Forks of the Ohio when Governor Dinwiddie ordered him to return to the western edge of the Blue Ridge Mountains with the Virginia Regiment, a unit that now existed more on paper than in reality, so fragmented were its companies. In the West once more, according to the governor's instructions, he should resume operations against the French. Taken by surprise, Washington objected and managed to postpone anything resembling compliance.

Washington, like most of his colleagues in the army and the legislature, would have welcomed circumstances favoring an attack. But they did not exist. After the battle at Fort Necessity his force simply faded away, wrecked by desertions and unable to replace its losses by recruiting. He explained the impossibility of mounting an attack to Dinwiddie in clear and forceful terms: He did not have the troops needed for further combat, and the few that remained to him were in deplorable condition and short of everything—weapons, clothing, and food. The men, he told Dinwiddie, were now "naked," a description that was not exaggerated by much. The supplies to feed and support an army were also missing; his commissary had little flour and less meat and few prospects of gathering the supplies required in a campaign. Most of all he lacked men—in August he wrote that if he were ordered to get under way, "I will [march], if not more than ten men follow me (which I believe will be the full amount)."[19]

Comments of this sort from Washington had circulated throughout the colony in August and September. He may have been an inexperienced commander, as he sometimes confessed, but he had a feel for the political realities that underlay public policy and military action in Virginia. His awareness of the need for the public's support led him to make a gloomy assessment of the possibility of taking the field soon after the defeat at Great Meadows. He also explained his discontent in person and in writing to members of the House of Burgesses and the Virginia Council. His judgment about what was to be done after the battle at Fort Necessity was clear, and his analysis was quite explicit and direct. It was also correct, as others, even those hot for assaults on the French, came to see. Neither the political leaders in Virginia, aside from the governor, nor those commanding the military forces in Virginia were prepared in military terms for a fresh attempt to take the Ohio. After rebuffs of his requests for money to support further military operations, Dinwiddie agreed to await better weather and a changed attitude in the legislature.[20]

But Dinwiddie also resolved to reorganize the army at his disposal by dissolving the Virginia Regiment and putting its officers and men into ten independent companies, each to be commanded by a captain. He explained to British officials that recent history of "disputes betwn the Regulars & the Officers appointed by me" had convinced him to make this change.[21] He did not say that Washington's complaints had played a major part in this decision, though there is little doubt that they had. Washington had also figured in tensions between regular forces from other colonies and the Virginia Regiment since the beginning of the crisis over the Ohio. He and Captain James Mackay, of the South Carolina Company, had managed to cooperate at Fort Necessity before their defeat, even though they had set up separate camps there, each with its own organization—separate sentries, separate passwords, and separate lines of command. But Washington and his officers resented being treated as inferior to the regulars. Mackay, a captain, had refused to accept the orders from Washington, a lieutenant colonel. Mackay's commission and those of his officers were from the king; Washington and his officers had been commissioned by the governor. In the rank-conscious army, this difference mattered, and the government in England approved of it. Colonel Washington regarded it as unfair, and the injustice of it all came home to him when he came to understand that British regulars expected that orders they gave to colonials, even those with a higher (colonial) rank, were to be carried out. Captain Mackay in this system would command Colonel Washington.

Colonel Washington, full of bitterness, resigned his commission in late October when Dinwiddie, attempting to resolve conflicts, announced the dissolution of the Virginia Regiment and the creation of the new Virginia independent companies. Washington would not accept the reduction in rank and all that it implied about the place of Virginia in the empire.

Resignation of his colonelcy, he told friends, should be understood as an intention to give up military life altogether. Whether he was really convinced that he was through with the military is not clear. There is evidence in his actions that his decision was firm, for he now leased Mount Vernon from his brother Lawrence's widow, Ann Fairfax Washington, who was to remarry soon afterwards. As 1754 ended, Washington began preparing himself as a planter.[22]

Washington was twenty-two years old and of much promise. Nothing could have prepared him for the plunge he had taken into military life. He emerged from the defeat at Great Meadows unbroken but also unwilling to remain a soldier unrecognized by the British establishment. For a few months a planter's life seemed to beckon. Whether he was ready for such a life is unclear, though at times he seemed prepared for anything.

In fact he was still largely unformed. Flaws in his judgment had appeared in the campaign against the French, and nothing in his limited experience in conventional tobacco planting suggested that he was ready to act as an estate manager. To be sure, he had a range of abilities that reassured men who had served with him. They not only respected him; they liked and admired him. He obviously had character, and though his performance in the military campaign of 1754 did not match his talent, he had, in fact, grown as a military leader—and a man.

But his sense that he was still something of an outsider or, perhaps, if not an outsider, a man on the fringe of Virginia society, remained. Coupled with his natural reserve, this sense reinforced his quiet drive and will, and was to remain an underlying condition that helped shape his mind and feeling in the years ahead.

2

The Making of a Soldier

Washington had hardly entered his new life when the British government changed everything. In February of the new year, Edward Braddock was sent to America as the army's commander. Braddock had no special qualifications or record justifying his appointment other than his friendship with Prince William, the Duke of Cumberland—the son of George II and the captain general of the army. He did have administrative ability, had headed British forces on Gibraltar, and knew his way around the two worlds of politics and military affairs, and no one else seems to have craved appointment to the American command.[1]

Once in America, Braddock learned that George Washington probably knew more about the Ohio Country than anyone else and that he had earned the affection and regard of many in Virginia. Washington's reputation recommended him for Braddock's immediate task: recapturing the Forks of the Ohio and driving the French out of the country. It was a mission with which Washington sympathized, and though he could not participate as an officer in the British army or as a colonel of the Virginia Regiment, he volunteered his services. He would serve without pay, he told Braddock, who made Washington a part of his military "family," as the staff of generals in the eighteenth century was often called.[2]

Washington could not help Braddock solve one of his most difficult problems: how to get his army of two regiments plus companies from Virginia to the Ohio Country. Braddock had trusted the governors of Virginia and Maryland to provide the wagons, horses, and forage for them. By April he had assembled an army of about thirteen thousand men, most of them in camp at Frederick, Maryland. He expected to find around two hundred wagons (there were twenty); twenty-five hundred horses (there were two hundred); and forage for the horses (there was almost none, the animals being turned out at night into fields and woods to fend for themselves). Not surprisingly, many wandered away. Braddock and his officers responded in anger that the expedition to take Fort Duquesne could not go forward; it seemed at an end before it started. News of this impending fiasco had made its way to the Pennsylvania General Assembly and to Benjamin Franklin, who paid a visit to Braddock just at the moment when all was to be given up. Franklin promised to supply wagons, horses, food, and forage; how he did this is another story, but he kept his word, and Braddock, with the army suitably supplied, began to move on Fort Duquesne.[3]

Washington soon took the measure of his leader and fellow officers. Braddock's chief of staff, Captain Robert Orme, impressed him, as did Thomas Gage, an officer he would face twenty years later when both were generals. The officers were the only ones, besides a company of Virginians, to whom he accorded respect. Though Washington recognized that the army was large for colonial wars, he soon lost confidence in its ability to get itself into battle. It crawled rather than marched as the June days passed one after another. Some days it managed to move only two miles. There were two reasons for this glacial progress. One was the bloated character of the army itself, consisting as it did of infantry, artillery, wagons, and a mass of supernumeraries—camp followers, including many wives and others of no discernible abilities, servants, and a mound of luggage, much of which would have no redeemable value in battle. The second reason for delay was the need to construct roads to carry this mass westward. The army possessed pioneers, as men who built roads and structures were called, but Braddock had not been able to recruit or hire men of great skill and energy. Then there were the horses. Franklin had performed wonders, but even he could not procure the number needed, and many, according to unhappy officers who examined them, lacked sufficient strength to pull heavy caissons and wagons.[4]

When discontent reached a near-breaking point, Washington advised Braddock to cut out a fighting force and compel the troops to leave behind most of their luggage and their artillery for a dash forward. A lean army could make it to Duquesne before the French there received reinforcements, which everyone with Braddock assumed were coming. Braddock accepted this counsel, and on June 17 some twelve to thirteen hundred men and officers, Braddock with them, left some six thousand behind, with orders to follow with due dispatch.

This flying force, not including Washington, who had recommended it, reached the Monongahela in early July. Washington had been ill, probably with dysentery, but he joined Braddock on July 8. He had been too feeble to ride, and the cart he rode in gave him agonies as it jolted over the road constructed by the pioneers.

Early on July 9, seven or eight miles from Duquesne, Braddock sent Thomas Gage forward with an advance party. He followed with the bulk of the infantry, trailed in the rear by his baggage party. Gage led his advance group out of camp early in the morning. Only a few hundred yards from the second ford of the Monongahela, he struck a combined force of French and Indians. Altogether, some nine hundred men—around 100 French regulars, 146 Canadians, and 637 Indians—had left Duquesne under the command of Captain Daniel-Hyacinthe-Marie Liénard de Beaujeu, a brilliant French officer who had rallied a collection of Iroquois and other Indians, who joined him despite suspicions of French weakness. The French in Duquesne under the command of Captain Claude-Pierre Pécaudy, sieur de Contrecoeur, had not known until July 6 that the British were close by, but the Indians, whose military intelligence surpassed that of both sides, had heard much about their enemy's advance. In particular they had received notice that the British force was large and that it had brought big guns.

When Contrecoeur and Beaujeu learned that the British attack was imminent, they naturally turned to their Indian allies, who had no good reason to welcome the English. But the Ohio Indians had not gathered in numbers in Duquesne, and the few there resisted calls to fight the British. Beaujeu appealed to the remainder in terms that challenged their honor, if contemporary accounts can be trusted. The Indians joined him, and on July 9 the battle was fought.[5]

The first exchange of fire occurred when Gage's advance party ran into the Indians on ground rising from the river. Both sides were surprised by this convergence, but the British fired before the French could get into any sort of fighting position. In all the confusion, the British got off three volleys, the third of which killed Beaujeu. His second-in-command, Captain Jean-Daniel Dumas, then took over, averting an early panic that apparently seized the Indians. This opening favored the British—just about the only good surprise the day held for them.

Recovering themselves, Dumas and his men began to use the cover the woods afforded. Though the area was filled with trees, there was not much brush, and the Indians moved swiftly down the slope on both sides of the rough British column. Historians of the engagement that followed usually argue that the British advance force collapsed in panic almost immediately and in pulling back crowded together with the main body. Certainly they were confused by the Indians' movement in front and along both flanks, and the advance party, in retreat, blundered into the main body coming forward. Contemporary accounts suggest that these soldiers tended to bunch up, in fact to form a tight mass that made it impossible for those at its center to fire effectively at the French and Indians around them. But fire they did—to disastrous effect, for their shots often struck soldiers on the periphery. Several of the Virginians and perhaps the regulars as well attempted to shoot from behind trees. In their confusion, the commingled advance group, the main body, and soon the rear guard shot at their fellows who had taken shelter behind trees or were shooting at the Indians from such positions.

Braddock, Washington, and other British officers made their way into the thick of the swirling center. Braddock soon received a bullet "in the shoulder, & into the Breast," reported Washington, who escaped without a scratch, though "I had four Bullets through my Coat and two Horses shot under me." Nothing that he tried could avert the catastrophe that followed. Three hours of confusion compounded by the fear of Indians—every member of Braddock's army had undoubtedly heard stories of scalping and other mutilations—the screams of the dying and the attackers alike, and the inability to fix the enemy, who seemed almost supernatural in his ability to hide and then spring out from trees and holes in the ground, were enough to drive the British into a mad effort to escape. Washington blamed the "English soldiers." They "broke & run as Sheep before the Hounds, leaving the Artillery, Ammunition, Provison, and every individual thing we had with us a prey to the Enemy, and when we endeavour'd to rally them in hopes of regaining our invaluable loss, it was with as much success as if we had attempted to have stop'd the wild Bears of the Mountains."[6]

The flight carried the mass of men back over the river to the camp of the major body of the army. Colonel Thomas Dunbar of Pennsylvania, in charge there, decided against re-forming the herd that poured in on him. His group and the stragglers made their way to Philadelphia. There was no thought of resuming the campaign, thereby leaving the Virginians exposed, as Washington pointed out to men not disposed to listen.

The defeat of Braddock temporarily shook Washington's self-confidence. His initial response was to ask again what he received by sacrificing himself to military service. He had lost two horses in the battle and was almost killed, as the holes made by musket balls in his coat attested. He was also still sick, and the pain reinforced his self-pity. Then there was another sort of pain: the humiliation felt at being beaten by an inferior force, some three hundred French and Indians. The defeat was "shameful," even "scandalous," he wrote his brother Augustine, and what was worse, it was a defeat "by a handful of men" who had not expected to do more than "molest and disturb our March; Victory was their smallest expectation."[7] His surprise is evident in his resort to a kind of literary excursion in his account to a friend: "see," he said, "the wondrous works of Providence! the uncertainty of human things! We a few minutes before, believed our numbers almost equal to the Canadian force, they only expected to annoy us: Yet, contrary to all expectation and human probability and even to the course of things, we were totally defeated, and sustained the loss of every thing." Others shared his surprise at the defeat—Governor Dinwiddie, for example, wrote the Earl of Halifax in November that Braddock's loss "appears to me as a dream, when I consider the Forces & the train of Artillery he had with him"—and in both America and Britain the public scorn piled up.[8]

Washington, who felt the humiliation of the affair, did not join the critics of Braddock. His restraint did not come from a sense of responsibility for the disaster; he had given advice to Braddock, of course, but he had not shared command. In fact he had fought bravely and seems to have led the rescue of Braddock when bullets cut him down. Turning on Braddock would not have been an honorable act, and then there was his concern for British officers, among them Captain Robert Orme, who were present and were comrades as well as colleagues.

Orme, an officer in the Coldstream Guards, served as Braddock's principal aide-de-camp and found a sympathetic friend in Washington. The two men liked each other and, if their letters can be trusted, talked with a candor unusual between regular and provincial officers. Orme mounted a defense of Braddock before leaving America for home, and Washington, though not so vehement in his assessments, agreed that Braddock should not be blamed for the defeat.[9]

He did not spare the regular British enlisted men. The Indians had overpowered everyone, according to all accounts of the battle, but the Virginians had never given way to panic. The regulars had lost their nerve and, flummoxed by the Indian skill and tactics, had run away, giving up despite the bravery of their officers, including their commander, who, refusing to run, lost his life. They resembled nothing so much as "sheep before hounds." The loss of battle tore at him, but it freed whatever penchant he had for invective, and the words "shameful" and "cowardice" filled his letters about the British loss—he would always hold that the loss itself was British rather than Virginian.[10]

Washington's pride was at stake in the days following the battle, and he appears to have been divided in his feelings about continuing a military career. His disposition to give it up, however, arose from more than the sense of humiliation; an awareness of self-interest also had a part, though he may have exaggerated this to convince friends who wanted him to remain in the army. He knew that they would react with sympathy when he listed his losses, such as the two horses killed in the battle, and the low returns that came to him as regimental commander—little pay and impaired health. He had also complained for months about the miseries of recruiting men who hated the thought of military service. Their lack of discipline once enlisted and their propensity to desert before, during, and after combat troubled him. The picture he painted for himself, his friends, and observers seemed to suggest that he was finished with military life.[11]

Yet within two months he accepted command of the Virginia Regiment, shortly after it was offered by Governor Dinwiddie at the end of August. He had not contrived a dilemma in his conversations and letters about the Braddock campaign; rather, he had revealed a variety of emotions, including a mild revulsion from further military service. What he really felt seemed unclear, even to him.

His deepest attachments, however, were to the army and the idea of command. Dinwiddie did not fully understand Washington's attitudes, and when Washington responded favorably but with certain caveats, the governor was relieved but also somewhat unhappy at having to accept these conditions. Washington's principal requirement was that he be allowed to choose his own officers. The regiment ordinarily was composed of ten companies, each with a captain. These officers were crucial to the army's success and in fact could make or break the regiment and its commander. Washington pointed this out to Dinwiddie, saying that his "honour" depended upon their "behaviour," a statement based on experience. His use of the word "honour" recurred throughout his life and seems to suggest that what people thought about him governed his conduct. To be sure, he was always concerned about his reputation and guarded it carefully, but "honour" had deeper and wider meanings. When Washington referred to his "honour," he was thinking of more than his standing with the public or his own kind, gentlemen or leaders in the army or Virginian society. All these relationships were important constituents of his place in the world. But "honour" lay deeper in his essential nature—his attachment to truth, honesty, and responsibility to others. The war forced a process that defined him, fashioning, in fact, what he was as a man. The process was in full action in 1755, and the next three years advanced it. What grew most in his character was his personal strength, a disposition to hold to his certainties, all summed up in a profound sense of "honour."[12]

Taking up his assignment as commander of the Virginia Regiment, he plunged into problems he had become familiar with in the previous two years. The first was basic: how to command a regiment that had few officers and almost no men of ability and experience. In the fall of 1755 he chose, with the help of the governor and others, the captains who were to head the regiment's ten companies. Recruiting soldiers for these companies proved to be a problem that defied solution. He tried during the next three years to solve it in several ways, the principal one an appeal to the governor and the legislature for money to lure men into his army and to pay them after they joined. This was a reasonable course of action that ran up against official inaction. Whether Washington understood the absence of public support for the militia is not altogether clear. He certainly recognized that Virginians did not wish to serve without compensation; he himself had complained occasionally about his own pay, but when men who had not been paid deserted, he rarely explained their action as arising from their financial needs.

To him, irresponsible conduct in the ranks—refusal to obey orders in a timely way, surly responses to orders, slovenly appearance, or sloppy handling of weapons, including firing them off when not in battle, among other unacceptable aspects of conduct—all were evidence of some lack of personal worth and not simply responses to the misery of military life. And when his troops ran away from camp or, worse, from battle, he may not have understood that the circumstances of their lives in the army drove their actions, not a lack of courage.[13]

At some level, he did of course understand that these underlying conditions of a soldier's life—training, pay, and food, shelter, and arms—had much to do with their performance. He was never indifferent to his soldiers' welfare, but he was impatient with their failures. To his credit, he was also impatient with his own, even though he generally demonstrated confidence and strength in his leadership.

The men under his command in these years were not satisfactory soldiers. Judging from his orders, Washington told his officers of his dissatisfaction and almost immediately laid down requirements for training intended to prepare men for battle. Accurate shooting appeared in his scheme of training, as did moving troops in and out of favorable positions for combat. (Before much time for preparation passed, he evidently gave up on the possibility of fielding an army capable of accurate fire if it recruited unqualified men.) What he most desired was men practiced in handling weapons. Find marksmen, he instructed recruiters; there was not much time to train men unaccustomed to shooting. He needed men who could kill Indians who fought from behind trees—"bush fighters," a term that frequently entered his letters and orders from 1755 on.[14]

Washington's desire to have a disciplined and skilled regiment was not shared by his troops. The regiment in 1755 was a skeleton force. Neither adding to their number nor training them proved successful, though he never eased up on either task. Early in his service as commander of the regiment, he wrote that his orders were obeyed only "with my drawn sword" and that inhabitants along the frontier sometimes threatened "to blow out my brains." Undoubtedly, there was some rhetorical excess in his accounts of getting compliance to his orders, but not much.[15]

There was no excess at all in his accounts over several years of his troubles with Captain John Dagworthy, the leader of the Maryland troops. Dagworthy had been with Braddock's forces in their disaster and had been left behind by Colonel Dunbar when he led the remnant of the defeated to Philadelphia. Dunbar ordered Dagworthy to Fort Cumberland, in Maryland, with small numbers of Maryland and Virginia soldiers. Dagworthy took his assignment seriously, perhaps with the sense that he had authority over the entire area of the Maryland and Virginia western settlements. The Virginians, especially Washington, defined the borders of power differently, and though Washington thought that Fort Cumberland was badly located, he believed his own claim to command there, as elsewhere, should not be challenged. What made matters worse at this time was Dagworthy's claim to a royal commission, which would make him more than Washington's equal. (Washington's commission was from Dinwiddie, a colonial governor.) Indeed, Dagworthy saw himself as a commander of the whole force, Virginians as well as Marylanders. The dispute over command was to linger for many months, and brought into focus for Washington his need of a commission as a king's officer.[16]

He had entertained such thoughts, of course, long before Dagworthy fouled the lines of command. Several of his officers in the Virginia Regiment shared his desire; holding a royal commission offered many advantages, among them higher pay and membership in an army certain of support of all kinds. There was also the matter of prestige. Whenever the two sorts of armies met—regulars and colonials—the regulars used every means to assert their superiority, and the colonials suffered in the fashion of inferiors everywhere. Neither group concealed its feelings, which sometimes led to foolish actions, as Washington had discovered at Great Meadows the year before.

If conflict with Dagworthy had not existed, Washington's nerves would not have been so ragged, but he would still have agitated for a change in the status of Virginia's regiment. He had hoped for a new policy when he took command in August, and in early 1756 Dinwiddie gave permission for an appeal to the commander of all British forces in America, Governor William Shirley of Massachusetts. Washington rode to Boston in February and received a sympathetic but cautious hearing. Shirley obliged him by agreeing that Captain Dagworthy's authority did not extend to command of the Virginia Regiment but did not agree to issue a royal commission to Washington.[17]

By this time concern over incursions by French-inspired Indians had again appeared, and Washington had little opportunity to persuade anyone else of his need for a commission from the Crown. Indeed, the immediate and persistent menace of the Indians proved intractable to all efforts to meet it. At no time in 1756 or 1757 did the Indians undertake an operation with a large concentrated force; instead they relied on small attacks, usually by less than fifty warriors. Such attacks were made at about the same time or within a few days of one another, by scattered and widely separated bands, hard to discover and harder to oppose with organized force because of the skill and speed of the attackers.

In April 1756, Washington thought that the frontier, as he called the edge of settlements in the West, was near collapse, and he predicted that unless the depredations of the Indians were eliminated, "the Blue-Ridge will soon become our Frontier." The fighting qualities of the Indians had drawn his respect, and he wrote Governor Dinwiddie that, "however absurd it may appear, it is nevertheless certain that five hundred Indians have it more in their power to annoy the Inhabitants, than ten times their number of Regulars. For, besides the advantageous way they have of fighting in the Woods, their cunning and craft are not to be equaled; neither their activity and indefatigable Sufferings: They prowl about like Wolves; and like them, do their mischief by Stealth."[18]

Washington never believed in fighting the Indians on their terms, but the tactic he favored—a major expedition in force against Fort Duquesne, an important base for Indians—could not be undertaken until 1758, when General John Forbes, by then the British commander, collected a major army. Forbes would gather in that year a fairly large number of soldiers and would be unencumbered by the suggestions and demands of a colonial legislature. Washington was well supplied with such burdens, principally from a governor and a House of Burgesses. At times he could count on troops from Pennsylvania and Maryland to lend support, but these times were brief, and the soldiers were under their own commanders.

What could he do in 1756 and 1757 to mount a defense of the scattered settlements of Virginians in the West? He found himself responding to the Indian raids through limited forays by his own undermanned regiment, almost always after farmers had been slaughtered, their houses burned, and their livestock and crops destroyed.[19]

The governor and the legislature had insisted that forts placed at important points on the upper reaches of the Potomac and its tributaries would afford protection against the marauders; Dinwiddie called them "stockade forts," but they usually were nothing more than palisades and a building or two. They were seen as places from which Virginia forces could operate, most often emerging on patrols or in pursuit of Indians who attacked farms located fairly close by. They did not prove to be of much value, as the Indians slipped by or around them whenever they chose not to attack the soldiers within the stockades. The troops frequently demonstrated that they preferred to remain within the forts rather than fight the Indians outside. Desertion offered a remedy to reluctant fighters when the forts failed to establish their worth. Washington had opposed their use, expecting that they would scatter the Virginia Regiment, not enable it as a cohesive unit to establish a useful defense.[20]

Fort Cumberland troubled him even more in 1756 than the smaller stockade forts and, he argued, ought to be abandoned, its garrison pulled back to Fort Loudoun, at Winchester, Virginia. His reason for this judgment was that Cumberland was useless against the Indians who slipped by easily and conducted their raids south of it. They did not attack it; they ignored it and made their way around it with ease. Although Washington did not spend much time pointing out that Fort Cumberland lay in Maryland, he did point it out, and noted that Virginia was supplying Maryland troops stationed there. This was not a minor matter. It was a continual source of resentment that festered until the war reached its climax.[21]

The old adage says that "failure teaches more than success." If so, Washington learned much in the mid-1750s, for he and his Virginia forces failed repeatedly. Their failures were not in spite of strength—they had little, and the weaknesses of their fighting ability overwhelmed all of Washington's skills, which were in the process of development.

Almost from the time he took over the leadership of Virginia's forces, he realized that he must learn the full extent of the problems of defending the West. But it was not until November 1756 that he made an inspection that carried him through the settlements, from Virginia into the Carolinas. He was not surprised by what he found; he was disgusted. By this time his convictions about the incapacity of the militia were well established, and he found nothing to change his mind. The militia in Frederick, Hampshire, and Augusta Counties simply appalled him, and he described their condition in a letter to Dinwiddie. In riding to the Augusta courthouse accompanied by militia, he found that they galloped along like a mob on horseback, heedless of security, "with order, regularity, circumspection and vigilance . . . matters of derision and contempt." That this group reached the courthouse in about seven days without being interrupted by the Indians he attributed to "the protection of Providence." Otherwise, he said, "we must have fallen a Sacrifice, thro' the indiscretion of these hooping, hallooing, Gentlemen-Soldiers!"[22]

These complaints about the militia covered only a small part of the indictment he drew up against them in the letters to the governor and others. He had long reported the difficulty of attracting them to military service. Some would agree to only a month's enlistment, and half of that time was spent coming to camp and going home. In the western settlements, militiamen lived off the inhabitants they were to protect. While riding with a militia company, Washington watched with revulsion as the group slaughtered cattle before every meal, eating only part of the beef and then, on resuming their march, refusing to take what was not consumed, instead killing more cattle when they next ate. They would "sooner starve than carry a few days' provisions on their backs," he said.[23]

His conclusions about the forts followed naturally from his analysis of the militia: They were virtually useless, their garrisons incapable of maintaining discipline or an alert watch for marauding Indians. Only one captain was present in the forts when he visited on his tour of inspection. Fort Cumberland took its place at the top of his list of supposed strong points—he, of course, regarded it as anything but strong and remarked on its faulty location in his report to Dinwiddie. With protections of this kind, the people of the backcountry were disappearing, and Washington predicted that in a little time, "scarce a family will live in Frederick, Hampshire, or Augusta Counties."

Much of what Washington desired in a policy designed to meet the threat from the Indians and the French was well known to the governor and the legislature. The most effective way of defeating these enemies in the West would involve an offense—a march to Fort Duquesne, destroying Indian settlements along the way and in the end defeating the French, who supported the Indians in their attacks in Virginia. He soon came to see that the government in Williamsburg would not adopt this policy—not out of a fear or love of the French, but because of a belief that it would cost more in money and men than Virginia could give.

Washington had pushed his plan whenever he could, in letters to the governor and to John Robinson, Speaker of the House of Burgesses, and in meetings with them and others in Williamsburg. He was an active but unpersuasive advocate. Knowing the limits within which he was expected to observe, he suggested that lesser means should involve the frontier inhabitants themselves. If they could be persuaded to abandon their isolated plantations in favor of nearby townships, defense of them could be provided by the small force in existence, presumably at Winchester.

Washington laid out the story of weakness in the West in detail on November 9, 1756, after returning from his tour of inspection. Dinwiddie reacted in anger a week later, characterizing Washington's charges against the militia as "vague." He claimed to want details (names of the offending militia, perhaps) about the behavior Washington had described. Dinwiddie insisted that he had heard it all before, and Washington's repetition of it failed to help him raise the militia to an effective level. The charge of vagueness apparently applied to only two of the three counties Washington had visited; as for the third, the "Charges attending the Militia of August is monstrous . . . a great Imposition on the County." On two points he seemed to agree with Washington: "the necessity of an offensive war" and that the use of the forts "will be a poor defense to our Frontiers."[24]

Dinwiddie's comments on all these matters were preliminary to the meat of his reply—a direct order to Washington to march one hundred men at Winchester to Fort Cumberland, which he was to make as strong "as you can in Case of an Attack." This order made it clear that Washington was to move his command himself—not leave the shift to a subordinate. As for the fort at Winchester, a "subaltern" officer was to be left in charge there. Dinwiddie delivered these orders, he said, with the backing of the Virginia Council, in Williamsburg, and enclosed the minutes of its meeting of November 15. About three weeks later he reported that John Campbell, Earl of Loudoun, now in overall command of British forces in North America, had written stating his emphatic agreement that Fort Cumberland should not be abandoned but, indeed, strengthened. According to Dinwiddie, Lord Loudoun had issued a warning against leaving supplies behind if Cumberland were abandoned. Such action, Loudoun purportedly wrote, "will not have a good Appearance at Home."[25]

Dinwiddie's rebuke, with its order to reinforce Cumberland, arrived a few days later, and Washington, on his way to Williamsburg, wasted no time in answering it. His letter did not evade any of the governor's charges, but explained all that Dinwiddie found objectionable. One such matter concerned Washington's tone in his letter of November 9, on the subject of the Catawba Indians, which Dinwiddie had considered "unmannerly." Washington said in this connection that he "intended" no insults to anyone, and that in fact he "endeavoured to demean myself in that proper respect due to Superiors." Nor did he intend to conceal anything about the misbehavior of militia officers—a charge made by Dinwiddie—but tried to hint in his comments that this was a problem for others to address. (Washington's authority did not extend beyond the Virginia Regiment to the command of the militia.)[26]

The most significant matter raised by Dinwiddie was Fort Cumberland, "an affair" he characterized as being "of great Consequence." So "great," apparently, that he convened the Virginia Council, which advised reinforcing it with one hundred men from Fort Loudoun.[27]

Washington's next letter, on November 24, 1756, told the governor that he did not have one hundred soldiers at Winchester to send to Cumberland. By Washington's count, he would have only eighty-one men available in early December to send off. But send them he would, he said, even if it meant leaving Fort Loudoun unprotected and the "Kings Stores" defenseless. The fort was not quite finished, and the materials there for completing the construction, he said, would be "pillaged & destroyed" by Winchester's inhabitants. Dinwiddie's surprise at Washington's report that shifting one hundred soldiers from Fort Loudoun to Cumberland would leave that fort and Winchester virtually without a defense was evident in his response. Surprised but not

moved to change his orders, he added to Washington's disgust by telling him that if he could not move the eighty-one from Fort Loudoun,
he should draw the men from the garrisons of stockade forts. Washington saw such a move as making matters worse, but he complied,
and the transfer was made in the next few weeks. He was to write
Dinwiddie three more letters in early December. The first reminded
Dinwiddie once more of the consequences of shifting so many men
and resources to Cumberland. Though the governor in the past had
expressed a concern for the suffering of settlers exposed to Indian
raids, his willingness to shift soldiers from Virginia to Fort Cumberland seemed to betray an indifference to the consequences for those in
and around Winchester. Washington's letter reported "the terror and
consternation" of the people under the protection of Fort Loudoun. It
also provided a list of material losses that could be expected if the fort
were stripped of its garrison. Ultimately, he concluded, Winchester
itself would be captured by the enemy.[28]

Despite his ragged protests against shifting headquarters and himself to Cumberland, he made his way there early in the new year. He
had declared that he would obey the governor's orders, and he did.

It was to be only a short stay, for in May John Dagworthy assumed
command of Fort Cumberland with Maryland troops. The British had
ordered the change, in part at least because the fort lay outside of Virginia, in a location that called for Maryland responsibility.

Washington had carried out his orders, but before he acted he went
behind the governor's back with a letter to the newly appointed commander in chief in America, Lord Loudoun. Here he elaborated without distortion the weaknesses in the regiment's structure and in its
public support. Its men were deficient in skills and character, thanks to
the method of their recruitment. Many of those taken from the counties' draft were "Vagrants" and "Miscreants," ill disciplined and prone
to desertion. Good and bad alike were frequently owed back pay and
were without clothing. Uniforms seemed to be nonexistent. Whatever
the soldiers' condition, there were too few of them, and he believed
that had there been greater numbers of troops, they would have been
no match for the Indians, who were skilled and savage in their tactics.
What he told Loudoun was a mixture of the history of the regiment's
struggle and an explicit statement of its grievances. Washington also
offered up flattery of Loudoun, awkwardly joined to a request that the

Virginia Regiment be made an official part of the British army, a "bet-ter Establishment," in Washington's term. He did not shrink before the task of recommending himself by invoking General Braddock's name, saying that had Braddock "survived his unfortunate Defeat, I should have met with preferment equal to my Wishes." Braddock had prom-ised "to that Purpose," he told Loudoun, and so had William Shirley.[29]

This claim for himself followed a discussion of the difficulties of waging war in America. The implication was obvious: He had per-formed well, and he deserved the recognition that a royal commission would confer. His recitation of the difficulties he had faced was not an exaggerated account, and the problems he laid before Loudoun were the same ones he had complained of to Dinwiddie. When the conflict with the French began, Washington wrote, it was greeted in Virginia as a "Fiction," indeed a scheme to "promote the Interest of a private Company." He was referring to the Ohio Company, an organization of investors, mostly American, who had organized to open up the Ohio Country. Skeptical of warnings that the French were at work to extend their power into the West, Virginia's leaders delayed a response, and before anyone knew it the French had seized control of the Forks of the Ohio by building Fort Duquesne.[30]

Loudoun was not inspired by Washington's letter to provide solu-tions to the problems of the regiment; indeed, he probably did not bother to read the letter, though an aide who replied for him wrote that the commander seemed pleased with Washington's account. Washing-ton had been determined to see Loudoun even before he wrote this report on his troubles, and in February 1757 he rode to Philadelphia to talk with him. Loudoun let him cool his heels until late March and then, in their meeting, snubbed him.

For the next two months, little was accomplished in pulling Vir-ginia's forces together or in creating a strategy that would provide a coherent defense against Indian raids on western settlers. Loudoun undoubtedly had much on his mind besides Virginia and Maryland. South Carolina seemed open to invasion by both the French and the Indians, and the colonies to the north required attention if the French were to be defeated.

Rather than confine his attention to Virginia, he now looked to the problems of all the southern colonies and ordered reinforcements for South Carolina, including a large contingent from the Virginia Regiment under Lieutenant Colonel Adam Stephen, Washington's second-in-command. He also ordered the placement of those remaining at Fort Cumberland in the scattered frontier forts. Fort Cumberland was to be turned over to Maryland forces under Captain Dagworthy, who now, by assuming its command, unintentionally did something that pleased Washington.

Instead of protesting against the scattering of the companies of his regiment, Washington followed the new arrangements carefully and urged on their chiefs, all officers who in a sense were responsible to him. He knew of course that the transfer of units of the regiment was temporary, and no doubt he also recognized that opposition to Loudoun would not advance the process of making Virginia's officers and himself regulars in the British army. He also seemed to allow himself to think again about leaving military service altogether. In these spring months, he shipped a small amount of tobacco—grown at Mount Vernon—to England, using a British firm as his agent. He also took more interest in the family's plantation, though he had little time to act as a planter.

He gave much more of his time to the affairs of the regiment. He pointed out to Dinwiddie that the power to convene courts-martial had lapsed, and he argued that it should be renewed immediately. The practice of the country people of abetting deserters was also troubling, and he looked for measures that would discourage or even prevent it. There was a natural sympathy between the small farmers and unwilling soldiers, and Washington strove to alter it by pointing to the army's need for men who remained on duty, not running away, if it was to defend settlers against Indian raids.[31]

These were matters that defied solution, but as persistent as they were, the need to keep friendly Indians on the colonial side was even more important. There were several tribes that had aligned themselves with the British; most important were the Cherokees and the Catawba in the Carolinas. There was also a scattering of others who preferred the British to the French; most in recent years had drifted westward as settlements of the Americans had gradually filled up lands that once were rich hunting grounds. The lives of all Indians were not easy, and the demands on them by the British and the French further complicated this. They had learned early on that neither European power kept its word, and they had responded for years with a mixture of defection and loyalty. Neither course proved satisfactory but their choices were limited.

Along with most white colonials, Washington regarded the Indians as "savages"—a word he used to describe them for many years—but he recognized their political skills. The Indians assumed their positions in the struggle according to how it would serve their interests, a way of judging that Washington shared. Both French and British Indians negotiated their allegiances carefully and with force. They knew that they were needed, and they did not disguise their motives. Washington did not expect anything else and he proved himself as demanding a party as the Indians in all the negotiations. The hand he held was often empty, however, and he pressed the governor and legislature to keep up support of the Indians. Their needs, especially those of the Creeks and the Catawba, came down to food, arms, and clothing—demands similar to those of the Virginians he led.[32]

For several weeks in midsummer 1757, the French-led Indians were especially prominent in his mind. For on June 14, Captain Dagworthy wrote from Fort Cumberland that he had received a report from six Cherokees that the enemy Indians were on the move from Fort Duquesne to attack in considerable force. This, Dagworthy's report implied, was not a small raid but a major effort to destroy the enemy and to capture Cumberland and other key points. Dagworthy's reports about this attempt suggested that the invading force included French troops and artillery. Washington wrote his superiors—Governors Dinwiddie and Horatio Sharpe, among others—and began establishing a defense appropriate to the threat. He also considered taking some countering action but did not have time to do anything before he learned that Dagworthy was the victim of a faulty translation of the Indians' report. There was not an expedition of the enemy coming down on them, and Dagworthy had reached conclusions based on incomprehension of the Indians' language.

Washington had never thought well of Dagworthy, but he restrained himself and made no comment on his old adversary's unreliability, instead writing letters to those who had shared his alarm that the Indians were preparing an all-out attack. Perhaps there was a kind of charity in his restraint; he had appealed to the governor for help in dealing with the Indians before Dagworthy's folly. He had become convinced of his own "incompetency" in understanding them; someone else and different methods were needed. Washington's clarity of mind and his willingness to learn from evidence were implicit in his suggestions on how to establish a new relationship with the Indians. He described his plan to John Robinson as "exactly agreeable to the french policy of treating them." The French "have a proper person appointed to the direction of these affairs; who makes it his sole business to study their dispositions and the art of pleasing them." Such a person would have the power to negotiate with them and "reward them for every piece of service; and, by timely presents . . . obtain very great advantages." The reason for confining the relationship with the Indians to one person was to escape from present practice, which saw Indian affairs as "every bodies business," with everyone attempting to please them, a situation in which "*one* promises *this,* and another *that,* and few can perform anything, but are obliged to shuffle and put them off, to get rid of their importunities." The Indians, Washington pointed out, respond by accusing us of "perfidy and deceit" and give little service.[33]

Washington nominated Christopher Gist as the agent to the Indian tribes. Gist was a longtime trader with the Indians who held him in "great esteem." He was "well acquainted with their manners and customs," honest, indefatigable, and patient. The Indians would respond well to him, and, though Washington did not say so, it was obvious that he would as well. Gist had been with him in the Braddock expeditions.

Shifting some of the responsibility of supplying the Indians to Christopher Gist seemed a good, though partial, solution to the problem of keeping them in the friendly fold, but whatever was done in late 1757 could not conceal the mindless drift in British policy and operations. Governor Dinwiddie, who may have been ill at this time, felt helpless and tended to blame Washington for the failure to stop Indian incursions. Washington, who was still sick, did not feel helpless and wanted to take action. He had by this time pretty well given up the hope that the governor would find the men and supplies to allow an attack on Fort Duquesne, or even a lesser attempt to shut down the raids by Indians. He had retained this hope for more than two years, and repeated his requests for aid so often that they seemed to Dinwiddie like demands. The two men were tired of each other, and when in September Washington asked for permission to leave Fort Loudoun for Williamsburg, in order to better explain himself, he received a flat denial accompanied by an accusation that he was ungrateful to the governor. The dispute between the two was old by this time and reflected little credit on either one. Dinwiddie seems to have suspected that Washington's motives in asking for leave rested on little more than a desire to have a good time with his friends in Williamsburg. Washington denied the accusation and explained that he wanted to settle his accounts before the governor, who had recently resigned and left the colony for England. A few weeks later, in October, he added that, "among many other reasons," he had wished to give "a more succinct account than I cou'd in writing the immovable determination of all the Settlers of this country" to leave the West in the face of the persistent Indian attacks. For, as he put it, "if we adhere to our destructive, defensive schemes, there will not long be one soul living on this side of the Blue-Ridge."[34]

Washington was not the only figure of authority pleading for a greater effort to protect frontier settlements. John Robinson, from his post as Speaker of the House of Burgesses, also urged that the colony come to the aid of a suffering West. Dinwiddie was packing his bags for England at this time and awaiting a ship to carry him away, but he remained committed to holding the frontier. The means he favored did not differ from Washington's, though he seems to have held more faith in the militia. What he never fully explained to his critics was that successive military commanders in chief in America failed to share the urgency felt in Williamsburg and the West. The British Empire was a creature of power, but both reluctant and, at this time, incapable of bringing it to bear in the southern colonies.[35]

By late summer Washington considered the possibility of securing the frontier almost lost, unless friendly Indians could be coaxed into taking a leading role in defense of Virginia. A buildup of the regiment would not occur, and he looked to Indians, in particular Cherokees, to furnish the reinforcement of the regiment, weakened by general neglect and a steady flow of desertions. The Cherokees were, he wrote Dinwiddie, a "brave people" who had "behaved nobly," but when they appeared at Fort Loudoun, they found almost nothing in material support—weapons, food, and clothing, all items that they expected to receive. How they were to be held in the British interest was a mystery he could not solve, and he expected them to return home. Some, he conceded, would find their way to the French.[36]

On the ninth of November, he was so sick that he went home. The regiment's doctor reviewing his physical symptoms had bled him a week earlier and then twice again on the eighth. The next day, apparently convinced that failure merited repetition, he bled him again. Washington, who the week before had endured the bloody flux and high fever, now was "seized with Stitches & violent Pleuretic Pains." The complications of this disorder "perplexes" the doctor according to Robert Stewart, temporarily Washington's second-in-command in Adam Stephen's absence. The doctor also recommended that Washington immediately change his "air" and go "to some place where he can be kept quiet." Keeping quiet was not one of the attractions of Fort Loudoun. Washington reluctantly consented to leave for home when the doctor declared that he might not survive if he waited until the governor gave his permission.[37]

Dinwiddie soon learned of the seriousness of Washington's illness and did not seek to punish him. That Washington had been sick for three months soon became known in Williamsburg. He did not offer excuses for his return, and when his condition was known, sympathy poured in. He wanted to be with his regiment, but five months of inactivity lay before him.

At Mount Vernon, Washington's illness gradually came under control, though early in his stay he seems to have despaired of his life. Friends, including George Mason, his old friend and neighbor, urged him to rest and not rush back to the army. In February 1758, he set out to consult a physician in Williamsburg but turned back when the travel strengthened his illness. Much of his stay was spent in bed, where he may have brooded over Virginia's troubles as well as his own. But by April his physical condition had improved and he returned to the army at Fort Loudoun. On his way back, he visited Martha Custis at White House, in New Kent County. This visit was a part of a quiet courtship, so quiet that few then or later understood its meaning.

He resumed command of the Virginia Regiment without the loss of a step—to his officers it must have seemed that he had never been away.

Washington, however, recognized that he had come back to a military charged with an order to drive out the French. William Pitt the Elder had taken office in Britain, and he wanted the war against the French accelerated everywhere in America. The Virginia legislature—Council and Burgesses—responded to the new circumstances by bringing a second regiment into being, and acting governor John Blair ordered Washington to fill the ranks of his regiment by recruiting.[38]

Washington saw the fresh activity as a chance to improve his own situation. His immediate commanding officer was Colonel—soon to be Brigadier—John Stanwix, an Englishman he felt comfortable with. To Stanwix and to Colonel Thomas Gage, a comrade from the Braddock expedition, he sent letters asking that they intercede with General Forbes, now the British officer running the American show. Washington was not looking for "military preferment," he told Stanwix, but only to be "distinguished in some measure from the *common run* of provincial Officers; as I understand there will be a motley herd of us." The letter to Gage used some of the same language and added that he did not consider his request "unreasonable," when it was remembered "that I have been much longer in the Service than any provincial officer in America."[39]

He was in fact looking for preferment, though perhaps he did not know exactly what shape it should take—nor can we be certain. A part of his wishes was surely that he and his regiment be made a royal regiment, a unit recognized as in the establishment. For himself, besides being a king's officer, he craved the standing and respect his long service merited.

On this last score he need not have worried. Both General Forbes and Colonel Henry Bouquet, Forbes's second-in-command, had knowledge of him and entered the American arena with favorable impressions of who he was and what he had done. Forbes gave his first assessment in a tone of regret, in March 1758, having heard that Washington had resigned his commission—he was "extremely sorry," he wrote in a letter to John Blair, as "Washington has the Character of a good and knowing Officer" in the western counties. Bouquet seems to have entertained a similar opinion, but he soon ran up against Washington's firm advocacy for the use of Braddock's Road in the attack on Fort Duquesne. How to approach the fort soon became the center of severe disagreements between Washington and the British command. When Bouquet first learned of Washington's argument in favor of the old Braddock's Road, he resorted to a style that bordered on flattery: Washington's ideas, he wrote, "were generous dispositions for the Service." Washington, he continued, "was above all the Influences of Prejudices, and prepared to go where Reason and Judgement Shall direct." The two men met and discussed their differences. Washington probably recognized what lay behind Bouquet's oil, and in any case held firm. Bouquet's judgment, like Forbes's, was that a route from Raystown, Pennsylvania, about thirty miles north of Braddock's route, offered the better course to Duquesne. It was shorter and direct, and did not present as many obstructions—impassable mountains and swollen rivers—but indeed ran through land more easily traversed and offered more forage for the army's horses. Washington discovered a variety of flaws in these arguments and insisted that such a road would have to be cut throughout its rugged terrain. Braddock's Road, by contrast, had already been carved out through mountains and valleys. Few trees along it, presumably, would have to be cut down, and the crossing of rivers would be easier, because they had been identified before. The knowledge was available, and the entire process of getting at the French would be eased if the old way were followed.[40]

The most powerful argument Washington had was that the season was late—these discussions took place in late July and early August—and cutting a road across Pennsylvania could not be completed before winter set in. The only route that would lead to Fort Duquesne for an attack in 1758 was the old Braddock's Road. Forbes listened, read Washington's frantic letters, and investigated on his own. Both he and Bouquet soon came to the conclusion that Washington was wrong and that a new road could be built before winter shut down operations. Washington received the bad news in early August and reacted with overwrought declarations that "all is lost," sometimes expanded to "All is lost, by Heavens!" This theme of loss preoccupied him for at least four months and filled his letters to two Virginia governors, the Speaker of the House of Burgesses, and assorted friends in and out of the regiment. He presented a quieter, less extravagant version of the idea to General Forbes and Colonel Bouquet, but their rank and position shielded them from his anger and despair. Inevitably they learned of the depth of Washington's opposition, and both concluded that his unrestrained anger had gone too far. By the middle of September,

Forbes had heard enough and summoned Washington and William Byrd, the colonel of the 2nd Virginia Regiment, to inform them that he found their conduct unseemly.

> I told them plainly that, whatever they thought, yet I did aver that, in our prosecuting the present road, we had proceeded from the best intelligence that could be got for the good and convenience of the army, without any views to oblige any one province or another; and added that those two gentlemen were the only people that I had met with who had showed their weakness in their attachment to the province they belong to, by declaring so publicly in favour of one road without their knowing anything of the other, having never heard from any Pennsylvania person one word about the road.[41]

Forbes did not hesitate to comment on his own reasons for choosing to approve building a new road. His choice, also Henry Bouquet's, came out of his devotion to "the good of the service . . . at heart, not valuing the provincial interest, jealousys, or suspicions." There were certainly a good many provincial suspicions at play in the controversy over the location of the road. They were at the center of Washington's explanation to Virginians as to how Braddock's Road—a Virginia road—had failed to become the road to Fort Duquesne. Washington convinced himself that merchants and others had exacted an unhealthy influence that backed the road through Pennsylvania. Forbes detected non-military influences, too, but he found them in Virginia, not Pennsylvania.[42]

Washington always denied that political interests to Virginia had shaped his preferences. His recommendation, made over and over again, was for military purposes; nothing else had entered his thought. After a lot of argument that noted the superiority of Braddock's Road over the projected new one—fewer mountainous obstacles, more easily crossed rivers, abundant forage for horses pulling supply wagons—he settled on the timing of the operation. Cutting a new road from Raystown in Pennsylvania, he insisted, could not be completed before the snow, ice, and cold set in, making a campaign impossible in 1758. Even using the old Braddock's Road, mounting an attack would be impossible. Delay of a year would destroy the support of the Cherokees, he maintained, and of other friendly Indians as well. The Cherokees would go home to South Carolina, and the others would scatter throughout the Ohio Country. And there was also the threat that they would attach themselves to the French. As for the French, a delay of a year might enable them to build up their forces and perhaps organize a campaign of strength themselves.[43]

Early on in the argument, Washington had pledged himself to the "law" that required him to obey his orders, even though his pledge did not rest on agreement with the strategy Forbes had devised. Thus, the campaign to take Fort Duquesne began in fighting, but not the sort anyone relished. During the months it took to settle on a road to the West, George Washington took defeat badly, but he meant what he said about following orders.

The orders were rather slow in coming. Forbes did not summon Washington and the Virginia Regiment to Raystown until September 21, perhaps thinking that beginning the construction of the road to the West should be left to officers better disposed toward the campaign. Even after reporting with his troops, Washington was given to evaluating what lay ahead with bleakness and pessimism, writing to Francis Fauquier, the newly appointed governor of Virginia, that "our affairs in general appear with a greater gloom than ever." On September 25, he wrote, "I see no probability of opening the Road this Campaign."[44]

He could not see the probability of opening the road "this Campaign," but he attempted to make it happen. He had artificers with the regiment and some equipment to use in preparing the way. He also commanded a significant part of Forbes's army. Throughout the march, the army was divided into three brigades, with Washington commanding one, made up principally of Virginians; Bouquet leading another; and Colonel Archibald Montgomery the third. Washington had the most experience in wilderness operations of the three colonels, and at times Forbes directed him to lead the way. His general orders, when he was operating almost alone, reveal a commander who gave attention not just to general purposes but also to important details. On the march up to Loyalhanna, near the crest of Chestnut Ridge, he was especially concerned about tools needed in opening the road, and ordered that those in use should be given to sentries, then delivered to a Captain Fields for safekeeping. If any officer received tools—axes are mentioned in orderly books—he was to see that they were returned to Fields at night. Weapons were not ignored in Washington's orders; rain fell daily in mid-November, a danger to the condition of both firearms and gunpowder. Such matters demanded careful supervision in all eighteenth-century armies—and in Washington's brigade they always received scrutiny.[45]

The march to Loyalhanna from Rayston consumed most of October. The move up gave Washington opportunity to assess the quality of the new road, which was, he wrote Governor Fauquier from Loyalhanna at the end of October, "undescribably bad." It was raining at this time, and the movement of men, wagons, and horses undoubtedly helped turn the soil into mud. About a week later, he told Bouquet that the campaign should be ended there.[46]

On November 12, some two hundred of the French and their Indian allies attempted a raid on the animals of the British at Loyalhanna. Forbes reported to James Abercromby that he sent five hundred men out to thwart this group. A skirmish followed, which Washington did not write about for almost thirty years; his report then described a small-scale encounter in which a second British force, led by himself, exchanged fire with the first, sent out by Forbes. Each of the two had mistaken the other for the enemy, a mistake that cost them forty dead or missing. The sources from which an account can be constructed are not altogether reliable; Forbes's letter did not mention Washington's part, though others say that upon realizing friends were shooting friends, he interposed himself in the middle of the gunfire and with his sword knocked upward the muskets of men he could reach. The existing evidence is not strong enough to establish the truth of this report; Washington's part in it remains largely unknown.[47]

In the firefight, three of the enemy were captured and questioned; they testified that Fort Duquesne was lightly garrisoned and short of provisions. The fort appeared ripe for the taking.

The day before the capture of the three enemy soldiers, General Forbes, who had just arrived at Loyalhanna, held a meeting of his principal officers—eight colonels in all. The question posed by Forbes was quite simply what should be done now, given what was known of the enemy's forces at Fort Duquesne and considering the strength and provisions of his command. Washington's opinion had been given to

Colonel Bouquet the week before, and he probably repeated its substance at this meeting. In talking to Bouquet—and writing him almost
immediately after the conversation on November 6—Washington had
argued for caution: British provisions were not ample, and a march to
Fort Duquesne would draw them down. Should a battle be fought in
the woods and should the British then put the French to "Rout[,] what
do we gain by it?" If the enemy were defeated in such an engagement,
he asked, could the British be certain that the French would give up
the fort? He did not offer a prediction then; but the tone of his attitude
was that Forbes's army was in no shape for a gamble to risk all. What
the eight colonels thought of this formulation, if in fact he gave it in
their meeting, is not absolutely clear. But they voted as if they heard it,
or perhaps for other reasons they shared his skepticism, voting against
a full-scale march to Fort Duquesne.[48]

Then the skirmish of November 12 occurred and the French prisoners reported on the weakness of the fort. That news was enough
for Forbes, who the next day ordered his army to take itself to Fort
Duquesne. The next two weeks banished doubts about the enterprise,
and Washington, along with his colleagues, plunged into action. The
three brigades moved as fast as they could, with Washington playing
a full part. For several days his brigade took the lead, Bouquet and
Montgomery following; but for much of the time he led his men in the
middle of the march, which, by necessity, saw the brigades slightly
separated from one another. Washington's brigade guarded the light
artillery, deep within the column—tents and the heavier guns had been
left behind. The three brigades took turns cutting the road toward the
fort, an uncertain task if for no other reason than that no one seemed
certain of how near, or far away, Fort Duquesne was. At the beginning
of the march, predictions of how far they would have to slog their way
were optimistic. When it became clear that Fort Duquesne was not
just over the next hill or ridge or stream, realism set in.

On November 25, they reached Fort Duquesne almost without
opposition—the enemy had fled and had burned the fort before leaving. No doubt some of the army, both officers and men, felt let down
at not getting a fight, but the feeling gave way almost immediately to
relief and happiness. Forbes, a generous and thoughtful commander,
sent Washington off to Williamsburg and Governor Fauquier with a

report of the army's success. In late December, Washington arrived home, with more than this news on his mind. He would resign his commission in a few days, and on January 6, 1759, he married Martha Dandridge Custis.

The war had served as George Washington's tutor, and it drove his development as a soldier and a commander of soldiers. When he accepted the commission as the head of the Virginia Regiment, he had some awareness of what he was taking on. "Some awareness," but not all, of what lay ahead. The chief problems that were to affect his life for the next three years began to take shape long before he took command. They lay in Williamsburg, the Ohio Valley, and the militia of Virginia.

Williamsburg—the governor and the legislature—was close enough to present problems, almost daily. The governor whom Washington had to deal with for most of the period was Robert Dinwiddie, a man of ability but unsteady in judgment. Dinwiddie meant well, as is often said of troublesome men, but he meddled in matters he could not know much about; and had he known more, his judgment might not have led to the right decision. Moreover, the governor was faced with a legislature in which one house, the Burgesses, took a dim view of his use of executive power. The House of Burgesses did what it pleased and often found much that was not pleasing in what the governor recommended.

The Ohio Valley, with its potential for growth in settlement, attracted people who expected too much from a colonial government with little military power at hand. Power cost money, and the colony looked for the Crown to pay for it rather than dig into its own resources. For Washington this meant chronic underfinancing. He had to defend scattered settlements ranging over several hundred square miles. His enemy in this undeveloped West knew the ground as well as or better than he did. The Ohio Indians proved themselves in the wilderness, using a style of fighting that Virginians, indeed all colonials, never really mastered. "Bush fighting" offered problems to Virginians that did not show up in European manuals, or in the traditional methods favored by Europeans and colonials alike.

The men in the Virginia Regiment commanded by Washington were sometimes trained in the conventional European ways: They knew something about moving in columns, firing on order, and the infantry drill. But most of them were not skilled in any form of combat; many were poor shots, and Washington came to beg for marksmen with genuine ability. The militiamen who came to his regiment when the Indians seemed about to overrun settlements in his first two years of command were especially troublesome. They usually were draftees, sometimes the unemployed, even vagrants, forced into service by counties in a halfhearted response to requirements of the Virginia legislature.

Washington pointed out their inadequacies but had no alternative to using them. He did not receive much help in his efforts—clothing, weapons, and food remained in short supply in these years. Understandably, a good many men deserted, some aided by the farmers along the frontier who pitied them.

By the time the war turned in the colonies' favor, Washington had become a soldier of considerable skill. He had learned much from the Indian and French enemy and also from the British army and political establishment, which denied him a royal commission. In this educational process, he had become a hardened professional knowledgeable in the military arts and experienced in combat with foes from the New World and the Old. The campaign along the Forbes Road was in a sense the icing on the cake of experience. He held his own with British officers, most notably Forbes and Bouquet. Leading troops in large numbers—his brigade was five or six hundred strong—called for and surely strengthened his organizational sense. He proved equal to all the demands imposed by a campaign with European regulars.

Washington's political skill was pushed to the limit in these years. Dealing with Dinwiddie found him stumbling on occasion, but most of the time his ability to read his superior served his and the army's interests. He had also to deal with British authority in the persons of absentee commanders in chief—most notably Shirley and Loudoun. Washington found allies in the House of Burgesses and the Council in John Robinson and William Fairfax. He wrote to them in difficult and dangerous times, but his tone in explaining his problems was not that of a man of fears or desperation. He did not whine or beg but provided a realistic account of what he faced, and his letters conveyed a sense of his own determination and personal strength even in desperate times.

He was twenty-seven years old when he resigned, a formidable man and a soldier of ability and experience. He was also brave and had much talent in reserve. He did not know it, but he was ready for a major challenge, one that would enrich his life but also transform the world.

3

From Planter to Patriot

Washington had married almost immediately after leaving the army. Martha was a widow with two children, twenty-eight years old, pretty rather than beautiful, and extraordinarily wealthy. Her children—Patsy, two years old, and Jack, four—were healthy and much loved by their mother. More than her money made Martha attractive to young men. She was a gentle person, thoughtful, free of pretensions—she once described herself as "a fine, healthy girl"—and apparently charmed by Washington when she first met him, in March 1758.

Although Washington at the time may have been in love with another woman—Sally Fairfax, his neighbor at nearby Belvoir plantation—he found Martha Custis to have attractions of her own. Yet they were not so good as to wash away the feeling he harbored for Sally. Sally Fairfax, the wife of his close friend George William Fairfax, seems to have felt affection for Washington, but she never hinted that she was willing to give up her marriage for him. Nor did he wish to endure the scandal, and the loss of George Fairfax's friendship, by engaging in an affair with her. They were neighbors, Washington and Sally, but they kept their love, if indeed either one felt passionate affection, at a distance.[1]

Washington took Martha and the children to Mount Vernon immediately after the wedding. The marriage had made him a wealthy man, and now he turned to the problems of establishing his new family in a setting he loved. Mount Vernon had been in his hands since late 1754, when he leased it from Ann Fairfax Lee, his brother's widow, recently remarried. (He was to inherit it in 1761, on her death.)

When he took up the life of a tobacco planter, Mount Vernon was in terrible shape, its buildings run down and its fields neglected. An overseer had managed it for Washington during the years he spent in the army. Washington had lived there for short periods while serving, but he had neither the time nor the energy during these years to make it a productive plantation. In fact, in his longest stays he was sick or recovering from illnesses that in one instance threatened his life.[2]

Now, in good health and with a wife and two children, he had to transform himself into an estate manager, one part businessman and one part farmer. This assignment seems to have been as different from the soldier's tasks as anything could be. On the face of things, running a plantation called for skills not ordinarily found in a soldier. War had called for physical and moral courage—qualities he had in abundance. It had taught him much about the organization of men and resources. It had also exposed his less desirable qualities, an ambition for the status that appointment in the British army would bring, and occasionally an impatience so strong as to evoke conduct bordering on immaturity. By themselves, impatience and ambition were not necessarily unfortunate characteristics: the ambition fostered hard work and commitment to military duty, and the impatience could trigger action needed in situations where lethargy and complacency were common. Though his resignation of his command of the Virginia Regiment in 1758 was understandable, a man less driven by his inner compulsions might have seen things through and emerged even stronger as the tide turned in the war.

But Washington had resigned, and he now was a married man facing the daunting tasks of making a new career as a planter. His powers of organization were soon very much in evidence. Marriage had brought new lands, slaves, and problems. The most prosperous of the Custis plantations now under his control were located eighty miles south on the York River, at a distance that prevented his direct supervision. Whether he would have supervised their operations closely had they been nearer is not clear, for their longtime steward, Joseph Valentine, had managed them well. In any case, he had plenty to do at Mount Vernon and his nearby properties.[3]

There were mouths to feed. His slaves numbered about fifty when he took up his new duties, and they had to be fed if they were to work. The responsibility for providing food he shared with his slaves. He allowed them to fish, indeed encouraged them to do so by lending them a boat and nets. Such work was not a regularly scheduled activity but was taken up when schools or runs of herring appeared in the

Potomac and nearby rivers and creeks. His slaves also raised chickens for meat and eggs, a practice common on all Virginia plantations. Most of the food for slaves came from systematic production of corn, turnips, fruits, and animals, especially hogs. In the early years after his return he bought hogs from nearby producers. His goal was, however, to produce a number sufficient for his own use.[4]

Until the middle of the decade, Washington's chief focus at Mount Vernon was the production of tobacco. It proved a frustrating task. The soil on the plantation was not quite right for tobacco, or for a number of other crops Washington hoped to grow. Several types of clay predominated, each with its own deficiencies—some of it drained too slowly and remained in a form almost marshlike; another type dried out, seemed to pack itself tightly, and resisted efforts to plow it up for planting and cultivation.

Soil—tough, resistant, or fertile—fascinated Washington and stimulated his venturesomeness. His experimental sense grew from his daring, a willingness to try some new expedient if what he had done failed. He began conducting experiments with soils soon after full-time planting became his life. In 1760, he moved "earth" from the field into the garden and mixed several kinds of composts "to try their several Virtues." This effort soon became a rather intricate trial, with earth, marl, cow bones and sheep dung, riverside sand, mold from the pocosin, and the clay from "just below the garden." He separated these components into ten separate "apartments" within a box. One of them was reserved for clay without any other mix. Once the soils were mixed, he "planted three Grains of Wheat 3 of Oats & as many of Barley, all at equal distances in Rows & of equal depth (done by a Machine made for the purpose)." Some grains yielded plants over the next few weeks, and on May 1 he tabulated the results in his diary.[5]

This experiment, carefully planned and executed, was about as intricate an exercise as any he undertook. In conducting it, he was looking for the kind of wheat best suited to Virginia. He began with the English red winter wheat, but he tried many others over the next few years. Awareness of his interest in wheat and his experiments spread over Virginia, and before long he received seed from other planters; when he was satisfied that he had found an outstanding strain, he sent samples to neighbors and to friends as far away as Jefferson's Monticello. Altogether he seems to have tried out a dozen varieties, finally concluding that white wheat suited Mount Vernon soil the best.[6]

There was design in this experiment, repeated in various forms with many plants as he searched for the most productive crops. In these early years he planted clover, alfalfa, and rye; he varied the times of the year in a number of these trials, and resorted to different composts and fertilizers. Whatever he planted received careful scrutiny, and the results of his trials were meticulously recorded. Most of his planting, of course, was not by nature an experiment, but the results were treated as if it were. The results proved enlightening, especially as they concerned tobacco. By 1766 he had concluded that profit lay in wheat, not in sweet-scented or oronoco tobacco. His tenants on several farms and the plantations on the York stayed with tobacco. At Mount Vernon he gave it up.

This result proved the weightiest of all his planting experiments. Throughout his years of focus on tobacco and for years afterwards, he continued his study of soils, seeds, crops, and all that went into agricultural production. Besides testing soil, compost, and seeds, he experimented with plows and fencing (with an eye to restraining hogs, which rooted up his garden) and showed himself willing to try any possibility that promised success in planting. He tried out several kinds of plows—including the "Duck Bill" and the "two Eyed"—soon invented one of his own, and finally ordered one from England.[7]

Looking to England for a plow was one aspect of his eagerness to learn and to profit from the experience of others. The revolution in agriculture was near its peak when he began his life as a planter, and he explored its findings with eagerness. In these early years, he relied on Jethro Tull's *Horse-Houghing Husbandry, an Essay on the Principles of Tillage and Vegetation* (1731) more than any other publication. The edition he used, published in 1751, was an American favorite, but few Virginia planters read in the scientific literature as deeply as he did.[8]

Before he gave up tobacco planting, he thought that he understood the process of its production and sale well, and in certain respects he was right. But it was a more complicated world than he recognized. The actual cultivation of the plant was probably better known to Washington than anything else in the system that had developed in the century and a half of the colony's existence.

Throughout most of the seventeenth century, Virginians had not completely cleared their fields, preferring instead to cut trees and bushes close to the ground and plant seedlings around them. They avoided much heavy labor in following this procedure, an especially important tactic when most fieldwork had to be done by white indentured servants. Planters also used fields that had been cleared years before by Indians and in most cases had lain fallow. In fact, these seventeenth-century practices constituted a "long fallow" system. The system—leaving fields unplanted—was not always a conscious attempt to allow the land to regain its fertility, though most planters recognized that allowing second-growth trees and bushes to grow would, after an interval of twenty or thirty years, make the once abandoned fields productive.

With the introduction of slavery, these practices changed, and early in the eighteenth century, as population increased and slavery was established, a new pattern appeared, involving better-prepared fields and the use of animal fertilizers. More tobacco-growing fields were put in and population expanded, with most of the new planters moving into woodlands to the north and west. Some of these planters were men who had abandoned their old ground, or, more commonly, men who held on to what they had, even in the face of its infertility, and looked to add to their holdings in the Piedmont.[9]

George Washington had long seemed to harbor a lust for land—he bought land whenever he could, and he took part in several ventures with other planters to claim lands in the West. One of these ventures saw him join a group of officials in Britain and big planters in Virginia; another, in which he took the lead, sought to bring into cultivation the Great Dismal Swamp, along the North Carolina border. In both efforts, he and his partners believed that there was money to be made; in both, planters acted as speculators. Claiming large bodies of land that could be broken up and sold to those easterners eager for their own plantations and farms was by this time an old story in the English colonies. This drive for owning land resembled a natural force, with its own history and rationale. The ownership of land had for centuries provided a measure for status and class, and animated the English as few things ever had.

There were other reasons for the strivings of Virginians to gather more acres for themselves. For all who planted tobacco suffered from the same disability: Fields in which tobacco was grown began to their fertility after two or three years of the crop. Over a long period, the loss of good plants became markedly serious.[10]

If tobacco drove the desire for land, so also did it affect the routine of day-to-day life. Growing tobacco taxed planters' patience, a feeling that often gave way to a realization that the whole process was beyond anyone's control. Resignation followed when, as frequently happened, nature failed to cooperate with planters' efforts. Little could be done in the face of drought that shriveled up a once promising field; nor could the effects of a sustained rain that virtually drowned the crop be avoided. Tobacco required a large labor force, careful planning in putting it in, and shrewd timing in its harvest. Early in the year, once the cold gave way to warmer temperatures, slaves under close supervision inserted seeds into planting beds. The sites for these plantings called for good soil and nearby water; hence, the banks of runs or small streams were favored places. The seedlings appeared a couple of weeks later, if the weather had warmed; they were then transplanted into small hills, usually knee-high, and carefully located. Once they reached a foot or two in height, they were topped, and excess leaves removed. Over the course of the next few months, slaves picked off worms and suckers and small limbs that yielded no leaves. Harvesting the crop required experience and judgment from the planter and his overseers. If timing was not everything in harvesting tobacco, it must have seemed so to those who had to gauge when stems must be cut. The color of leaves gave some direction—the right shade of green was decisive. Plants that remained in the ground too long often proved to be brittle and the leaf in danger of flaking off; plants taken too early might suffer mildew.

Once cut, the stems, leaves attached, were stacked in bunches and then hung from rope for curing in a tobacco house. Some time later—from a few days to weeks—they would be pushed into hogsheads and shipped to warehouses to be inspected by colonial authorities. Shipping from the coastal areas—the Tidewater—found the hogsheads transported in drays pulled by horses. Planters in the Piedmont sometimes improvised by driving pegs into the ends of hogsheads and then rolling them to the houses of storage and inspection.

The difficulties in cultivating tobacco were well known, and most of them—the doubtful gifts of nature, excessive rain, drought, the

cts—were inevitable. Slaves did most of the work
roblems, as well as the ordinary labor of cultiva-
the transport of hogsheads to the points of exporta-
e time, they did these tasks well, though some slaves
ig ignorance when they were ordered to do some tasks.
y some fell sick or died, and still others ran away. On
owever, tobacco planters declared themselves satisfied
with ᵤ. laves and after slavery was well established showed no
desire to find another system of labor. As for the burdens an unreliable
natural world imposed upon them, these planters remained steady in
the knowledge that there was little they could do but carry on. Man
and nature in Virginia may have been troublesome, but most planters
thought they could bring them under control most of the time.[11]

There was no such assurance in the cycle that began with harvesting and ended with selling. That part of the world of tobacco, the marketing of the crop, offered obstacles that often could not be avoided.
The market, after all, was overseas in Britain, and by the middle of the
century primarily on the European continent. Under the terms of the
Navigation Acts, tobacco had to be shipped to a British port; it was an
enumerated commodity under a parliamentary statute. Planters new
to the business found it intractable in one major respect: They had no
sure way to control prices.

For much of the seventeenth century and during the first decades of
the eighteenth, most planters relied on British firms to sell their crop
under a consignment system. Merchants they never laid eyes on sent
ships to the Chesapeake to transport the tobacco to Europe, where
they sold it. Under the consignment system, the planters owned the
tobacco until it was finally sold by these British firms to whom it was
consigned. The British merchants assumed none of the risk in this process, and if a ship went down or in times of war was captured by the
enemy—almost always the French—or was damaged in transit, the
planter took the loss of cargo. As for the price received when it was
sold, the far-off merchant firms decided on when to sell, and to whom,
and collected a commission as the planters' agents. Planters bore all of
the costs of the system—insurance, duties imposed by the English state
under the law, and, when the merchant provided additional services,
paying bills on planters' accounts (when in effect they acted as bank-
ers). The English firms frequently served as suppliers as well, buy-

ing on planters' accounts a large variety of goods, clothing, medicines, tools, leather goods, and much more.

In performing these services, they made life easier for planters. The English firms knew the retailers in London and elsewhere who sold the goods the planters wanted. Some planters developed close relations with merchants, but they were always at a disadvantage in dealing with them. Relying on a consignment house may have cut through their ignorance of English markets and prices and saved them the inconvenience of writing many letters with orders for a vast array of goods. But in placing orders with British firms, planters rarely knew what prices they would pay, and if they spent more on goods than their tobacco brought in, they incurred horrific debts. It was the rare planter entangled in the webs of the consignment world who did not find himself in debt.

Changes involving the marketing of tobacco and the buying of European goods came not so much from a concern about the precariousness of planters' financial lives as from business conditions in Britain and the Continent. The European market grew in importance in the eighteenth century, and as it did, fresh ways of tapping Chesapeake production appeared, or more accurately were strengthened. For, from seventeenth-century beginnings, British firms came to acquire tobacco by a second method: A factor who lived in Virginia bought the planter's tobacco and sold him British goods in his store. Initially the factors were English, or occasionally Americans with ties to English houses, but by the middle of the eighteenth century they commonly were Scots, as Glasgow entered the business, purchasing the crop in the Chesapeake and reexporting it to the Continent, usually to France.[12]

Although Washington had given up the planting of tobacco in his Mount Vernon fields by 1766, he remained deeply interested in all aspects of the business, from planting to selling the crop; for his tobacco plantations in York and neighboring counties continued in the old way. They had always brought greater profits than his own efforts, even after Joseph Valentine, the skillful manager of his York plantations, died. James Hill, Valentine's successor, seemed capable of carrying on much as Valentine had, and he suggested to Washington that tobacco grown in the York River plantations should not be abandoned. There was a second reason to stay with tobacco there: Washington was responsible for the estate Martha Washington's children would inherit, and their fortunes were tied to tobacco. He had no intention of taking chances with their property or their futures.

Yet the business of tobacco often turned Washington's eyes away from the York plantations to the British merchant firms in London and also, at times, to merchants in Liverpool, Glasgow, and—in the half-dozen years before the Revolution—the West Indies and the Chesapeake. For most of the period before the Revolution, Robert Cary and Company, a London consignment house, took most of his tobacco. In a sense, he inherited his ties to Robert Cary's firm, for it had handled the tobacco shipped from the York River plantations that came to him when he married. Joseph Valentine was accustomed to dealing with the captains of the ships sent out by Robert Cary, and Washington, though he seems not to have solicited Valentine's advice, slipped easily into the groove running from Virginia to Cary's London.[13]

Enough of Robert Cary's communications to Washington survive to justify the conclusion that Robert Cary and Company was better at selling English goods to Washington than it was at selling his tobacco. Washington did not hesitate to sound his complaints to the firm, and he continued to express them until the Revolutionary War broke the connection. It did not take him long to discover that at times his tobacco was sold by Cary for lesser prices than others received. He compared prices with George William Fairfax, his friend and neighbor, finding in this case that he was the loser. More commonly, he relied on what he learned from the English market itself. The subject drew the interest of planters in Virginia, and he had a variety of sources of information—ship captains, for example—who sailed up the Chesapeake and into the Potomac. Williamsburg, which he visited several times every year, was an even better source. Planters held most of the seats in the Burgesses, and Virginia merchants also congregated in the town several times a year to discuss business. Robert Cary and Company itself gave him the most exact information about the sale of his own crop, information that provoked responses ranging from patient disappointment to bitter comments, including threats to find a British house that commanded higher prices.

The longer Washington shipped to Robert Cary and Company, the longer his list of complaints about the price paid for his tobacco became; and with every justification Cary offered, Washington's response grew harsher. At one point in their correspondence, Cary asked that the stem be removed from the leaf before it was packed into Washington's hogsheads. Removing the stem reduced the weight and, perhaps as important, took more labor. Washington insisted that he should not be required to prepare his tobacco in such a way—many others did not—and implied that Cary's request was one more example of the unfair treatment meted out to him. He clearly felt that there had been unfairness in their business relations, and he drove home the point by saying that his loyalty to the firm had cost him money. Part of his dissatisfaction arose from the fact that ships from England—at least Cary's ships—were sent only to the lower bay, where they loaded York River tobacco but did not venture to the Potomac. What could a planter such as himself do if the ships did not come up the bay? The answer, usually not given by Robert Cary, was that Potomac River tobacco should be shipped down to the York or wait, sometimes for months, until ships sailed up to collect it. The uncertainty spurred Washington's anger; as he reminded Cary on one occasion, "I have refused such of my Potomac Tobacco as was intended for you, to other Ships upon Liberty by which means I shall miss the Convoy, & enhance the Insurance I fear."[14]

Managing an estate filled Washington's days with work of surprising scope, as did buying and selling, and it tied him into local and British networks. He bought land all over Virginia and in the West, but the needs of consumption found him looking overseas more, trying to obtain the best price for his tobacco and, soon after his beginning in business, his wheat, corn, and fish. It also found him buying and buying—seemingly everything a wealthy planter wanted: clothing, household goods, plantation equipment, wine, fine foods, and much more.

To meet these requirements of the planter's life, he was frequently in the saddle riding in his fields, or in his coach on his way to Williamsburg or the York River plantations that marriage to Martha Custis had brought him. Judging from the extent and size of his correspondence, he sat at his desk as often as on a horse. For most communication, if not face-to-face, happened through the post, and he wrote and heard from neighbors as well as merchants and others across the Atlantic.

This short summary only hints at the levels of activity in his daily existence. There were other occupations. His family—his wife, Martha, and her children, his wards—gave him his greatest satisfaction and happiness.[15]

John Parke Custis, usually called Jack, absorbed more of Washington's time than Patsy did, and in the course of his short life worried him in ways that his sister did not. Martha Washington loved both children with a passion marked by fear that she might lose one or both. It was a common feeling among parents in Virginia, in Martha's case perhaps more than usual because she was a widow.

Jack was a boy of five years when his mother married Washington. His formal education began in earnest a few years later. Who taught him to read and write is not known, but not long after coming to Mount Vernon, he was put under the tutelage of Walter Magowan, who lived on the plantation. Magowan, a Scot, introduced Jack to Latin and seems to have begun to open up Greek for him as well. Magowan left Mount Vernon in 1761, creating an opening for a new tutor.

After canvassing at least a part of the field, Washington decided on Jonathan Boucher, a clergyman who was angling for appointment to a church in Virginia. He would be ordained in 1769, and he would gain his own church soon after. Meanwhile he kept himself alive as a tutor in Latin and Greek to the sons of planters before moving to Annapolis, Maryland.[16]

Washington, though fond of Jack, held no great hopes for him, but despite his doubts about his mental ability he wished to see him master the learning expected of a gentleman in Virginia society. His first appraisal of Jack for Boucher's benefit described "a boy of good genius," that is, of good character or spirit, "about 14 yrs of age, untainted in his Morals, & of innocent Manners." He took the boy to Boucher in June 1768 and shortly after received a letter in which Boucher confessed that he had initially feared that Jack—"of so exceedingly mild & meek a Temper"—might be made uneasy "by the rougher Manners of Some of his Schoolfellows," but he was later reassured that Jack was "happy" in "his new Situation." Yet Boucher's concerns lingered and were of more importance than how Jack responded to leaving the security of Mount Vernon for the rough-and-tumble of a boarding school. He asked Washington if Jack were not "more artless, more unskill'd in a necessary Address than He ought to be, ere He is turn'd out into a World like this?" By "Address" he meant "bearing," thinking of the confident attitude men in the eighteenth century expected of its gentlemen. What was desirable in an educated man went beyond knowledge of Latin and Greek, the conventional conception of education; indeed, more than "intellectual powers" required development—it was the "Heart" he aimed at, in the hope that what Jack lost in "Gentleness, Simplicity, & Inoffensiveness" would be replaced by "Address, Prudence, & Resolution." He had found that Jack "posess'd all the Harmlessness of the Dove" but the boy "wanted some of the Wisdom of the Serpent."[17]

These early impressions proved unreliable, and in the next three years, if Boucher did not exactly decide that the Serpent had found a home in Jack's breast, he soon concluded that the "Dove" did not reside there, either. Jack never proved to be turbulent or disrespectful; he did not lie or steal, he did not drink or debauch girls, but he did not give any more of his time to his studies than he had to, and when he found a way to leave boarding school, he took it and remained away, usually at Mount Vernon as long as possible. Washington hoped for more and remarked on several occasions that Jack seemed to have added little to his stock of Latin and Greek, a failure that especially disappointed him, since there had been so much room for improvement.

Washington indeed wrote Boucher several times in disappointment with Jack's performance. His own desires accorded well with Boucher's—up to a point. He felt much less disturbed about Jack's lack of style or the less-than-impressive manner with which he carried himself; the surface of the boy he believed would take care of itself. He was looking for evidence of learning and the discipline required to get it. At one point he even reminded Boucher that a gentleman should have French, though he himself could neither read nor write the language. Boucher's reply to these comments could not have pleased him, though he said little in response to Boucher's statements that more than a schoolmaster's education was needed to make a gentleman. But after a few months of Jack's sloth, Boucher seems to have come around to Washington's opinion that Jack should work harder. As for Jack, horse racing, and an awakening interest in young women, soon replaced whatever interest he had in learning and discipline. "His Mind," Washington wrote, was "a good deal relaxed from Study, & more than ever turnd to Dogs Horses & Guns; indeed upon Dress

& equipage, which till of late, he has discovered little Inclination of giving into." Without saying anything explicitly in contradiction of Boucher's intention of shaping Jack's bearing or "Address" in accord with his conception of a gentleman's worldliness, Washington warned against permitting Jack to act in ways "derogatory of Virtue, & that Innocence of Manners which one coud wish to preserve him in." For the most part, in writing Boucher, Washington maintained the posture of a parent who would not presume to tell an expert schoolmaster how to run his educational program, but by late 1770 his patience showed wear, though it never yielded to querulousness. He was obviously displeased with Jack and perhaps with Boucher as well. To Jack, he said in effect, Get to work. And to Boucher, a flat requirement: Keep him close to those useful branches of learning, for if Boucher did not, Jack "will too soon think himself above countrol." Nor should he "be suffered to Sleep from under your own Roof, unless it be at such places as you are sure he can have no bad examples set him; nor allow him to be rambling about at Nights in Company with those, who do not care how debauchd and vicious his Conduct may be."[18]

Boucher, now made aware of Washington's anxiety, wrote immediately, agreeing that Jack needed discipline and offering an assessment of his own: Jack was "indolent" and "surprisingly—voluptuous—one would suppose Nature had intended Him for some Asiatic Prince."[19]

These discussions of Jack's learning and discipline were carried on throughout his stays with Boucher. While they occurred, Boucher raised the possibility of a grand tour of Europe by Jack, suggesting that travel abroad would help form and polish his manners and presumably establish the "Address" Boucher had initially found so lacking in him. Boucher generously proposed himself as an appropriate guide, though he had never made such a tour himself. In one of his most forceful letters of advocacy, he also reminded Washington of Jack's aversion to study and his fondness for a life of indolence. Although Boucher insisted that Jack was "indolent, & voluptuous," the boy was not so far gone as to be unredeemable—redemption obviously coming from travel abroad, which would break down provincial prejudices and make him a man of the world.[20]

As the two men explored the possibilities, it became clear that Boucher himself relished the opportunity to see more of Europe. It was also clear that he had failed as a teacher, and that all of Washington's urging that "classical knowledge" was the thing for Jack, because gaining it would come only through the self-mastery and discipline required in such serious study, had not affected the teacher any more than the boy.

Jack did not go to Europe, and in 1773 entered the King's College, New York—later Columbia University. He did not take a heavy load of classical learning with him, nor was he well qualified for studies in a college. But he was George Washington's ward, and that connection was enough.

Jack received the treatment he thought he deserved—he was in fact much favored, as he explained "There has Nothing been omitted by the Professors, which could be in any means conducive to Happiness, & contentment; during my residence at this place, and I beleive [*sic*] I may say without vanity that I am Look'd upon in a particular Light by them all, there is as much Distinction made between me, & the Other Students as can be expected." He expected a lot and got it—for example, he dined with President Cooper and the faculty, not with his fellow students.[21]

Washington's military service made him a familiar figure in Virginia and rounded out his reputation as a man who could be counted on. Already famous locally and to some extent outside the colony, he stepped forward early in the revolutionary crisis brought on by the changes in colonial policy instituted by the British government. Though he had never been abroad and would never see the British Isles, he knew much about the system that underlay the tension between the mother country and her American colonies.

In fact, the British Empire in America held few mysteries for him. He had seen it close up from 1752 on. He knew its governors in Virginia, and he had dealt with others from Maryland, Massachusetts, and Pennsylvania. He had seen close up the British army in action, and he had fought alongside its troops. A number of British officers were friends, and one, Thomas Gage, led the army that would fight the opening engagements of the Revolutionary War.

Another source of his knowledge was newspaper accounts of the operations of Parliament and the relations the king's government managed in the world. Even more important was the information he gained in talking with captains of British ships that sailed up Chesapeake Bay. These men and British travelers could give him accounts of the affairs of the British Isles and the events that affected policies of colonial governance—and much more.

On the surface of things, he and most planters seemed isolated. But almost all were interested in the world around them, including the world of the empire and the mother country. They might be surprised by what Parliament and the Crown did, but they knew something of the mechanisms of empire—how things worked, even those things across the Atlantic.

Early in the first colonial upheavals of the 1760s, he expressed his dismay that the British seemed unaware that what they proposed to do in Parliament would cost their merchants money. His experience with those merchants, rocky as it sometimes was, led him to distinguish their exploitation of commercial advantage from that of the government. That government, the ministry and Parliament alike, seemed heedless of American rights under the British constitution and of imperial welfare in its determination to tax the colonies for revenue. The first attempt, in the North American Revenue Act of 1764, known since as the Sugar Act, aroused few in Virginia. It had no immediate effect there, for its central provisions reduced the old duty on molasses of six pence per gallon to three pence and came with plans to collect it. The original duty, levied in 1733, had been prohibitive, designed to exclude molasses from the French West Indies; it was in modern parlance a protective tariff—protective of British sugar planters in the islands.[22]

American distilleries, virtually all located in the New England colonies, New York, and Pennsylvania, had responded since 1734 by bribing customs collectors, who were British imperial officials, to look the other way. The new statute was not to be easily evaded. The king's minister, George Grenville, ordered the collectors in America to do their jobs and replaced most of them with men he knew would comply with his orders. Americans caught trying to avoid paying the taxes by smuggling in the molasses would be tried in vice-admiralty courts, which sat without juries, leaving their fate in the hands of English judges appointed by the Crown.

If Washington knew of these new arrangements at the time, he failed to reveal his knowledge. He soon became aware of them, but in 1764 and probably for several years afterwards, most Americans, including political leaders in the southern colonies, said little about the new statute. It contained other regulations that had nothing to do with taxes, and thereby presented a rather obscure, even murky, picture of what it was actually about.

The Stamp Act, passed in 1765, was another matter entirely—a clear attempt to tax and to extract revenue. It imposed a tax on legal documents, business papers, newspapers—a reach into economic and political life that left no doubt about what was intended or who was affected. It was to take effect on November 1, 1765. Long before that, the House of Burgesses had made known its displeasure in the Virginia Resolves, passed at the end of May. Washington, a representative from Fairfax County, was not present, nor were most of the members who ordinarily ran the House. A rump group, led by Patrick Henry— then a young man well known in the colony through his legal pyrotechnics in courtrooms but new to the Burgesses—presented at least four resolutions, which were eagerly passed by his followers. Most of the burgesses, decidedly not his followers, had gone home before he offered his resolutions. The essence of Henry's draft resolutions held that the people of Virginia possessed "all the Liberties, privileges, Franchises, and Immunities, that have at any Time been held, enjoyed, and possessed, by the People of Great Britain." Much followed from this premise, most notably that only a legislative body in which the people were represented could tax them. This body in Virginia was of course the House of Burgesses; in it, the people might tax themselves through their representatives—"Persons chosen by themselves to represent them, who can only know what Taxes the People are able to bear, or the easiest method of raising them, and must themselves be affected by every Tax laid on the People." Such an arrangement, Henry's third resolve stated, did more than offer protection to the people—it was "the distinguishing characteristick of British Freedom, without which the ancient Constitution cannot exist."[23]

The fourth resolve claimed that this constitutional right had enjoyed long-standing approval—the king and his subjects in Great Britain had always favored it. Henry wrote at least two other resolves, much more controversial in wording, one insisting that anyone outside of the burgesses who said that any other "person or persons" had the authority to impose a tax on the people should be considered an enemy of the colony. This statement, along with the others, found its way into most colonial newspapers up and down the coast. The *Maryland Gazette* printed them all, as if they expressed the received wisdom of the House of Burgesses.

It is not clear when Washington heard—or read in the Virginia or Maryland newspapers—of the action of the Burgesses. He had a variety of sources of information besides the newspapers—the records of the House and the testimony of visitors to Mount Vernon, as well as conversations with neighbors, near and far. By late summer and probably before, his own ideas were clear, and they were expressed in his letters of September. "The Stamp Act," he wrote, "engrosses the conversation of the speculative part of the Colonists, who look upon this unconstitutional method of Taxation as a direful attack upon their Liberties, & loudly exclaim against the Violation."[24] He repeated this statement in different terms in the years that followed. He did not mention Patrick Henry and he did not quote the reports in the newspapers, but his initial reaction was to see British action, in its implications for American freedom, just as Henry and his radical young colleagues had. But Washington looked further into a more complicated future that included the effects of political action on the empire's economy. What would occur, he asked, if the British government persisted in its course? The colonies, moved by the threat to their freedom, would not pay the tax—indeed, *could* not, for they lacked the money required. Rather than comply, they would forgo imported luxuries and manufacture the necessities they required. In such events, British merchants and manufacturers would suffer as their profits disappeared.

Washington did not speculate on the political import for the empire if commerce dried up and colonies took to satisfying their needs themselves, but he was clearly aware that the relationships that sustained the empire were becoming of interest to Americans. The first "bad consequence" of the British action would see that "our Courts of Judicature will be shut up, it being morally impossible under our present Circumstances that the Act of Parliament can be complied with."[25]

In 1765, Washington's feelings about the empire were in flux. He had announced his dissatisfaction with the prices his tobacco brought almost from the time he first began shipping it to Robert Cary and others. He had trapped himself in a financial arrangement that found him scrambling to pay the debts he had incurred through his large appetite for British goods. The prospect of cutting back could not have displeased him—the reasons would not be beyond his control—and a life of at least some frugality had its attractions.

The repeal of the Stamp Act in Parliament brought relief but—because the Declaratory Act accompanied the repeal—not complete satisfaction. Parliament's declaration that it reserved the right to "bind the colonies in all cases whatsoever" could not have explained its action more clearly—it was repealing the stamp tax only in response to merchant insistence that financial disaster beckoned if it were enforced. American protests influenced some in Parliament, but as they came from colonists, inferiors who should be put in their place, most thought they could be disregarded.[26]

Washington wrote little about the repeal, beyond acknowledging the congratulations from Robert Cary and Company. The 1767 passage of the Townshend Acts, another attempt to raise revenue, in the form of duties on tea, painters' colors, paper, and glass, banished whatever pleasure he had felt the year before and provided proof that the British government meant to put the colonies on another footing. If there was any doubt in Virginia about the danger the new statutes embodied, action in Massachusetts taught Virginians and colonists everywhere in America what the Townshend Acts implied for colonial liberty. The most vivid lesson the New England radicals sought to impart came in the form of a "circular letter" from the House of Representatives in Massachusetts, sent out in defiance of the secretary for the colonies, Lord Hillsborough. The letter bore in on constitutional questions, taking the standard position that only representative bodies could levy taxes on the people who elected them. The threat to liberty stood out as its main point. What made this assertion, indeed the entire "letter," more powerful than the bare statement of colonial rights was that it came from a body that had defied orders from an imperial official who warned them not to write.[27]

Rioting in Boston had preceded the circular letter by almost a year. By the time Virginians took official notice, in a protest in April 1768 by the House of Burgesses against the Townshend duties, organization in Pennsylvania, New York, and Boston was far advanced. In the crisis of the Stamp Act, Virginia had taken the lead that Massachusetts and other parts of New England eagerly followed; in the next couple of years it was Virginia that fell into line, following, up to a point, the example set in the North. The House of Burgesses delivered a memorial in opposition to the taxes, but neither it nor any other organized body in Virginia proposed that mobs riot or directly pressure customs collectors. The crowd in Williamsburg that had greeted George Mercer, the stamp distributor, on October 30, 1765, had not come to the town for such a purpose. It had gathered from all over the colony for the opening day of the House of Burgesses meeting. Several of the crowd's members took advantage of the coincidence of the Burgesses meeting and Mercer's arrival to pressure him to resign.

Washington was not in attendance when the Burgesses approved its first declaration against the duties. He soon made his approval known, and in April 1769, a year later, he indicated his agreement with plans for a nonimportation agreement. The plans established nonimportation as a tactic intended to lead British merchants to call for repeal in Parliament once more.

Action joined words the next year, a conjunction Washington encouraged and played an active part in forming. The stimulus seemed to have come from the northern colonies once again. Merchants in Boston and Philadelphia provided the model in agreeing among themselves that nonimportation associations offered the most effective means to bring grief to their fellow traders in England, who in turn could be expected to advocate repeal to Parliament. Washington carried the letters from four groups of northern merchants to a meeting of the Fairfax County Court in April 1769. There he talked with George Mason about the tactics of opposition, and the two men agreed on the principles of Virginian freedom. Such constitutional ideals had been at the center of their agreement ever since the crisis of the Stamp Act.[28]

The temperature of meetings against the Stamp Act had never achieved the level attained in Boston, New York, or Philadelphia. Virginians of Washington's persuasion who deemed the act unconstitutional were rarely in one another's presence, and they also lacked an urban mob that could do the rough work of changing the minds of royal officials and their supporters. The Williamsburg group that forced George Mercer to resign his Stamp Act distributorship was an exception and acted with unusual force.[29]

By the time of the passage by Parliament of the Townshend Acts, in 1767, Virginians with few exceptions had returned to their quiet habits, and the pace of resistance barely matched the routines of ordinary life. For Washington, the routines included such matters as recording his "Cash Accounts," shipping tobacco from his York River plantations, reading and writing letters regarding his son, John Parke Custis, and calling together the veterans of the militia who had survived the disaster at Fort Necessity to report on his efforts to secure land for them. During these early years as a planter, he had also "ridden to the hounds," as foxhunting was often called, entertained his neighbors and other visitors, played cards with friends, and participated in the usual ways in the social life of northern Virginia. But the crisis, slow as it was in coming, gradually intruded on the old and familiar.[30]

If the year 1768 offered no great excitement, it was followed by the fevers of 1769 and 1770. In those years, a new scheme for pressuring British merchants took form, in the hope that these worthies in turn would complain to Parliament in their behalf. Interrupting trade with the colonies was the action sought. Merchant groups in Philadelphia, Maryland (chiefly Annapolis), and Virginia furnished the power to start protest on its way. Washington thought that the tactic chosen— the nonimportation of certain British goods, tried once before—held promise in Virginia. The merchants wrote one another proposing joint action, an idea difficult to realize in a large colony such as Virginia, with little by way of concentrated settlement and with few means of communicating. In Virginia virtually every planter acted for himself in commerce, a one-man firm that imported goods not for customers but only for its own use. Of course, there were local merchants throughout the colony who kept shops and sold to others, sometimes in large numbers. But the usual pattern of trade across the Atlantic saw a planter ship tobacco of his own production and import goods for himself—not a retail trade. Washington at times pointed out that this made it difficult to enforce a ban on the importation of British commodities.

What to do about such a problem? In April 1769, Washington and his neighbor George Mason, both justices of the peace in Fairfax County, put their heads together at a regular meeting of the county's court in Alexandria. Neither man was given to excess in emotion or expression, but in this meeting they agreed that a protest against the Townshend taxes should be drafted, and in the process the colonial constitutional position be explained once more. The Stamp Act, though dead, remained fresh in their minds.

Mason did most of the writing of the resolutions, which embodied the reasons for protest and the recommendations for action designed to bring repeal of the statutes. On May 16, 1769, Washington, now in Williamsburg for a meeting of the House of Burgesses, voted in favor of the resolutions, along with all others in the body. The governor, Lord Botetourt, did not attempt to dissuade the House and instead dissolved it on the spot, whereupon its members simply walked down Duke of Gloucester Street and met in the Raleigh Tavern. There, Speaker Peyton Randolph formed a committee charged with establishing a nonimportation association for Virginia and named Washington to this committee.[31]

A man as accustomed to giving orders as Washington had been for many years might not be expected to be an ideal committeeman. Committees usually work by consensus and compromise, and this one in May operated under instructions to devise a scheme to thwart the will of Parliament, an institution at the heart of the British Empire with enormous power and little patience with opposition outside its walls. Washington joined the opposition with no doubts about the propriety of extralegal moves against the power and glory that Parliament manifested.

Over the course of the next year, he watched this effort to clamp down on imports of English goods slide away from its original purpose as planters, merchants, and others discovered ways of bringing in such goods. By June of 1770 he and apparently most of his colleagues in the Burgesses had had enough of such backsliding. Tighter enforcement of non-importation rules seemed called for, and Washington proposed a new association, which would require Virginia counties to form inspection committees with the authority to act against violators. The Burgesses adopted the plan, and Washington went back to Fairfax County determined to carry out the wishes of his colleagues, something he did as a member of an inspection committee.[32]

Washington had led, as well as followed, in this attempt at resistance. There was no hint of weakness, no note of indecision in anything he did in these years. He listened to George Mason, who had most of the ideas about what should be done in the face of actions that most burgesses and most planters considered unconstitutional. And he acted decisively, and though he had none of Mason's eloquence, he explained clearly his own reasons for resisting British measures.

By summer of the next year, 1771, the trial at stopping imports had fallen apart, and Washington gave it up. News of the repeal by Parliament of the taxes on all items except tea finished off what had been only a partially successful attempt. Elsewhere in the colonies, success came easier, and the effects were felt sufficiently in Britain to persuade Parliament to give up much of its original program.[33]

The pace of disaffection in Virginia slowed considerably in the three years following the retreat of the British government from the Townshend Acts. Washington, like most thoughtful planters in these years, went about his usual business; he had little leisure time, given the demands made on him by his business, as well as by his family and community, which seemed to turn to him with increasing requests for help. He said little in his letters about his conviction that Parliament and the ministry had resolved to get their way in disregarding an old constitutionalism that had recognized American liberties as the same as the liberties of subjects at home.

He said little but thought much. He had decided, in the crisis over the Stamp Act, that there was something afoot in Britain, most likely a conspiracy to revoke the essential rights Americans had enjoyed under the British constitution. "Oppressive" had been an adjective he used to describe British action, and in his statements following the passage of the Townshend Acts he expressed an understanding of the imperial system as one that embodied mercantilism in economic life and liberty in the governance of the colonies. All of that seemed at risk in the new measures, and nothing indicated that the British government had yielded its underlying plans even in repealing most of the statutes passed by the ministry of Charles Townshend.[34]

Had Washington been asked in 1773, before the upheaval opened up by the Boston Tea Party, if he foresaw war and revolution ahead, he likely would have denied any such prospects. If he had then been asked if he was satisfied with the definition of the British constitution that Parliament and the ministry seemed to hold, he would have said no and then described the political environment as threatening American self-government and American liberty. But until he was aroused to action early the next year by the Intolerable Acts—the American term for legislation passed by Parliament in spring 1774 in response to the Tea Party—he took no action and urged none.

Washington had referred to Virginia's protests in the 1760s as "the cause," meaning an organized defense of the rights of free men. The cause at that time apparently did not imply a movement that led to rebellious acts such as had occurred in Boston and other northern cities and towns. To be sure, there had been the small-scale "riot" that forced George Mercer to resign his commission as stamp distributor for Virginia, and there was coercion on a small scale to force some recalcitrant merchants to honor the nonimportation movement. But all in all, the most dramatic moments had come early on in the House of Burgesses, when Patrick Henry had presented the Virginia Resolves. Since then, there had been protest and organized boycott and nonimportation, but for the better part of three years—between 1771 and 1774—there had been little change, little open alienation or estrangement.

Washington resembled other planters who thought about such matters, matters of political liberty and the health of the imperial system. But he remained quiet—at least publicly—in the Burgesses, the county, and the vestry, all of which offered venues for expression. Nor did he write often about his underlying uneasiness about the colonies' relations with the British government.

He lived in a patriarchal society, as one of the patriarchs. Such societies and men change the ideas that guide them slowly, and, when they do, only reluctantly. Washington did not want to believe ill of the king and the king's government. Before the crises of the 1760s and 1770s, he had never given royal government much thought. His world was made up of men uninterested in change that bent the proprieties, but they were sensitive to challenges to their rights and to their liberty.

In the early 1770s the rhythm of planters' lives followed the cycle of crops. The slowness—by modern standards—of transportation everywhere, but especially across the Atlantic, reinforced this measured pace. On the most basic level, these circumstances enforced a kind of stability.

In referring to the defense of American liberty in these years of the Townshend crisis as "the cause," Washington meant the defense of the right of Americans to govern and tax themselves. He thought of the right as a central part of the British constitution, and he came to believe that governing authorities in Britain had abandoned that constitution, while in America he and others like him insisted that they could not under its terms be taxed by any body in which they were not represented.

The three years following the repeal of the Townshend duties saw no fresh outrage, no act of terrible oppression against the constitution he prized, but he did not believe that the cause was now out of danger. The British government had ceased oppressive action, at least for the moment, but it had not given up its claim to do whatever it chose to do. So matters rested, or drifted.

In this lull until 1774, Washington wrote little about Virginia's rights, though he did not suspend thought about them. He gave his time, however, to his planting life. That life sometimes led him to extraordinary ventures; one, in 1772, embodied his long-standing hope of opening up the upper Potomac River to navigation "from Fort Cumberland to tide water." Land in the Ohio Country remained in the front of his mind, especially the grant Governor Dinwiddie had authorized in 1754 for Washington and the veterans of the disastrous campaign that ended at Fort Necessity. He reported to his old officers and soldiers on the division then under way of those lands, said goodbye to George William Fairfax, who was moving to England, and agreed to take on Fairfax's power of attorney in America. Since Belvoir was not going to be sold, this responsibility included supervising the overseer of the plantation and looking after the house. Washington's own work in business demanded more than ordinary energies, as he sought better services for his increased stake in the market and bought additional slaves for his new mill. He also built a ship to carry his flour to Barbados, a venture that led to protracted trouble with the ship's master, who proved unreliable.[35]

In June 1773, while Washington juggled the responsibilities of farm, field, and sea, plus service to widows who had had difficult husbands, he faced even greater responsibilities in his family. He had traveled with Jack to the city, got him settled in lodgings and studies, and returned to Mount Vernon. He had not been home long when Patsy Custis died in epileptic seizure. She had endured such episodes for several years, events that aroused the sympathy of her stepfather and mother, as well as their dread that one might kill her. When that occurred, her mother, filled with grief, needed desperately the love of her husband. Washington gave it unstintingly and, for several months, devoted much of his time to her care. Martha Washington rallied a few months later, but for as long as her suffering demanded his attention, Washington withdrew from all but necessary business. A very different sort of family concern had nagged at him throughout 1773: Jack had told his family in April that he was engaged to be married. The news had surprised everyone, including his teacher Jonathan Boucher. Jack had quietly courted Eleanor (Nelly) Calvert, who proved early on to be much more interesting to him than his studies with Boucher and the faculty of King's College.[36]

The rhythms of ordinary life changed radically in 1774, when Parliament acted in response to the Boston Tea Party. When Washington first heard of the destruction of the tea, he felt both disapproval and dismay. These feelings soon gave way to stronger feelings of anger at Parliament, which had responded with the Intolerable Acts, closing up the port of Boston and transforming the government of Massachusetts into one with no place for liberty or the British constitution. In May, summoned to Williamsburg, he voted with most of the burgesses in favor of resolutions calling for a day of fasting and prayer in protest against British actions.[37]

The pace of opposition to British measures now picked up. At first the Boston Port Act had seemed to Virginians to be the most shocking aspect of what Parliament had done. Washington expressed his dismay on learning of the act, but he soon realized that Parliament had broader measures under way that threatened "American liberty." This term appeared in his writings and that of others early in the spring. It was American liberty and American rights that were at risk, not simply Boston's or Massachusetts's; and the oppression prospectively included all of America. There were hints in Washington's letters even before this crisis that a plot had been started in Britain to reduce the liberties of Americans. Now, with the assault on Boston, it was out in the open. His part in organizing Virginians and Americans throughout the colonies rested on this premise that a plot existed, designed to end long-standing freedom in America.[38]

As a member of the House of Burgesses, he took part in generating support of the first Virginia statement calling for a repudiation of the British action. Though the Burgesses set the tone, most of the action in Virginia early in 1774 took place on the county and provincial levels.

After the House of Burgesses met as an informal body in the Raleigh Tavern—a site selected after Governor Dunmore dissolved the body—official fetters could be thrown off. Lord Dunmore thought he had sent the House packing on May 26, but the next day it designated itself the "Association," composed of members who would manage the opposition to official action for the next two years. On May 30, the Association called on its members to meet on August 1, when an agreement to ban trade with Britain would be made. The Association reported in a broadside that prevailing opinion was that nonimportation would be the first step, followed by nonexportation if the first failed to persuade Parliament to withdraw its Boston policies.[39]

The organizations that swung into action after the dissolution of the House of Burgesses served Virginia well into 1775. Washington chaired one in July, "a general Meeting of the Freeholders and Inhabitants of the County of Fairfax." He was of course a member of the House representing the county and widely known throughout the colony. The meeting in July resembled similar meetings all over Virginia and eventually produced a set of resolves that recounted the history of the controversy with Parliament and proposed a detailed course of action in response to the Intolerable Acts. Its strictures and prescriptions were to find their way into the decisions of both Continental Congresses. These were the Fairfax Resolves.[40]

George Mason wrote the Fairfax Resolves, not his neighbor George Washington. Mason, who lived about twenty miles away in Gunston Hall, was a good friend of Washington. The two men wrote each other and spent time together working their way through the problems common to all the colonies. Mason visited Washington the day before the July meeting for Fairfax County, and his influence on Washington remained strong throughout the year.

The first ten of the Fairfax Resolves laid out in some detail the basis of colonial grievances, insisting that "the most important and valuable Part of the British Constitution, upon which it's very Existence depends, is the fundamental Principle of the People's being governed by no Laws, to which they have not given their Consent, by Representatives freely chosen by themselves." It was Mason's sentence, but Washington might have written it. In all of the protests emanating from the Fairfax meeting and all the Virginia Conventions that followed, preceding the First and Second Continental Congresses, the fundamental issue in Washington's thought was the right of the colonies to govern themselves. He did not advocate independence in 1774; the right to consent—or not to consent—to measures bearing on colonial liberties was an example of the freedom he had in mind. He, along with virtually all colonial leaders, denied that they were looking for independence; they believed—some, like Washington with many doubts—that freedom to govern themselves was possible within the British Empire. This belief and a sense of honor led them to offer to pay for the tea destroyed in the Boston Tea Party. Mason, with Washington's support, argued in the Fairfax Resolves that the British Parliament's claim to "the Power of regulating our Trade and Commerce" was necessary for "the general Good of that great Body-politic of which we are a Part." Mason added that this claim and its exercise in the past were, however, in some "Degree repugnant to the Principles of the Constitution." He was willing, temporarily it seemed, to compromise liberty for the general good of the empire—a willingness that, being repugnant, soon disappeared.

The Fairfax Resolves and the discussion and revision in the months that followed all contributed to Washington's political thought before independence. He took part in the discussions in this extended period, and as far as anyone in Virginia could tell he agreed with their development in the Continental Congresses, a development that gradually claimed more power for the colonies as it rejected that of Parliament. For a time the rejection of Parliament's claims, while maintaining the fiction that the colonies were loyal constituents of the empire, depended on a distinction between king and Parliament. It was the king's ministers and Parliament that threatened colonial liberties—not the king. Eventually this idea of separation crumbled as the king showed himself as an enemy of America.[41]

Throughout the process of rejecting every part of the British policies, Washington held firm. There was in almost all his statements, especially in letters to friends and family members, harshness, even bitterness, in his judgments of Crown and Parliament. His friend Bryan Fairfax, who had worked closely with him on other matters, disagreed with the measures of resistance adopted by the Burgesses that followed its dissolution in May. In the exchange of letters between the two friends, Fairfax said that "the Majority of the english Parliament, or a great part, [acted] from honest tho' erroneous principles."

But Washington saw corruption in the policies, and described British actions as "a regular Plan at the Expence of Law & Justice, to overthrow our Constitutional Rights & liberties." A month later, after the meeting on the Fairfax Resolves, he insisted in an argument with Bryan Fairfax that if the colonies submitted "to every Imposition that can be heap'd upon us," such submission "will make us tame, & object Slaves, as the Blacks we Rule over with such arbitrary Sway."[42]

The meetings of the First Continental Congress, in September 1774, followed by the Second Congress, in May 1775, brought the process of alienation on the part of the American colonies to a head. Washington served in both meetings, though he left the Second long before it declared independence to assume command of the army.

In September, Washington had arrived in Philadelphia with a reputation as a man of great wealth and a military leader. The wealth was real, but a story that was told concerning an offer he supposedly made to finance an army to fight the British was not. His military background had brought him a reputation that had generated such fantasies. He seems always to have impressed others with his bearing; he stood out among the delegates and elicited comment. Silas Deane, of Connecticut, described his countenance as "hard," but added that he had "a very young Look, & an easy Soldierlik Air." Deane knew something of Washington's history in the previous war, noting that Washington "was the means of saving the remains" of Braddock's army. Deane also praised Washington's speech in public: "he speaks Modestly, & in cool but determined Stile & Accent." There were other comments about his style and bearing, all favorable to him.[43]

Washington played a limited role in the First Congress, but in the Second he found himself the delegates' choice to lead the Continental Army. He had arrived at its meeting in May dressed in civilian garb. Within a few days, as talk of war increased among the delegates, he began appearing in the meetings wearing a military uniform, probably that of a special volunteer company formed in Virginia just before he left for Philadelphia. The uniform reminded delegates of fame earned in the war against the French. It's likely no reminder was needed, given his soldierlike bearing and his record.

Washington himself had misgivings about his ability to command successfully a large army. He wrote Martha of his desire to avoid accepting the command "from consciousness of its being a trust too great for my Capacity." But he also felt that he must accept it, "as it has been a kind of destiny that has thrown me upon this Service, I shall hope that my undertaking of it, is designed to answer some good purpose." There was another dimension to his feelings about the command—turning it down, he felt, "would have reflected dishonour upon myself, and given pain to my friends." His reflections reveal the complications for him of the call to duty, and it is not too much to say that he both wanted and did not want to command the army. Whatever satisfaction this new responsibility—this calling—gave him owed much to his glimpse of destiny and his sense of honor. His musings did not reach brooding about it. He escaped that state of mind by recognizing that he was in the hands of Providence, as he said. That belief was enough—he would be George Washington, American commander in chief, guided by Providence.[44]

PART TWO

American

4

Boston

George Washington rode into the camp of the New England Army in Cambridge, Massachusetts, on July 2, a quiet Sunday afternoon. He had left Philadelphia on June 23, escorted by a detachment of cavalry, the Philadelphia Light Horse. Generals Philip Schuyler and Charles Lee were with him, as well as two young men: Joseph Reed, who would serve as his military secretary, and Thomas Mifflin, who had been named his aide-de-camp. Schuyler, a wealthy New Yorker, had been given the New York command; Charles Lee, a former officer in the British army now living in Virginia, would serve Washington in operations around Boston. Both had genuine strengths, and both would serve Washington well and ill.[1]

Reed was better educated than Mifflin, having been graduated from Princeton and having spent two years at Middle Temple, a legal institution. He knew more than the law, and before the Revolution had received an informal education in British politics through frequent attendance at parliamentary debates in 1764 and 1765 when he should have been immersed in his legal books. Mifflin, like Reed born to a good Pennsylvania family, also graduated from college, the College of Philadelphia (1760), and entered business soon after. His political experience before the Revolution saw him serve four terms in the Pennsylvania legislature and then the Continental Congress, from 1774 until called into the army when the war began.

The Philadelphia horsemen on the ride remained with Washington until New Brunswick, New Jersey, where he spent the night of June 24. He rode to Newark early the next morning—his practice was to travel early, even giving up breakfast, in order to spare his horse and himself the heat of the day. Because of uncertainty about the strength of loyalty in New York, he entered that city the next day by a circuitous route that saw him proceed up the west side of the North River in order to cross at Hoboken. He was told the day before that the royal governor, William Tryon, who had been in Britain, was about to sail in, carrying unknown intentions and instructions from the king's government.

In New York, Washington proceeded cautiously. He met with members of the New York Provincial Congress and sampled local opinion. The New Yorkers were eager to learn more about Bunker Hill, and told him of a letter that had come into their hands, written by Massachusetts authorities for the president of the Continental Congress. Undoubtedly it contained information about the battle; would Washington open it and share its contents with them? Washington hesitated—the letter, after all, was addressed to the body to which he reported—but gave in when it was pointed out that perhaps the letter also brought military intelligence. The local seekers were right on both counts—the letter told of the killing on Bunker Hill, and it reported that gunpowder was lacking in the New England Army. This last finding was one Washington would grow weary of hearing. For the moment, he kept this matter to himself.

The New York Congress had other things on its mind besides a desire to discover what had gone on in June at Bunker Hill. It presented a memorial to Washington in a quiet ceremony in which it claimed to "rejoice in the appointment of a gentleman from whose abilities and virtues we are taught to expect both security and peace."[2] With fine sentiments, but ultimately vague, the memorial was probably wise, given the setting of its presentation—a few doors away from the New York meeting in Washington's honor was William Tryon, royal governor of the colony.

The next day, July 3, 1775, Washington assumed command of the army. It was still a New England Army in most ways—its commander, Artemas Ward, was a former Massachusetts militia officer, and most of its troops were from the New England colonies. Ward, five years older than Washington, was a graduate of Harvard and had made his living in business, keeping a store soon after his graduation. He turned over his command without complaint—perhaps even with a sense of relief.

For as Washington soon discovered, the New England Army, now officially the Continental Army, was not a fine-tuned instrument. It did not know itself well, an ignorance exposed when he asked for a report on its numbers and on the supply of ammunition available to its troops. His request for an accounting met silence, for neither General Ward nor his staff knew. A week later, the report came in and reinforced his worries. According to what he was now told, the army numbered 16,600 enlisted men and noncommissioned officers, of whom not quite 14,400 were present and fit for duty. He believed that he needed a little over 22,000 soldiers to maintain the Siege of Boston and to repel any British efforts to lift it. Estimates varied of the size of the enemy's force; at this time, the best held that the British army had 11,500 in Boston. Besides the army, which was much better than the one he commanded, the British navy controlled the waters around Boston; indeed, the Atlantic Ocean was mostly theirs, enabling them to move forces around and concentrate them at strategic points.[3]

Discovering with any exactness how much powder and lead was available in the various regiments of the colonies proved to be impossible, but all reports suggested that shortages of both were common. Washington concluded in a few days that the supply would not allow even limited use of the field pieces he had. This shortage persisted for months, and there never was a time in 1775 when he felt secure in the knowledge that his soldiers had the ammunition they needed. His first letters to John Hancock, president of the Continental Congress, revealed his disquiet at this circumstance.[4]

Even though more ammunition would arrive, it was a feeling that never really left him while he remained near Boston, for in the early months of the siege his army was very much a work in progress. It did not look like an army: Most regiments lacked uniforms; all needed camp equipment; some needed arms, and those who had them had little powder and sometimes fewer musket balls. Discipline was also in short supply. Some soldiers fired off their guns apparently for the pleasure of the sound, while others wasted powder in taking shots at British soldiers in out-of-range outposts. American soldiers made a practice of leaving their own outposts before being relieved, thereby exposing their fellows to attack. Many soldiers were dirty—bathing was not a favored activity of many, and a layer of grime did not trouble them in their slovenly appearance.

Behind all these deficiencies stood bad organization and management. Militia duty in many New England towns by this time made few demands on anyone, and the many officers had not prepared themselves to lead men. In peacetime, training days frequently were social occasions. New England regiments were led by officers who differed little from their men, in that they were all imbued with a spirit of equality. Status counted—education, family background, wealth, and occupation made a difference—but even though these social differences set men apart, and set some above others, a spirit of equality often undermined such distinctions. The practice by which common soldiers chose their officers made it difficult for officers to issue orders and to train their men, who often were neighbors. If familiarity did not breed contempt, it inhibited forceful measures in training and disciplining men.

"Discipline" was not a word most men in the New England Army wanted to hear. Discipline required that they stay in their camps when they wished to go home, unless given permission to leave. Officers who lived nearby sometimes took advantage of their rank and went home to sleep in their own beds. Washington learned of this habit and forbade it—several times. Discipline also required men to carry out the orders of their officers, a requirement made harder to stomach when the officers giving the orders had no great skill that suggested they were qualified to do so.

The troops Washington led appalled him at times. That they were nasty, dirty, and disobedient was bad enough, but he recognized immediately that their officers were equally deficient, for they had failed to provide the leadership essential to an effective army. They, in a sense, were more responsible than the men for the disorder and confusion that marked the army.

Washington initially felt a certain revulsion when he looked at these soldiers—"nasty," "dirty," and "raw" were all words he used to describe them. The overall condition of the army evoked a more dramatic characterization—it was in "chaos." As far as he was concerned, the source of this condition lay in New England society itself. Its equality of condition—or the absence of gentlemen of status—explained much, he thought, for the officers, cut from the same cloth as the soldiers they commanded, hesitated to give orders that might not find favor in the ranks. Whatever Washington's convictions about the army he had taken over—and its officers—he was determined to make it into a fighting force. Not all of its officers were irredeemable, and not all of its men ungovernable. What was needed, he decided early in July, was to purge the army of its weak officers and to drive out its cowards through courts-martial.

The group he most despised were an inheritance from Bunker Hill. Though the Americans had lost the ground, they had won the battle, if British losses were taken into account. Still, the behavior of a handful of officers in the battle festered in the memories of some of the officers (and probably men) in the army that surrounded Boston. A number of those who had quailed in the face of the British attack, some even deserting their troops, remained in command. Those who had not run now brought such conduct to the attention of their new commander. Washington responded by ordering courts-martial and approving sentences already handed down in the three weeks following the battle. These cases gave him an opportunity to instill in the troops the code of a soldier. One notorious case involved John Callender, a captain in a Massachusetts regiment who had been convicted of refusing to return up the hill with his cannon when ordered to do so by Major General Israel Putnam. Only the threat of immediate death at General Putnam's hands had convinced him to go up the hill again, but once back up and out of Putnam's gaze, he deserted his post and abandoned his cannon. The court-martial found Callender guilty and sentenced him to be "cashiered and dismissed" from service in the army. Washington seized the opportunity to state, in the general orders announcing the sentence, that cowardice was "A Crime of all others, the most infamous in a Soldier, the most injurious to an Army, and the last to be forgiven; inasmuch as it may, and often does happen, that the Cowardice of a single Officer may prove the Destruction of the whole Army."[5]

Callender's court-martial took place early in July, less than a week after Washington's arrival. By August 20, five captains had joined him in disgrace, and two colonels were under arrest. One of the two was acquitted. The other, Colonel Samuel Gerrish, compounded his difficulty a few weeks later by failing to repel an attack on Sewall's Point. Gerrish had refused to order his soldiers to fight and paid for his curious behavior by being charged again with cowardice.[6]

By the end of December 1775, more than fifty officers had faced courts-martial, and almost all were convicted. Their offenses— additional cases of cowardice, fraud in handling provisions for their soldiers, "beating" their troops, "profane swearing," striking a superior officer, abusive expressions, neglect of duty—suggest that Washington had good reason to regard his officers with worry.[7]

His feelings about the troops were divided. "The Men would fight very well (if properly Officered)," he wrote in late August, "although they are an exceeding dirty & nasty people." In fact, he went on the say, "had they been properly conducted at Bunkers Hill . . . or those that were there properly supported, the Regulars would have met with a shameful defeat."[8]

Nothing in the conduct of the enlisted men during the remainder of the year softened Washington's estimate of them. Some of their offenses were typical of those in almost any army at any time: Drunkenness, stealing, being absent without leave, and insulting their officers are representative samples. A persistent source of distress for Washington was the number of those who left their posts without authorization, and another was those who fired their muskets to no purpose. Not all of such behavior brought offending soldiers to courts-martial that were reviewed by Washington. Regiments sometimes dealt with conduct of this sort within themselves—noncommissioned officers undoubtedly corrected with their fists many of those who strayed from the path of military righteousness. Still, other offenses, such as stealing, were punished by courts-martial under the army's control. Throughout its life in 1775, the army was a ragtag affair, often badly fed, clothed, and paid. Perhaps these circumstances account for the variety of things ordinary soldiers stole—clothing and food were most often chosen—but whatever the reason, when caught they usually felt the lash thirty-nine times.

By the end of the year there were fewer cases of unauthorized abandonment of posts or sleeping on duty. This circumstance reflected the imposition of tighter discipline and better training. Yet there were several instances in which courts-martial found soldiers guilty of "mutiny." The largest instance—thirty-three riflemen of Colonel William Thompson's Pennsylvania regiment—had acted on the evening of September 10, after one of their sergeants had been confined for neglecting his duty. These riflemen had joined the forces around Boston well after the siege began, and they seem to have come into the army thinking very well of themselves. Or, more likely, they simply had not been trained thoroughly and they resented the imposition of normal duty and discipline. Their company commander had not seen fit to crack down on them when they refused to perform ordinary fatigue duties, including work on entrenchments and fortifications on Prospect Hill, in the northern sector that faced Bunker Hill. Their regiment lay under General Nathanael Greene's command, and he had in the days before their outburst learned of their disaffection—they were, he wrote Washington, "very sulky," but "there is little to be feared" from them.[9]

Greene was right in this judgment, though he must have wondered at it when he learned that some of the riflemen had set off with loaded muskets for the main guard in Cambridge to free one of their own from the guardhouse. Greene, Washington, and Charles Lee, with several companies from nearby, set out to stop them. One of the generals, probably Greene, ordered the mutineers to ground their weapons, which they did immediately. One of their colleagues who refused to take part, and who was thoroughly ashamed of his fellows, commented three days later that "these thirty-two rascals" had surrendered without a fight and were frightened at the "proceedings" they had set afoot.[10]

The courts-martial that followed in a few days recognized that, shocking as the affair might seem, no deep plot was involved, but apparently only troubled spirits. The punishments were light—twenty shillings per man in fines, with one man sentenced only to time in the guardhouse. Washington, who had an instinctive understanding of such upheavals, approved the sentences.

There was one other unspoken circumstance that encouraged light punishment in this case, and Washington felt it more acutely than anyone else: the morale of the army. The "greater Part of the Troops are in a State not far from Mutiny," he reported to John Hancock. One source of poor morale was low pay—or no pay. If the troops were not paid soon, and if they were not paid "more punctually" in the future, "the Army must absolutely break up." There were other reasons, of course, for the discontent of the soldiers. The army was not badly fed then, and its troops, though soon in need of winter clothing, were not ill clothed, but they needed uniforms; without them their appearance was not smart, not even military, and many of the men did not feel like soldiers. Sitting outside Boston often prevented them from marching or drilling, and the absence of such military actions robbed soldiers of the feeling that they were a sharp outfit fully prepared for anything.

Troops in trenches, behind breastworks, or standing watch in outposts undoubtedly recognized the danger in their positions, for they could see the British enemy, at times almost within musket range and usually never more than a mile away. Standing watch had few rewards, and Washington's army, no more than most European armies, did not patrol vigorously. Had they done so, their spirits might have been higher, but after Bunker Hill there was not much fighting—few skirmishes that kept men on edge and gave them reason for what they were doing. In place, the army did not improve substantially—discipline continued to be elusive, and skills were undeveloped.[11]

Washington explained, at least in part, the disappointing character of the rank and file of the army as a consequence of the weak corps of officers. The officers he inherited on taking command of the New England Army had given him difficulties almost immediately. The trouble began at the top. Congress had reserved to itself the power to appoint all general officers. Legislatures or provincial congresses of the states were to appoint field- and company-grade officers. In the case of vacancies occasioned by the death or removal of a colonel or lower-ranked officer, Congress authorized Washington to appoint, by "brevet or warrant," a replacement who would serve until the provincial congress chose someone else.[12]

Officers with the rank of general were another matter—Congress, attuned to the sensitivities of their constituencies in the states, reserved these appointments to themselves. The problem arose in the ranking of these officers, all of whom had reputations and standing locally. The most serious case involved John Thomas and William Heath, of Massachusetts, both appointed as brigadier generals, with Heath standing at fourth in the list of eight brigadiers and Thomas at sixth. This ranking conflicted with the order of the two in the Massachusetts service, where Heath was junior to Thomas. It so happened that the Massachusetts order reflected the competence and abilities of the two men, a fact apparently widely known. Thomas, convinced that he had been shabbily treated, threatened to resign. Washington did not know either man and, understandably, hesitated at first to resolve the conflict, but in a few days he came to see that Thomas's abilities were greater than Heath's. Fortunately, two powerful leaders in Massachusetts,

James Warren and Joseph Hawley, stepped in and persuaded Heath that Thomas deserved precedence. A means of changing the ranking presented itself when Seth Pomeroy, of Northampton, who had been placed first on the brigadiers' list, failed to respond to his own appointment. Washington waited to hear from Pomeroy, and, when nothing was forthcoming from him, put Thomas in the top place. Congress itself had reconsidered the rankings at the instigation of representatives from Massachusetts and sent Thomas his commission in early August.[13]

Not all of the strife among officers arose from their ranking, and not all found solutions so easily. Rather, there were petty jealousies in evidence throughout the army. Many of them revolved around provincial rivalries and did not call for intervention by Washington, but the existence of these rivalries, and the local pride they revealed, troubled him. Washington wished in effect to erase state lines, to make the army truly continental. But at Boston, and especially in the first years of the war, he found that officers wished to remain with their own state's troops. Their vision clearly was narrower than his, and the troops in the commands of the various states tended to agree with their officers.

Washington attempted in these milieus to banish provincialism in favor of unity. With his army surrounding Boston, it was more than unity of command he sought—it was unity of feeling and morale, and indeed a unity that implied the existence of a national union. He did not mean to destroy provincial loyalties, and he remained a Virginian to the core throughout his life. But he believed that the preservation of American freedom—his most profound purpose—could not survive policies that placed the states first.

Transcending state loyalties and their expression in the army and the Congress required careful diplomacy. Working his will in his command found him dealing with the states, usually governors and provincial congresses, with sensitivity and care. If Washington realized that he was widely regarded with something approaching awe throughout America, he gave no hint of it. There was no talking down to the governors or the various members of the Continental Congress whom he met or corresponded with. All were regarded with respect, their concerns listened to and responded to when a response was possible.

Congress had made Washington commander of the Continental Army and charged him with defending the American states; it had

not given him complete jurisdiction or power over all military matters. It could not have made such a grant had it wished to, for the
thirteen states would not have allowed it. Washington's dealings with
the variety of powers on the American side revealed his own recognition that much was expected of him both in using his power and in
making room for the states to use theirs. His understanding of these
realities—political realities—is nowhere better illustrated than in his
careful attempts to supply his army with the materials it needed to
maintain itself and to fight the enemy in Boston.[14]

The lack of gunpowder was one of the realities. Shortly after his
arrival in the Cambridge headquarters, Washington was given a
report that was mildly reassuring, but a month later a second report,
stating that the total amount of powder would provide "not more than
9 rounds per Man," caused him to describe the army's situation as
"melancholy." This term, he soon realized, might properly be applied
to almost the entire stock of supplies available to his army. In the
months that followed, he used every means he could think of to equip
and supply his army without revealing to the British across the lines
his woeful circumstances.

It was the Continental Congress and its president, John Hancock, to
whom he turned most often. His letters to Hancock and nearby governors, especially Nicholas Cooke, of Rhode Island, and Jonathan Trumbull, of Connecticut, betray neither panic nor uncertainty concerning
the American cause, and they are devoid of any expression of disappointment in Congress or the governors and their states. But while
these accounts never wander into the personal, they are rich in facts
that made clear to Congress that Washington regarded the army's circumstances as unsatisfactory for a fighting force.[15]

Hancock, in Philadelphia, did not have to question Washington
about what was going on around Boston, for Washington took pains
to keep him informed of the circumstances of the army as well as the
condition of British entrenchments, their supplies, and the movements
of their ships in and out of Boston Harbor. These letters to Hancock
made him in effect almost a brother officer at headquarters, a trusted
colleague, and a friend. Yet they were always respectful and offered
reassurance, if any was needed, that Washington, the commanding
general, knew where power lay in the young republic and was determined to carry out the policies of its government.[16]

The lines of his authority were not as clear as his responsibility for the American military effort, and in the exchanges between him and Hancock, they were only gradually made clear. If Washington's restraint was much in evidence in these letters, he used them to gently educate his superior. His sense of the importance of concerted action by all of the states was frequently a subtext in his reports to Hancock when he did not disclose explicitly his concern.

Yet it may not have been clear to his masters in Philadelphia what Washington was actually doing in the siege of Boston: giving the army its form and being. The Congress understood enough to join in deciding on the regimental organization. A regiment, one of its committees decided after conferences in camp with Washington, would have 728 officers and men. An infantry regiment would differ from an artillery regiment in numbers of officers and men. (The numbers specified changed throughout the war.) Washington proved receptive to such definitions coming from a civilian body, and not simply because he helped it decide on such matters. He believed in civilian control, and he also saw that implicating civilians in such decisions gave them a stake in the support of their creation.[17]

Sometimes in these months Washington explicitly taught Hancock to understand what else was required if an army was to be a whole—a rounded and complete institution. In an army "properly organized," he wrote about three weeks after his arrival, "there are sundry officers of an Inferiour kind, such as Wagon Master, Master Carpenter." He confessed that he did not know whether his powers "are sufficiently extensive for such Appointment," but if they were he would—he promised—establish such places and fill them with "a strict Regard to Oeconomy, & the public Interest." There is in this letter a fusion of tact and determination—no talking down to Congress, or its president, but a thoughtful explanation of how things should work in an army, with an implicit question (or request) that he might possess the authority to take an administrative action.[18]

The letters Washington wrote to Congress and others in the six months after he assumed command might be read as statements crowded with administrative and political matters. Such a reading would be fair, but not altogether accurate. For though Washington gave almost all of his time to the creation of an army, he yearned for the opportunity to use it, to drive the British from Boston. Neither he nor anyone else on the American side anticipated with any sureness how the crisis with Britain might end. He was not alone in supposing that force would end the conflict, but others, including some in Congress, believed that simply holding on in Boston would compel the British government to come to accept the colonies' desire to govern their own affairs, with the exception of those that pertained to some vague idea of imperial interests. For several months into the new year, 1776, some Americans clung to the fiction that the crisis was between themselves and the British ministry, sans the king. This feeling found expression in such terms as "ministerial" troops—not the king's, or even the Crown's. Some even expected the king to step in and ease recalcitrant ministers out of office. But when the king agreed to the Prohibitory Act, which barred trade with the colonies and then issued the proclamation that declared them in rebellion, such feeling in America largely vanished. For his part, Washington had given up on peace within the empire when he assumed command of the army, and he had in letters to friends berated British actions as the king's actions. He faced many men who still cherished ideas of accommodation, but there was in him a growing clarity that nothing important could be accomplished until he drove the British out of Boston. Doing so, however, would not be easy, and his first steps toward fighting were taken to secure his army's defense.[19]

The day after Washington's arrival in Cambridge, he rode the lines. Something far from expelling the British was on his mind; the question, rather, was whether he could hold his position and maintain what seemed to be a siege. To that end, he began straightening his lines, which amounted to moving several redoubts and strengthening others. These steps entailed the construction of heavier fortifications, with more gabions and fascines added to existing positions. Washington worried in these early weeks about being surprised by the British attacking in such force as to carry the American defenses. Knowing the weakness of his own army and suspecting that it might not be able to withstand such an attack, he asked himself and others why the British were not coming out of Boston to destroy the American force. This worry also led him to strengthen his outposts, usually a small contingent of soldiers (and sometimes only a soldier or two) stationed in front of the American positions. These men, sometimes close enough to talk to British soldiers in outposts of their own, were intended to give warning to the main forces should the British emerge in a surprise assault. The American sentries sometimes left their outposts before being relieved, simply taking off to attend to their own purposes, heedless of the damage their desertion might inflict. Washington believed that some means of tying these soldiers to responsible action might be found by assigning such duty only to men "Native of this Country," that is of New England. He added that a man who "has a Wife, or Family in it, to whom he is known to be attached" would be acceptable. Whether such choices were always reliable is doubtful; what is clear is that Washington also complained about men who obviously lived near Boston and went home on occasion to visit wives and families.[20]

Washington's uneasiness about his enemy's intentions never left him, though there were moments when he speculated that Howe's army might actually fear their American opponents. He was close to being right in this opinion, for under Gage (who was relieved of his command on September 26) and then William Howe, who took over from Gage, the army regarded the Americans with a concern that bordered on fear. Gage and Howe both believed that their soldiers constituted a force better than the Americans, but a large-scale attack against their enemy would inevitably bring heavy losses. The British did not have an army of such size as to allow a costly victory. Their reluctance to engage the Americans was reinforced by their experience at Bunker Hill, where they had traded a thousand casualties for a piece of ground that offered scant protection for the city in which they found themselves.[21]

These British leaders could not believe that Washington might actually push them out of Boston and felt that nothing much needed to be done until reinforcements from Britain arrived. They did not know that minds no clearer than their own ruled the British government. The king wanted the rebellion to be put down and told his ministers so, but they did not know with any exactness what Gage and Howe had in mind. Uncertainty and even confusion abounded: What, beyond a few noisy radicals, was driving this rebellion? the ministers asked. When they attempted to answer that question, they found themselves appalled by anxious wails from men on the scene: "all is confusion, anarchy, and wretchedness—a whole country in rebellion—for such it is now." Washington, historians have often pointed out, had never led an army; the opposition leaders at home in Britain and in the field in America had never faced a major rebellion—in fact, a revolution—in the empire. All of the British generals in America had far more experience of large-scale operations than Washington. But they, like their superiors at home, were puzzled by the problems they faced while sitting in Boston.[22]

So the two sides sat and watched one another. The British had a spy in Washington's headquarters, Dr. Benjamin Church, director or surgeon general of the army's hospitals. Church, who as a boy had attended Boston Latin and Harvard College, was a fiery patriot in the years of protest, giving speeches on behalf of the American cause and indicating his opposition to British measures. In these years he formed friendships with British officers and evidently changed his mind about the grounds of conflict between Britain and America. Someone in General Gage's command helped along this change of mind by bribing Church. His treachery was discovered when a letter he wrote to friends in the British army was discovered. Washington had Church jailed and then deported, not knowing just how much had been revealed. The intercepted letter had contained intelligence about the army's size and condition and provided some information about a projected invasion of Canada. Just how much Church had conveyed to Gage before he was discovered is not clear. What is clear is that other spies operated in the American sector. Gage kept a close watch from his lines, but seems never to have learned the true state of the Continental Army.[23]

Washington was no less assiduous in learning all that he could about the British in Boston, their strength, their activities within the city, the size of their forces, and the extent of their power. He was never able to find out with any certainty what they planned to do. Washington, like his counterpart, attempted to place spies within British lines. He was no more successful than the enemy in their use, but he had other means, including placing observers in the hills and harbor around Boston. Throughout the siege, they informed him of the ships that entered the harbor and reported on troop movements, several of which he pondered as forecasting a major British effort to end the siege.[24]

To strengthen the army's fortification, Washington on several occasions ordered attacks of some size. One such action occurred in late August, when he sent General John Sullivan and 2,500 men to take Ploughed Hill, then unoccupied, in order to prevent a British capture. Ploughed Hill lay just west of the Mystic River, standing near Bunker Hill, and was of obvious tactical importance. The Americans moved onto the hill on August 26 and dug in under the cover of darkness. The British, usually quite attentive to what their enemy was up to, did not notice the changes in the American lines until 9:00 A.M. Their response was a fairly heavy cannonade that lasted most of the day. The entrenched Americans suffered only light casualties. Washington took satisfaction in this maneuver, but did not gloat.

Rather, he asked questions, which he would repeat throughout the remainder of the siege, until late winter 1776: When will the British come out—or why haven't they come out, presumably in a full-scale attack? Before long he revised the question to: Shall we attack them? Or, in more urgent terms: Why shouldn't we attack them?[25]

He raised this question to his generals in a formal "circular" on September 8, saying that if the British will not come out and fight, why should we not go in? He gave no detailed plans of what he had in mind—no plan of attack that placed his regiments in any sort of formation beyond indicating that he thought that the American move should have two prongs: one on land, up the neck from Roxbury, and the other on the water, by troops carried in boats across the bay from American lines, presumably those at Cambridge and to the north. If he laid out no tactics of attack, he indicated with great clarity the reasons underlying his proposals. These justifications said nothing about the British fortifications, or the troops in them; rather, they all centered on the problems of maintaining the American army in the approaching winter. American soldiers, he reminded his commanders, were badly clad, fed, and housed. They seemingly lacked everything, including pay, firewood, and gunpowder. As if these deficiencies in the army were not enough, the army itself would begin to evaporate as men went home when their enlistments ran out around the beginning of the new year.

All this was reasonable enough and true, but perhaps his most powerful point was one that he did not make much of: his feeling (for feeling it was) that "the expence of supporting this army will so far exceed any Idea that was form'd in Congress of it, that I do not know what will be the consequences [of not attacking the British soon]." In offering this assessment, he confessed that he wished to have "a speedy finish of the dispute." He asked his officers to consider all of the circumstances in favor of an assault but not "to loose sight of the difficulties—the hazard—and the loss that may accompany the attempt—nor, what will be the probable consequences of a failure."[26]

The council of generals turned him down, "at present at least," citing the "state" of British lines, meaning the formidable defenses the British army had thrown up. It also noted that "some important Advices from England" were expected, a reference to a rumor then current in the army that the government of Lord North would soon fall, to be replaced apparently by one sympathetic to the American cause. This expectation was of doubtful merit, but it probably helped reconcile the generals to their advice, which smacked of timidity in the face of their commander's desire to take a chance. Still, the generals had a reason to recommend caution, for Washington gave no argument based on the realities of American fighting qualities. He did not argue that the American troops were better than the British, for he did not believe that they were; he did not suggest that the defensive works around Boston were weak or badly placed. He knew, as everyone did, that the British artillery was better, to say nothing of British infantry; he did not claim that Greene, Ward, Heath, and the others were superior to the likes of Gage, Clinton, and Howe. What he argued concerning the military realities came down to the certainty that his army would soon vanish as its enlistments ran out. Therefore, if the dispute were to end favorably, he must strike immediately and in surprise. The reality he counted on was surprise—as he told his generals, "the Success of the Enterprize (if undertaken) must depend on a great measure upon the suddenness of the stroke."[27]

The council of generals advised him not to risk the army and then turned to another reality outlined by Washington: the maintenance of the army at hand. Washington had warned Congress of what faced them, but Congress could provide only limited help. The governors and legislative bodies in the states could do more, and in several respects did. But finding more men and money for Washington's army remained difficult. Their problem—and, most immediately, Washington's— was how to persuade men who suffered and struggled to survive and on occasion, in the autumn of 1775, to fight while short of virtually everything, including food and housing, muskets and ammunition. An attack on Boston that was successful would have made all such problems disappear, and when Washington wrote Hancock of the decision to withhold an attack, he admitted that though he had been advised to give up the idea, he had not "wholly laid it aside."[28]

Spoiling for an all-out offensive against the British, he had to settle, three weeks later, for a conference with a committee sent by Congress to see how things were going in the army. Congress, often criticized since the Revolution, had, like its army's commander, felt frustration at what seemed to be a stalemate in Boston. It did not in its dissatisfaction blame Washington. There were men of great perception in the Congress, men who understood that the provincialism that prevailed in the states made concerted action almost impossible. Others, unable to dismiss their suspicions of a central power, found it difficult to agree that the states should put aside their differences and provide the army with the means to drive the British from Boston. Thus, there were at least two camps in the Congress regarding war policy, with deep roots in the states. All factions, or groupings, in and out of the Congress and in the states, thought, argued, and sat quietly in the darkness of ignorance concerning what the states were doing. Were they taxing themselves in support of the war? Were they raising regiments for Washington's use? Were they making gunpowder and uniforms or providing other supplies so necessary to the campaign? Not knowing the answers to these questions and uncertain about the national effort—or even if there was one of any promise—the state legislatures moved slowly when they moved at all.[29]

The Revolution demanded that they create a wartime union—a national state—but they were a collection of provinces accustomed to thinking only of local affairs. In the previous ten years, they had done much in resisting British measures that they thought deprived them of liberty. They had done well, so well that they were on their way to creating a sovereign state. But they had much to overcome in constructing such a state, with its own structure of government, its own army, and a policy regarding the empire of which they had been a loyal part for almost two centuries.

Congress did not send a lightweight committee to confer with Washington. Its three members included Benjamin Franklin, the best-known American in the world and also surely the most accomplished man in America. Sixty-nine years old, he had rejoined the Congress after a long stay in Britain, during which he had learned much about the ways of the empire and its rulers, military and political. He had lost all hope by this time that the imperial connection could be repaired, though he did not reveal all of his disenchantment even to his colleagues in Congress. He probably knew more about how the political world worked than anyone there, but he was not complacent in this knowledge. He had come to Washington's camp to listen and, once informed, to help the army find ways to organize and sustain itself. His two fellow members—Thomas Lynch and Benjamin Harrison— were much younger than he, but both were five or six years older than Washington. They, like Franklin, arrived in Cambridge more than well disposed toward Washington.

Thomas Lynch, of South Carolina, was an early advocate of the American cause, had attended the Stamp Act Congress (1765), and from that time on had impressed others with his learning and clarity. John Adams had described him the year before, in the First Continental Congress, as "a solid, firm, judicious man," an appraisal shared at the time by Silas Deane of Connecticut. Benjamin Harrison, who later aroused Adams's displeasure, had earned his praise when they first met in Philadelphia by remarking that "he would have come on foot [to the First Congress] rather than not come." Harrison was an old hand in Virginia politics, having sat in the Burgesses in key committee roles for fifteen years before the war.[30]

How these three felt about an attack on Boston before the Continental Army's enlistments expired is not clear. But it is known that many of their colleagues in Congress favored such an attack. Whatever the committee might have said, it soon discovered that informed opinion—that of Washington's generals—held that their troops were not prepared for such action.

Washington recognized that any attempt to use the committee—or, more important, the Congress—to force the issue could only destroy his standing among the generals who served under him. But the committee's visit and its reputation in the Congress offered an opportunity to inform the Congress of the complexities he faced in creating an army in the new political world. A natural impulse would have been to cover up obstacles, especially when they could have convinced the committee and the Congress that failure was in prospect.

The complexities were many. Washington presented them to the committee in a list of twenty-nine questions; several included secondary questions. The maintenance of an army in the face of its dissolution by January 1 was primary in all of the discussions with Washington. The governance of the army—rules and regulations—occupied much of the deliberations; so also did such matters as pay of troops and officers (the latter a major concern of Washington and his circle), rations, supplies, and tentage for the soldiers. There were surprises for almost everyone: What, Washington asked, should he do about Christopher French, a British officer who had been captured and was being held in Hartford, and who insisted that he should be allowed to wear his sword, a demand that elicited little sympathy in Hartford and Cambridge? This matter was not made a formal part of the agenda, but it did come up, with the committee refusing to give advice. There must have been some hilarity over French, if Washington displayed the letters that he wrote. The important questions took several days to review and included requests that the committee give advice on where the army might obtain a variety of essentials: more ammunition, in particular flints and lead, and artillery (from Crown Point and elsewhere in New York, the committee responded), as well as engineers (the committee suggested that Henry Knox and Israel Putnam Jr. be made assistant engineers and promoted to the rank of lieutenant colonel). Indians, captured British soldiers, and blacks provided another sort of focus. The British captures should be humanely treated and exchanged when possible; the Indians who had volunteered should be kept in readiness; and the blacks should not be enlisted into the army, the committee advised. Ships and privateers were also subjects of discussion, as was Tory property. The committee gave sound advice on all these matters. On several questions, it simply responded by saying that Congress would have to decide; the committee's own responsibility had its limits. Perhaps the most formidable example of such a question concerned the possibility of destroying the city of Boston by fire if an assault was not made.

The policy emerging from the discussions had a clear focus: the existence of the army itself, an army that legally had a little more than two months of life left. The committee recommended that the army continue to reenlist its present members, officers and men, for a year, and that it resort to new enlistments and militia if necessary to bring its number to 20,372. This force was to be divided into twenty-six infantry regiments, at least one of artillery, and companies of riflemen, each of sixty-eight men. That the committee devised, or more accurately drew on, Washington's careful plan is very much in evidence in this reorganization. When Washington bade them farewell on October 24, he knew that he had achieved much, though he was left with the task of replacing or reenlisting most of the troops who made up the army. In the next few weeks, Congress examined what its committee of conference had done and approved in detail virtually all that it had recommended.[31]

Washington had urged in his conversations with the committee that one of the needs of the army was a higher degree of professionalism. His letters to friends in and out of Congress in the three months since his arrival in Cambridge had pointed to the ragged—in fact, raw— character of troops and officers. Many of the men by their behavior offended his sense of what a soldier was; many, he implied, though enlisted in the army, were not really soldiers, and for weeks they had given very little evidence of becoming so. At least a part of the fault lay with their officers, who had no sense of themselves as a caste apart. He was disgusted, even repelled, by their failure to maintain a line between themselves and their troops—as he called it, their "familiarity." Separation born of a sense of their difference was necessary for discipline, for leading and sometimes driving their men in battle. Killing, as he knew well from the war he had fought in the 1750s, did not come easy to men, nor did persistence and steadiness in the face of the likelihood that the soldiers in continental ranks would die even as they killed their enemy.

To improve the quality of the officers, he looked to attracting a better class of men and to strengthening the resolve of those he had. Paying officers more would help set them apart, help them act as gentlemen of honor and character, even if they had demonstrated little of either; it would in a sense establish—or contribute to—"subordination," another word he favored, essential to discipline.[32]

Washington got his way with the committee and with Congress. That he had forcefully explained his ideas about a professional army is clear in a letter from Thomas Lynch, who wrote notifying him "that Congress has agreed to every Recommendation of the Committee and have gone beyond it allowing the additional Pay to the Officers." Lynch had contempt for "the officers who failed to support Washington— the "pityfull wretches who stood cavilling with you when entreated to serve the next Campaign"—and who "will now be ready enough," even though they probably didn't deserve more pay. Lynch's hope was that Washington "will be able to refuse them with the Contempt they deserve and to find better in their room."

The picture Lynch painted of the weakest of the army's officers was of a group that had failed to display the spirit that honored distinctions among officers and their soldiers. With the new Articles of War and the increase in pay, he told Washington, "you will not now suffer your Officers to sweep the Parade [with] the Skirts of their Coats or bottoms of their Trowsers, to cheat or to mess with their Men, to skulk in battle or sneak in Quarters, in short being now paid they must do their Duty & look as well as act like Gentlemen. Do not bate them an Ace, my Dear General, but depend on every Support of your Friends here."[33] To "bate them an Ace" meant to make the slightest abatement, or ease up on the demands made of officers.

Washington knew that with the new regulations he could use a stronger hand in dealing with officers and soldiers, but he knew also that his immediate assignment to create a new army from the old would not be easy. The major obstacle was quite simple: His army had subscribed, or enlisted, in agreements that expired on December 31, 1775. Rhode Island and Connecticut troops had signed on until the first of December.

Massachusetts troops served under Articles of War originally agreed to by the colony's provincial congress on April 5; these regulations, which by any standard were inadequate, furnished the basis of a second version drafted for the Continental Army and established by the Congress on June 30, after Bunker Hill, when in effect it took over the war from the legislatures of the New England colonies/states. At the time of Congress's action in June, many soldiers refused to sign the articles, for fear that they would extend their service beyond the date they originally had agreed to. Now, in early November, they were asked to subscribe to new articles approved by Congress, which would extend their service until the end of 1776.[34]

Washington had dreaded the problem of holding the army together almost from his first day in Cambridge; desertions were at an unacceptable number as winter approached, and the period for recruiting was short. Not knowing what to expect from Congress, he had begun the process of reconstruction of his force before it disintegrated. In August he ordered all officers and men to sign the Articles of War approved in June by the Continental Congress. (The Congress had made the Massachusetts regulations its own, with slight changes here and there.)

Wary soldiers proved reluctant to sign. Congress had anticipated this reluctance and in issuing instructions to sign gave Washington the authority to retain soldiers whether they signed or not. But uncertainty about the length of service remained, with many officers and men wondering whether they would be compelled to stay under arms past the expiration date of their service.

Washington wanted them to stay as long as possible, ideally until the war ended but, at the least, well into the new year, when he hoped to have a new army under his command. In early October, his concern had risen to the point that he sought reassurance from the troops themselves. He seems to have been slightly more concerned about the officers and in late October asked that all officers declare whether they would remain in the service until the end of 1776. A few days later, it was clear that a third to a half of them would remain in the army. In the general orders of October 26, he repeated an argument for continuing service in terms he had used before—with one difference. The usual exhortation had seen Washington refer to the "great Cause," sometimes "the glorious cause"—"When Life, Liberty, & Property are at stake." This late October appeal had an extraordinary timeliness in his linkage of the cause to a recent atrocity—the burning of Falmouth by the British navy. Falmouth was a town on the northern coast of the District of Maine, and virtually nothing of it survived this calculated action. In Washington's phrasing:

> our Country is in danger of being a melancholy Scene of bloodshed, and desolation, when our towns are laid in ashes, and innocent Women & Children driven from their peaceful habitations. . . . Where Calamities like these, are staring us in the face, and a brutal, savage enemy (more so than was ever yet found in a civilized nation), are threatening

us, and everything we hold dear, with Destruction from foreign Troops, it little becomes the Character of a soldier, to shrink from danger, and condition [bargain] for new terms.[35]

The use of the word "condition" referred to demands for better compensation, food, and clothing made by soldiers and their officers in the final months of 1775. Washington wanted more pay and better support of all kinds for his soldiers, but he hated having them ask for it. So urgent was the need to keep the ranks filled and led by competent officers that he now coupled his patriotic appeal with the claim that "the General also thinks that he can take upon him to assure the Officers and Soldiers of the new army, that they will receive their pay once a Month regularly."[36] (Early in January he was to find that he could not pay his troops at all.)

Throughout these months, his anxiety about the army seems not to have lessened. His efforts to keep as many soldiers as possible and to replace those who would leave never let up. In several ways he showed a surprising flexibility in the means to hold his men. He agreed to temporary furloughs to enable soldiers to go home for short periods in order to find winter clothing for themselves; he offered a month's pay for those in desperate need; he advised men who were paid to spend it on shirts, stockings, shoes, and leather breeches, not, he added, on coats and waistcoats, which the army would provide at cost. He also continued his appeals to Congress for more money with which to pay his troops.[37]

All these efforts were made in circumstances that suggested that the new army would face problems equal to or greater than the old. Weapons and powder had to be found for new recruits, who frequently arrived in camp without them. Washington demanded that soldiers who refused to reenlist should leave their muskets behind when they left camp. When that demand was ignored, he threatened to withhold pay from those who carried off their muskets. He also offered to buy back such muskets, and then ordered his regimental commanders to send officers into surrounding towns to buy weapons. Recruits to the new army who came bearing muskets were rewarded one dollar per musket.

By the middle of January 1776, his army—its soldiers coming and going—numbered around 10,500 men. A part of this number were militia, temporary substitutes from Rhode Island and New Hampshire for the regulars who had gone home. A month later he estimated that his army had two thousand men without muskets, and gunpowder for those with weapons was difficult to find.

Slowly men came into camp, and by the end of February he could count something close to fifteen thousand in camp. More arms trickled in, among them a shipment of muskets from France and small numbers from most of the colonies. When Congress accepted six regiments from Virginia, the men came bearing arms.[38]

Yet he felt little reassurance as he saw their numbers climb. They were far from the size that everyone in the army and the committee of conference had agreed was necessary for either offensive or defensive operations, and many of the men were not really soldiers. "Raw" had been the adjective Washington used when he regarded the force he commanded in the summer. It took months to make a soldier, and it took time to train units to fight in a coordinated manner as an army.

Nonetheless, in the middle of February, he convened his generals once more to seek their approval for a full-scale attack on Boston. He would use this new army—undersize, raw, and undisciplined as it might be—to smash his enemy and, perhaps, end the war. At this time, he still felt "wonder and astonishment" that General Howe had not attacked him. It was a feeling he had entertained for months, and particularly so since the beginning of the year, when soldiers in his original army began to go home. Howe, he speculated many times before, either did not know of the disintegration of Washington's force or was under orders to delay until reinforcements arrived. What Washington took to be either Howe's ignorance or his paralysis gave the Americans an opening that they could not ignore.[39]

Washington's generals disagreed. The British were too strong, they said—the British had more troops than Washington recognized; they had more artillery, powder that would allow its use, and a fleet in the harbor that would lend its support to the army; and of course everyone knew that they were entrenched in well-prepared fortifications. An attack by the new army, still short some three thousand muskets, would, the generals implied, fail, though they did not use that word. The words they did use were bleak enough, and a little starchy in the context of the cold response they gave.

Washington could not have been surprised, and he did not argue with these men, though he was clearly disappointed. He was feeling pressure from the world around him when he made his proposal for an attack and received a negative response. Of course, he had received rejections from generals before, but this time he seems to have resented it even more. Reporting to John Hancock about the generals' advice— and his decision to take it—he halfway confessed that in proposing an attack, he was moved by questions from others in America and in the Congress about why he had not carried the war to the British in Boston. He explained his own thought processes in rather oblique terms:

> Perhaps the Irksomeness of my Situation, may have given different Ideas to me, than those which Influenced the Gentlemen I consulted and might have inclined me to put more to the hazard than was consistent with prudence—If it had, I am not sensible to it, as I endeavourd to give all the consideration that a matter of such Importance required.

This reluctant concession to outside influence soon gave way to the admission that he found it hard to ignore the opinions of others,

> for to have the Eyes of the whole Continent fixed with anxious expectation of hearing of some great event, & to be restrained in every Military Operation for want of the necessary means of carrying it on, is not very pleasing, especially as the means used to conceal my Weakness from the Enemy conceals it also from our friends, and adds to their Wonder.[40]

The "wonder" he referred to existed in Congress, along with worry about the consequences of any American attack, successful or failed. Hancock had sent him the resolutions by Congress of December 22, 1775, authorizing an attack even if it resulted in the destruction of the city. It had not reached its conclusion without hesitation and doubt, as Hancock noted of a speech given by John Dickinson, of Pennsylvania, with its references to "Cromwell's massacre at Drogheda" and "Louis XIV burning the Palatinate." Dickinson had also apparently warned that "we may destroy the town and its people one day, and hear of proposals of accommodation the next." How much of this sort of thing made its way to the Cambridge camp is unknown, but it is likely that Washington heard accounts suggesting that Congress believed he should get on with the job and others that suggested he should not. Though he was far from being indifferent to civilian casualties and the destruction of property, he was more pressed by hints that he lacked the will to fight. Such hints came to him through his former aide Lieutenant Colonel Joseph Reed, now a representative in Congress who heard the muttering about failures to act in Cambridge. In January, Washington responded to such news by saying that had he anticipated the refusal of the old army to reenlist—"a backwardness . . . in the old Soldiers to the Service, all the Generals upon Earth should not have convinced me of the propriety of delaying an Attack upon Boston till this time." In February, he was resigned to the criticism by "Chimney Corner Hero's," but he had not given up the idea of an attack. His cooler moments introduced realism to his thought—he expected "considerable loss" in an attack, but he believed it would succeed "if the Men should behave well."[41]

After further consultation with his general officers, the conclusion Washington reached seemed inescapable. There was simply too much weight in the generals' objections to an assault: There was the persistent shortage of gunpowder; the new troops themselves were at best of unknown quality, and there was not the number needed; and the British remained too strong, in fortified positions. Thus did the generals argue, and Washington gave in to them, though privately—to himself and to Joseph Reed—he still professed certainty "that the Enterprize, if it had been undertaken with resolution must have succeeded."[42]

The generals, in their reluctance, were not immune to the notion that defeating the British might end the war. Washington advanced this theory more than once during the siege, and others, perhaps more in hope than certainty, had taken it up. It was an idea based on the feeling that the ministerial government lacked resolution and the will to send another army to America if its force in Boston were destroyed. There seems to have been little discussion in the American army of the British government's purposes should its army fail. That it would give up its intention to establish a tyranny in America was an agreeable idea, even if there was not evidence in support of it.

If attacking the British would not succeed, why not draw them out in an attack on the Continental Army? This was an idea that Washington and his generals had talked about informally for several weeks while they assessed the possibilities of their own attack on Boston. The means to draw the British out lay in the high ground of Dorchester Heights, which comprised several hills to the south of the town, then unoccupied by either army. Fortified with heavy cannon and mortars, they would be an ominous presence for the British army in the town and its navy in the southern part of the harbor.

Placing troops on the heights, where they could fight from entrenched positions—simpler fighting than complicated attack—was attractive to the generals for still another reason: It would please Washington, who almost visibly ached for battle and the resolution he thought it might bring. With little additional deliberation, the generals endorsed the idea, while they turned down the proposal for an American offensive. So it would be Dorchester, an offer to the enemy of a fight.[43]

The American army's officers expected the British to accept the challenge. Washington used several phrases to describe what he was undertaking—such as "I am preparing to take Post on Dorchester to try if the Enemy will be so kind as to come out to us." The gallantry embodied in this sentence was typical of eighteenth-century officers. Washington's succinct name for the combat he expected, the "Rumpus," was more down-to-earth, but lighthearted and solidly in the officers' lexicon.[44]

The name and the language describing the expected combat concealed the careful planning that now began. There were at least two problems to be solved: how to entice the British to come out, and how best to receive them. A bombardment of Boston before troops moved onto the heights would force the British to a decision: either to fight or to run. A second attack across the bay, now clogged with ice, would help in bringing them to destruction as their army, or a part of it, set out to drive the Americans from the hills of Dorchester. For the bombardment, Washington could call on about fifty cannon and mortars recently transported from Fort Ticonderoga by Henry Knox, colonel of artillery. How to meet British regulars coming up the hills aroused greater concern in Washington, for doubts remained about the Continentals' willingness to stand in place as massed British infantry approached them. Traditional entrenchments, redoubts, and forts could not be dug in deeply frozen ground, and such entrenchments would probably be necessary if the Americans were to hold steady. Lieutenant Colonel Rufus Putnam, cousin of General Israel Putnam, gave the answer to the problem posed by the frozen ground: Fortifications should be set upon the ground, not dug out of it.[45]

Washington found Putnam's solution persuasive, and with his staff of generals he fashioned a plan that included beginning the "Rumpus" with three days of bombardment of British works in Boston, to be followed by an occupation of the heights, with an assault across the bay should the British come out with a heavy attack. This part of the plan required careful coordination of American efforts. Washington appointed Israel Putnam commander of this second force. It had two divisions; the first was headed by Nathanael Greene, who would land south of Barton's Point, their objective Copps Hill, and then join the second division, under John Sullivan, who would lead eight regiments of five hundred men each. The combined force was to drive to Boston Neck, destroy the British posts there, and open the way for American troops at Roxbury to cross the Neck into the town. This assault on Boston would require precision in timing and movement and would be undertaken only if the British sent a major part of their army against Dorchester Heights. In a real sense, the Americans would slip in behind the British.

Washington set the plan in motion on the night of March 2 with a light bombardment by his batteries of Lechmere Point, Cobble Hill, and Roxbury—British posts in Boston. Only a few shots were fired—the shortage of powder limited the barrage—and to no effect, except on American pride, when "Old Sow," a heavy mortar, ruptured. The shelling resumed the next night, answered, as on the night before, by the British. The third night, the fourth of March, saw the artillery on both sides open up without restraint, and shortly after 7:00 P.M., in darkness, Brigadier General John Thomas took an expedition up the heights—twelve hundred men in a working party—to set up the breastworks and a force of eight hundred men to provide cover. The timber works for the fortifications, called chandeliers, had been made weeks earlier and, as they were emplaced, were filled with gabions, bales of hay, and whatever dirt and stones could be dug up. Barrels filled with dirt and stones were emplaced as well—they had a dual use, to help shield the troops but also to be rolled down the hill on the infantry that would be marching up. Abatis—sharpened stakes and branches—ringed the fortifications.

Most of the work had been accomplished when, the next morning, the British discovered their enemy looking down their throats. Howe muttered something about the rebels doing more work in a night than his entire army could do in months and resolved to clear the heights of Americans. The next day was spent in preparing his force, which was to number more than two thousand, and arranging for the navy to transport them to a point on Dorchester peninsula from which an assault up the slopes could be made. Howe's fast reaction to meet the challenge head-on had been stiffened by the navy's warning that, should the Americans, with their heavy artillery, be left in place, its ships would have to pull out of the harbor. Howe decided to land troops that night and send them up the heights the next day. A heavy storm made this impossible, and the next day, as the storm continued, he canceled the attack and resolved to evacuate Boston altogether. He had been looking forward to leaving the place for months, and so, apparently, had his officers. The general opinion of these officers held that operations from Boston had very little to recommend them. New York would serve better than any place on the coast, and presumably, once he was reinforced, Howe might begin anew there.[46]

Washington watched his enemy pack up over the next week, a process marked by destruction of heavy guns and a good many supplies. The actual loading of troops, loyalists, and materials of various sorts was done in a haphazard fashion—the army and navy both wanted to escape before Washington attempted to destroy them in their vulnerability—and when the ships reached the outer harbor, they put down their anchors and shifted cargoes for almost ten days. On March 27, they were done and sailed off for Halifax. Washington did not know where they were going, but he was delighted to see the last of them.[47]

5

New York

New York was not Boston, but the city presented problems that had plagued Washington in Boston. First, there were the troops. He took many of the New England soldiers with him in April 1776, when he moved his command to New York, but he had to raise others, replacements for those he'd left behind or who had gone home. So his New York army was in several respects new. It was composed largely of militia from New York, though it also included troops from New Jersey, some from Pennsylvania and Virginia, and still others from nearby states. But wherever they were from, they manifested the behavior of the group he had left behind.

Throughout the summer his soldiers, in defiance of all good discipline, left their units, wandering around, apparently visiting friends or going home for short stays. They also found the city alluring for its women of doubtful virtue, no doubt of such attractiveness that stories about them were circulated in nearby towns and villages. One of Washington's officers, Captain Nathan Peters of the 3rd Massachusetts Continentals, was informed by his wife, Lois, then living in Preston, Connecticut, that a post rider had told her that almost "all" of the soldiers in the army had "a Lady at their Pleasure." The result was "that allmost the whole of our army was under the Salivation"—that is, in treatment for venereal disease.[1]

In Peters's case and others, the stories were false, but they indicated one source of the problems Washington faced in holding his troops in line: Unreliable while out of combat, what would they do when they faced the regulars? To drive home his point about the importance of discipline—obeying officers, training seriously, and saving their powder until the battle began—he resorted to his usual exhortations. He demanded that officers crack down on delinquents, lead or force their men in getting fortifications prepared, punish offenders against military order, and enforce the rule against the random firing of muskets. Not all of these officers satisfied him.

He had not come to New York with a full complement in any case, for the group of generals under him at Boston contained several who either did not want to go to New York or were not worth taking. Among them, Major General Artemas Ward had resigned on the eve of the move to New York, pleading bad health, but then retracted his resignation. Washington had never been entirely happy with Ward, and Ward had never fully reconciled himself to the fact that Congress had preferred having Washington rather than him in overall command. When Ward indicated his intention to resign, Washington had not objected—a month later he attributed Ward's desire to leave the army to his discovery "that there was a probability of his removing from the smoke of his own chimney."[2] (This was a phrase Washington used several times to describe men who showed no enthusiasm for the hardships of army life. In Ward's case, he referred to a man who wanted to live at home while holding command.) The sardonic note in this dismissal of Ward was mild compared with his characterization of Brigadier General Joseph Frye, another New England officer who left the army when he learned that it would not remain in Boston. Frye, "that Wonderful Man," in Washington's account, received his appointment on January 11, but remained at home thereafter, without doing "one days duty." In late March he resigned, effective April 11—exactly three months after he accepted appointment, in order to collect three months' pay, though he had "scarce been three times out of his House." Washington's scorn is evident in the explanation he offered of Frye's conduct. Frye, he wrote, "discovered that he was too old, and too infirm for a moving Camp—but *remembers* that he has been young, active, and very capable of doing what is now out of his power to accomplish; & therefore has left Congress to find out another man capable of making, if possible, a more brilliant figure than he has done."[3]

There were two others he would not have mourned had he lost them: Joseph Spencer, a Connecticut brigadier general, and William Heath, the brigadier general from Massachusetts. Neither had distinguished himself; nor had either suffered disgrace. Washington's standards were high, and mediocrity, he thought, should be avoided. For the time being, Heath and Spencer remained. Only John Thomas and

Nathanael Greene drew complete approval from Washington, and both held important positions until Thomas was called to Canadian command, an almost hopeless assignment. Greene continued to serve as adjutant general. Charles Lee, more than acceptable to Washington, had been sent to the South to assume command there even before the main army left Boston for New York.[4]

He could take comfort, at least for a few weeks before fighting for the city began, that rations, gunpowder, and clothing were not lacking. The weather was sometimes marred by rain, but temperatures did not require that camps furnish permanent barracks. There was sufficient tentage for many of the troops, and though digging trenches and throwing up redoubts and parapets was heavy work, it progressed from April through June.

Having outstanding commanders by his side seemed more than ordinarily desirable when Washington took a reckoning of the problems he faced in defending New York. At Boston he had been the besieger, charged with taking a city in a compact area; in New York he was the defender of a city spread out over three islands and on the edge of a major harbor. The central part of the city lay on New York Island, also known as Manhattan, abutting the North River, which opened the way through northern New York to Canada. Control of this corridor was vital, he thought, to holding New England. He was not alone in his assessment that New York and the corridor to Canada possessed great strategic importance. British commanders shared this conception, though they gave precedence to the West Indies, for reasons of economic policy as well as strategy for containing the French. Washington and congressional delegates also recognized the importance of the West Indies, but if at this time the leaders had a strategic obsession, it was Canada.

They converted the obsession into strategy in the summer and autumn of the year. Congress itself stepped into the planning with an order to General Philip Schuyler to mount an attack. The two points of importance for such an operation were the cities of Quebec and Montreal. Benedict Arnold headed a force put together to subdue Quebec, and Brigadier General Richard Montgomery was selected for Montreal. Washington, the supreme commander with no control of these

efforts, approved of them nonetheless and supplied troops and equipment. Arnold badly miscalculated the obstacles between Massachusetts, from which he set off, and Quebec. But he bravely persevered
and on December 31—joined by Montgomery, who earlier had captured Montreal—he led an assault against British forces in the city. It
was a romantic effort, made in a snowstorm by men who had endured
a terrible march through the Maine wilderness, and it failed after a
bloody struggle. Montgomery, fatally, took a bullet in the head, and
Arnold one in a leg. Arnold pulled his troops back and besieged the city.
But by mid-1776 it was clear to everyone that the Americans would
not take Canada. The disappointment in Congress and the army was
great; and the army and Washington knew that bleeding of a sort had
not been confined to the North. Washington's strength in troops and
weapons was one of the casualties of the Canadian campaign, for he
had, over the months of the siege, sent both north in support.[5]

The problems in holding New York were great, and not much had
been done to ready its defense before the Continental Army arrived.
General Charles Lee had begun the process of planning fortifications
but had made little progress on the ground. Washington studied New
York's vulnerabilities carefully and ordered the digging of emplacements. But more work was needed before the British arrived.

Such work indeed took precedence over everything else. Washington did not acknowledge that Congress had declared independence on
July 4. He had expected its coming—the demand for such action by
Congress had grown increasingly loud in 1776—and many in the army
shared this popular feeling. On the ninth, officers read the Declaration
to the troops standing in formations. There is no doubt that it received
the soldiers' approval.[6]

William Howe and his fleet arrived in late June and early July. Some
100 to 150 ships brought his troops, making their way into New York
waters over several weeks. Besides coming over an extended period,
the ships carried men of varying quality and readiness. They numbered
some thirty-two thousand when all came ashore on Staten Island, and
included four thousand Hessians. A voyage at sea had left the men
tired and, in many cases, sick. Getting them prepared for operations
required time, and their officers did not press them into shape quickly.[7]

But by August they were ready. General Howe put his force in motion from Staten Island to Gravesend Bay, Long Island, early on the morning of August 22. They sailed on small craft manned by sailors from British frigates in nearby waters, and by midday some fifteen thousand men had reached shore, supported initially by forty fieldpieces. These soldiers were all British regulars; a second group of Hessians, who had arrived in America on August 12, pleaded for time to rest and gather themselves. On August 25, sufficiently refreshed, two brigades of Hessians under General Philip von Heister, a veteran of the Seven Years' War, joined Howe's command. These landings went unopposed, as the Americans lacked the numbers to fortify all the beaches of Long Island.

Howe knew that his army outnumbered Washington's; he knew also that most of his enemy were militia, not regulars, neither well armed nor well trained. But Howe and his officers did not expect a lark. Howe in particular acted with a feeling of some restraint—not fear or trepidation, but the knowledge that, while he could drive the Americans from Long Island and New York Island, he might lose his military superiority in the victory. For Bunker Hill had reinforced skepticism he and the professionals in his command felt about battle, especially in America. His force was finite—the casualties he might suffer would not soon be replaced, as reinforcements were an ocean away, and not sure to be sent in any case. And battle, as a German officer had said, expressing a widely shared belief, was the remedy of the desperate. Howe had endured one terrible fight with Americans who were entrenched, on Bunker Hill. After it was over, he commented that his losses in his victory were a "success . . . too dearly bought."[8] General John Burgoyne agreed, and Gage, the overall British commander in Boston at the time, pronounced the deaths of his troops "greater than we can bear. Small armys cant afford such losses, especially when the advantage gained tends to little more than the gaining of a post." General James Murray, another observer from afar—in Minorca—wrote after Bunker Hill that the "Americans' plan ought to be to lose a battle every week, til the British army was reduced to nothing: 'it may be that our troops are not invincible, they certainly are not immortal.'" Murray summed up Howe's problem in a classic eighteenth-century military sentiment: "The fate of battles at the best are precarious."

Howe's restraint did not hobble him completely nor stay his hand in taking a chance in getting his troops across the water to Long Island. Though the sailors who sailed the small craft from Staten Island were among the best in the world, their task was not easy, for the night before, a storm filled with thunder and lightning had dumped a "prodigious heavy rain" on New York Harbor, and no one knew what the new day would bring. The weather turned out fine, as did the landing, and the army moved without opposition toward the American lines.[9]

Washington had visited those lines on August 26 and made no changes, though the disposition of American troops was faulty. The original plan of defense called for a series of entrenchments, redoubts, and other fortifications built around Brooklyn. Those defenses were well placed and well constructed. The commander of all American forces on the island until just a few days before the British landing was Nathanael Greene, an able man with knowledge of the ground he was to defend. But in a terrible piece of bad luck, he fell ill with a high fever; Washington replaced him with Israel Putnam, a fighter of spirit but little tactical savvy. On taking up his new duty, Putnam decided to change the placement of his troops—now throwing forward a line along the Heights of Guan, a range of hills 100 to 150 feet in height, covered by heavy brush and woods. The south side rose abruptly to eighty feet in places and was thought to be impassable by troops in formation because of the rough, wooded terrain. The woods would also prevent horse-drawn artillery from being moved up through the hills. Four passes breached the Heights of Guan: the coastal pass near Gowanus, with its creek and salt marshes, on the American right; Flatbush, about a mile to the east; Bedford Pass, another mile farther east; and Jamaica Pass, almost three miles beyond.[10]

Howe, ever cautious, felt out the American positions carefully, sending a patrol up the road near Bedford. A unit of Sullivan's force repelled them—the British were not interested yet in a serious attempt to break the line, and pulled back almost immediately upon contact. Sullivan's soldiers followed and burned three houses that they believed the British had occupied. When Washington heard that Americans had destroyed American property in this encounter, he rebuked them, through Putnam. Burning the houses was shameful, he wrote.[11]

This skirmish told Howe where the Americans were, but he was not yet in the mood to act on this information. In Boston he had mastered the art of the inactive, and now on Long Island he adhered to familiar practice, doing what he did so well: nothing. Nothing on the day after the landing, nothing on the next day, the twenty-fourth, nothing on the twenty-fifth.

Late on August 26, he at last moved. Inspired by a plan laid out by General Henry Clinton, he decided to outflank the American forces stretched along the Guan Ridge. He first fixed the bulk of Americans in place by sending James Grant against the American right at Gowanus Pass and Philip von Heister's Hessians against the center of the ridge, where Flatbush and Bedford Passes cut through. These attacks were diversionary and held the forces of Sullivan and General William Alexander, Lord Stirling, in place. On the east end of the line, where Jamaica Pass lay, there were only five American officers, who, taken by surprise, could not notify the force down the ridge that Howe's main body would be marching down the north side of the ridge. The Americans were dreadfully exposed but knew nothing of their danger, because the British moved swiftly but carefully on back roads until they reached the end of the line, which was defended by only the five befuddled officers. The British poured through the pass—Henry Clinton in the van, with dragoons and light infantry; General Charles Cornwallis at his heels, with two regiments of foot and artillery; and Howe, with the main body. The initial breach of the American line occurred about midnight, and by three the British were on the Bedford Road, securely behind their American enemy.

The tactics they used allowed them to widen the road so that wagons and fieldpieces might be drawn along. Sawing down trees that blocked their movement would make less noise than troops pushing over ground with trees and brush, they believed, and they did not wish to be discovered until they had trapped the American army.[12]

They need not have worried. Sullivan's forces collapsed soon after Heister's gunners began the work of holding the Americans in place. The process of disintegration accelerated as Howe's troops struck their flank and Stirling's regiments—principally William Smallwood's Marylanders and John Haslet's Delaware Continentals. Raw and untried as they were, these American soldiers fought bravely. They had never fought anyone before; they could not have learned much about the terrain, having been boated over only the day before, but they held their places under severe fire for two hours. Stirling did not deploy them behind trees and rocks, but stood them up in the open and had them fight in European fashion. By late morning they were almost surrounded. Stirling then sent most of his command across the Gowanus Creek, through the "impassable" marshes into Brooklyn. To cover the rear, he held a part of Smallwood's Maryland regiment in place and stayed with these soldiers himself. Just before noon, with Cornwallis at his rear and left flank, Stirling—with the Marylanders, 250 strong—attacked, assaulting Cornwallis's grenadiers six times until he and his men were finally broken by overwhelming British fire. By noon it was all over. The British had cleared the Heights of Guan and pressed the shattered Americans back into their lines at Brooklyn Heights.[13]

Washington watched part of the action on the American right, but he did not insert himself into the fighting. Remaining out of it was hard for him, but he was wise in keeping his distance in order to gain understanding of the battle. Riding to that sector of the battlefield would have not brought him there in time to affect the action. Because of the rough ground and a wooded ridge, he did not recognize until it was far too late what had happened to that part of his army outside of Brooklyn. It is not known when he discovered that he had been outflanked; but as his soldiers streamed off the ridge and ran into Brooklyn, he saw that what might be considered the first phase of the defense of Long Island had ended in defeat.

There was not to be a second phase. The next two days, August 28 and 29, he brought three more regiments over from New York Island in an attempt to brace for an all-out British assault. It did not come on either day, as Howe, more than respectful of his enemy's ability to fight from fixed positions, abandoned any idea of an assault with bayonets carried by massed infantry. Instead he began "regular approaches," as construction of trenches and breastworks toward enemy lines was called. By August 29 the British were about 150 yards from an American fort. Rain fell that day and the next.[14]

Washington knew that his army's situation was desperate, and so did his senior commanders who met with him in a formal "Council of War" during the day of August 29. These generals could not avoid the conclusion that their soldiers were so dispirited as likely to be overrun when British infantry dug their trenches a few yards closer. The Americans' morale lifted at least for a few hours in the two days after their flight, when they held their own in skirmishes provoked by light British probing. But these feelings of hope were not widely shared and soon passed as the rain continued and the British advanced their trenches inexorably. The council of generals voted unanimously in favor of abandoning their hold on Long Island. For the record, they admitted that their troops had lost their spirit, and rations and tentage were in short supply. They also conceded that their Brooklyn lines were not as strong as they might have been had a serious effort to dig in been made. Washington, ever the realist, put down whatever he retained of the impulse to fight and ordered the retreat.[15]

That day—August 29—he rarely dismounted from his horse; he reported later that he had not slept for two days. Instead he spent those hours in the saddle, supervising preparations for removal of men and supplies to New York Island. There was much to take across the river—fieldpieces, provisions, gunpowder, and lead for muskets, to name the principal items. There were also horses, a few tents, blankets, and medical supplies to be saved. During the night of August 29, the troops moved carefully out of their trenches and into the formations for entering the boats that Washington had ordered for their use. There were few mishaps, and their skill and care allowed the move to be made without discovery. Howe's troops found their enemy gone early in the morning; the Americans had left behind little except their pride and several heavy cannon that had sunk into the mud up to their hubs. Howe revealed little disappointment that he had failed to overrun his enemy. Far from such feeling, he probably secretly felt relief, for even an overpowering assault on Washington's fortification would have been bloody.

Washington took the army off Long Island in good order, but as soon as it landed on New York Island, it fell into shambles. Climbing into boats and sailing across the river had entailed a certain degree of order, as men and weapons were confined and static; ashore, freedom of movement prevailed, and Washington's army was one that valued freedom and movement. Its soldiers were soon in motion, mostly outward, bolting from camp and going home. The militia, most of whom had only recently arrived, were the major deserters. Washington reported that "Great numbers of them have gone off; in some Instances, almost by whole Regiments—by half Ones & by Companies at a time." Others who remained refused orders, and wandered about as they chose, in defiance of their officers in some cases, and in others the officers took themselves off, as eager as their troops to leave the army.[16]

Recruitment of an army had preoccupied Washington for months, indeed since the move from Boston. The defeat on Long Island made this task even more difficult, and he despaired of succeeding as long as short-term enlisted militia made up the bulk of his force. He needed men for the duration of the war; six-month or six-week militia could not meet the requirements of the stable and disciplined force he needed if he were to hold off the British. Moreover, the militiamen were a negative influence on the discipline of the regulars. An appalled Washington wrote Hancock that the militia "have infected another part of the Army. Their want of discipline and refusal of almost every kind of restraint & Government, have produced a like Conduct." It was a sad confession he made in this letter to Hancock: "I am obliged to confess my want of confidence in the Generality of the Troops."[17] None of this could have surprised Hancock. Both the style and the substance of the comment had marked Washington's reports since he assumed command in Cambridge in the summer of 1775.

Before the month was out, he was to expand this analysis of his troubles in command and explain why something needed to be done before the army and the Revolution collapsed. Much of what he said in his appraisals of the militia also applied to enlisted men. They made up the army, of course, but they were not really soldiers. They were simply ordinary men who had reacted with irritation and "inflamed Passions" when the British had begun trampling on American rights. But, as Washington read the circumstance of such "emotions," it was "foolish to expect . . . such People," who composed "the bulk of the Army," to be "influenced by any other principles than those of Interest." In fact he concluded, on looking at common soldiers, that those who "act upon Principles of disinterestedness, are, comparitively [*sic*] speaking—no more than a drop in the ocean." What was required to bring such men to the army "upon a Permanent establishment" was good pay and at least 100 or 150 acres of land, a suit of clothes, and a blanket.[18]

If there was no high regard for the mass of men in Washington's assessment, there was not much more for the officers serving in New York. To recruit officers, good pay would have to be given, but it was not. Officers, whatever their pay, had to be of higher quality, Washington insisted. He had made this argument the year before, and in repeating it he stressed a familiar line: An officer differed from his men—he should be a man of good "character" and "Principles of honour." The group then in the army had been chosen by the states for their ability to recruit; that was their "only merit." Unfortunately, such officers differed from their soldiers in no other way, and their men treated the average officer as an "equal"—and regarded him as "no more than a broomstick."[19]

Indeed, Washington at every opportunity made clear his preferences for gentlemen to make up the core of officers. They had to be of a different quality if they were to lead men—the difference enabled them to insist on what Washington almost always called "due subordination." There was nothing romantic in Washington's conception of an army in battle. Gentlemen made officers who were trained to lead men in action, and action might well result in deaths and wounds. Only men who recognized the superior quality of their leaders and who were willing to do as they were bidden could make an army an effective force.

The militia did not rise to the level of conduct necessary for an effective army. Those Washington observed in New York—especially in the defeats of August and September—were clearly, in his eyes, "a broken staff." They did not consider themselves subject to the "Rules and Regulations of War." They took liberties in defiance of good order, and they corrupted—Washington's word was "infected"—others. He had little faith in them, and he, in the ruins of the battles and retreats of these late summer days, wondered if the war could be won.[20]

The despair in these ruminations he hid from his command, though he revealed much to Hancock at the beginning of September. Writing in this bleakness did not paralyze him, and, far from abandoning his responsibilities, he set about preparing for a British onslaught that would come from Long Island. He thought he had little time to get ready and, hence, he began immediately to pull his regiments together, seeking in his orders to clamp down on soldiers he suspected were almost out of control. This suspicion led him to remind colonels of regiments to count their men, perhaps as often as three times a day. When men were out of camp, they sometimes plundered the civilians who lived on New York Island. He detested such practices, but he might have been placated by the knowledge that across the river Hessians, more often than British regulars, were doing the same thing to the people of Long Island.[21]

Troops who were out of control made getting regiments into proper defensive positions difficult, and defending New York Island was the immediate tactical problem. Washington did not wish to attempt to hold the island, but Congress gave him no real choice. Washington turned to recently promoted Colonel Rufus Putnam for advice and also talked the matter over with Nathanael Greene. He lacked the conviction present in Congress that New York Island could be held, but he believed that he could extract the enemies' blood in their attempts to take it. More than anything he feared entrapments by British attacks in the north, at Kingsbridge or in its vicinity. The British would, according to his and Putnam's anticipation, attack to the south to hold his army in place and then cut it off by a movement from the northwestern shores of Long Island. To contain such attacks—and to keep open a way to escape from the city—Washington broke his army into several parts: one, the smallest, near the base of New York Island; a second up the island around Kips Bay; and the third, with large contingents, at Kingsbridge and Fort Washington. A fourth part served as a reserve intended to provide support for any section of the line repelling the invaders from Long Island.

These dispositions were not tested until September 15, when in the morning the British placed five ships in the East River, about two hundred yards offshore from Kips Bay, to soften up the American defenses. They opened fire at about eleven o'clock in the morning with broadsides to, as Washington described it, "scour the Grounds and cover the landing of their Troops."[22] This they did to the dismay of the Connecticut militia there in trenches and earthworks. The Americans had never encountered such firepower and took to their heels almost immediately. Washington, who was with units to the north, rode down just in time to see the pell-mell flight of his soldiers. In a sense he should not have been surprised, given that he had complained for more than a year about the lack of discipline. Perhaps it was disappointment, not surprise, that overtook him, but in any case he lost control of himself in his eagerness to hold his position and took to using his riding cane on the officers and men who were running away from the cannonade. British soldiers landed amid this confusion and might have captured him had one of Washington's aides not grabbed the bridle of his horse and led him out of danger.[23]

General Henry Clinton led the troops landing on Kips Bay, a site he had recommended against. He now found the way open to cut across New York Island, trapping the American force to the south. But his orders from General Howe stifled whatever impulse he had to take advantage of his opportunity, for Howe's instinctive caution had led him to restrain the landing force to the site.

The beneficiary of his enemy's sluggishness (or addiction to following orders), Washington pulled his army from its vulnerability and retreated up the island to Harlem Heights. The heights, a plateau between the Hudson and the Harlem Rivers, was a part of the island still sparsely settled—rough, wooded ground that seemed made for the defense. Washington set up two lines about three-quarters of a mile apart and planned to establish a third. He had about ten thousand men on the heights; the remainder he soon placed at Kingsbridge, where the two rivers came together.

The next day, September 16, British carelessness and contempt for their enemy produced what the Americans called the Battle of Harlem Heights, hardly more than a skirmish between several hundred light infantry and Colonel Thomas Knowlton's Connecticut militia, just forward of the southernmost American lines. As Lieutenant Frederick Mackenzie confided to his *Diary*, the light infantry pursued the Americans on the heights without "proper precautions or support" and blundered into an unfavorable position, where they "were rather severely handled by them." This affair gave American soldiers at least a shred of confidence, but at the cost of Knowlton's life. He had been one of the best regimental commanders in the army.[24]

The battle had one other effect. It reinforced Howe's reluctance to engage the Americans in a frontal assault, especially when they held ground that favored the defense. Howe's delay in attacking his enemy sometimes degenerated into paralysis, or so it seemed to Washington, puzzled by Howe's inaction and wondering when he would attack again. The answer was slow in coming, but on October 12 Howe put four thousand troops ashore from Long Island at Throgs Neck, which jutted into Long Island Sound almost due east of American lines. The neck, sometimes a point or peninsula and sometimes an island, depending on tides, was guarded by American troops at its points of exit. There was an exchange of artillery fire from both sides, but the British had made no real effort to drive their enemy from their positions. Washington then decided to march from Harlem Heights to White Plains, about twenty miles to the north. Howe's intentions now seemed clear: The effort to trap Washington's army on New York Island would be through a wide swing from Long Island.[25]

The campaign that followed for the rest of the year saw Washington fall back from one post to another. The move to White Plains proved slow and difficult, for horses and wagons were lacking. The troops themselves pulled most of their heavy guns, and it is safe to say they felt fatigue when they arrived at White Plains. Their stay was short after October 28, when the British assaulted and captured Chatterton's Hill, on the far right of their defensive lines. Three days later, Washington withdrew his army back to North Castle and a new line of entrenchments. Howe followed as far as the old lines, but on the night of November 4, he led his army southward—a retreat, according to Washington—to the area near Fort Washington, the American strongpoint on the east side of the North River below Kingsbridge. The fort lay on high ground and held promise of dominance over the river and the land around it.

On his way to Fort Washington, Howe looked in on Dobbs Ferry, on the North River, a stop that helped confirm Washington's suspicions that the enemy's objectives included the capture of Philadelphia. But no one in the American army could be absolutely certain what Howe's purposes were. Speculation ranged over possibilities that the British were also going to plunder the New Jersey countryside. Underlying all thought about what was afoot was also the concern to deny the British full control of the North River. The Canadian campaign had compelled Washington to think of what might result if the British focused all their efforts on opening up the corridor between New York and the St. Lawrence.[26]

The two forts on the North River, Lee and Washington, had seemed critical to keeping the British from establishing the linkage to Canada. Evidence of such intentions had mounted since the summer, when the Howe brothers returned with powerful naval and military forces. They had in fact sailed up and down the river whenever they liked. Additional evidence now appeared as they forced their way past Fort Washington, on the New York side, and Fort Lee, almost directly across in New Jersey. The American gunners in both forts proved unable to stop such passage, even though their cannon on both sides of the river fired on British ships. Obstacles created by sinking old hulks in the river also proved porous.

Early in November, when Washington learned that two British warships had made their way past the forts, he concluded there was little reason to defend them. If they could not be made to deny the British the river, why attempt to hold them? He wrote Nathanael Greene early in November with this question and added, "I am therefore inclined to think it will not be prudent to hazard the Men and Stores at Mount Washington, but as you are on the spot, leave it to you to give such Orders as to evacuating Mount Washington as you judge best, and so far revoking the Order given Colonel Magaw to defend it to the last."[27] Not being on the spot may have, to some extent, stayed Washington's hand. He was a commander who wished to see the ground on which he was to fight, an understandable desire undoubtedly shared by most leaders who sent men into battle. In Washington's case, the desire was born from experience as much as from prudence. He was a man who had studied the earth, surveyed it as a youth, farmed it as a planter, and bought and sold it for much of his life. As a commander, he used maps, but sketches on paper of the terrain were not enough; he wanted to see the sites of action for himself. Thinking of what decision to make about Mount Washington, a place he did not know well, he naturally listened to Nathanael Greene, a bright young man whom he had come to trust.

Greene in turn relied to some extent on Colonel Robert Magaw, a Pennsylvanian, in command of the fort. Magaw was not certain that Howe would attack the fort; nor was Greene. Shortly before the attack occurred, Greene reinforced the garrison, apparently to help convince himself and perhaps Howe that the fort could not be taken. But taken it was, in a battle on November 20 that lasted less than a day.

Washington watched the woeful collapse of the Americans from across the river at Fort Lee. He was not inclined then or later to blame Nathanael Greene for this debacle. Had he known that the enemy's casualties were not light despite the brevity of the battle—about 69 dead, 335 wounded—he might have felt better, temporarily at least, but that knowledge, after it came to him, could not ease his disappointment. He had lost more than 3,000 men—2,858 captured and 150 killed or wounded—as well as valuable pieces of artillery and much ammunition.[28]

Cornwallis, Howe's second-in-command, apparently under orders to allow Washington to yield, unintentionally allowed him to pull together his forces, which were split between Hackensack and Fort Lee. On November 20, the British had loaded Hessians and their own regulars into boats and crossed the North River at Lower Closter, New Jersey, about six miles above Fort Lee. The American army lacked the strength to hold Fort Lee or to make any realistic attempt to stop the enemy, and on November 21 it began its retreat. From that day until it crossed the Delaware River at Trenton, on December 7, it barely held itself together and on several occasions barely escaped attack by its pursuers. Its route led it to Newark on November 22; there it rested for five days, its rear guard pulling out just as Cornwallis's van arrived. The following day it entered New Brunswick, and the day following it said farewell to two thousand militia from New Jersey and Maryland whose enlistments had expired. Others came into the American camp at about the same time, but they carried no promise of staying for any lengthy period. Three months was the limit of service for most.[29]

During a part of this period, the weather slowed Cornwallis's pursuit—rain was frequent, the roads muddy, and he was burdened by a heavy baggage train. Washington made it to Princeton on December 1, his men tired, cold, and hungry. Reaching Trenton on the seventh, he took his troops across the Delaware River, a formidable obstacle. He made it even more of a barrier by clearing the river up and down from Trenton of all small craft. When the British arrived they were in effect stuck—no way to get at the Americans unless they manufactured boats. They seem not even to have considered this option, and in a few days Howe returned to New York City, leaving several regiments at posts along the river. These troops were mostly Hessians, and Howe placed Colonel Johann Rall as the commander.

The retreat from Fort Lee and Hackensack can be plotted easily on a map, with the route taken, the days of rapid flight and near disaster, and the eventual respite offered by the crossing of the Delaware. Washington exercised his command effectively in these weeks, and his withdrawal to temporary safety appears to be a simple story. Within the story, however, were other stories of much greater complexity, which demonstrate that his escape called on his ability to manage disparate problems on the run. For while he was clearing out of Fort Lee with his army, he was also recruiting another as the troops he had begun his march with finished their service and went home. When he left Fort Lee, he had a small number of Continental regiments in his army, but these units had been badly depleted by fighting on Long Island and New York Island. It soon became clear that he would have to rely on soldiers he considered unreliable: newly recruited militia sent to him by Governor William Livingston of New Jersey. Their tour of duty would end in six weeks. The authorities in Connecticut and Massachusetts promised to provide additional militia, who had been lured into military service by promises of advanced and augmented pay. Washington dreaded the effects of such terms on men already under arms. He had reason to feel concern—there was already rivalry among the soldiers of various states, and all, whatever their condition, felt underpaid and badly supplied. Most needed better food and clothing soon after they arrived, and many found themselves living in the open even when they were not on the move—tents were lacking, and no one believed that barracks would be put up for them. Washington feared that if these conditions produced low morale and genuine grievances, an attempt to pay some better than others might yield a violent reaction, even "mutiny."

When he first ordered his army out of Hackensack, he knew that adding to its numbers through enlistments presented him with a challenge. But for a brief moment he believed that he might strengthen his force by pulling together those units that had been detached for special missions. There were several of these detachments, one of which was at times as large as the force immediately under Washington's command. Charles Lee had led this unit in northern New York since February, and for several months afterwards had tightened patriot control in the city and the waters around it. With Governor Tryon acting to protect the Crown's interests, maintaining a government sympathetic to the policies of the Continental Congress was impossible. The arrival in the summer of British naval and military forces stopped whatever consolidation of authority the state's council could claim, which Lee had supported.

Lee had enjoyed his New York command but had not managed to do anything important for American interests after Washington brought the body of the Continental Army to New York in April. He was in the Highlands when Fort Washington fell in November, and he soon worked out his version of his mission when Washington began his retreat across New Jersey. Washington wrote him on November 21, suggesting that Lee bring his part of the army to Washington's in New Jersey. Lee, whose army was in North Castle, had objected to the idea that he leave New York, writing that "it wold give us the air of being frighte'd [and] it wou'd expose a fine fertile Country to their ravages."[30] Lee composed this letter on November 19 and may not have received Washington's until November 23 or 24. If he had received this letter earlier, it would have made little difference in his conduct; nor did the letters Washington wrote—at least six—in November and December telling him to come. In his letters Washington observed the proprieties of gentlemen. He was the commanding officer, but he remained polite as he sent letter after letter commanding Lee to join him in New Jersey. He also explained the necessity of adding Lee's army to the main force: He was losing troops as militia enlistments expired, and he could not depend upon recruiters to find replacements. He was also on the run, with Cornwallis pressing on his heels. To help explain the urgency of joining Lee's troops to his own, he told Lee that Philadelphia was Cornwallis's objective. Congress had met there since its beginnings in 1774—and the loss of the city would be such a blow that the Revolution itself might collapse.

Lee's replies nowhere indicate explicit refusal to follow his commander's orders, but instead offer reasons for delay. He was remaining in northern New York to protect its people from the Tories who, he implied, abounded there. About the time he made this answer, he was also ordering General Heath, who was in command of forces Washington had left at Peekskill, to send two thousand of his men to Washington. Heath refused, though Lee informed him that he, Lee, was second-in-command of the Continental Army and that Heath was obliged to follow his orders. Washington knew nothing of Heath's difficulty with Lee, and his own problems must have seemed intolerable when he read Lee's magisterial pronouncement that he hoped Washington would "bind me as little as possible—not from any opinion, I do assure you, of my own parts—but from a persuasion that detach'd Generals cannot have too great latitude—unless They are very incompetent indeed." This detached general promised to cross the river "the day after tomorrow," December 2, but actually did not do so until December 5.[31]

The reasons for Lee's disobedience in the face of Washington's orders cannot be known, shrouded as they were by his various promises and claims. Through it all, he let Washington know that he thought the most productive course would be to hang on the rear of the British army, a tactic that would allow him to operate free of the encumbrance of his chief's orders.

During the effort to entice Lee to join the main army, Washington opened a letter Lee had sent to Joseph Reed, his aide, that seemed to be on official business, only to discover that it was private. In it Lee criticized Washington's "indecision of mind which in war is a much greater disqualification than stupidity."[32] Had Washington read Reed's letter to which Lee's was a response, his shock would have been greater. Reed's was obsequious, despite claims that "I do not mean to flatter, nor praise you at the Expense of any other" (which he then proceeded to do). It urged Lee to "go to Congress & form the Plan of the new Army," a suggestion that, if followed, would have openly challenged Washington's appointment as commander of the Continental forces.[33]

Whatever Washington felt, he had little time to lick wounds inflicted through letters. He had barely squeezed his troops out of Fort Lee, and in fact had almost been trapped between the Hackensack and Passaic Rivers. He and his army arrived at Newark the next day, November 22, without cannon or much of anything else. His rear guard had given him some time in which to pull his force together by destroying the bridge over the Hackensack.

Cornwallis, now delegated by Howe to bring Washington to bay, allowed his enemy to rest for almost five days. There was no kindness or mercy intended by this act, for Cornwallis had some regrouping of his own army to do. There was also the problem of the roads, difficult to march over accompanied by artillery and supply wagons because of their mud and roughness.

When Cornwallis got under way from Fort Lee, Washington resumed his flight. The British almost caught him as he left Newark, but he made it to New Brunswick on November 29. There were reinforcements of a sort in New Brunswick: two thousand men in General Stirling's brigade, which had gone ahead a few days before Washington's retreat from Fort Lee began. Fortunately they were fine troops—five regiments of Virginians and another from Delaware, about twelve hundred new soldiers in all. Unfortunately, they too were largely without equipment, lacking tents, blankets, and in some cases shoes. Still, their presence gave comfort to the weary men who marched in, and over the next few days this augmented force received militia from Pennsylvania.[34]

Then it was off to Princeton for the army, and then to the Delaware River and Trenton, where boats were collected to transport Washington's group across. Cornwallis had not pursued him out of New Brunswick. Howe had given up the idea of catching Washington, who had proved to be elusive and faster on his feet than expected. Never a venturesome man, Howe had decided on winter quarters for his troops. He would resume his operations in the spring, as any good eighteenth-century general would.

Washington made no such decision about his army, as there was no certainty that he would have an army after his long retreat following the debacle at New York. He did not know Howe's intentions, in any case, but thought that the chances were that the British would continue their advance and not stop until they had taken Philadelphia. Scooping up all the boats in the Delaware would slow the enemy down, but they could build small craft. Given that, there was no certainty that the British would not attempt a crossing soon.

Meanwhile, he pulled his troops together and decided on the locations of defenses and camps. He also tried to add to his forces with new enlistments. While he was attempting to cope with his situation along the river, he watched his enemy closely, trying always to anticipate what the British were plotting.

These were defensive measures. While fashioning them, Washington thought of another kind of tactic, a surprise attack across the river at Trenton. Such an attack by his forces was for him more than a strategic (or tactical) move; it was political action. He had felt concern, throughout the days of his retreat from Fort Lee to the western bank of the Delaware, about the effects of his movements on the Revolution. He asked himself in these desperate days if the revolutionary cause could survive the loss of New Jersey and Pennsylvania. General Howe had, on November 30, offered pardons to Americans who declared their loyalty to Britain, an offer that, Washington learned, many in New Jersey were accepting. The prospect of a colony returning to the British fold seemed dangerous, and Pennsylvania might fall if Howe sent his army across the Delaware River. By mid-December intelligence reports—at least one from a Tory who wrote from New Jersey to a friend in Philadelphia—suggested that Howe waited only for an opportunity to close with Washington's army. The prospects did not look promising: If the ice froze over, the British would cross; and if they found boats or made them, they would cross.[35]

To avert such a strike would not be easy. The best way seemed to be to strike first, a big risk at best. The surprise of such an attack would give him an advantage, and, given the precariousness of his situation—an army weakened by defeat and reduced by the departure of its troops—what did he have to lose? The decision to attack thus grew out of his political as well as his military sense. It is not known when he came to his decision, but it is clear that his military thinking and his political understanding were linked in what he planned. He had about fifteen hundred men in five Continental regiments and a handful of militia; a few more militia might come to his camp, but there was no certainty in his estimates of their coming.

What Washington had in soldiers did not make an imposing force. But he had made up his mind to risk these men. If he was to preserve the public's faith in the Revolution, he had to act to hold the tenuous attachments of the people in the Mid-Atlantic states and perhaps all over America.

There was feeling besides political calculation in his decision to go across the river, the old passions and instincts that could be satisfied only by an attack for glory and honor. He did not show much of how he felt to the troops at this time. He recognized their physical discomfort—many could not stay warm in the cold weather that had set in weeks before, for they lacked warm clothing, and some still had no shoes. A summons to glory would have seemed barren of meaning to such men. Yet some also yearned to get at the enemy that had forced them to run all the way across New Jersey. Washington insisted that the people of New Jersey would be satisfied if the army simply looked the enemy in the face, and his soldiers seem to have entertained the same feeling. They were tired of showing the British only their backsides. Challenging them may have appeared foolhardy, but they too wanted some action favorable to the American cause.

The Hessians across the Delaware were actually less formidable than they looked, strung out from Trenton to Burlington, near Philadelphia. This was where Colonel Carl von Donop stationed himself, near the southern end of these posts at Mount Holly; Colonel Rall with three regiments held Trenton, and General Alexander Leslie remained at Princeton. The British forces in New Jersey were now commanded by General James Grant, who reported to Howe.[36]

To the surprise of the Hessians, who had a dismissive opinion of their enemy, the Americans around them on the east side of the Delaware resented their presence. It should not have been a surprise, given the plundering they did wherever they were. Like most occupying armies in the eighteenth century, they were in the anomalous position of simultaneously protecting and exploiting the inhabitants around them. They needed meat, grain, and forage and took what they found, despite the protests of New Jersey farmers. Before long there were reprisals, and Hessian commanders complained that the security of the chain Howe had strung them along did not exist. To get a letter to Princeton, Colonel Rall had to send a heavy patrol of fifty men. Hessian patrols, foraging parties, and outposts were regularly mauled by local partisans and raiders from both sides of the Delaware. Rall did not, given these conditions, even bother to throw up fortifications about Trenton; the enemy surrounded him, he explained, and he could not cover such outposts adequately.[37]

Neither Rall nor his chief expected Washington to attack on Christmas night. The weather brought rain and snow, and the Delaware River, though not covered with ice, carried large blocks of it downstream. Washington planned carefully, though he had not expected the weather to conceal his movements. He ordered an attack of three prongs: Brigadier General James Ewing, with seven hundred men, would cross at Trenton Ferry and seize the bridge over the Assunpink Creek, just south of the town. Lieutenant Colonel John Cadwalader, farther to the south, would strike over the river at Bristol and hit Donop's force at Mount Holly, a diversion to keep the Hessians so occupied there as to prevent reinforcement of Trenton. The main objective of the attack was Trenton, and Washington himself would lead this attack, which, if all went well, would push through Princeton and beyond, perhaps as far as the main British magazine at New Brunswick.

After dark on Christmas night, the main force, some 2,400 soldiers, assembled behind the low hills overlooking McKonkey's Ferry, about eight miles upriver from Trenton. Washington wanted to cross them all by midnight and march south to Trenton by five in the morning, well before daylight, but the storm, the rough water, and the ice prevented him from holding to this schedule. Knox's artillery, eighteen pieces in all, proved difficult to handle in the snow and sleet and was not put ashore until three in the morning. Washington, who had crossed with the advance party in Durham boats, stood on the bank and watched—he knew that his presence would not go unnoticed even in the dark. By four o'clock all of his troops were on the east bank and assembled for the thrust into Trenton.[38]

Two columns formed, one on the upper road, Pennington Road, the other on the lower, River Road. Washington, with Nathanael Greene, commanded the force on the Pennington, and General John Sullivan led on River Road. By skill or by good luck, both forces reached Trenton within minutes of eight o'clock. The lower road curved into the southern end of town; the upper carried the troops to King and Queen Streets, running north and south, the main thoroughfares of the town. Washington's van drove in a company on outpost duty on the north edge and in a few minutes had unlimbered their cannon on King and Queen Streets. Two young captains commanded the fire of these guns: Thomas Forrest and Alexander Hamilton.

Gunfire brought two Hessian regiments pouring into these streets, and a third remained unengaged for the moment, in reserve at the southwestern edge of town. Colonel Rall, who had celebrated Christmas night with the usual enthusiasm, took charge on the streets, but a bullet cut him down almost immediately, and his men never formed to fight effectively. Much of the village was empty, the inhabitants having fled three weeks earlier, and its houses and stables were soon turned into arenas for vicious bayonet fights. The American artillery prevented the Hessians from fighting as organized units, and American infantry gradually forced their surrender after a short period in which they showed their proficiency with muskets and bayonets. In an hour it was over, with twenty-two Hessians dead, ninety-eight wounded, and almost a thousand prisoners. Two American officers and two privates were wounded.

These were satisfying figures, but there was disappointment too, for Ewing had not been able to make it over the river, leaving a route of escape across Assunpink Creek that five hundred Hessians and a handful of British dragoons used. Nor had Cadwalader crossed in force farther south. Washington took his tired but triumphant men back across the river to Pennsylvania in the afternoon. He had learned of Cadwalader's failure, and there seemed nothing else to do. Without Cadwalader in place, Washington anticipated that the enemy downriver would be coming up in number to attack him. He was wrong on this score, as in the next few days the Hessians abandoned every post on the river in favor of withdrawal to the east.

Two days later, somewhat rested, Washington took his troops back over the river, directly into Trenton. Once in the town, he ordered Cadwalader up and gave General Mifflin, who had occupied Bordentown with 1,600 militia, the same order. As the year ended, Washington had an army of 5,000 and forty howitzers in Trenton.

He now faced a greater challenge. On the news of the debacle, Howe ordered Cornwallis, then sitting in Princeton, to move quickly against Washington, and Cornwallis responded by marching out with 5,500 regulars and twenty-eight fieldpieces. Washington expected him and did not ease his way south. The British had to use Princeton Road, which was churned into mud, and as they marched, small parties of Pennsylvania and Virginia Continentals harassed them with musket fire and quick strikes along their flanks. Late in the afternoon of January 2, Cornwallis found Washington's army drawn up along the ridge of Assunpink Creek. The British sent advance units against Americans in an effort to cross the creek. They failed, punished by American artillery and infantry fire. Several unsuccessful attempts convinced Cornwallis that he should delay a major assault until the next day. A subordinate or two protested, arguing that Washington would not be there in the morning. The answer to that was a question: Where would he go? He had no boats to carry him back across the Delaware. He was trapped.

Washington answered the question that night by quietly taking away his army on a new and lightly used road southeast of the main highway to Princeton. He masked his departure by leaving behind several hundred men who in the darkness kept campfires ablaze and made noise by digging into the ground. The British across the creek saw the fires and listened to what they assumed was an army preparing for an assault when daylight came. But by daybreak Washington had reached the outskirts of Princeton. There the Americans found two regiments of British infantry under Lieutenant Colonel Charles Mawhood. The fight that followed did not last long. Mawhood's troops, at first giving a good account of themselves, seemed on the verge of breaking the American van, but Washington, with most of his troops, soon recovered control—it has been commonly said that resisting Washington on horseback was too much for any enemy—and in this case he had the advantage of surprise. Mawhood pulled back and escaped, his army in near disintegration as it made its way to Trenton. He had left behind a third regiment, which failed at first to give battle and then retired to New Brunswick. It, too, took severe losses, and Washington captured almost two hundred of its soldiers.[39]

New Brunswick had figured in Washington's plans, for it contained a large supply facility that he hoped to seize. He soon discovered that his own soldiers were just about as tired as those under Cornwallis, and he gave up all thought of fighting his way into the town. Cornwallis, fearing the worst from his slippery enemy, had in the meantime marched his command from Trenton to New Brunswick. He was taking no chances on losing his supply depot. Hackensack and Elizabeth Town fell to other American forces detached from Washington's command on January 8, the day Washington's army entered Morristown. Howe, who had dominated New Jersey two weeks earlier, now saw his forces there confined to Amboy and New Brunswick. He decided to spend the winter in the relative comfort of New York City. Washington would be thirty miles to the west in Morristown.

Washington now had an army that had fought well after disastrous defeats in the previous six months. More of his officers and soldiers now believed in themselves. As important as this belief was the
renewed faith of the nation in the army and its general. All agreed
that Washington's victory at Trenton had transformed the Revolution,
which once again was a cause that could be won.

6

The Philadelphia Campaign

Washington's strike at Trenton and Princeton revealed a side of his character not often seen: a willingness to take chances. He had allowed a part of his fierce energy to come out, and the consequences were especially pleasing to him, not simply because his daring paid off, but also because he had thrust himself into the heart of the fighting. Much of what he had done as a commander up to this moment fell into the category of administration. He had to pull together an army when he arrived in Cambridge in 1775, and that assignment compelled him to act as a manager virtually every day. The big battles of the beginning of the war had been fought at Lexington and Concord and at Bunker Hill; he was not present at either. Nor did the end of the Siege of Boston or the beginning of the New York campaign bring him under gunfire. He planned the move onto Dorchester Heights, but the need for overall coordination had moored him to his headquarters. In the New York campaign he had watched, but could not prevent, the collapse in Brooklyn. To be sure, he led the escape of his army in the fog and rain from Long Island to New York Island. His fierceness finally found full expression amid the shelling and musket fire the British poured into his troops at Kips Bay, but whatever satisfaction that engagement brought to his combative spirit vanished as his troops, sharing nothing of his eagerness to get at the enemy, fled for safety.

After the weary run across New Jersey, the Battles of Trenton and Princeton, at the end of December 1776, transformed his spirit. He had smelled gunpowder again, his soldiers fought well, and this time he and they emerged from battle convinced that they could defeat their enemy wherever they found him. For troops who had been in retreat for months, the victories of Trenton and Princeton assumed enormous significance. The mode of these attacks, with their swiftness, deception, and force, confirmed for many soldiers their own skill. In effect, American soldiers defeated their enemy in the way the enemy had grown accustomed to defeating them.

Washington did not exult in his victory, but others did. Members of Congress wrote of their pleasure at the news, though several remained dissatisfied at the strategy Washington had followed since taking his command. John Adams was among them, and he, as Nathanael Greene remarked, did not have "the most exalted opinion" of any American general.[1] Washington's unguarded deprecation, two years earlier, of the slovenliness of New England troops probably still rankled Adams, but on the other hand it may not have had anything to do with his later unhappiness with the conduct of the war. Adams did not like many people and had even less regard for the way things were done anywhere. Adams aside, most Americans in and out of Congress whose opinions survive declared their satisfaction in the outcome of the Trenton and Princeton attacks.

As for Washington's reputation, it seems clearly to have been solidly favorable before these battles, and this includes regard for his military skill. Nicholas Cresswell, a Virginia planter, recorded in his journal the change of heart of a friend in Leesburg, Virginia, who had been a critic: "Six weeks ago this gentleman was lamenting the unhappy situation of the Americans and pitying the wretched condition of their much-beloved General, supposing his want of skill and experience in military matters had brought them all to the brink of destruction. In short all was gone, all was lost. But now the scale is turned and Washington's name is extolled to the clouds."[2]

Washington did not read Cresswell's journal. But he did read, in a letter from Bartholomew Dandridge, his brother-in-law, "that it is plain Providence designed you as the favorite Instrument in working the Salvation of America." Dandridge offered this estimate "without flattery," and coupled it with a warning "against exposing your Person too much," advice that might have produced a smile in Washington, who seems not to have ever felt physical danger.[3]

In fact, he acted as if he had no time for congratulations or for taking care of himself. His descriptions of Trenton and Princeton played down American prowess and his own, but he did acknowledge that "these succeses" [*sic*] had improved the morale of the people of New Jersey and Pennsylvania. Whatever pride he might have felt was carefully disguised in his dismissal of his army's quality. To Jonathan Trumbull Sr. he began his account of what had happened in this way: "Our success at Trenton has been followed by another lucky blow at Princeton on the 3d instant," phrasing repeated almost exactly in a letter to Philip Schuyler: "The Enemy by two lucky Strokes at Trenton and Princeton, have been obliged to abandon Every Part of Jersey except Brunswick & Amboy." Elsewhere he deflected responsibility for fashioning victories in the battles, simply saying that "Providence has heretofore saved us in a remarkable manner, and on this we must principally rely." He was under no illusions about the strength of his army; nor did he believe that it had become the reliable professional fighting force he had long craved.[4]

Yet he had been affected by the success at Trenton and Princeton. He was now a more confident commander, one who recognized that his own abilities were equal to his assignment. Such conviction had lived uneasily within him since he took command of the army. The uneasiness led him to pay attention to the recommendations of his council of generals, which always counseled caution and restrained action, usually warning that the enemy was too powerful to fight head-on. Washington talked with these commanders in December before deciding on his bold strokes and found agreement that an attack across the Delaware should be made. There was no doubt that the officers' agreement pleased him, though in actuality he had made up his mind before such consultations were made, and before any advice was given.[5]

In deciding to strike, he yielded to the frustration that had built up as defeat and one retreat after another occurred. But his motives were not based on unthinking anger or a sense of desperation that implied that rolling the dice was the only action left. He did feel a desperation, but it was softened by a mature sense of how the war should be fought and a recognition that the political being of the new nation was in peril, linked as it was to military operations. He was no longer shocked at the conduct of the militia; nor was he surprised at the unevenness of the operations of the Congress. These were problems he could do little about. His immediate dread in the weeks leading to Trenton and Princeton was that Howe would take Philadelphia. With New Jersey in British hands and its people apparently lacking the will to help in taking it back, could the Revolution survive the loss of Philadelphia and, perhaps, all of Pennsylvania? These fears provided the context for the decision—so redolent of frustration and fury—to strike across the Delaware.[6]

The success of the attack gratified him and released some of the anguish of earlier defeats, but he felt that the British would respond with their own attacks as quickly as possible. This belief was mistaken. Howe may have wished for one more chance to crush the rebellion before winter closed down operations, but he soon fell back into conventional actions and sent most of his army into winter quarters at New Brunswick and Amboy (later Perth Amboy). His proclamation at the end of November 1776 had brought a number of loyalists out in the open—these people wanted to escape violence, not commit it—but by early January of the new year they had had enough of the peace the British and Hessians brought them. For these troops plundered friend and foe alike, without regard to the oaths New Jersey loyalists had taken to support the British king.[7] British commanders, confined with their forces in New Brunswick and Amboy, found that they had to resort to local supplies of food and forage if they were to sustain their troops. They soon discovered that enemy militia, who had shown themselves incapable in previous months of fighting in conventional ways, were quite adept at taking on foraging parties, which were necessarily clumsy and difficult to maneuver, encumbered as they were with the horses and wagons necessary for transporting grains and hay back to their camps. Foraging parties also attempted to collect local cattle and horses. Bloated with their plunder, they proved to be easy targets for the angry militia. When the enemies collided, the British seemed usually to get the worst of the damage, and in flight back to friendly lines they sometimes left behind not only what they had collected but also prisoners, dead, and wounded. They soon attempted to even the odds by sending heavily armed forces along with the foraging parties, and sometimes added fieldpieces to these forces. Not even such strenuous efforts stopped militia attacks, and in these months of winter and early spring, British soldiers in Amboy and New Brunswick lived on salted beef and bread, with very little else.

Washington had ordered several of these attacks and approved of them all. He knew they would keep the British on the defensive and would also raise the morale of the people of New Jersey, a consequence that boded well for sustaining the Revolution.

The need to deny food and forage to British troops, important as it was, had to give way to one even more urgent: recruiting and maintaining an army. As usual, short enlistments were the key to this problem, presenting Washington with a mixture of soldiers, some serving for only six weeks, others on three-month tours, still others in the service for a year, with a few signed up for three years or for the duration of the war. He needed men, and he made his preferences known throughout the months that followed Trenton. Although he had no high opinion of the fighting ability of ordinary people, he thought that with training and discipline, the common run of society in America could be made to yield the soldiers he required. But how to go about finding them remained an intractable problem.[8]

Congress had heard him on the subject more times than most delegates probably desired. Late in 1776, Congress had responded by authorizing him to raise sixteen more regiments, in addition to the eighty-eight it had agreed to about a year earlier. A good step, Washington believed, but an authorization brought no one into camp. Congress did call upon the states to raise these regiments, just as it had in approving the original eighty-eight. Washington added his voice, but he knew that he faced reluctance among most men to venture themselves by joining Continental regiments. Most preferred service in state militias if they had to serve at all.

There was no recruiting service available, but Congress had eased his task somewhat by allowing him to name the colonels who would command the sixteen fresh regiments—and the other, lower officers as well: the lieutenant colonels, the majors, captains, right down to the lowest lieutenant, if he chose to exercise his right to choose. Washington, as recruiting proceeded in the winter, soon came to permit a colonel who had agreed to head a regiment to name all the officers in his command. This right was an important inducement, and a necessary one on several scores, for no regimental commander wanted officers in his command whom he did not know, and in many cases regimental officers turned out to be men who knew one another. Washington did make clear that should a colonel's choices of subordinates dissatisfy him, he retained the right to reject them.[9]

Filling the ranks was even more difficult than finding officers. In this assignment he received limited help from Congress, which proved unwilling to require long-term enlistments and could not bring itself to pay, feed, and equip ordinary soldiers in any but the most miserly style. Washington recognized that the paltry rewards offered to recruits stopped many from coming in, and he told Congress that such parsimony could gut the army and forestall attempts to replace those who departed. What he proposed by way of rewards was hardly magnificent: In January he suggested paying every man who volunteered a twenty-dollar bounty, and added that a suit of clothes would be necessary. Congress agreed and added a promise of one hundred acres, presumably to be carved out of the West, and half pay for the disabled for life.[10]

Armed with such lures, newly commissioned colonels set out to fill the ranks. They could not accept anyone simply because he volunteered, for Washington had clear ideas about who should find acceptance and who should not. The rules he laid out provided that no one under seventeen or more than fifty years of age should be accepted, and only those "free from Lameness or other bodily Infirmity" that might make them incapable of standing up to the rigors of camp life should be enlisted. To make certain that no weakling might slip through for the bounty, Washington also instructed his new colonels to take only men of sufficient stature to carry out the duties of a private in the army. He was emphatic in demanding that no deserter from the British army be enrolled; nor should anyone of suspicious principles, a warning to steer clear of Tories or the lukewarm. He also demonstrated knowledge of an underhanded practice sometimes used by recruiters by requiring that no one already in the army in another regiment be accepted. All of these requirements imposed standards that would not likely slow recruitment, but the term of service he insisted upon surely did. A recruit who signed up must agree to a minimum enlistment of three years—and preferably for the duration of the war. This requirement probably discouraged more men than any other.

Competition came from the states that were also engaged in filling militia battalions and the original eighty-eight state Continentals. Such efforts also undercut attempts to put together the additional sixteen

Congress had approved.[11] In January, just as Washington's attempts to establish these regiments began, he discovered that the Connecticut legislature had authorized payment of a bounty of thirty-three dollars "over & above what Congress have given" for regulars, and not long afterwards Connecticut's generosity had drawn men from New York, to the dismay of recruiters there. John Trumbull, governor of Connecticut, when reproved by Washington for his state's action, explained that because the cost of living was higher in the New England states than elsewhere—in particular the South—the higher bounty was justified. Washington replied that the southern states manufactured little and paid "most extravagantly" for what they imported. Trumbull did not extend the dispute—he and the Connecticut legislature held Washington in high esteem, and saw the cogency of his desire to fill the additional regiments. They could be helpful, they believed, by agreeing to pay the difference between the congressional bounty and Connecticut's, thereby making equal the amounts paid to recruits to the additional congressional and state regiments.

This enlightened action helped to gather in soldiers in Connecticut, but the fact remained that it made recruiting more difficult in next-door New York. There were similar disparities elsewhere in the United States, which undoubtedly slowed the entire process of expanding the size of the army. There were other sorts of competition for recruits: The militia attracted men who might have entertained patriotic sentiments, as service in such units was always of a short duration—sometimes as little as four weeks and virtually never more than a year, and a year was seldom required. In Massachusetts, William Heath, who took over the Eastern Department in March 1777, after Artemas Ward resigned, despaired of meeting the state's quota and reported to Washington that the state had taken the congressional bounty of twenty pounds and increased it with a subvention of twenty-four pounds. The towns of Massachusetts sometimes added even more to the bounty, raising it to the point that he feared it would make the troops "Uneasy," a euphemism for "envious," for it created a system that could only be considered unequal in its treatment. This pattern seemed especially destructive in a part of the country in which equality was taken seriously.[12]

Washington himself unintentionally contributed to difficulties in recruiting by requiring that as men were brought into the ranks they be inoculated against smallpox. This was more than a prudent measure—it was a necessity. Smallpox in an army would kill the troops faster than the enemy, and an army with many infected men would threaten civilians in towns and cities. His order in these winter months of 1777 to the commanders charged with bringing their soldiers into the larger camp always included the requirement that they make certain that all of their men be inoculated, and to bypass Philadelphia if they had not.[13]

At least some of the men who volunteered aroused Washington's suspicion when he learned, early in the process of putting an army together, that enlisting, accepting the congressional bounty, and then disappearing was not an uncommon practice. His remedy was incorporated in his suggestion that colonels looking to fill the ranks of their regiments pay each man only a part of the bounty when he joined. Later, presumably when a soldier had received part of his training, it would be safe to pay the remainder.[14]

In late winter through the early months of spring, despite difficulties and failures, Washington never let up. He wrote the new regimental officers often, urging them on and reminding them of the need to rebuild his force; he kept Congress informed of the process, especially of its flaws; and he reminded state governments of the overriding importance of a national effort. At the beginning of April, after months of strenuous effort, not a single soldier had been added to his army in New Jersey, but two weeks later they began marching in, inoculated, many actually equipped with muskets, and adequately clothed. By summer Washington could look upon an American army of regulars, though these soldiers were still not fully trained, and militia from several states made up almost half the total force.[15]

This army resembled its predecessors in most ways. Its men were largely untrained—a few hardy souls stayed with it, and more than a few commanders remained with their regiments. Washington added new brigadiers—his desire for more officers in that rank had resided with him all winter. The core of major generals stuck with him, Nathanael Greene, the best of the lot, among them.

This new army did not perform as a smoothly functioning machine, or even as a machine with all its parts in place. When Congress created the army in 1775, it had not really known what an army looked like, had not indeed known what its staff should be, or how they should work in relation to its regiments or to Congress. A handful of delegates had read a few guides for army commanders; a smaller number had any experience in military life other than the attenuated version provided by conventional militia service. Despite their ignorance of military organization, the delegates in Philadelphia plunged ahead.

A number of departments had to be created at once, and no great knowledge of armies was needed to decide that action had to be taken to feed, clothe, arm, and otherwise supply the new organization. To a limited extent the New England Army that swarmed around Boston after Lexington and Concord provided a rough, if provisional, model. It was no surprise, then, that within a couple of days of appointing Washington commander in chief, Congress established five staff departments: a commissary general of provisions, a quartermaster general, a commissary of musters, a paymaster general, and an adjutant general.

Filling these posts was left to Washington, a recognition of his judgment that set John Adams on fire with worry that such an arrangement would encourage concentration of power in the army's command. These "officers," he wrote his friend James Warren, "are checks upon the General, and he a Check upon them: there ought not to be too much Connection between them."[16] Only Adams seemed troubled by this delegation of power, and in the weeks given to devising a command structure, his colleagues in Congress, far from such concerns, turned their attention to finding places in the army's staff and the auxiliary organizations growing up around it for their friends and political allies.

Other departments were fashioned in the months that followed and all through the New York campaign. One part of the army was often in transit between the camp and civilian life, and another part simply remained incomplete—or not conceived of—with responsibilities left to some temporary arrangement made by Washington and his staff. Getting any sort of clothing on his soldiers remained a problem. Washington never solved it satisfactorily, despite appeals to state officials, or to any authority with a supply. At times the competition for clothing, blankets, shoes, and socks led to conflict. There were occasions when Washington thought he had secured a supply from a British transport, its cargo having been sent on its way to the Continental Army by the privateer captain, but local authorities, hearing of the captured supplies, seized and diverted them to their own militia as the cargo was crossing the state.[17]

Desperate for a reliable system, Washington appealed to Congress to create a department with a clothier general in charge. In late December 1776, Congress named James Mease to the office. Mease was a Pennsylvania merchant, a civilian, and remained a civilian, though he reported to Washington. He was not notably successful in his job, if the men he was charged to clothe in uniforms are to be trusted. They, often afflicted with sickness they associated with inadequate dress, joked that they were "dying of the Meases." The possibility exists that Mease was color-blind—how else are we to explain that one of the regiments was given red uniforms? This embarrassment undoubtedly angered Washington, though most of the time he probably would have been grateful had Mease found uniforms of any color. He asked Congress to remove Mease in 1778, but Congress did not act until the following year.[18]

That appointing an official to supply uniforms for Washington's troops required so many months indicates something about the organization of the Continental Army and the Congress. The army's incomplete character lingered far too long and diverted energies better given to making disciplined fighting men. Incompletion marked the army in almost every way, and Washington strove month after month to fill such holes. His methods were almost always ad hoc: appeals to state governments or directly to Congress, but also to private sources, usually men of property who could give of themselves or find others who could. The commissaries were not lavishly staffed; in time, deputies and other assistants were authorized by Congress, but they proved to be of limited value. The fault, or the limitation, has to be traced back to Congress. Like almost all legislative bodies before and since, it was not designed to function with speed and decisiveness. Its strength lay elsewhere, and it could not find the means within itself to act as an executive. For executive authority and an underlying unity of purpose were needed to carry on the war.

The deepest problem of organization and drive arose from American society itself. The Americans, even after two years of war, were a divided people. Only a few delegates to Congress believed that in Phil-

adelphia they had a political center. For most, their provincial capital
or the town, parish, or county served as the organizing point of governance. Their economies were only gradually coming together—usually
through coastal trade. The big producers of tobacco and rice sent their
crops overseas, and much of the fish and naval stores also found their
way abroad. If a farmer raised grain or milled flour or baked bread, he
often dealt in local markets, but he might also send a considerable proportion of these commodities to the West Indies. Local trade usually
took second place to European and British productions, especially in
books, fine clothing, guns, and hardware of various kinds. A sense that
an American society existed that transcended the societies of the thirteen states barely breathed in 1776, when independence was declared.
Over the next few years, as the states struggled to bring their scattered
spirits together, the outlines of such a society, with different purposes
from those of the states, began to appear. No revolutionary leader surpassed Washington in the attempt to lead Americans to think and act
together; nor was any more pleased than he when they did.

Throughout his time dealing with the morass of administrative
problems, Washington had also to fight a war. Operations as a category did not overpower the demands to find, feed, clothe, and arm the
troops he led; there were no large-scale operations until September of
1777. Small-scale operations—attacks on British foraging parties and
moving soldiers from here to there in anticipation of a British strike—
were challenging enough. And underlying all that he did in this time
was his concern about what the British were going to do after their
noses had been bloodied at Trenton and Princeton.

Washington thought most of the time that General Howe would act to
capture Philadelphia. This belief was widely shared in his army and
in Congress. There were other possibilities, of course, such as a drive
up the Hudson River to meet Burgoyne bringing an army down the
lakes from Canada. Howe was a baffling man to American commanders and, in fact, to several of his colleagues. General Henry Clinton
could never figure him out, and found his own advice about strategy
rejected with little discussion.[19]

Howe's head may not have been entirely clear while he sat in New
York. There were stories at the time that he was so dazzled by Eliza-

beth Loring, wife of the British commissary of prisoners, that he had no will to take on his American enemy. (The story is given much too much importance.) For a short period in late winter, he roused himself sufficiently to recruit loyalists for service around New York and in New Jersey. But he did little to entice nearby Indians into British service. By this point in Howe's service in America, suspicion had arisen of his ability to exercise overall command of the army. No one doubted his bravery, for he had shown that on a number of occasions. The best known of his exploits in America had occurred in 1759, in the French and Indian War, when he led the advance force that climbed the Heights of Abraham and captured Quebec. He looked the part of a warrior—he was tall, good-looking, and he carried himself quietly; no bragging or display of the sort that Burgoyne favored.

Howe, like his brother Lord Richard, probably came to the Revolutionary War with some sympathy for Americans. Massachusetts had erected a monument in Westminster Abbey to their brother George Augustus, 3rd Viscount Howe, who had been killed at Ticonderoga in the French and Indian War. But neither William Howe's sympathy nor his principles had kept him out of the war. Other British officers had refused to join the effort to subdue the Americans. But William and his brother had agreed to serve, and their commissions from the Crown to offer a peace had not stayed their hands from making war.

The suspicion toward William Howe owed more to doubts about his capacity for command than to such matters as his sympathy for a people who had honored his brother. There was his record in the war—his delay in using his army, after his return from Britain in July 1776, with an overwhelming force. His failure to attack Washington when he had him trapped in Brooklyn raised doubts about his leadership. Howe had also appeared sluggish after Kips Bay and White Plains, and most emphatically in the march across New Jersey that ended in the defeats at Trenton and Princeton.

The feeling that Howe lacked something essential in a commander in chief grew in late 1777 and continued to dog him. It is difficult not to conclude that he lacked the intellectual power to understand the war he was fighting. Coupled with a disposition to take his ease, to wait rather than act, there was a feeling that for all his courage and his long years of experience in the army, he was out of place—in over his head—as commander.

Howe's chief task in 1777 was to plan a new campaign and to carry it out. He had informed Lord George Germain, the minister in Britain charged with running the war, that he needed reinforcements if he was going to carry the war to the Americans once again. He did not explain exactly how he would use his army, but mentioned that fifteen or twenty thousand additional troops would be needed. Germain let him know in March that only 7,800 would be forthcoming.[20]

The correspondence between the two men in these months had a curious quality, almost as if each man had not read the other's letters. The distance between Germain's Colonial Office and the headquarters of the two overseas armies—Guy Carleton's, in Canada, and William Howe's, in New York, made clear communication difficult, and the peculiar personalities involved often led to fuzzy understandings. In the case of the 1777 campaign, problems of planning were more than intrinsically complicated, and proved impossible to work out. That General Burgoyne, who was to lead the northern army marching down from Canada, did not leave England until April 3 compressed the period for consultation and clarification. What Germain thought was clear to everyone on the British side—that there would be a coordinated effort to cut the colonies in two, with Burgoyne driving down from Canada and Howe moving north up the Hudson, presumably for a meeting of forces in Albany—was not clear to the commander in America. Germain also apparently believed that Howe could take Philadelphia as a first step in his operations.[21]

Whatever Howe understood about Germain's instructions, he acted as if he were fighting on his own, without regard for the northern theater. His second-in-command, Henry Clinton, who had been in England, returning to America in early July, now attempted to persuade him that Germain's strategy should be followed. Howe dismissed all such appeals and loaded his army onto his brother's transports in July, with the intention of getting at Washington by way of the Chesapeake. After looking into the mouth of the Delaware, he resumed his voyage and finally began putting his troops ashore at the head of the Elk River on August 25. He had landed an army unprepared to fight: Its soldiers were worn out, weakened by living in dreadfully close quarters without exercise and on a diet insufficient for a life of marching and fighting. The cavalry had watched many of its horses on board wither and die and knew that its animals required rest and nourishment even more than the men. Given the condition of horses and men, Howe had little choice but to rest both. Not until September 8 did he make a serious move to engage Washington.

Howe's plans were now clear, dispelling the ignorance that had kept Washington and his army on edge for months. Although there had been time to get ready for the resumption of combat, these months had not been profitable to readiness. Recruiting a new army after Trenton had dominated every other activity. There had been some fighting, as we have seen, most often on a small scale—what Washington and his officers called the "petty war." This was for horses, cattle, food, and forage; and there was nothing grand about it. There had also been the annoyance of having to turn away eager but unqualified French officers, almost none of whom spoke English or had the experience of war they claimed. Even worse in Washington's judgment was the insistence of Massachusetts that it should be allowed to keep at home newly raised Continental regiments, on the expectation that the British would soon make another attempt at conquering New England. Washington, in a carefully phrased letter in response, examined the fear felt in Massachusetts, showing a willingness to consider such a suggestion, but then stripped away its foolish gloss by concluding that "it would be the most wretched policy to weaken the hands of the continent, under the mistaken idea of strengthening your own."[22] He was saying once again, in this diplomatic but lucid argument, that the common cause demanded common—not parochial—measures.

Washington could not be certain of what his British enemy during these months was doing. In late May, intelligence came from spies and other friendly observers that Howe was moving his forces to the north—perhaps for a major campaign up the river?—but in June, he gathered much of his army at New Brunswick. This movement was followed by what Washington assumed would be an attack on the American army then dug in at Middlebrook, New Jersey. Howe, who marched his men about ten miles west of New Brunswick, had not carried portable bridges with his forces, which suggested to Washington that his purpose was to destroy the Americans, not cross the Delaware River to take Philadelphia. But he could not be certain of Howe's purposes at any time, for, as he had written to Hancock two weeks earlier, "the actions of the Enemy have, for a long time past, been so different from appearances, that I hardly dare form an opinion."[23] Howe, in this instance, changed his mind about an attack and a few days later pulled his forces back all the way to Staten Island.

The rumors and reports about British intentions continued well into August, when Howe finally emerged from his excursion on the Atlantic. Then and only then could Washington send his troops into battle. He did so in anger at his enemy, extreme even for him. The British had abandoned their forward positions outside New Brunswick with a brutality far from anything Howe had intended. Whatever William Howe and his brother had favored in dealing with the Americans opposing them, they had not approved of brutal measures. Ordinary British soldiers and probably their officers as well had not agreed with them, and in pulling back from Middlebrook in late June, "they had behaved as they were wont to do, leaving nothing which they could carry off, Robbing, Plundering, & burning Houses as they went." Washington's final assessments at this point reveal a growing hatred: "were they to take up the business of Scalping they would much resemble Savages in every respect! so much is the boasted generosity, and glory of Britains fallen."[24]

There were other lessons from this part of the war. Washington had learned much from the beginning of the New York campaign about the importance of a navy in New York waters. Watching Howe embark his troops and sail away in July brought home again the importance of sea power and what it meant for the land-restricted Continental Army: "By means of their Shipping, and the easy transportation that Shipping affords," he ruefully remarked, "they have it much in their power to lead us a very disagreeable dance."[25]

The dance began a few days after Howe's army shook off the effects of its confinement in transports. Washington watched the first slow steps on August 26 from a hill near the British encampment, and spent the night in a farmhouse very near his enemy. Nathanael Greene and the young Marquis de Lafayette, who had recently joined the army after his arrival from France, were with him. At dawn on the twenty-seventh, he and his small party of officers rode back to headquarters in nearby Wilmington, convinced that a real effort to destroy their forces was about to be made. At least one of his commanders, Brigadier General Anthony Wayne, urged that Washington "not wait" for Howe's attack, but rather "make a Regular and Vigorous Assault on their Right or Left Flank." Wayne, who was sometimes referred to as "Mad Anthony," did not claim that this suggestion was original; indeed, it was "no new Idea," he said, having been "Often practiced with success" by such commanders as "Caesar at Amiens when besieged by the Gauls," and at Alesia. The tactic had brought victory to Caesar, a result attributed by no less an authority than Marshal Saxe to the "terror and surprise" it creates in the enemy, which the marshal observed "proceeds from the Consternation which is the Unavoidable effect of Sudden and unexpected Events."[26]

Washington, who might have pointed out that militia and Continentals in his army lacked the fighting skills of the Roman legions, did not accept this advice. Instead, as the British picked up their advance on September 8, he chose Brandywine Creek for his battle with Howe. By September 10, the two sides seemed to be in place.

Brandywine Creek, in Pennsylvania near the Delaware state line, was not a stream that one could step over; in fact, it could be crossed only at a number of fords. Washington placed his army on the east side of the stream: At Pyle's Ford, close by Chadd's Ford, he stationed two brigades of Pennsylvania militia commanded by Major General John Armstrong. Greene's division held the position east of Chadd's Ford, with Anthony Wayne to his right at Brinton's Ford. This position straddled the road leading to Philadelphia, twenty-five miles away. On Wayne's right, Colonel Thomas Proctor set his artillery up on low-lying hills overlooking Chadd's Ford. The overall command of emplacements stretching from Brinton's Ford, just to the right of Wayne, was given to John Sullivan, with General Adam Stephen and Lord Stirling extended farther on, almost to Painter's Ford—a line almost two miles in length. Birmingham Hill, two miles to the east of these placements, was left unoccupied, as were fords farther up the Brandywine, including Trimble's Ford, on the west branch, and Jeffries, on the east. As a precaution, these positions were given some attention by small numbers of militia placed to give warning should the British appear. The size of the two armies is not known with any certainty. Howe seems to have commanded a force of about fifteen thousand, Washington something close to that if militia and light horse are included.[27]

The battle that began early in the morning of September 11 opened with Howe in motion at five in the morning. Perhaps with the tactics of the Battle of Brooklyn in mind, he marched northward from Kennett Square with eight thousand troops up the Great Valley Road. He had been told of fords at the split of the Brandywine; crossing them would put him in position to roll up the right flank of the American army. The march, quietly undertaken in fog, was covered to some extent by a force of 7,800 left behind under the command of Lieutenant General Wilhelm von Knyphausen, who had been ordered to hold the Americans in place along the creek. Knyphausen carried out his mission by moving to the east from Kennett Square, where he drove back American outposts that had been established across the creek. His appearance implanted a conviction among several commanders that the main British attack would come at Chadd's Ford or its vicinity.

Washington was not sure: Remembering the surprise Howe had given him along the Brooklyn Heights, he half-expected that outflanking tactics might be used again. His uncertainty lasted until early afternoon. In midmorning, he received some intelligence that the British were on the move to the north. He had been told that fords far up the Brandywine did not exist, implausible information on its face, but he hesitated to strip the army facing Knyphausen before the report of a flanking operation was established. While hesitating, he appealed for reliable intelligence and sent scouts to the north to look for the British.

By early afternoon, sometime between one thirty and two, no one could doubt that Howe had succeeded in pulling off another surprise. The British in force were then sitting on Osborne's Hill, a couple of miles south of Jeffries Ford, which Washington had not known of, and they were preparing to destroy the American line from its flank and rear. Washington had been with Greene while this was going on, and he immediately began an attempt to shift his troops to counter the British stroke.

Sullivan, with Washington's approval, began moving his own troops and Stirling's and Stephen's from the creek to Birmingham Hill, a mile southeast from Osborne's, where the British sat resting before making an assault. The American soldiers of these three commanders had marched—sometimes running—to their new positions along the hill. The ground they moved over was rough and wooded or brush-covered in several places, conditions that made getting into a proper alignment extraordinarily difficult. The British began their move before the Americans were fully realigned, and in fact found that there was a gap of several hundred yards between Stirling and Stephen. The Americans in Stephen's division, discovering that they had not hooked up with Stirling on their left, attempted a lateral movement to cover the distressing hole. They did not succeed, but the British did not exactly pour through them in good order, for Nathanael Greene, ordered to repair the damage, had led his troops in a quick march from behind Chadd's Ford to the rescue of the American force on Birmingham Hill. Greene's soldiers moved at a pace that carried them almost four miles in about forty-five minutes.

Greene's brigade, as well as Stirling's, Stephen's, and Sullivan's, was aided by the terrain, for the ground was broken by trees, brush, and small rises that impeded the drive of Howe's force, which had begun its march from Osborne's Hill in regular order. Indeed, they had stepped out to the tune of "The British Grenadiers," played by a band that accompanied them at the start of their attack. The music of the band soon disappeared, swallowed up by the explosive sounds made by muskets and fieldpieces. Nor did the good order achieved at the beginning of the attack survive, but gave way to confusion and horror on both sides. The British maintained the integrity of their units much better than the Americans, who often lost theirs yet managed to fight well until late in the day, when they gradually gave way. Greene's force performed the best of all the Continentals and in so doing gave Washington and others time to direct stragglers to the road at Dilworthtown, leading to Chester and Philadelphia.

The battle at Birmingham Hill was soon heard at Chadd's Ford by the British and the Germans commanded by Knyphausen. This part of Howe's army now crossed the Brandywine, where they ran into Anthony Wayne and William Maxwell. The Americans fought with spirit for a time but were soon pushed back by the large enemy force. A German officer later remarked on the bloody hue the Brandywine took on as his soldiers wading across were shot down. They could not be stopped for long, however, and the retreat of the Americans along the creek soon merged into the larger flow on their right flank.

An exhausted Washington almost fell into bed at about midnight that night. He had helped rather than led the disorganized men who fled the field. Part of those hours of pulling men in retreat together occurred in the hands of Nathanael Greene and his subordinates, who managed to retain unit integrity. The darkness of the night gave cover, but it also made it more difficult to reestablish company and regimental organization. Had the British troops not been exhausted, they surely would have killed more of their enemy and made the retreat even more disorderly than it was.

Though he was near exhaustion, Washington told his staff as he prepared to go to bed that he must report something about the battle to Congress. The task fell to his staff—in this case Colonel Timothy Pickering—to write the dispatch. As in almost every other instance, Washington read what was written and added a word of his own. Pickering had not disguised the defeat, saying that it left "the enemy masters of the field," but Washington felt that he had not conveyed anything about the morale of the army, and therefore added, "Notwithstanding the misfortune of the day, I am happy to find the troops in good spirits: and I hope another time we shall compensate for the losses now sustained."[28]

It was an important addition, though it probably described his own feelings better than those of his soldiers. In any case, there was no way of accurately assessing how the defeated felt. Washington himself knew that his troops had taken a pounding; he knew also that he had not performed with brilliance—or success. But at least he was between the British and Philadelphia, which was their objective, he now realized with certainty. Keeping them from Philadelphia would not be easy, and none of his commanders had clear ideas about how to hold them off.

The immediate task for the army was to collect its stragglers and equip itself for further fighting. In the days that followed, Washington organized both efforts while attempting to block Howe's army from Philadelphia. He did not know whether Howe would pursue him; the British had not suffered the casualties that the Americans had taken, but their army had marched seventeen miles in order to bring on the battle, and they had fought all afternoon just as the Americans had. Howe rested his troops for three days and took care of his wounded.

Washington took advantage of this respite from fighting to summon regulars under Major General Alexander McDougall at Peekskill and militia located in nearby New Jersey. His strategic aim of defending Philadelphia and defeating Howe required, he thought, that he keep his army between Howe and the city. Howe, he believed, would attempt to cross the Schuylkill at Swedes' Ford, about twenty miles above Philadelphia. To make certain that some other ford not be used, he established outposts at several of the most likely places. But he could not make effective preparations on the Delaware River below the city, and if Howe took the city, American fortifications below might choke off the line of supplies the river offered.

The first task was to keep Howe out. On its face, given the condition of the American army, this assignment looked almost impossible. The army remained fragile, with stragglers only slowly returning, and those remaining in camp were in miserable circumstances—as many as a thousand lacked shoes, and almost all needed fresh clothing, blankets, and tents. At least its generals had accumulated valuable seasoning at Brandywine, though one, John Sullivan, seemed on his way out. Congress was dissatisfied with his performance, both on a raid against Staten Island in August and at Brandywine on September 11, where, the delegates believed, he had failed to protect the right flank of the army stretched out along the creek. Congress, in an act of imperfect timing, demanded that Sullivan be recalled from Washington's army in order to answer its questions about his performance and his bravery. When the demand came to Washington to produce Sullivan, he wrote back that he understood the summons by Congress but refused to comply with it, saying that Sullivan was needed for the next great battle. Congress, out of respect for Washington, backed down.[29]

That battle, satirically called "The Battle of the Clouds," was not the one Washington expected to fight. It occurred as the two armies approached each other near Goshen on September 16. Howe's army had renewed itself after the strain of Brandywine, and now, with Cornwallis leading one column and Knyphausen another, it marched toward the Goshen meetinghouse fully expecting to find its enemy awaiting. Small units of Americans on reconnaissance did await the British, but Washington had pulled the main body out before any major collision could occur. Rain began falling heavily as the two sides closed in, and American troops soon discovered that their powder could not be kept dry. Ordinarily an American infantryman, equipped with a pouch or cartouche for carrying powder and shot, could keep his powder dry, but this rainfall proved too much for the usual equipment. The estimates at the time held that around 400,000 cartridges were ruined, and the Americans were effectively disarmed by nature.

The rain, a sustained torrent, impressed officers in both armies, and no one among the Americans complained when, late in the storm, Washington ordered a retreat. The rainfall may have done him a service: His army had not fully recovered from Brandywine, and the additions of McDougall's Continentals and Dickinson's militia had not brought it up to a fighting standard. There were too many men without shoes, too many dressed in clothing hardly better than rags, too many sick or weakened by illness, and undoubtedly too many who were simply tired out by the almost constant marching. And when they rested, too many found no shelter in tents, and too many slept uncovered by blankets.[30]

Washington led this tattered lot to Yellow Springs, then to Warwick Furnace, and finally on September 18 to Reading Furnace, where they set up camp. They were there only long enough to clean their weapons and to replace powder and cartridges. The next day they resumed their march, in a vain effort to keep the British out of Philadelphia. The rain three days earlier had taken them out of any useful blocking position, and Howe seemed bent on turning the American right; virtually every move he made suggested to Washington that his enemy aimed to execute a tactic most recently employed at Brandywine. In response to British moves, he took his army to the northwest, intending to prevent a grand flanking operation but actually opening the way behind (or under) the Americans to the city. Howe crossed the Schuylkill on September 23, and rode into Philadelphia on the twenty-sixth. Congress, warned days before, fled for Lancaster, and Washington now hoped to trap Howe by cutting off his supplies coming up the Delaware.

With Howe ensconced in Philadelphia, Washington made camp along Skippack Creek, twenty-five miles to the west. He had no intention of sitting quietly, however. The old desire for action worked within him, drawing strength from his conviction that his troops, young and inexperienced as they generally were, would fight well if given half a chance. By early October that chance had appeared. Howe had not found life in Philadelphia full of comfort and ease. The American forts on the Delaware River blocked all traffic and denied British ships the opportunity to bring in supplies and reinforcements. In his isolated circumstances, Howe, not wanting to spread all his troops throughout Philadelphia in inns and houses, had bivouacked around nine thousand at Germantown, on the east side of the Schuylkill River five miles to the north. Another three thousand had been sent to protect the transport of supplies from Elkton, Maryland, which involved a slow move over land. Four battalions remained in Philadelphia, and two more had marched off to attack Billingsport, twelve miles below the city on the Delaware. Howe was now spread all over the map.[31]

When Washington learned of the scattered condition of the enemy, he decided to attack the largest concentration, at Germantown. His troops probably needed no persuasion to fight, but Washington felt compelled once more to review the reasons why they should. The preamble to his general orders to the army conveyed something of his own eagerness and, what is probably more important, just how far his understanding of the Revolution and of his army had proceeded. He now recognized that a professional pride existed in at least several of his regiments, and he appealed to it by reminding them that far to the north their comrades had delivered a heavy blow to Burgoyne at Freeman's Farm. He coupled this reminder of the northern success with invocation of the cause of America:

> This army—the main American army—will certainly not suffer itself to be out done by their northern Brethren; they will never endure such disgrace; but with an ambition becoming freemen, contending in the most righteous cause, rival the heroic spirit which swelled their bosoms, and which so nobly exerted, has procured them deathless renown. *Covet!* My Countrymen, and fellow soldiers! *Covet!* A share of the glory due to heroic deeds! Let it never be said, that in a day of action, you turned your backs on the foe; let the enemy no longer triumph.[32]

These appeals to pride, to heroism, to honor had been made before, but their linkage to a cause that was "righteous" as well as glorious, and that was shared by the "Country," marked a subtle departure, a broadening understanding. Washington ended by bringing these grand concepts into conjunction with the immediate and personal interests of his troops. The enemy, he reminded them, "brand you with ignominious epithets. Will you patiently endure that reproach? Will you suffer the wounds given to your Country to go unavenged?" These questions concerned his soldiers' families, especially since a revolution that failed would undoubtedly be regarded as treason: "Will you resign your parents—wives—children and friends to be the wretched vassals of a proud, insulting foe? and your own necks to the halter?"[33]

Perhaps only in a revolutionary war do soldiers go into battle with a conception of a "righteous cause" competing with an image of their own necks in a halter. These men could have no doubts about what they were fighting for, though they may have blurred some of the fine distinctions in republican theology. What they had to understand was that their fight was for themselves, not for an overmighty lord and master.

The first task at Germantown was to surprise the British. Washington took care to give Howe no warning by taking a leisurely march to the village. Rather, he broke his camp twenty miles to the west and, by a forced march during the night of October 3, got into position. At 2:00 A.M., he stopped two miles away from the British pickets.[34]

Germantown, five miles northwest of Philadelphia, extended two miles on each side of Skippack Road, which ran between Philadelphia and Reading. All of the British there were east of the Schuylkill, as indeed was most of the town. Most of their camp lay at the south end of town, though of course they had placed pickets along its northern edge. The four roads that led into Germantown seemed to make an attack on a broad front possible, and Washington decided that his army should converge on Howe's camp in overwhelming strength. Accordingly, he drew up a plan that provided that four prongs of the American army would push into Howe simultaneously at 5:00 A.M. Major John Armstrong and his Pennsylvania militia would advance down the Manatawny Road on the American right and behind the British left. Sullivan, with his own and Wayne's reinforced brigades, would deliver the main blow down the Skippack Road, which cut the town in two; Greene would lead his force, including Stephen's division and McDougall's brigade, along Limekiln Road, to the northeast of Skippack; and a mile farther to the left, Smallwood, with Maryland and New Jersey militia, would march down the Old York Road and if all went well cut into the British right and into the rear of their main encampments.

On the map the plan looked brilliant, and it very nearly worked on the ground. Once the American troops had positioned themselves, at two o'clock in the morning, they moved forward to within a few hundred yards of the outposts, and at around five, in the early light, they struck. Washington's order called for an assault by "bayonets without firing" along all four roads. Sullivan's force, which Washington rode with, hit first at Mount Airy and drove over the pickets. There was firing, apparently from both sides—American fire discipline was almost never tight—and the British in confusion gave ground. A heavy fog that made seeing ahead more than fifty yards impossible created some of the confusion, especially about the size of the attacking force. Howe rode up through the fog to scout the ground for himself and immediately berated his light infantry for yielding. "Form! Form!" he called, and added that he was ashamed of his soldiers for running before only a scouting party.[35] The scouting party turned out to be Sullivan's infantry, accompanied by light artillery, which soon disabused Howe of the notion that only a probe was under way. The fog also confused Sullivan's troops, who had trouble maintaining contact with one another. And within the first hour they experienced greater confusion when they ran into a strongpoint on Skippack Road. This point was the Chew House, a large, old house constructed of heavy stone, which Colonel Thomas Musgrave of the 40th Regiment occupied with six companies. After failing to take it, Sullivan sent his men on, but the delay had given the British time to form.

Even this delay might not have proved detrimental to the attack had Wayne, leading Sullivan's left, not been fired upon by Stephen, coming in on Greene's right. Greene had attacked about forty-five minutes after the designated hour, because he had to move two miles farther than Sullivan in order to reach his position of assault. This delay has often been blamed for the confusion at the center and ultimately for the loss of the battle. Of itself, Greene's delay was probably not important and may indeed, had fog not covered the ground, have been desirable. For when Sullivan struck, the British sent their troops forward to meet him. Greene might have been able to cut behind them had he been able to see. In the fog, however, Sullivan's left remained uncovered for an hour, and Wayne moved to secure this flank. Stephen, uncertain where he was to link his flank with Wayne's, drove behind him and then, his vision obscured by the fog, opened fire. Wayne returned fire, and before the two groups discovered their mistakes, casualties mounted and the left-center was thrown into disorder. Whether through good luck or shrewd timing, Howe then delivered a counterattack with three regiments. A major part of this attack hit Sullivan's left and poured through almost unopposed. This drive blunted the American effort, and within minutes the impetus in the battle had swung to Howe. The Americans retreated, despite Washington's efforts to re-form the troops. Thomas Paine, who had accompanied Washington, later called this retreat "extraordinary, nobody hurried themselves."[36] They were much too tired to hurry and resembled nothing so much as a slow herd in motion. Greene too pulled back, for Sullivan's collapse had left him terribly exposed. One of his regiments, the 9th Virginian, which had taken around a hundred prisoners, was now trapped itself and surrendered, four hundred strong. On the American right, Armstrong survived intact—he had not sent his force into battle. And on the far left, Smallwood arrived much too late to exert pressure on the rear of the British, and retired almost as soon as he'd arrived. By late evening Washington's bedraggled army had pulled back some twenty miles to the west, to Pennybacker's Mill.

The failures of the day undoubtedly arose in part from a plan that was much too complicated to fulfill. The plan called for coordinated attacks by four widely separated forces. Their failures of coordination are often cited as the reason for the defeat. Washington blamed the fog for a lack of coordination, but the mounted messengers and the flankers each column was supposed to send out might have kept the brigades in touch with one another even through the fog. There is a possibility, too, that the fog enabled the attack to get off to a good beginning, as the British could not determine just who or what they faced. Moreover, American troops usually fought at their best from cover, and the fog afforded cover of sorts. What might have occurred in bright sunshine, with clear visibility, is anyone's guess. The British explained their recovery and victory on rather different grounds: Discipline and the counterattack won the battle, as far as they were concerned. Still, they and foreign observers conceded that the battle that had been won was almost lost. The Americans again had taken serious losses, but they had fought gallantly, as Washington remarked. And, as always, the British had fought bravely. Perhaps Washington's army derived most from the battle: the knowledge that they could carry the attack to a fine professional army and carry it well. They lost the battle, to be sure, and for reasons that we will never completely understand, given the possibilities in this engagement. But even in defeat, they had absorbed another valuable lesson.

7

Valley Forge

The George Washington who rode from the Germantown battle-field was a defeated commander but an undefeated man. He seems never to have admitted—or believed—that his plan for the battle had been too complicated for his army to carry out. Nor did he believe that he made a mistake by allowing his troops to be distracted at the Chew House and thereby to squander energy and time better spent pressing ahead in the assault on the main lines of the enemy. A few weeks after the battle, he was blaming the fog for the defeat. In a sense, he never banished the fog in his thinking, and indeed may not ever have looked deeply within himself for the responsibility for this failure.

The facts of the war in October gave him little opportunity for self-analysis—or analysis of any part of the recent past. He had much to do, and his inherent preference was for action, to begin to face the new problems left to him by Germantown. There was, after all, still a chance to force Howe out of Philadelphia; the city had to find food and supplies of every kind, and the British, with thousands of troops crowded into its houses, still relied on the Delaware River to feed themselves and the several thousand civilians still remaining there.

Besides the ever-present problem of holding his army together, keeping the British army in Philadelphia cut off from food and forage occupied his time more than any other problem in the six weeks following Germantown. He held two strongpoints just below Phila-delphia: Fort Mercer, at Red Bank, on the New Jersey side, and Fort Mifflin, on Mud Island, in Pennsylvania. Lieutenant Colonel Samuel Smith, an experienced officer in a Maryland regiment, commanded the garrison in Fort Mifflin after Washington decided that a challenge by an officer leading a Virginia regiment to Smith's rank and right to command was not justified. David Forman, a regimental commander in the Continental Army and also a brigadier general in the New Jersey militia, headed the force at Fort Mercer. He too faced a challenge to his authority, from a general in the militia, a challenge that he met after weeks of frustration by resigning his New Jersey commission. Washington was caught in the middle of these disputes, an annoying circumstance that repeated itself on several occasions in the war. Both Smith and Forman were men of ability and courage, and in these weeks of fighting along the Delaware, Washington had attempted to provide them with all the support available.

He could not, however, throw his entire army into the effort to deny Howe supplies sent up the river. He had an army numbering a little over eight thousand Continentals, not large enough, or skilled enough, to drive the British from the river. The militias of both Pennsylvania and New Jersey composed an uncertain force—uncertain in quality and, as the weeks passed, uncertain even in being.

At first, shortly after the British took Philadelphia, the struggle for the river seemed to go Washington's way. Howe spent most of his early weeks in the city settling his troops and building redoubts facing to the north, from which, he assumed, attack might come. On the twenty-second of October, Howe sent Colonel Donop and twelve hundred Hessians against Fort Mercer. The battle—or heavy skirmish—that followed was not one of the major engagements of the Revolution, but it was significant. Before he attacked, Donop, in old-world form, summoned the Americans to surrender—the reply came back with the officer who had carried the initial message: "Colonel Greene, who commands the fort, sends his compliments and he shall await Colonel Donop."[1] In the fighting that ensued, Donop had his right leg shot apart, and almost four hundred Hessian officers and men were either killed or wounded. Donop, captured by Americans, died a week later.

This defeat did not end matters on the Delaware. The British had hoped to take Fort Mercer and then Fort Mifflin shortly after, but Fort Mercer held out, and the British warships that had hoped to provide the support of heavy guns found themselves the target the day following. They had maneuvered up the river to the chevaux-de-frise that the Americans had installed close by Hog Island. Fort Mifflin sat just to the north on Mud Island. The ships—the *Merlin,* with eighteen guns, and the *Augusta,* with sixty-four—went aground while the battle was being fought and the next morning, while seeking to escape, caught fire and blew up, whether by shells fired by American galleys or by other means. Before the day was out, they were hulks, and the British were clearly stymied.[2]

There was little likelihood that the British would ever give up their attempts to establish river communication to Philadelphia. If they were to remain there, they had to clear Americans from the forts; no other way to supply the army in the city existed and, having just captured it at the cost of considerable blood and misery, they did not intend to be starved out. Their efforts over the next three weeks eventually paid off as they gradually pounded the fortifications of the Americans to pieces. Washington watched with anxiety and hope, and with reinforcements led by General James Varnum. A pattern of struggle soon established itself. The British brought up heavy guns—howitzers and mortars—and proceeded to fire shell after shell. Most of the shelling took place during the day, with the American forces firing back as long as their ammunition lasted. The nights were given to repairing the forts as much as might be done, and all the while the British brought up more cannon and fresh shells and powder. By mid-November both forts had given in, their garrisons exhausted and their walls battered down, apparently beyond repair. Most of the men who could escape did so, knowing that nothing more could be asked of them.[3]

Washington praised the survivors and the dead. But he had other things on his mind—principally how to get at the British army in Philadelphia. So had his commanders, and when he asked them whether the army should attack Philadelphia to drive the British out, or even destroy them, almost all of the American officers—brigadier and major generals—had an answer ready. It was not unanimous, but most agreed that the Continental Army did not have the strength to defeat Howe in Philadelphia. Nathanael Greene proved especially flexible—not in his judgment of the prospect of a success in attack, for he doubted that Howe could be defeated by such an action, but in his willingness to back anything Washington wanted to do. He was clear, however, in his judgment of an attack, saying that "I think it a hassardous attempt and will terminate to the injury of the Continent and disgrace of the Army." No doubt his memory of his advice to Washington to defend Fort Washington, on the North River, the year before remained vivid and bitter. Anthony Wayne gave a qualified yes to the idea of attack, and, as was his wont, gave Washington a little lecture on the subject informing him that the "eyes of all America are fixed on you," mentioning also that the "Country & Congress" expected an effort similar to the one responsible for Burgoyne's surrender in October. Whether the country expected Washington to destroy or capture Howe's army is not clear, but Wayne was probably right about Congress's expectations.[4]

All members of Congress, of course, wished for Howe's destruction, and some, perhaps many, wanted another attack by Washington's army. The wish was natural and so was the hope that Washington could bring success just as General Horatio Gates had in New York. Quite naturally, they griped that Washington was doing little and that he should act. Realistic members recognized that Washington's circumstances differed greatly from Gates's and, given the losses at Brandywine and Germantown, believed that he could not defeat Howe's army.

Washington's motives in asking advice from the generals leading his army were not as clear as they seem. He had no intention of seeking another major engagement with the British hard on the heels of Germantown. His army did not possess the strength for such an effort: It had suffered much since early September, and it was now losing men at a depressing rate—militia and regulars continued to go home, including nine Virginia regiments, and those who remained included an inordinate number without shoes and clothing. Just about everything was in short supply, as he feared it would be after he learned of Congress's reorganization of the commissary and quartermaster departments. Reorganization had not included increased compensation for the officials of those services; indeed it had produced resignations, not eager efforts to clothe and otherwise equip Washington's troops. Among those who took themselves out of the army was Thomas Mifflin, a brigadier general, who resigned in November. He had not shown much energy even before Congress tried to make supplying the army an effective operation, and his anger at Washington's lack of success in defending Philadelphia further diminished his energies for finding food for men expected to fight.[5]

The resignation of Joseph Trumbull, commissary general, proved more serious. Trumbull, who resigned in August, had performed as well as circumstances permitted. Circumstances included a group of deputy commissaries discontented almost from the beginning of their service at Congress's refusal to allow them compensation on the basis of their purchases. Most of these men argued for a small percentage that would have yielded a large sum for their pockets. Their resignations followed Trumbull's, and Congress responded slowly with new deputies. The real sufferers in this contest of policy and will were the soldiers. Washington pointed out to Congress that his troops were again without steady supplies of food, clothing, and other equipment but found that, as was Congress's practice, little of substance would be done as 1777 neared its end. Had Congress produced commissaries who bought the necessary supplies, it would have faced still another problem: finding the means of getting them to the army. For many teamsters had almost simultaneously refused the use of drivers and teams of horses until their pay was increased; and Washington's army had too few wagons and horses of its own.[6]

Logistics in late 1777 were—to put the matter plainly—in crisis as Washington strove to maintain the army as a military force and to find a place for it to spend the winter. His appeals to Congress for support of all sorts did not uncover a receptive audience in that body. For in early December, Congress responded to his requests for support with resolutions that revealed either ignorance of the army's condition or a determination to paint a picture of the war that defied Washington's accounts of it. Earlier, on September 16, Congress, on the eve of fleeing a Philadelphia about to be captured by Howe's army, had approved resolutions authorizing Washington to seize private property that might serve the army's interests. There were restrictions on the use of this power, but the grant by Congress did strengthen Washington's hand, should he need to use it. In mid-November, Congress confirmed authorization and reported that it had requested that neighboring states provide allotments of clothing for his troops.[7]

Congress's allotment of power to impress supplies was an act born of the recognition that the delegates' own flight from the British deprived them of the capability to give Washington aid. It was, all things considered, a strange form of testimony of confidence in him. By mid-November the confidence had begun draining away—a consequence mostly of the defeat at Germantown. By early December, disillusioned and discontented, Congress began lecturing their general. Their new president, Henry Laurens, did not agree with the charges and complaints made by Congress, but he could not stop them.[8]

Congress took the easy way out of problems it had failed to solve by telling Washington that he had not used his powers to seize the needed supplies; nor had he used supplies of grain and forage available in the counties near his army's camp—Philadelphia, Bucks, and Chester. His "forbearance" in failing "to use his authority may, on critical exigencies prove destructive to the army and prejudicial to the general liberties of America," it insisted. According to Congress, Washington had resorted to "distant quarters" for the food to sustain his army. These charges annoyed Washington—they were indeed shocking in their inaccuracy, to say nothing of their crudity—but he replied with clarity and calmness.[9]

What Washington felt as he read these rebukes cannot be known. What he thought can be. His thought took two forms: the first was a quiet account of the facts about army efforts to supply itself; the second, a brilliant assessment of the people's opinions of military governance. On the first question—the collection of food and forage might have elicited a question—"What do you in Congress know about it?" Such a sardonic reply probably did not occur to Washington, and if it did, he put it aside, contenting himself by telling the Congress that it was mistaken in assuming that he was surrounded by abundance— for "Forage for the Army has been constantly drawn from Bucks & Philadelphia Counties and those parts most contiguous to the City," and it was "nearly exhausted . . . entirely so in the Country below our Camp." Flour from these same counties had also been collected. The millers in these areas had been reluctant to grind grain, out of "disaffection" or "fear" (presumably facing the British army), which made for a low level of supplies. As for livestock, he did not know whether there was much available or if much had been taken from close by.[10]

This reply to Congress's sniping relied on knowledge of what had actually been done. That the implications of these actions had not been examined by Congress or anyone else besides Washington was clear. He made those implications stand out in the most thoughtful part of his answer to President Laurens and the Congress, written in mid-December. He had not revealed his assumptions about what underlay civilian reactions to military force, but now, in a letter to Laurens, he did. "I confess," he began, "I have felt myself greatly embarrassed with respect to a rigorous exercise of military power." His reasons for this feeling, he explained, began with an "Ill placed humanity perhaps and a reluctance to give distress [that] may have restrained me too far." These were explanations he drew from examining his own feelings, and they referred to the suffering that was brought to a peaceful society. There were others that had little to do with how he felt but everything to do with what he understood to be deeply held attitudes of the American people. There was, he argued, a "prevalent jealousy [he might have used the word *suspicion*] of Military power." The "best and most sensible among us" harbored this attitude and considered such power "as an Evil." Recognizing this attitude had induced a "caution" in him, lest his actions in the use of power should increase the fear of the military. At the same time, he added, he wished Congress to understand that "no exertions of mine," as far as "circumstances will admit, shall be wanting to provide our own Troops with Supplies on the one hand, and to prevent the Enemy from them on the Other." What had hampered him in providing the supplies to the troops, he said—in a mild phrasing—was "the change in the Commissary's department at a very critical & interesting period."[11]

All of Washington's explanation of the failure to supply the troops up to this point in his letter to Laurens had stayed close to the actual circumstances in which the army found itself. His conclusion to this long explanation was similarly down-to-earth, and arose from a wish that "Civil authority" in the states, perhaps encouraged by recommendations from the Congress, would "adopt the most spirited measures" and do the job. It would be a most appropriate action, he suggested, because it would be in keeping with the deepest values and a long tradition in America. For, he said in a probing statement that revealed his knowledge of the public's disposition, "the people at large are governed much by custom. To acts of Legislation or Civil Authority, they have ever been taught to yield a willing obedience without reasoning about their propriety. On those of Military power, whether immediate or derived originally from another Source, they have ever looked with a jealous and Suspicious Eye."[12]

Understanding the problems of getting supplies and the deep-seated reasons for not simply impressing them were not strictly helpful in improving the army's condition. It remained hungry, badly clothed, and literally out in the cold as both tents and more substantial housing continued to be elusive. What to do with this army, poorly provisioned as it was, was a question that had to be answered.

The loss of Forts Mercer and Mifflin had at least simplified Washington's strategic problems. He knew that he would not make an attempt to expel Howe from Philadelphia; he knew also that he had to find winter quarters for his troops, a problem that was as much a political matter as it was military. The Congress now sat in York, to which it had removed just before Philadelphia fell to the British, and the government of Pennsylvania, such as it was, had retired to Lancaster.

The main body of the army, at Whitemarsh, was far enough away from Howe's troops to avoid a surprise attack, and smaller units gave some protection to lower New Jersey. The Pennsylvania authorities in the state council and assembly were clamoring for defense of the country east of Schuykill. Fortunately for the Americans in Pennsylvania and New Jersey, General Howe did not feel strong enough to make still another attempt at destroying his enemy anywhere, and he had his own problems in supplying his army. Opening up the Delaware had made his life and that of his troops much more comfortable, though few British officers found the army's situation to be much more than tolerable.

The logistical problems of the Continental Army were to persist for many months—intractable problems that affected virtually every action Washington took in the next year. Coupled with the difficulty in holding the army together as a fighting force, they were familiar to him. But their intensity grew as the supply services fell apart; and it seemed, at the end of the year, that as commissaries and their deputies resigned or went home to look after their own affairs, the army would shrink into nothing.[13]

In late October, Washington received reliable news of Burgoyne's surrender at Saratoga; he had received reports a few days earlier, but nothing from Gates, and nothing in fact from anyone in the Northern Department. The opportunity to add to the strength of the "main army," his army, now seemed feasible if, as the reports implied, the military threat from Canada had been ended with Burgoyne's surrender.

The surrender itself marked the greatest triumph of American arms in the war up to that time, and Washington was delighted. (He did not use the word "delight," but his pleasure was clear.) It did not give him rest, however, and among his reactions was a suggestion to Israel Putnam, commander of forces just north of New York City, that he lead his troops down one side of the North River and Gates begin to move down the other, in order to drive General Henry Clinton, who had recently marched up to support Burgoyne, back into the city. And if Putnam should find it possible to insert himself between Clinton and the city, he might then actually take it. This was a suggestion made in haste and, as Washington himself admitted, without much knowledge of what was happening on the ground. It soon disappeared from his mind, not to be heard of again.

His primary reaction was simply to use the victory to get more done in the war against the British. Among his first reactions, one stood out: With Burgoyne's army in captivity, he could draw on the northern American force to strengthen the main army. He did not remind his commanders or Horatio Gates that he had, since 1775, sent many of his best soldiers to the North. He had, after all, favored the strategy that called for such shifts of regiments, and he had been among the first American leaders to define the areas of battle, with the northern corridor being a point of extraordinary importance. Even as he thought of how to exploit the new situation in the North, he could not avoid comparing his army's record with that of Gates. Recent experience in New Jersey as well as Pennsylvania had sharpened his awareness of the weakness or unreliability of militia. But the militia in the northern sector had proved to have ability not present in those available to him. The northern group fought with spirit, standing up to British regulars and Hessian mercenaries, while those he called up shirked when they did not actually desert before battle. The North offered an instance in which militia performed with distinction, and Washington said so— privately—in a letter to his friend Landon Carter. The northern militia, he wrote, "shut the only door by which Burgoyne could Retreat, and cut off all his supplies. How different our case! The disaffection of a great part of the Inhabitants of this State—the languor of others & internal distraction of the whole, have been among the great and insuperable difficulties I have met with, and have contributed not a little to my embarrassments this campaign." As if aware that this recitation of his trials might disillusion Carter, he ended with "but enough! I do not mean to complain, I flatter myself that a superintending Providence is ordering everything for the best—and that in due time, all will end well."[14]

He was complaining, of course, and he did not stop with this letter to Carter. He had already written Gates, expressing his disappointment that he had not received the news directly from him, but in letters from others, thereby reminding Gates that he, Washington, was his superior officer, and he was not pleased with the neglect of the chain of command.[15]

Gates, in fact, had been strengthened by his victory over Burgoyne and for several months acted almost as if his command were independent of Washington's. Almost, but after he felt Washington's displeasure he gave way to his commander's will. The displeasure was made clear to him by Lieutenant Colonel Alexander Hamilton, whom Washington sent to Gates in early November to explain that he was expected to release two brigades to the main army, plus other units. In all they numbered five thousand Continentals and twenty-five hundred militia. Gates struggled against the inevitable for a few days—Hamilton reported to Washington that Gates's ideas "did not correspond with yours"—but he soon agreed to provide some troops. He was taken aback by Hamilton's forceful presence, and though he knew that he was popular in the New England states and in New York, he did not wish to test his newly won renown against Washington's. Still, he tried to deflect criticism Hamilton brought, by pretending to have an attack on Ticonderoga in his plans. His agreement came in a surly spirit in a passage he seemed to cross out, in a letter to Washington, saying that "I believe it is never practiced to Delegate that Dictatorial power to One Aid de Camp sent to an Army 300 Miles distant." Wounded pride spoke clearly in this letter—and a strong antipathy to Hamilton, who had not hidden his disgust at Gates's inflation of himself.[16]

For a brief moment, Brigadier General Thomas Conway, Irish by birth but at this time an officer from France, seemed to threaten a more serious dissatisfaction. Conway had been with a Pennsylvania regiment at Brandywine and had performed well under fire there, and soon after at Germantown. He was agitating at this time for promotion to major general, and he may have thought that the way up the ladder was to attach himself to Gates. In any case, in a letter to Gates, he compared him with Washington in terms denigrating Washington. The letter—or a copy—fell into the hands of Lord Stirling at Whitemarsh. Stirling, always a loyal admirer of Washington, sent this excerpt to him: "Heaven has been determined to Save your Country; or a Weak General and bad Counsellors would have ruined it." In the context of the letter, the designation "Weak General" meant George Washington.

For Conway to have written in such fashion would not have surprised anyone who knew him. He was a man who did not guard his tongue.[17]

Historians have sometimes assumed that Conway was at the center of a cabal—one that included delegates to Congress—that aimed to get Washington removed from command. This group presumably had selected Horatio Gates as Washington's replacement. Belief in conspiracy comes easily to men under tension, and Washington may have been such a man, though how seriously he took the possibility of a Conway-Gates alliance is not clear. What is clear is that he despised Conway and felt no affection for Gates. That Conway had genuine ability made no difference to Washington, nor to most officers in the army. Conway had the annoying habit, common to many of the officers who came to America from France, of letting his provincial colleagues know of his superior qualities. Nor did he conceal his ambition for higher rank, and as a brigadier general he agitated for promotion to major general. Such agitation was unseemly in American eyes, especially to those around Washington, who had little regard for either Conway or Gates.[18]

Washington himself was not disposed to approach either man with charity in his heart. On reading the dismissive comment by Conway, he responded to him with a crisp reproduction of the offending sentence that indicated that he expected an explanation from its writer. There followed a back-and-forth exchange between the two men that drew in Horatio Gates, who issued various denials that he had been a voice in the criticism of Washington and a complaint that someone had pilfered his letter. Conway veered from a defense that included a professed respect for Washington to a sardonic linkage of "the *Great Washington*" to the "*great Frederick* in Europe," clearly a remark intended as insult and understood as such.[19]

The whole matter seemed to take an important turn in December 1777, when Congress promoted Conway to major general and then appointed him inspector general of the army. The promotion evoked a protest from at least nine brigadier generals who let Congress know of their anger. Washington simply ignored Conway when he presented himself, apparently eager to whip the remnants of the army into a fighting machine. Gates soon lost heart and abandoned any pretense of respect for Conway, and Congress, realizing that the advancement of Conway to the rank of major general had offended many officers, accepted Conway's resignation from the army. Conway may not have submitted his resignation with the expectation that it would be accepted. Disabused of any hope of winning in a contest with Washington, he returned to France in the spring.[20]

The decision to go into winter quarters was kept from the British and from the American army itself until just before the actual move from Whitemarsh, later in December. The British, of course, received no formal notification, and the army was informed only after it was put on the road to Valley Forge. Weeks before Washington wrote Laurens of his intentions, the Congress, accepting the necessity of winter quarters, had discussed what the army should do after Germantown. A few delegates, apparently immune to facts when thinking of the war, urged that an attempt be made to destroy Howe and take Philadelphia. The simplicity of these suggestions did not trouble their makers, but they did trouble Washington, who had to explain that reality could not be made to conform to such wishes. Most members of Congress, however, required no explanation that the condition of the army made going into winter quarters unavoidable. A committee from Congress visited the camp at Whitemarsh early in December and spent its days there in a serious probe. The condition of the troops was a sobering surprise, and Washington drove home to them the lesson of a poverty-stricken army. The chief lesson was familiar, and for some tiresome: He had close to three thousand men in need of shoes, and almost everyone in camp was hungry.[21]

Where the army should go for the winter was another matter, and once the idea sank in that the army was going to settle in, Washington began hearing from members of Congress as well as others, in particular members of the legislatures of Pennsylvania and New Jersey.

In Pennsylvania, there were many men who thought that Washington should use the winter to recapture Philadelphia; others advocated spreading the army around in cantonments in order to give protection across the state. No planning for such a dispersal proceeded very far, but there was a feeling in the Pennsylvania legislature that if an attack on Philadelphia was impossible, the army should not be allowed to do anything that would deprive inland towns and hamlets of its protection.

The move from Whitemarsh to Valley Forge took six days, owing to the physical condition of troops, horses, and wagons. The soldiers marched, some on bloody feet. Many horses were sick or weakened by the thin supply of forage, and wagons to carry supplies were also scarce.[22]

Valley Forge, about eighteen miles northwest of Philadelphia, had been chosen because it was close enough to permit the army to move effectively in response to British forays into the countryside. It was also far enough away from Philadelphia to prevent a British force there from surprising an army in camp. No barracks stood ready in Valley Forge, but the surrounding hills were covered with trees, many large enough to be cut down and turned into lumber for housing. Washington issued orders to cut down the trees and gave the specifications for huts that would provide shelter from snow and low temperatures. Officers organized their soldiers into work parties, and by early January most of the men had roofs over their heads.[23]

Washington had promised in his general orders that he would share the troops' lot and did so, living in a tent until the huts went up. He then found quarters for himself and his staff in a house nearby. The weeks that followed differed in one major respect from those of later summer and autumn: They offered to some the opportunity to sit and even rest, but Washington worked with diligence all through his stay at Valley Forge. At least he did not have to ride a horse much of the day or lead soldiers into positions from which to fight and perhaps die.

He soon also had Martha Washington at his side. She found her way to Valley Forge early in February, escorted from Virginia by several officers, and was met near camp by Lieutenant Colonel Richard Kidder Meade, an aide to the general. She had made a similar trip to Cambridge early in the war, but there her accommodations had been much more comfortable. In Valley Forge, she and Washington occupied a small farmhouse that also served as his headquarters. At times its bedrooms were called into service as sitting rooms or were used for other official purposes. Martha took all this in stride with her usual quiet charm and courtesy. Not long after her coming, Washington had a small cabin built where meals could be taken, a space that made day-to-day life a little more comfortable—though not in any fashion luxurious or stylish in the Virginia manner. Entertainment, when Washington could find time for it, consisted of conversation and singing. There were no parties or dances, but the atmosphere was enlivened in the evenings by the presence of other wives—in particular Lucy Knox and

Caty Greene—and by occasional dramatic productions in the nearby bakehouse. No doubt Washington and others at headquarters appreciated the infrequent diversions from the scarcity-dominated lives of everyone in Valley Forge.[24]

"Scarcity" is in fact probably too mild a word to describe the conditions. When the army arrived at Valley Forge, it carried almost no rations, and the promise of getting any seemed remote. The commissary and quartermaster departments remained idle, in part because their leaders, Joseph Trumbull and Thomas Mifflin, had resigned earlier in the year. Their deputies, for the most part with less energy and indifferent abilities, did not exert themselves to solve the problems that fell to them. The deputies had long felt underpaid and had urged that their merits be recognized in a different system of payment. What they wanted was compensation based on a percentage of the value of the supplies they bought. It was a system that held great possibilities for high incomes, and with such arrangements filling their heads, they shirked their duties. Some near Trenton were accused of consuming a large proportion of food, ostensibly collected for the troops they supposedly served. Corruption and stealing undoubtedly were practiced in the supply departments, sometimes with the cooperation of line officers. Washington hated such behavior, but his main interest, he knew, was in getting a reliable and active set of commissaries to meet their responsibilities, which were to feed and clothe his soldiers.[25]

A supply apparatus indeed seemed so remote to Washington that he turned to Congress—not because he believed that action-producing supplies would come immediately from them, but rather because he knew that only Congress could provide organization for the long term. Meanwhile he would look out for the army himself.

He began with a proclamation issued just as the army marched into Valley Forge, calling on all farmers within seventy miles who raised grain to thresh half of it by February 1 and the remainder a month later. The proclamation stated that if any grain was left in sheaves, not threshed, it would be seized and paid for as if it were straw. To make certain that no one with grain could plead ignorance of the requirement, the printer of the proclamation in Lancaster, one John Dunlap, was ordered to reproduce it in the next issue of his newspaper and to keep reprinting it until the deadline expired. Washington also called on Dunlap to print the proclamation as a broadside, with one hundred to be distributed in Lancaster and two hundred sent to headquarters in Valley Forge. Because many farmers in central and western Pennsylvania were Germans and might not read English, Washington requested that the proclamation also be printed in German.[26]

In the absence of commissaries and quartermasters, Washington sent his troops up and down the Delaware and Schuylkill river valleys to seize grain, horses, pigs, cattle, and forage. In the last days of December, these foraging parties did not consist of large numbers of officers and soldiers. They were ad hoc groups, born of a terrible necessity, and contained hungry and angry men. On one of the early occasions, December 22, Washington discovered firsthand just how desperate some of these men felt. For that night a small unit of foragers, the exact number unknown, were ordered out to collect what they could find, but instead of leaving Valley Forge as ordered, they mutinied. They were quickly put down in the knowledge of the danger such an attempt presented. There were no repetitions, no imitators; the army—hungry, cold, and barely clothed—held together, and small units were dispatched into the countryside. They found little nearby to collect or to seize.[27]

The army at this moment seemed to Washington close to a catastrophic collapse, and his own feelings approached desperation. He was not, of course, a man given to extravagance in either actions or expression. He had up to this point made only quiet appeals to Congress, all through communications to its president. Henry Laurens, like John Hancock before him, had expressed genuine sympathy in response, but nothing by way of aid had been forthcoming. Delegates from Congress had visited Washington's headquarters and listened to his appeals, but none of his suggestions, complaints, or requests for supplies had produced any of the food and clothing so badly needed in the army.[28]

Washington had observed the proprieties in his appeals; he did not go over the president's head to the whole body of Congress; he did not enlist the help of friendly newspapers or publish tracts or broadsides of his own. His letters to his friends in Virginia were private matters, written for their recipients and not intended to be leaked to the public. Indeed, he avoided exposing the army's condition to those outside for fear that any British observing the American army closely would take advantage of its weakness and mount a major attack. But he now changed his tactics, and began seizing what his troops needed. By early February he had mounted a much more systematic campaign of searching by sending several of his most enterprising generals into the surrounding countryside. Anthony Wayne took a brigade along the Delaware River close to Philadelphia and then into New Jersey; Nathanael Greene worked the farms and hamlets between Brandywine and the Schuylkill in Pennsylvania; and Henry Lee began in Delaware. All branched out as they heard of previously unknown supplies.

Each of them encountered farmers resistant to the idea of parting with crops and cattle for the benefit of Washington's army. Where American commissaries had bought food supplies before, the generals heard complaints that compensation had never come to the farmers. These same farmers were now hiding their cattle and other animals in nearby marshes and woods. Henry Lee may have felt the most sympathy among American officers and wrote Washington of the need of "humanity" in the process of seizing what they wanted. Nathanael Greene listened to the pleas of the farmers but proceeded to take all the supplies he could, saying of himself, "like Pharoh I harden my heart."[29] Taking food away by force, or its threat, intensified the disaffection every American officer found in the Mid-Atlantic states. It did not take long for hearts to harden, as Greene said, and the language of intention changed as the effort went on. Lee reported that his purpose was to "drain" the countryside of its supplies; Greene remarked, similarly, that these rural areas in Pennsylvania had been "gleaned." Though all noted that scarcity prevailed, they expressed little sympathy for inhabitants who were left little of what they had produced.[30]

While his troops searched the ground near and far, Washington urged governmental officials, mostly governors, to look within their states for supplies. Connecticut, because of the abundance of cattle and horses there, was a favorite target, and Washington appealed to New York and New Jersey as well.

These and other efforts paid off. By late February enough food had come in to feed most of the soldiers. Getting any supplies to Valley Forge remained a problem, however. The wagon master had warned weeks before that wagons were lacking, and when they were found, horses to pull them were not available. There were also problems of storage; Washington had anticipated this problem—at least in theory—

by urging Congress to provide salt, which was used to preserve freshly slaughtered meat. But as he reminded Congress of this need, he sought to collect as much fresh beef and pork as possible. Winter would gradually ease up, and by March his fears for the present supply disappeared. He had no large amount of food for the troops, but he had enough for the short term.

As Washington had explained to Laurens on December 23, he felt restrained by the danger he would be exposed to should he reveal to Congress just how crippling his lack of food and clothing was. The British, everyone knew, kept their eyes and ears open, and any confession of weakness would be taken as an invitation to attack. In the last week of December, his desperation had mounted to an intolerable point. Quiet appeals to Congress had failed; even the observations by delegates visiting his army had yielded no result. In fact, nothing—no suggestion, no request, no testimony—had brought action to supply the army with basic essentials. Given these abortive efforts to awaken the Congress, and their failure, he resorted to an open threat: This army, he wrote Laurens in a letter that could not be kept from the British, must "Starve—dissolve—or disperse" if nothing was done for it. In this letter and in others he wrote in the final days of 1777 and early 1778, his anger broke through his usual restraint, prompting him to expose much of what he thought about the war and the soldiers who were fighting it.[31]

The failure of logistics—by itself so serious as to imperil the American cause—was not the only failure that shook him to the point that he was willing to cast aside his usual silence. Washington had always been disposed to conceal his doubts about the prospects of success in whatever engaged him. His usual practice was to repress his feelings and to get on with the job. Why talk, or explain what one thought, if the task at hand could be done without words? Now he had to do more than explain or talk—he had to give his passions an expression that would force others to do what they did not wish to do.

That many of his officers did not share his resolve to keep going became clear late in the year. At that time they began leaving the army, resigning their commissions or simply going home. In these days surrounding the new year, he did not have an exact count of the number of officers who had resigned or taken leave. Early in 1778, he told Laurens that at least ninety had left the army; the number on leave had increased so rapidly that he had issued orders that no leaves were to be granted without his permission. He also ordered two brigadier generals who had gone home to get themselves back to camp. But by March he was reporting that, since August 1777, "between two & three hundred officers have resigned their commissions and many others with difficulty dissuaded from it."[32]

Whenever the opportunity came up to keep officers in the army he took it, but the opportunity was almost always limited and usually appeared in a letter of resignation sent in by the officer concerned. He answered such letters with degrees of conviction that varied with his judgment of the officer. If he thought well of the officer, he argued in his response that he should not resign. Some resignations he simply rejected. Most junior officers did not submit letters to him—many, perhaps most, simply took off, after telling their regiment's commander that they had had enough.

Providing the army with able leadership was a part of a larger problem: the nature of the army itself—that is, its organization, skill, discipline, and fighting spirit. One of Washington's strengths as a military commander was his sense of the need for the army to plan carefully—its operations, the organization of its units, and its relationship to civil authority. He was always a man who gave attention to detail; indeed, at times he appeared in his instructions to subordinates to micromanage their assignments. Such a man might have lost himself in details; Washington did not. Thinking about the Revolution in its largest terms, what was at issue in the war, as well as the problems of leading the army, occupied his consciousness—indeed never seemed to leave his awareness, even as he struggled to discover the means to keep his soldiers fed and clothed.

Moving the army to Valley Forge after its bloody engagements at Brandywine and Germantown brought an intensified focus to his sense of responsibility. His immediate problem was how to implant the same sense in Congress. By this time Congress had deteriorated as a body of legislators. Much of its talent had gone home by late 1777, if not earlier, tired by the slow pace of work and the poverty of decisions it made. Lacking power, Congress did not do much, though the best of its members recognized that inaction would not move the war toward a victorious end. Then there was the personal side of service: Most delegates had families that needed them. If a delegate did not have a private fortune, keeping a family going at a distance was impossible. And finally, there was the loneliness of being far from home. Philadelphia at least was a city, with some of the attractions of urban life. But Congress had been forced to flee when Howe advanced in the summer, and of course he had captured the city in September. York, inland and small, proved to have little charm and, on top of everything else, was crowded and uncomfortable.

Washington tried to get along with the delegates in York, though he soon came to see them as difficult to contend with. Their lectures to him about seizing the abundant food supplies it supposed existed all around him in Philadelphia County tried his patience. The Pennsylvania Supreme Executive Council, the upper house of the legislature, struck him as especially unreasonable. Several of its members blithely urged him to attack Philadelphia, and others accused him of wasting his time marching around rather than fighting the British.[33]

Washington held his anger at these absurdities, and took pains to explain himself to both Congress and the Pennsylvania authorities. His belief in the cause was such that he felt it necessary to listen to civilian authority and, more, to follow its instructions as faithfully as possible. Interpretation of what the Congress wanted gave him some freedom of action, however. Congress, Washington knew, would complain about his decision to station the army at Valley Forge, but it would not overturn it. On more complicated matters, such as reorganizing the commissary and quartermaster departments, it would delay. Money was involved in any matter concerning the supply service—money and politics. There was money to be made in running these agencies, whatever form they took, and there were men eager to make them return a profit. Washington argued for responsible action, knowing that he must compel or persuade Congress to create a workable system if the army was to survive.

Through all of his problems—food, logistics, officers who seemed to be willing to give up their commissions—he came to recognize that a major reorganization of the army was needed. If it could not be attained, the Revolution would fail. By the end of January 1778, he had a plan. Several senior officers, including Nathanael Greene, could claim to have written its big provisions. Months earlier, Washington had canvassed the officers he trusted most for ideas about a reorganized army, and of course even before asking for advice, he and others had worried over the task of making the army an effective fighting force.

Whatever its origins, the document he presented to the camp committee covered a variety of problems in the army at hand. Its most important provisions had something to say about how the army should be recruited and how its men should be organized, as well as how they should be equipped, fed, and cared for. Several matters bore Washington's forceful and familiar impress. The first, which in a sense underlay all the others, concerned the social psychology of the army. Patriotism might bring men together, according to Washington, but it could not sustain them for long. Soldiers, like all men, were moved by self-interest. This was an assumption that he had insisted on when the Revolution began, and he never abandoned it. In the plan, he began by noting that the officers of the army were leaving its service largely because their service imperiled their own interests. They were, after all, badly paid, and they had no assurance that they would have any income when they returned to civilian life. The expectation had been that they would remain in the army until the war was won. Most had no thought of becoming professional soldiers, and if they had such ambitions, they were holding commissions far different from those of their enemies. Most British officers were professionals and had bought their commissions, and when they left the army they might sell them. Americans had no such opportunities. If they should die during their service or suffer disabling wounds, their families would be bereft of any support. The American army was a fresh creation—it lacked conventional commissioned officers and possessed no pension system or, indeed, any means of taking care of its servants during or after their duty ended.[34]

Though Washington acted as a professional and had once aspired to an officer's place in the king's army, he understood and sympathized with the men who served under him in a way a European officer would not. His was a strange set of sympathies by old-world standards. On the one hand, he demanded that his officers conduct themselves in a fashion expected of their European peers. They should lead their men in battle as if their own lives were of little importance. Courage, sacrifice of self, and gallantry should shape their actions; but they should regard the Revolution as a contest different from those fought in Europe. It was a "glorious cause," created in the name—and defense—of liberty, a cause, in other words, different from those in ordinary wars. Such wars were fought for narrow purposes: royal glory and imperial power and territory. The American Revolution, he once said, and repeated on several occasions, was different, "a Defence of all that is dear & valuable in Life,"[35] a war, in other words, that put at odds the American people and a monarch who was interested only in his prerogatives and reach. A British officer would have said the same thing about his army's relationship to its king—that it was fighting for him and for royal interests. Their own glory arose from that purpose, and their pride in it made their sacrifice glorious. The Americans, by contrast, as Washington pointed out early in the war, saw themselves engaged in an effort in which "every Post ought to be deemed honourable on which a Man can serve his country."[36]

A definition of patriotism resides in this statement, and Washington never retreated from his insistence that officers should regard their service in these terms. Neither did he disavow his contention that officers, like all men, were moved by their sense of self-interest. Those two assumptions are not easily reconciled, and he never tried to bring them together in one coherent statement.

The plan of January 29 put its emphasis on the leadership provided by the army's officers. In this emphasis, the plan reads like an elementary primer: "without officers no army can exist," and unless steps were taken to put Continental Army officers "in a more desireable situation, few of them would be able, if willing, to continue in it." The argument underlying this conclusion, familiar to many delegates and officers who knew Washington, was that "Motives of public virtue" may lead men to "conduct purely disinterested"—but not for long. For "few men are capable of making a continual sacrifice of all views of private interest, or advantage, to the Common good. It is vain to exclaim against the depravity of human nature on this account—the fact is so, the experience of every age and nation has proved it."[37]

Washington then gave a history of the army's officers in the Revolution. At first they were full of zeal, assuming that the war would not last long. (He himself, he might have added, had held this assumption about the length of the war.) But as time passed, their ardor diminished as they received little compensation and their worry rose about their families. They naturally thought ahead, and, lacking an income "even of a competency to supply their wants," they inevitably feared the future. They were, he argued, "losers by their patriotism."[38] Their subsequent actions could not have been a surprise given Washington's essential assumptions. Officers had begun resigning in considerable numbers when he wrote; others announced they would follow their colleagues out of the army. Still others awaited congressional action, and if Congress did not begin to meet their demands, they too would return to civilian life.

The loss of ardor for service in the Revolution found its way into the ranks, where disenchantment with the army was high anyway. The defeats in Pennsylvania, at Brandywine and Germantown, undoubtedly figured in enlistments and soldiers' attitudes, though Washington did not mention this possibility in his plan. But he did call attention to the "apathy, inattention and neglect of duty which pervade[d] all ranks." There was not much that could be done about the decline in morale within the ranks, though Washington had sought better logistical support for many months.

The plan proposed new means of filling up the regiments, however; the principal tactic would be to draft from the militias and in ways that would obligate men to serve for longer periods. Longer service coupled with better pay and a reliable system of feeding, clothing, and arming the troops would of course allow a tighter discipline, a means of fostering a more effective fighting army.

The officers offered a different problem—and solution. Discussions of a pension system had occurred before the army moved to Valley Forge. They grew more intense there, and the January plan proposed a system that included half pay after the completion of service, compensation that would be extended to families after the death of an officer. Exactly how this system would work was not clear in the plan, but its outline there was meant to reassure officers and their families that military service would not end in financial want.

The bulk of the plan concerned the organization of infantry regiments, the cavalry, and artillery. The number of regiments would be increased, and special provisions for the specialized units added. The sum of effects of the changes proposed would lead to a more unified army, though shifting the structural base from the states to the nation—or "continent"—was not done. Washington would have been delighted by any changes that involved shifting authority over state units, in all respects, to Congress. Such a change would have brought these regiments under his control, from their enlistment to their discharge. A change of this sort was not in the cards, and no serious planning was undertaken to make it possible. Congress itself was a creation of the states, and until it could draw significant power from the states, no comparable change could be made in the army.

Leaving Valley Forge had been discussed for weeks before it occurred. The occasion for departure turned out to be decisions taken in Britain and America. In Britain, the ministry decided in January 1778 to replace Howe with General Henry Clinton, his second-in-command throughout his service in America. The ministry acted in the knowledge that Howe wanted to resign his command, and that arrangements in America to cope with the anticipated war with France called for drastic change. The French decision in March to come into the war transformed British policy and made the Revolution into a world war.

For the United States, the impact of the new policy was felt almost immediately, with the British government ordering Clinton, who would assume command in May, to send five thousand men to St. Lucia and three thousand to the Floridas. The focus of the American war would now be the West Indies, not Philadelphia, which Clinton was ordered to evacuate. In the West Indies, the British navy was expected to lead the efforts to thwart the French. But naval strategy proved indecisive—even fumbling—at key points in the lead-up to the expansion of the war. Earlier the British had been slow to mobilize in the American war, and failed to bring the navy's strength in big ships up to the standards reached in the Seven Years' War. The navy had conducted a successful blockage of the French fleet in that war, thereby preventing it from bringing its might to bear against imperial trade. In 1778, the British navy did not possess the strength for a blockade, but it might have kept the Toulon fleet bottled up in the Mediterranean. That it did not do this was a costly failure, more than a little painful to a number of admirals. The cautious British strategy at this point arose from a profound disagreement between the Earl of Sandwich, First Lord of the Admiralty, and Lord George Germain, secretary of the colonies, the key official guiding the army's action. Sandwich was defensive-minded, and reluctant to expose the British Isles to invasion should the French enter the war. The home fleet therefore remained in home waters, guarding against the French—and, from 1779 on, the Spanish as well—while Germain urged its use in combined army-navy operations in the American war. The caution that underlay the decision to hold a powerful fleet out of the war against the Americans cramped much of the planning and effort to put down the Revolution.[39]

When the French came in, these two men agreed that the British army in the colonies should provide reinforcements for forces in the West Indies. By that time the French fleet in the Mediterranean had sailed through the Straits of Gibraltar, its exact destination unknown but constituting a menace to the British West Indies. No one in Britain now doubted that the demands of the war had shifted away from the thirteen colonies.

Henry Clinton began the evacuation of Philadelphia on June 18, an assignment complicated by the need to transport three thousand loyalists out of the city. They would go by ship to New York; the army, about ten thousand soldiers, would march to the same place. Lord Richard Howe, who retained naval command until early autumn, handled the loading of the loyalists onto ships in the Delaware River.

The army began its march with fifteen hundred wagons filled with supplies—some essential and some not, including the baggage of officers, soldiers' possessions, and a variety of things such as bakeries and blacksmith shops essential to eighteenth-century armies. There were other items in the wagons—tools of various sorts and ammunition. This great bloated mass set out at 3:00 A.M.; it took seven hours to cross the Delaware at Gloucester, New Jersey. On the east side of the river, it covered twelve miles of road. Six days after the crossing, the army had crawled thirty-five miles to Allentown, near Trenton.

Washington, who learned of Clinton's departure from Philadelphia the day the British pulled out, resolved to follow his enemy. Within a few days the entire American army had left Valley Forge, though Washington did not have a clear idea about how to deal with Clinton on the road. His preference was for an attack, a desire to inflict as much damage on men and matériel as possible without committing all of his force. He had between ten and eleven thousand troops. As he often did, he consulted the general officers in the army and found that most did not want to take on such risk. There were exceptions:

Greene and Lafayette were quite willing to lead an attack, and Wayne and Brigadier General Charles Scott advocated making a strong effort to strike Clinton, but the predominant sentiment among the generals was to avoid risk.

Two foreign officers, Baron Steuben and Charles Lee, by their professional standing seemed to be most qualified counselors. Steuben proved to be more than a counselor. A former officer in Frederick the Great's army, Friedrich Wilhelm von Steuben had come to Valley Forge in February, recommended by Benjamin Franklin and accepted as a volunteer by Congress. He was in his claims for himself a fraud, having apparently told Franklin that he had been a lieutenant general in Frederick's army, serving in a number of capacities, such as quartermaster general. It may be that Franklin misunderstood—he had little German, and Steuben even less English. Steuben did not reveal that he had never risen above the rank of captain and had been only a minor aide on Frederick's staff in the Seven Years' War. The title of nobility, which he gave himself, was also false. But he was an unusually qualified and capable fraud, and in late winter and early spring in Valley Forge, he taught the Americans much about the movement of soldiers in large units. He was more than a drillmaster: Though he evidently was excellent in drilling raw troops, he taught more than the simple skills of the parade ground, imparting a sense of discipline and professionalism. And when Washington took his army out of Valley Forge, they were a much improved force.

Steuben advised caution in following the British, but was not averse to an attack if the opportunity showed itself. Lee, as was his wont, was firm and at the same time puzzling in his opinion. He was at first almost dogmatic in his insistence that the British should be unmolested by Continentals on their way to New York. He apparently believed that the American army could not stand up to the British, but his advice was probably stained with disloyalty. He had in April returned from captivity in British hands—he had been captured by a British patrol in December 1776—a captivity in which he wrote a plan for ending the war in which British interests were served, not those of America. When offered the command of forces that were to lead the attack on Clinton's forces, he refused; Lafayette was appointed in his stead. Soon after this difficult occasion, Lee managed to scramble arrangements for battle by requesting that the command be given to him. Washington probably should have denied him, but he did not.

The battle that began June 28 covered the ground near a small village, Monmouth Court House (modern-day Freehold), New Jersey. Before it began, Clinton's force was strung out on a road that divided near the courthouse, a branch going north to Amboy and a second to Middletown and Sandy Hook. Clinton hoped to embark his troops from Sandy Hook to New York City; he was not looking for a fight on his way there, but he was not surprised when Washington contested his passage. The battle began near Monmouth—mostly pine barrens, sandy, rough, and broken by small streams that had cut three ravines just north of the village. The road ran over the West and Middle Ravines—each could be crossed by a bridge or causeway.

Lee had about four thousand troops. Clinton spread out his army in three main divisions: Knyphausen's Hessians in the van marching to the east, Cornwallis with the central position in the west, and Clinton with still another body of soldiers roughly in the middle of the great train of wagons and horses. Lee hit elements of the British covering group first, just southeast of the East Ravine. From that point on, for several hours, there were skirmishes, shifts of Lee's group almost impossible to chart, and finally a disorderly retreat by the Americans until it was stopped when they ran into Washington's army, which had come up to the west side of the West Ravine. Washington, dismayed and angry, had stopped the first regiments in flight when Lee rode up. He immediately confronted Lee with questions apparently liberally spiced with scorn and, perhaps, profanity. Little of this encounter is clear; what is clear is that Washington restored control, pulled Lee's troops into fighting order, and stopped the British.

For the remainder of the day, the battle swirled near the West Ravine and the village. It was not good fighting weather—the British infantry wore heavy woolen uniforms even as the temperature hit ninety-plus degrees. These men had been marching for several days in the heat, and many had fallen from it, as well as from American artillery and infantry fire. Clinton and Cornwallis in these hours ordered one attack after another, four in all, and all failed to dislodge the Americans. Losses were heavy on both sides, until exhaustion and darkness took over. Cornwallis was apparently especially active in leading several attacks, and Clinton himself was under fire. Though British officers later asked about the wisdom of these attacks, no one questioned the bravery of the troops involved or their officers.

The Americans had expected to resume the combat the next morning, but during the night the British quietly pulled out, and Washington did not attempt to follow. The British soon reached Middletown and by June 30 had arrived at Staten Island.

In the aftermath, questions were raised on the American side about Lee's performance, and Washington soon brought charges against him. No one questioned Lee's courage, but his judgment was a genuine issue. His career did not survive the court-martial, though the sentence was absurd—a year's suspension from duty.[40]

Neither side could claim victory, though some American officers did. In fact, it was a draw. One thing was clear in the aftermath: Steuben's training had had good consequences. The Americans had at times shown that they had absorbed his training in their movements in and out of battle. They still lacked full control under fire, but many would show the ability to resist panic when confronted by the enemy's glittering bayonets. That circumstance could be developed—and could stiffen American pride.

PART THREE

Citizen of the World

8

Citizen of the World

Britain's General Clinton, now Sir Henry, emerged from the Battle of Monmouth in a spirit far different from Washington's. He did not feel defeated, but neither did he consider himself a victor of the battle. He was not really surprised that he had led his army to New York without crippling losses, though the "butcher's bill," as knowledgeable British commanders referred to a casualty list, was not small. In fact, it grew longer every day after he gained separation from the Americans, the increase coming in the form of enlisted men who deserted. German soldiers, who left the army in numbers, had come to despise service in America, and the countryside in New Jersey and Pennsylvania proved attractive.

William Howe had been a popular man in the army. His officers in America seem always to have liked him, though more than a few complained quietly of his propensity to enjoy himself when they thought he should be leading an army looking for combat. Henry Clinton never drew his officers' affection, never showed his ease in military or other society, but also never displayed a preference for rest over action, as his predecessor had. Clinton in fact was a difficult man, uneasy with himself, sometimes aggrieved, often offended, under Howe's command, that his chief rejected or ignored his suggestions, which sometimes became pleas to accept fresh plans. Clinton described himself as a "shy bitch," a reference to the anxiety he felt in putting himself forward by pushing his own ideas in the war.[1]

Clinton, an English aristocrat born in 1730 in New York, spent his first nineteen years there, a period that included a stretch during his father's service as governor. At nineteen he went to England and a commission in the army. In the Seven Years' War he served Prince Charles of Brunswick as an aide, and though he never had a command, he emerged from the war with a good reputation as an officer. He returned to America with Howe and Burgoyne to suffer through the first year of the war at Boston and New York. Those campaigns were not happy ones for him as he spent his time in perpetual impatience with Howe.

Now, in May 1778, the army in America was his, just as it was shrinking in numbers, both by detachments and by desertions of its soldiers. No British officer liked the idea of his troops melting away in America, and Clinton hated the idea. But he was gratified to have the command, even if he knew that in a short time his soldiers would serve other commanders. He had been ordered to send off some five thousand of them to the West Indies and soon after to detach three thousand for the Floridas. These instructions, drafted in March, reached him in April.[2]

That he was to be on the defensive soon became clear to him. At home early in the year, even before the ministry learned of the decision by France to ally itself with the Americans, fear increased that Saratoga would bring the French into the war. That feeling was just about the only conviction Germain, the colonial secretary, and Sandwich, First Lord of the Admiralty, held in common. But Sandwich felt a caution about using the fleet overseas that was not shared by Germain and the army. Fear of invasion by the French filled naval heads, and to counter what they feared, they relied on a strategy of keeping the French navy preoccupied, or even bottled up in European waters. In the Seven Years' War the French never managed to concentrate their sea power because of British action. French naval strength had begun that war divided between bases in the Mediterranean; Toulon, at the mouth of the Rhône; and the Atlantic, the main base being at Brest, on the Brittany peninsula. For the most part, the British navy had established its supremacy early in the war and continued to hold it throughout. That supremacy was evident in the blockade they imposed upon the French navy, which was largely confined to European waters.

British strength at sea had declined somewhat, and the French, who had undertaken a naval rebuilding program, were stronger than they had been twenty years earlier. Looking at their enemy's force on the water, the British—with Sandwich sounding a warning concerning its potency—doubted that the strategy of the previous war could be resurrected. Germain and Sandwich, along with most others in the government, also believed that British holdings in the West Indies were more important to the empire than the thirteen continental colonies.

Shifting forces to the West Indies cramped efforts on the mainland in fundamental ways. If the French entered the war, there could not be a major campaign to crush Washington's army. The British navy was not only stretched thin off the American continent, but it now had to retain a considerable fleet in home waters to counter a possible invasion by the French. The next year, 1779, this problem grew enormously when Spain joined the war against Britain.[3]

Henry Clinton possessed a quicker intelligence than William Howe, and he had been impatient with him, though he followed orders loyally right up to the time of taking over. Not without protest, however— Clinton had questioned virtually every major aspect of Howe's strategy. Howe's penchant for inactivity depressed Clinton; his own energy sought an outlet in battle: in striking the Americans where they were weak, in conducting operations up the North River and in the southern states, in short doing something, someplace; and as second-in-command before Howe was relieved, he sometimes let his superior know that he had plans for action. It was Clinton's plan that Howe had used in 1776 in Brooklyn—reluctantly, for he found Henry Clinton irritating in his demands that he carry the war to the rebels. He simply ignored Clinton's opposition, in July of the following year, to his taking the army to Philadelphia by way of the Atlantic while Burgoyne struggled in the northern wilderness, only to collapse at Saratoga.

Not surprisingly, Clinton approached his assignment in spring 1778 with apprehension. His first responsibility, after all, was to evacuate Philadelphia and take his army out of any action that seemed promising. To be sure, Germain and his colleagues gave him some flexibility. When he abandoned Philadelphia, he might lead his army to Halifax or Rhode Island, but only after he had shipped much of it off to the West Indies and Florida. He could remain in New York, a depressing possibility, given his depleted force, but at least he would be in the fight that, had he not been directed to send his troops to another's command, he thought he might win.

Washington's mood during the spring brightened as Clinton's darkened. The change in how he felt about the war began when he heard that on March 13, 1778, the French had announced that they had allied themselves with the Americans, an action taken in secret early in February. The British government had learned of the new alliance almost as soon as it was made, and expected war to commence soon.

The news trickled into Washington's headquarters with a note of uncertainty, until Henry Laurens early in May sent word that confirmed his hopes. Though Washington was uncertain of what it portended for the war, he allowed himself to hope that it might mean the war's end, at least in America—an end that included American independence. "Hope salted with uncertainty" describes best his feelings during the summer months. He wanted to believe that the British would pull out all their troops concentrated in New York and Rhode Island. His hopes increased when he heard of the arrival of a French fleet under Admiral Charles Hector d'Estaing. The admiral himself had informed Washington of his coming, in a letter brimming with the extravagance so common in the vocabulary French officers used addressing one another. What Washington thought as he read d'Estaing's compliments is not known, though he must have felt wonder and embarrassment as he read the following: "The talents and great actions of General Washington have insured him in the eyes of all Europe, the title, truly sublime, of deliverer of America."[4]

This was only a sample of the French inflation he was to experience over the next few months, but there was substance too, as d'Estaing promised to establish communication with Washington; and of course—most important—he brought naval power to what both the Americans and the French intended to be a force to smash the British.

Washington answered with the suggestion that the French on the sea and the Americans on land together strike their enemy in New York City. D'Estaing carried four thousand soldiers, who would of course add to the Americans' strength on land. Such matters engaged the two commanders' attention in July, but before serious planning could begin, d'Estaing discovered that his ships drew too much water to cross the bar at the mouth of the harbor. New York obviously was out of reach for the French, and the Americans were not strong enough to make a move on their own.

American generals, including their commander in chief, had wished to push their enemy out of New York but had concluded that without a navy they lacked the strength to make such an effort. As was his practice, Washington had consulted almost all his generals after Monmouth about a course of action. Almost all favored staying in place outside New York or sending an expedition to Rhode Island, where the British seemed vulnerable. General Clinton and Admiral Sir Peter Parker had established a naval post at Newport—an ice-free port—in December 1776. D'Estaing's ships made an attack possible, and American discussions with him in July confirmed Washington's judgment that a joint effort—the Americans by land, the French by sea—might lead to the destruction of British forces in Newport and the islands around it. Major General John Sullivan commanded American forces near Newport, and, following orders from Washington, soon had gathered about nine thousand men. D'Estaing had an impressive number of regulars on his ships and, more important, their big guns.

All seemed well, even though Admiral Lord Richard Howe followed d'Estaing to Rhode Island waters soon after he learned that d'Estaing was on the move from New York. Early in August, the two fleets maneuvered cautiously, each attempting to gain a favorable position against the other. They had not yet begun the heavy action that the number of ships and guns promised when nature intervened. Winds had been ominously strong for several days while the enemies confronted one another and then on August 11 the high winds turned into a gale. Neither side could hold its position, and soon they were scattered all along the coast, with sails and rigging giving way and masts and spars crashing down.

When the American militia in Rhode Island recognized that d'Estaing no longer could provide support, its men began deserting. When it became clear that he would not return—his ships were making their way to Boston, where repairs could be made—the trickling away of men became a heavy tide, and Sullivan discovered his army numbered after this rush only around four thousand. Full of bitterness over the French action, Sullivan evacuated his position on Rhode Island after fighting a successful rearguard action on August 29. In this action the American Continentals distinguished themselves, holding steady and then retiring under control. Nathanael Greene, who commanded the "right wing" of the army, praised his troops and their officers for their "great spirit." Washington was delighted to read that Lieutenant Colonel John Laurens stood out—"its not in my power," Greene reported, "to do justice to Col. Laurens who acted both the

General and the Partizan." The Americans had behaved well, but they were forced to leave the island in British hands, with Sullivan in a fury at the abandonment by d'Estaing.[5]

Washington's disappointment at the French departure approached Sullivan's, but he could not allow it to be known. The Americans needed the French almost desperately, and Washington saw immediately that he must not allow local anger, such as Sullivan's, to turn away d'Estaing and his force. Sullivan was always a blunt instrument, and on learning of d'Estaing's action, he and other officers permitted their anger to run free. These officers used language not commonly found in communications to French admirals. Among the most cutting expressions was their opinion that the withdrawal in fact had been "derogatory to the Honor of France, contrary to the Intentions of his Most Christian Majesty & the Interest of his Nation & destructive in the highest Degree to the welfare of the United States of America & highly injurious to the Alliance formed between the two Nations."[6]

The loss of French naval strength in American waters upended Washington's strategy, and he feared that the criticisms of American officers in Sullivan's command might inhibit plans for a Franco-American campaign in the future. He therefore concealed his own disappointment and sought to soothe irritation d'Estaing felt at the criticisms from Americans. The irritation was clear, though muffled, in d'Estaing's letter of September 5, in which he says that it is "too common" for those in "Naval War to be judged with a degree of prejudice— especially when such prejudice is supported by the interested opinion of some individuals, who tho good pilots and worthy men in other respects have no idea of what a squadron is—however successfully they may have acquitted themselves in conducting small barks." The muffling appears in the remainder of this sentence, in which Washington of course was exempted from the group accustomed to sailing small barks. Nor was he likely "to give way" to "passion."[7]

Washington did not stagger under this load of praise, and he recognized that a response that included understanding and praise of d'Estaing and his fleet was called for. Incandescent prose was beyond his powers; for that he relied on John Laurens, of his staff. What emerged in the letter that Laurens wrote for him reassured d'Estaing that his American colleague saw in him "the virtues of a great mind . . . displayed in their brightest luster," and that the disappointment in Rhode Island waters "can never deprive you of the glory due you."[8] Besides this inflated admiration, Washington carefully explained to d'Estaing the disposition of the American army, which was in the process of moving itself so as to be able to maintain communications along the North River and protect the French fleet in Boston, should the British attempt to land troops there. His letter, in fact, takes the French into his confidence with an account of the sources of his food supply and a review of the strategic situation in New York and New England. His own judgment is clear in these comments and reveals a thorough assessment of the possibilities open to the British enemy and its American foes.[9]

For all its invocation of glory and its attention to French pride, there was another purpose behind Washington's reassurance of d'Estaing. He wanted d'Estaing to understand that the Franco-American effort did not simply consist of joint warfare against the British. What they were fighting for was glorious, and glory was not simply confined to the men engaged in the struggle, a point he usually made in his letters only obliquely. In his effort to assuage American anger at the withdrawal of the French and the injury the French felt was done to them by the Americans, he knew he had to act quickly and to use a vocabulary comforting to them. Hence the reference—really an echo—of the grandness of the war, and the glory it returned to the men who fought it well.

The dismay of the French at the crassness of the protests against their leaving Rhode Island by Sullivan and his officers could be dismissed more easily than these officers' objections. Washington recognized that in d'Estaing's affronted sensibilities there was an eagerness to belittle his American critics. These officers, d'Estaing sniffed, were small men used to sailing small craft, and as such were uncomprehending in what it took to lead a squadron. Washington recognized the bruised spirit that underlay French sneers, and he wished to soothe it in all possible ways. One such way—pointed out to Greene—was to appeal to Lafayette, whom he asked to intercede with d'Estaing and the French naval officers. If Lafayette could be "pacified," Washington believed, the other "French Gentlemen will of course be satisfied as they look up to him as their Head."[10]

However offended Lafayette was by the protests from General Sullivan and his officers, he could not resist the reassurances of Washington, one of the idols in his life. Washington's summation of the brouhaha in Rhode Island subtly appealed to Lafayette's prejudices. While seemingly declaring that he shared Lafayette's reactions ("I feel everything that hurts the sensibility of a Gentleman; and, consequently, upon the present occasion, feel for you & for our good & great Allys the French—I feel myself but also at every illiberal, and unthinking reflection which may have been cast upon Count d'Estaing, or the conduct of the Fleet under his command") he added, "I feel for my Country." This last sentence was not meant to suggest that Washington regarded the American people as exemplars of perfection. The reality was far from perfection, as he told Lafayette: "in a free, and republican government, you cannot restrain the voice of the multitude—every Man will speak as he thinks, or more properly without thinking—consequently will judge of Effects without attending to the Causes."[11]

Washington's letters to General Sullivan, a subordinate in a way Lafayette was not, sounded a different tone. Always polite, Washington gently reminded Sullivan of the sensitive nature of the Franco-American relationship but also made it clear that he did not wish to have the uproar in Rhode Island continue. American interest required a "cordiality" with the French, "a people old in war, very strict in military etiquette, and apt to take fire when others scarcely seem warmed."[12] It was necessary to cultivate "harmony" and good agreement with them, and along this line it was also necessary to keep knowledge of the protest from American soldiers in the ranks. Though Washington knew that his wishes would be difficult for Sullivan to accept, he also knew that Sullivan would follow orders—and he urged Sullivan to do "all in your power to forward the repairs of the French fleet."

While this first collaborative effort with d'Estaing was in progress, Washington faced a problem presented by French officers who had begun arriving in America on their own almost from the beginning of the Revolution. With the French alliance, they seemed to come in droves. Serving in the American cause appealed to the idealism of many, perhaps most, for its identification with liberty and the opportunity to strike the British, an ancient enemy. Some—Washington came to believe that there were many—arrived with the expectation of collecting pay for their service and enjoying military rank not available to them at home. Many in this self-regarding group did not have much, or any, military experience; what they had, Washington believed, was an absurd sense of their own talents and a desire to run things.

Congress did not share his skepticism of these exotics and too often took their descriptions of themselves at face value. Out of such assessments came commissions to men whom Washington found lacking and his American colleagues abhorred. The American officers objected openly to such appointments; hardly a day passed without such protests coming to him. At first they had little effect, but by late July 1778 he was telling Laurens and Gouverneur Morris, a friend in Congress, that the practice of accepting "military fortune hunters"[13] had to end. His own revulsion from such men was increased by his officers' threat to leave the army. Rank had been a sensitive issue among American officers since 1775—they were often jealous of one another, and the additional example of inequities in both appointments and promotions not only subverted morale, but thinned the cohort of officers.

For Laurens's edification, Washington identified a number of French interlopers by name, with details about their self-seeking actions. In this summer after Monmouth, perhaps the self-promoter who most irritated him was Louis-Pierre Penot Lombart, chevalier de La Neuville, a major in the French army. He and his younger brother Noirmont de La Neuville had come to America in late summer of the year before. Their presence did not alarm Washington at first, but when the elder Neuville sought appointment by Congress as a brigadier general, his earlier irenic reaction disappeared. He was shown "a very handsome certificate . . . in favour of Monsr. Neuville written (I believe) by himself," an endorsement that made him suspicious immediately. The chevalier fell into the way of one of those "Men—who in the first instance tell you, that they wish for nothing more than the honour of serving in so glorious a cause, as Volunteers—The next day solicit rank without pay, the day following want money advanced them—and in the course of a Week want further promotion, and are not satisfied with any thing you can do for them."[14]

When Baron Steuben, whom Washington admired for his service at Valley Forge, went off to Philadelphia in search of a line appointment at about the time that the Neuvilles made their move for advancement, Washington had had enough. He wrote his friend Gouverneur Morris that, though he considered Steuben an "excellent officer," he thought such a move for an appointment so widely prized would only add to the discontent of the army's brigadier generals. Washington summed up his feelings at this time, saying, "I do most devoutly wish that we had not a single Foreigner among us, except the Marquis de la Fayette, who acts upon very different principles than those which govern the rest."[15]

In writing Henry Laurens in late July about the discontent in the army over the appointment of foreign officers, Washington referred to himself as a "Citizen of the World." He was obviously concerned that Laurens not think of him as a provincial, bound so tightly to local interests that he missed the importance of the Revolution to the world. But if he was not, as he said, "easily warped or led away by attachments merely local or American," he had to "confess," he wrote, that "I am not entirely without 'em, nor does it appear to me that they are unwarrantable, if confined within proper limits."[16] Washington was always a harsh critic of those in the army who failed to do their duty; he hated slackness and lack of discipline, and despised action on behalf of the self when sacrifice for the public interest was called for. Yet he also felt enormous sympathy for officers and men who were reduced to wearing rags and who had families at home who suffered in their absence. And then there was the matter of justice not done for American officers who witnessed incompetent foreigners attaining high rank and commands simply because they were foreign. As he pointed out to Congress, complaints about such circumstances assailed him every day.

He did not propose to expel French officers from the army, and cited "principles of policy" as one of the reasons for welcoming them to service in the Continental Army. The principles he had in mind all came down to a recognition that French aid was essential in the war. Thus, though he yearned for simpler arrangements in American command, he exerted himself in justifying the inclusion of French officers in important assignments—Lafayette was the primary example—and acted to protect them whenever he could. Was d'Estaing going to give up the campaign in Rhode Island and repair his ships in Boston? Then he, Washington, would move his army from the North River to head off any attacks the British might make on the French in Boston from the land. Were the French likely to sail off from Boston to the West Indies when their vessels were fit? If they did, he said, Americans should accept their strategy because of the importance of the French islands. To John Sullivan, the American general in Rhode Island who found d'Estaing's movements hard to understand, Washington furnished a short introduction to the realities of Franco-American foreign relations.

The recognition of the importance of France to the American cause was only a part of what underlay Washington's reference to himself as a citizen of the world. He held the prevalent belief that the movement for independence expressed a sense of the American nation as a free people. Since the beginning of his first uneasiness with Britain's attack on the old imperial constitution in the 1760s, Washington's affections had become enlarged with a conception of the American cause. What constituted that cause had changed as a national feeling came to life. In Washington's thought at this time, the nation's independence assumed a far greater importance than the individual's liberty. He was not indifferent to the individual's concerns, but in his mind the individual was far less important than the union. This sense of proportion is not surprising, given that he conceived his assignment as commander of the army as one requiring him to cultivate joint or collaborative action, not the freedom of the individual to express himself. Justice also seemed to him much more essential in a free nation than equality. He was a slave owner in a society that thought about men in a vertical order, and though he felt uneasy about owning slaves, his uneasiness did not undermine his belief that the vertical order of men in society was a natural order. He saw slaves as occupying the bottom of that order.

As far as can be established, Washington did not give much thought to nature as a source of men's rights. The rights he was accustomed to were simply a part of the social order, and if rights expressed anything about society, they owed their value to the claim to real property that they embodied. Thus, it had been easy for him to join in resistance to parliamentary taxation that, after all, threatened not just the free individual's rights but the collective character of a free society as well. But there had been nothing in his early commitment to the opposition to parliamentary oppression that suggested that he valued individual liberty over that of the Virginia planting class. He enlisted in the cause of men like himself—free men who owned land and men. He was anything but the champion of the lone, free individual.

As a citizen of the world, he had no idea that the principles he and other leaders of the American Revolution espoused would eventually lead to democracy and individualism. A citizen of the world, by his definition, did not conceive of the world stretching to include the mass of men, except in certain limited ways. But he did not see it as a closed order, either, one that oppressed men without property or intelligence. His characterization of most men—unthinking men, he called them—as unable to judge well in most matters that served virtue or even affected their own interests was an insight shared by most such citizens of the world.

Washington had few illusions about human conduct. What he himself had in abundance was virtue—and virtuous standards. At times his sense of honor or virtue in action threatened to separate him from other, less virtuous men. Yet even as his principles strengthened him under pressure, the experience of the Revolution broadened his outlook, and if it did not make him more tolerant, at the least it induced patience in the face of terrible adversity.

This patience and tolerance proved their worth often to Washington, a commander facing daunting challenges, but they did not extend to slaves or provide the strength to banish inequality of opportunity in a society claiming freedom for its citizens. Washington recognized early in the conflict with Britain that he and others like himself, slave owners, stood on ironic ground. They claimed liberty for themselves and all the rights of free men while they held hundreds of thousands of blacks in slavery.

Washington had been a slave owner since the mid-1750s. He was a conventional master in most respects: He looked upon his slaves as property and took care of them in the usual ways; he fed them the usual diet; when they were sick, he treated them himself or summoned a medical doctor; he did not ordinarily have them whipped when they resisted their condition, but he did sometimes sell those he could not control or have them shipped off to the West Indies.

There is not much comment about his slaves in his letters, and he did not admit the horror of their condition until the beginning of the crisis with Britain. At that time, having become engaged in measures of resistance, he admitted to himself and to others that what he was doing could not really be reconciled with owning slaves. To some extent, George Mason, his neighbor and friend, helped him see the anomaly of a slaveholder's position. Mason in 1774 wrote the Fairfax

Surrender of Lord Cornwallis at Yorktown, Va. Oct. 19th, 1781
by Franz Venino, after a painting by John Trumbull, lithograph

Continental soldier in the background of a
Portrait of George Washington (detail) by
Charles Willson Peale, Philadelphia,
Pennsylvania, 1780, oil on linen ticking

General Thomas Gage by John Singleton Copley, ca. 1768,
oil on canvas mounted on masonite

Washington Rallying the Troops at Monmouth by Emanuel Leutze, 1853–54,
oil on canvas, from a color film transparency, Benjamin Blackwell, photographer

Portrait of Sir Henry Clinton,
engraving by Francesco Bartolozzi,
after John Smart

John Laurens by Charles
Willson Peale, a miniature,
after Charles Willson Peale,
ca. 1784

*Friedrich Wilhelm Augustus,
Baron von Steuben,* by
Charles Willson Peale,
after Charles Willson Peale,
1781–82

General Nathanael Greene
by Charles Willson Peale,
from life, 1783

*Jean-Baptiste Donatien
de Vimeur, Comte de
Rochambeau,* by Charles
Willson Peale, from life,
ca. 1782

George Washington
Following the Battle of Princeton,
after a miniature by Charles Willson Peale,
1780, oil on canvas

General Sir William Howe
by Charles Corbutt,
1777

George Washington at Princeton by
Charles Willson Peale, 1779, oil on canvas

Resolves, Fairfax County's declaration of opposition to British policy following the Boston Tea Party. He condemned the trade in slaves in the seventeenth article of the resolves, declaring there that planters in the county wished "to see an entire Stop for ever put to such a wicked cruel and unnatural Trade."[17] There was, however, no resolve in the document calling for an end to slavery. Washington willingly signed the Fairfax Resolves and played an important role in gaining their approval by the county. At about this time, in a letter to Bryan Fairfax, he revealed that the terrible lesson of black slavery had bitten into his mind. Somewhat ruefully, he explained Virginia's reaction to British policy by insisting that "we must assert our rights, or submit to every imposition, that can be heaped upon us, till custom and use shall make us tame and abject slaves, as blacks we rule over with such arbitrary sway."[18] Planters' rule over their slaves may have been recognizably "arbitrary," as he wrote, but he did not disavow such rule.

There were blacks in the New England Army when he took it over in summer 1775, but they were freemen, and their service was given far from the southern states where, had they appeared with muskets, they would have been thrown back into slavery or killed. In the following years, an occasional northerner proposed that blacks, free or slave, be enlisted, and a Rhode Island regiment took shape with most of its numbers coming from black freemen.[19]

Washington accepted these regiments without comment on the status of their black soldiers. The blacks were free when they were recruited, and they would remain so after they fought the British. They were fighting for the Revolution, his purpose as well as theirs, though he left unsaid what he might have felt about black freemen in America.

The example of such regiments did not stimulate emulation, and the ranks of the Continental Army remained predominantly white. By the middle of 1778 the ranks had grown thin of any men of color, and Washington wondered if he could maintain an army in the field large enough to carry on the war. The problems he faced in luring men into joining the army did not arise simply from weariness with war, though that certainly increased. Lack of pay for months took some men out

of service and made finding their replacements extraordinarily difficult; these same men had also wearied of the rags they wore, the lack
of shoes, blankets, tents—a multitude of lacks. The same insufficien-
cies kept men from enlisting and perhaps even more men from staying
in when their terms ended. The bounties offered by Congress were
not great, but Congress increased them, and the states tried the same
inducement. Patriotic men had once joined because they believed in
the "glorious cause," as Washington did, but that motive gradually
faded as the war ran on, and the depreciation of the currency with
which they were paid almost killed it. A bounty of twenty to fifty dollars held little appeal when paid in useless currency.[20]

To say that Washington suffered from the depreciation of currency
in the way his soldiers did would be a gross exaggeration. But he was
affected by the collapse in the value of the local currency. His difficulty
was different from most: He was a creditor who had lent money and
conducted business buying and selling land. Washington did not take
kindly to such transactions that saw him paid in Virginia currency
when what he was owed was in sterling. He was, like most men of
business in Virginia, both a debtor and a creditor.

For months in 1778, he thrashed about over this problem. Even in
the midst of a war that he was fighting, he had maintained a close
watch over his financial affairs, though at times his plantations in Virginia and what he owed and was owed had to be thrust aside. His
estate manager in Virginia, Lund Washington, showed no great flair or
imagination in his handling of his master's money, having had more of
a feel for the ground and crops than for money obligations and debt.
He clearly hesitated in acting in such matters, and he had little insight
to offer.

There proved to be no fully satisfactory resolution to the problems
of inflation and depreciated currency. Washington settled for a single
but effective resolution to his need to pay what he owed and to collect
what his debtors owed him. He would pay and collect on the terms
that had prevailed when these financial obligations were made. Since
he was owed far more than his debts, he had found terms that protected his own interests, provided of course that the men in debt to him
agreed to pay back on the terms they had originally agreed to.[21]

Washington's ruminations and ultimate decisions on his finances were made while he had to fight a war that seemed to offer no end. His early belief was that when the French joined the United States openly, the British would have to pull their forces off the American continent. By late 1778 this belief had evaporated. Getting out of Philadelphia did not mean that the British army, soon concentrated in New York, would take off for the West Indies—a likely destination, many American officers believed. To be sure, the British did carry thousands of men to the islands of the Caribbean and a lesser number to Florida. When these events occurred, Washington hoped to drive the British from New York, but to his dismay, his enemy managed to remain formidable in New York while coping with the French and using its strength in the new theater in the Carolinas.[22]

Given the strategic situation in the autumn of 1778, with concern rising about what the British army was going to do, to say nothing of the French naval force of d'Estaing, the annoyances presented by Congress and some of his own officers were minor. Congress offered the most interesting array of irritations, dithering for months at a time and ignoring the problems Washington faced as the army's officers pressed for more money—in their current pay and in pensions when they retired. These officers also demanded better medical treatment, and they insisted that they needed an allowance for uniforms.[23]

Recruiting was still a challenge as well. Drafting soldiers in the states was hard, and Congress did not really try. It did increase the bounty it would pay, authorizing Washington's regiments to offer twenty dollars above the usual amount. But this sum was not enough; the states and counties that raised militias paid more, and service in the militias was always of shorter duration. Almost no one wanted to remain in arms for three years or the duration of the war, the length of time Washington favored.[24]

There were some officers who wished to remain in the army despite inflation of prices and the depreciated currency. Congress, however, could not keep them all, because the reorganization it had agreed upon at the beginning of 1778 called for consolidating regiments, that is, reducing their number. This would require fewer officers, and what was to be done with those who had served in regiments going out of existence? Congress gave one answer in its silence: The officers who could not find billets in other regiments would go home.

While Congress and the army were trying to adjust to the reorganization of the army, the British government, in a strange twist of policy, decided to try to wean the "colonies" from rebellion by sending a commission armed with an offer of what it called peace. This initiative, the Carlisle Commission, arrived in June. Headed by Frederick Howard, the Earl of Carlisle, this group soon demonstrated that it had no real authority and need not be taken seriously. The North administration, in sending it, had not bothered to reveal the planned evacuation of Philadelphia, an indication of a lack of interest in the commission's work. The commission's own flaws would have crippled it even if its instructions had allowed genuine negotiations. Before it was through in America, Lafayette had challenged Carlisle to a duel—the commission had issued a statement describing the Franco-American alliance as unnatural and insisting that France was the enemy of liberty. Carlisle was not a dishonest man, but his colleague George Johnstone, once governor of Florida, was. Johnstone offered a bribe to a delegate from Pennsylvania; exposed in this clumsy and dishonest attempt, he drew scorn upon himself and the commission. The only really able member of the commission, William Eden, could do nothing on this mission of futility but cool his heels in frustration until the group departed, almost a year after its arrival. Throughout this affair Washington watched quietly, certain that this latest British effort would fall on its face.[25]

The French, despite all the reassurance d'Estaing had offered concerning joint action with his American ally, soon disappeared, leaving Boston for the West Indies to forestall British action there. Before leaving the North American coast, d'Estaing took his ships to the South, intending to destroy the British in Savannah and elsewhere in Georgia and the Carolinas. He failed and—to Washington's dismay when in November he learned of the dismal news of French failure—sailed off for French possessions in the West Indies.[26]

Washington had his own problems with his enemy, ensconced in New York. Late in 1778, he asked his generals what they recommended for 1779, in the campaign ahead. The senior officers in the army, as always, had ideas—in this instance, another campaign. As usual, they did not agree among themselves on taking action but, as always, agreed that the army should act, if act it must, with caution. Washington's question had been posed just as news arrived of d'Estaing's debacle off Rhode Island and his retirement to the protection of Boston's waters. Washington saw immediately that the French had unwittingly created another problem. The British, he speculated, might force their way into Boston Harbor, where the French, bloody and battered by the storm, might not be able to defend themselves. This situation had an ominous meaning for the Americans, who wished to protect their new ally. If Washington felt obliged to cover the French from the land—the British commanded the sea—he might weaken his forces that held the British in place in New York City. The British, if they should sense a diminished army, would thrust their army up the Hudson, thereby breaking New England's communications with the rest of the union. What Burgoyne had failed to do, the French would unwittingly make possible.[27]

The American council of generals had little knowledge of such possibilities when they answered Washington's request for advice on the campaign ahead in 1779. They were almost always inclined to go along with anything he proposed, and in the face of a future even more inscrutable than usual, they fell into a line of support for the plan he laid out in early September for the year 1779.[28]

That plan prescribed an unusual disposition of his forces, which would now be stationed in an arc of cantonments from Danbury, Connecticut, to Middlebrook, New Jersey. Washington had long felt uneasy about British intentions regarding the corridor up the Hudson, and he now resolved to add to the detachments on both sides of the river near West Point. He had regarded cantonments with suspicion the year before, but now he saw the necessity of dividing his army. The arc of garrisons from Connecticut to New Jersey was intended to give protection to the French in Boston, and it had another advantage as well, for it created sites from which supplies might be sent to the French. Besides feeding his own army, he believed that he faced the prospect of needing to provide rations for d'Estaing's fleet, some twelve thousand sailors and soldiers. He did not complain at the size of this requirement, though it was probably well beyond his means. It remained, however, only a prospect, for d'Estaing stayed only as long as it took to repair his fleet in Boston and then sailed in early November to face the British at St. Lucia.

For his part, Clinton, now fully in charge of the army, had not felt strong enough to attack anywhere. Lord Howe had given up his naval command to Vice Admiral John Byron and sailed for home in late September 1778. Byron had brought only thirteen ships, a number that strengthened British naval power in America, but not to the point of establishing superiority on the sea.[29] Byron was only a temporary replacement, in any case, and Clinton refused his offer to attack d'Estaing while the French were repairing their ships in Boston.

Washington learned of the change in British naval command soon after it was made. By this time he had almost concluded that the British intentions were to stay on the American continent, and though in September he had described British intentions as "mysterious," his most pressing fear then was that they might throw their naval and military power on d'Estaing where he sat locked up in Boston waters.[30] When d'Estaing repaired his ships, he did not seek out Washington for joint operations. By early autumn he had fresh instructions from his French superiors, and he proceeded to carry them out without informing Washington of his intentions. In a sense, d'Estaing's actions were as mysterious as those of Clinton. The winter that followed was much easier than the previous one at Valley Forge, for American troops were now spread out in several posts. There was enough food to prevent hunger; the hospitals, though busy, did not overflow with sick soldiers; and the number of soldiers lost as enlistments were completed did not diminish the army's power.

Spring 1779 brought hope and the news that Spain had entered the war against Britain. Washington of course received this report with pleasure, but he still wondered what to do in making another campaign. He lacked the strength to drive the enemy from New York, but he knew that troops lying idle in garrison would lose their fighting edge. The question was how to use his army without losing it.

The British themselves gave him an answer to that question in the new year. Henry Clinton, always suspicious and fearful of the future, had by early 1779 thought through the problems he faced with his diminished army, and had conceived a plan for bringing his enemy to a campaign—perhaps even a major battle—in which the British army would destroy Washington's force and end the rebellion.

Clinton would begin his effort by raiding the Virginia coast. The navy was amenable to such an activity. Admiral Richard Howe's permanent replacement had not arrived yet, but the navy in and around New York was commanded by a man respected and liked by Clinton, Commodore Sir George Collier. In early May 1779, the fleet transported an expedition under Major General Edward Mathew to Portsmouth, Virginia, on Chesapeake Bay, where they swept in, surprising the Americans, and proceeded to take supplies, destroying much they were incapable of removing to New York. The whole business took about two weeks.[31]

Clinton did not allow his soldiers to remain idle for long. His next step was intended to draw Washington into vulnerable territory, up the Hudson River. As May ended, Clinton moved against Stony Point and Verplanck's Point, both of which the Americans had been fortifying, but not with large numbers of troops. Washington, long sensitive to the Hudson River corridor, had given more of his attention to West Point, a position that commanded the entrance to the northern reach of the river in a way Verplanck's and Stony Point did not. Clinton's troops captured both with ease, and their commander hoped this would draw Washington into a major battle to reclaim them. Washington saw the intended trap and responded with care by strengthening West Point.

Clinton expressed no surprise at his enemy's caution. His plan at this point depended upon reinforcements from Britain, but the failure of such a force to come in June—they actually arrived in late August—ruined his hopes for a major battle with Washington. He did not take his enemy lightly, and he concluded that without a larger army he could do little more than appease loyalists, who wanted action, and General Tryon, the former governor of New York, who shared this desire, by authorizing raids along the Connecticut coast. Tryon's raiders included a number of soldiers from the points just captured on the river.[32]

The raids accomplished little, and throughout June Clinton waited expectantly for reinforcements. Washington waited, too, but then decided that he might strike a blow by retaking Stony Point. He first ordered Anthony Wayne to find a way to evaluate British defenses; Wayne sent a young Delaware officer into the fort, disguised as a workman in the company of an American lady in search of her son. The officer, Allen McLane, discovered the fort's weaknesses, and Washington himself followed up with close reconnaissance a few days later. Satisfied that his troops could capture the fort, he sent Wayne to assault it. Wayne led twelve hundred men through a network of abatis and trenches. This striking force, in two columns, did its tasks with skill and bravery—most carried unloaded muskets, but with bayonets attached. There would be no overeager firing by the Americans that might give the alarm to the enemy, who were surprised and soon defeated. Wayne's troops captured almost five hundred enemy soldiers and then withdrew. At the time, all agreed, including British officers, that it had been a brilliant strike. The British also praised their American enemy for not putting the garrison to the bayonet; as it was, about fifty British soldiers died before the garrison surrendered.[33]

Washington, without regret, ordered Wayne's force out of Stony Point—he saw no point in staying, for he held reinforced positions above on the river, which, now strengthened, could help keep the enemy from breaking the American hold on the Hudson River–Canadian corridor.

But he was not through responding to the initial British move, and on August 19 Major Henry Lee—called Light-Horse Harry by his friends—led a special detachment against a British fortification on Paulus Hook, a prominent point extending into the North River across from New York Island. There was no intention of holding this post once it was taken, and Lee's men, about three hundred in all, made short work of the attack. Stealth characterized this assault, just as it had the month before in the success at Stony Point. The American attackers resorted to the bayonet, again emulating the Stony Point force, and killed fifty of the enemy. The British commander surrendered most of the remaining defenders, 158 in total. Only two Americans died; three others suffered wounds. Lee left about fifty Hessian soldiers in a small blockhouse when they refused to yield. Taking this small fortification would not have been worth the cost in lives.[34]

Neither Washington nor Clinton knew it at the time, but the blows against these two fortifications on the river would end operations for the year. Clinton decided on a campaign in the Carolinas, solace for injured feelings over his inability to destroy Washington's army. The reinforcement from Britain, having finally arrived, was added to the garrison now withdrawn from Newport, plus the force in and around New York City, giving him about 29,000 soldiers. A significant number would have to be kept in the city in case Washington attempted its capture.

Washington's army, as had become customary, began falling away, thinned by the expiration of enlistments and the failure of recruiters in the pay of the states and Congress. By the end of the year it numbered less than half of Clinton's.

There were irritations of lesser magnitude that troubled him as 1779 ended. One, especially annoying, concerned Charles Lee, who had been convicted for offenses committed in the Battle of Monmouth. Court-martial and virtual banishment did not remove Lee from Washington's consciousness. Lee never really recovered from what he considered the injustice of it all, and in July he sought revenge in the *Maryland Journal and Baltimore Advertiser*. There, in a letter, he sneered at Washington as a "military genius," a characterization Washington would never have claimed for himself. Washington resented such scorn—his skin never toughened when his reputation was the subject—but he did not answer.[35]

General John Sullivan's complaints to Congress were another matter, because they seemed to question Washington's competence, though Sullivan did not directly indict his commander. In March, Washington, after failing to persuade Horatio Gates to lead an expedition against the Iroquois along the New York and Pennsylvania frontier, had appointed Sullivan to the command. Gates had pleaded ill health and a want of energy in turning down the command. Sullivan did not want to lead the troops to the West, and when he could not escape the task he proposed an attack of two prongs: one up the Mohawk River and the other along the Susquehanna. Washington pointed out the disadvantages of the Mohawk and noted that logistical weakness made two parallel efforts impossible. There was another reason for Washington to deny Sullivan's wishes: The plan Sullivan offered included a request for more soldiers than could be spared by the main army. As it was, Sullivan had received almost a third of that army and, with these troops, more supplies than anyone had counted on.[36]

Hardheaded, querulous, and probably insecure, Sullivan erupted with complaints well before he really launched his campaign. Once under way, he discovered that the Indians were hard to find, as they faded deeper into the wilderness with every advance of their enemy.

They could not take their villages and gardens with them; Sullivan destroyed habitations and fields everywhere and claimed that he had also destroyed many bushels of corn.

This grisly campaign had hardly begun when Sullivan insisted that the plan of operations was not his and was presumably inadequate. He also insisted to Congress that his expedition was too small, with only 2,312 rank-and-file at his disposal. From this total, the actual fighting force numbered 998, he reported. The absurdity of this conclusion was in the count—somehow Sullivan's arithmetic had him arguing that the 1,300 men unaccounted for were drivers of cattle, drummers, fifers, and undesignated support troops. Washington did the arithmetic almost without comment but pointed out how lopsided these apportionments were.[37]

Congress found the accounting and the complaints to be without merit, and seemed satisfied that the Indians had received a severe blow. Washington answered Sullivan's whining with fact, but the annoyance lingered.

As the year ended, the war remained, in effect, in a long pause. Since the spring of 1778, when the French entered the war, the operations of armies and navies had failed to produce decisive swings of power on either side. This was true even though the French had sent d'Estaing with a small fleet to America, for he was unable to win even a small-scale victory. To be sure, the British army replaced its commander in America, William Howe, with Henry Clinton and began to transfer troops from North America to the West Indies. They had also sent a commission headed by Lord Carlisle, ostensibly to secure peace. Each side had raided the other, to little perceptible effect.

Washington's operations against the British in New York also took on a pallid cast, and though he watched the British carefully, he knew that he could do little more until reinforcements arrived, including the French. By the autumn, he again had another version of old problems to confront: where to spend the winter and how to feed, clothe, and house the troops who had remained with him.

9

Weary but Resolute

The raids on Stony Point and Paulus Hook invigorated Washing-ton's soldiers, pleased Congress, and raised his spirits, but he rec-ognized that the change in mood at the time was temporary and that the limits on the army's power were still set by the enemy—what the Brit-ish could do in operations, especially those of its navy—not by himself or his generals. The army's ability to defeat the British remained what it had been for months, and not even the accession of the French had changed that. In the last two months of summer 1779, he had in mind the idea of joint operations: The Continental Army and d'Estaing's naval fleet might together win an overwhelming victory against the British in New York. It was an idea that invigorated his thought when-ever the French sailed into the waters off the American coast. But by November he had given up hope that d'Estaing would return for joint operations, and news that the French navy had taken a beating in its attempt to take Savannah, Georgia, did not evoke much comment from him, though, of course, he was disappointed.[1]

But d'Estaing's failure did not send Washington into a depression. As was often the case, he sustained his spirits by acting. What he had to do was not dramatic, not filled with the smell of gunpowder, hardly even warlike. What he had to do was remove his troops into winter quarters—to find a place to live that would not take his army far from profitable action. He had done this before, and his orders to his com-manders to take up a familiar position showed the value of experience.

The main body of the army would lodge itself in Morristown, New Jersey, or close to it in Jockey Hollow, about three miles southwest of the town. Most of his infantry took up quarters there; his artil-lery, under Henry Knox, camped closer to Morristown—a mile to its west—and other units set up in nearby spaces. Morristown's location served the need to keep within striking distance of the enemy should they decide to drive on Philadelphia or sail up the Hudson. In a rough sense, Morristown sat on the British flank; closer in, where the British could be watched more easily, was a series of outposts occupied by smaller detachments living on the lines at Springfield, Rahway, New Brunswick, and Amboy, among others; altogether these watching points required about two thousand men. Ten thousand men found shelter at Morristown, building huts for themselves that were small—fourteen feet on all sides—cramped, and without windows. A fireplace at one end gave some heat, but the men had to find their own firewood. Though better than nothing, the huts must have been depressing.[2]

British enlisted men in New York City did not reside in luxury, but at least most of them lived in places that had been constructed for civilian use: houses, warehouses, and public buildings. They too found their quarters were tight, with many men in spaces designed for fewer men. They faced an added irritation: The civilians they displaced did not take to the limited space remaining for their use. There is no record of the grumbling evoked by the rubbing of elbows and other body parts in such quarters, and any fistfights were not noticed in official army reports.

Washington moved himself and Martha to Morristown on December 1, 1779. According to his aides and to others who saw him up close, his temper flared from time to time. He and Martha moved into the house of a widow, Theodosia Ford, who was not intimidated by having a great general under her roof and continued to live in two of the four downstairs rooms. This might not have mattered had the house been large and comfortable. It was neither, and to add to the Washingtons' distress, several of the upstairs rooms had not been furnished. Washington arrived with eighteen servants, an excessive number for a man who had pledged to make the army's standard of living his own. No one, of course, expected him to construct a hut or to live in one, and no evidence exists that there was unhappiness at the number of servants in his household. The servants themselves, however, were unhappy in their housing—many, perhaps most at first, worked in the kitchen with those of Mrs. Ford. Washington complained bitterly in late January 1780 to his quartermaster general, Nathanael Greene, saying that although he had been in the camp almost two months, he still did not have a kitchen "to cook a dinner in," a circumstance he found unaccountable because he knew that other officers had such kitchens. None had been built for him, for lack of boards. Greene, he knew, had his own kitchen, an arrangement Washington forgave him for because, as he said, Mrs. Greene was pregnant.[3]

Greene escaped Washington's wrath because he was a man Washington liked and admired. Others were not so favored. Major Caleb Gibbs, his captain of the guard, does not seem to have been directly rebuked for the lack of a suitable kitchen, but he felt his general's displeasure and passed it along to his subordinates. Several weeks after Washington's complaint to Greene, his anger cooled, but life in Mrs. Ford's house never became pleasant.[4]

Writing Nathanael Greene of his annoyance at the arrangements surrounding his living in Mrs. Ford's house probably reduced the heat of Washington's anger. To complain of such circumstance was a rare act for him at any time. He had more to think about, and even as he complained, he continued the unceasing assignment of finding provisions for his army.

The army went into winter quarters without much in the way of food or clothing, a lack that continued well into 1780. It also made the move without any certainty that it would be able to replace the men whose enlistments were expiring. And then there were the deserters who simply took off for home, time remaining on their tours of duty be damned. Fortunately, this last group was not numerous, and those who scorned desertion were often tough-minded veterans.[5]

But, as ever, men had to be recruited and food procured. Washington discovered while moving his troops into position that though the British would not try to stop them, the weather might. The winter of 1779–80 proved to be one of the worst that longtime residents in New York and New Jersey remembered. Washington talked with these people himself; looking at the ice on the ground, the frozen streams—rivers and creeks alike—and watching the snow pile up in drifts five feet in height, he could not have been surprised. His soldiers, meanwhile, felt the sting of the wind—sometimes, as Washington reported to Congress, without shirts on their backs.

It was a familiar story he told in letters and dispatches from December 1779 well into the spring of the next year. Along with his appeals for provisions and clothing came attempts to find wagons to carry flour and other foodstuffs to the camps scattered around New York

City and up the North River and the Highlands. His appeals for wagons failed more often than they succeeded. At times he knew that what he asked for would not be given. Late in the year and again in early 1781, the river offered a means of getting supplies north, after the British sailed most of their warships down to the main harbor, in part as a counter to anything the French might attempt. Boat owners along the river sometimes seemed willing to help the Continental Army without compensation, but such generosity proved to be rare. When conditions on the river were dangerous—the threat of the British navy or floating chunks of ice—the owners either refused or demanded guarantees that the army give full reimbursement for any boats lost.

By necessity, most of the provisions the army needed originated in inland farms, and Washington looked almost weekly to the countryside for aid. Few weeks passed in which he did not explain the army's needs in near-desperate tones. The army, he reported in a typical appeal, had gone six days without meat, and for three of those days without flour as well. During the winter months, when streams froze over, gristmills could not turn, and grain, if it was available, could not be ground. As hunger mounted, he ordered that soldiers take wheat from mills, beat and husk it, boil it, and "make a tolerable substitute for Bread."[6]

Such means were a desperate resort in the middle of winter and available only if wheat could be found. Hungry, the army turned to means Washington did not approve. As early as January, soldiers plundered nearby farms for meat and flour—and firewood as well. Washington refrained from condemning such means—"men were half starved," he wrote, "imperfectly clothed, riotous, and robbing the Country people of their subsistence from sheer necessity"[7]—but he required his officers in the field seeking provisions to consult local magistrates in their private capacity to set quotas of supplies that might be seized from farmers. The farmers were to be given certificates of payment, at prices presumably approved by local authorities. Later in the month of January 1780, something must have worked, for Washington described the army's "situation" at present as "comfortable and easy on the score of provisions." The comfort soon vanished and he resumed the process he despised—begging for support of all kinds.[8]

Help of another kind, he hoped, would arrive from France. While he occasionally moved troops along the edge of the North River, shadowing British moves, he looked for an opportunity to strike at New York Island itself. When Clinton sailed for South Carolina in December 1779 with almost eight thousand men, Washington thought that perhaps the remaining British garrison might be defeated, a feeling that grew when, in March, a second detachment of twenty-five hundred left New York. But he feared that the British remaining across the river were powerful enough to protect New York against a weak American army.[9]

He worried about what his enemy might do as much as he did about their number. Each army, of course, sought information about the other. From early in the war, Washington looked for information about the forces he faced. It was an essential interest, and he used every means that might lead to discovery of the full extent of the opposition. Besides questioning deserters and the civilians who crossed back and forth across the river, he relied upon spies when he had them in place, but as far as the movements of the British were concerned, he depended more on reports from small units, or the reconnaissance conducted by watchers sent out from the detachments scattered around New York. When Admiral Marriot Arbuthnot brought his squadron into New York in August 1779, Washington learned of its arrival almost immediately. Sailings of warships and transports out of the harbor were of equal concern. At such times, Washington eagerly read the reports of how many soldiers were aboard and of course attempted to learn the destination of such movements.[10]

Clinton used the same types of sources, though he may have relied more on the loyalists who traveled across the lines. Such travel occurred through the use of passes both armies issued, presumably for non-military purposes—visits to the sick for example. Whatever the means, the results often proved surprisingly reliable. The British at times seemed to know exactly what the Americans planned. Washington, too, learned much about his enemy, though immediately after Monmouth he found Clinton's strategy baffling.[11]

Had Washington known of the disorder in the higher command of British forces in America, he would have felt much better. William Howe, Clinton's predecessor, had not enjoyed good relations with Lord George Germain, the colonial secretary, who held primary responsibility for the conduct of war. The two had not communicated clearly in the years of Howe's command, and the tangle of orders and silences in 1777 had led to the disaster at Saratoga.

Things did not improve when Clinton took over. Clinton wanted to end the war with a great battle that would leave Washington's army in ruins and his own in control on the land while the navy dominated the sea. But the French entrance into the war deflated such desires, and Clinton soon came to favor lesser measures. At first he ordered coastal raids, their purpose being to force a scattering of Continental regiments—widely spread troops could not make a concentrated attack on New York City. A slightly varied version of such actions would have him moving heavy forces of his own up the Hudson in an apparent attempt to take the Highland forts. Given the American fear that the loss of the Highlands would split the New England states off from the South, this tactic promised much.[12]

These were small steps in Clinton's strategy. The big step, actually an enormous leap, entailed the major battle with Washington's army that Clinton dreamed of. If the British could lure Washington into a large-scale combat, they would need large-scale reinforcements and naval supremacy. Naval superiority would also have to be found in the South, where Clinton envisioned another great battle.

Dreams of great battles danced in Clinton's head until the spring of 1780, when he actually fought one: the capture of Charleston, South Carolina, in a siege of almost five months. On May 8, he accepted the surrender of about 4,500 men—2,500 of them Continentals and the remainder militia. Washington learned of the loss of the city two weeks later.

Clinton delivered this blow with the aid of the navy, under Arbuthnot, who had arrived with ships and about 3,500 troops in August 1779. Arbuthnot would not have been Clinton's choice had he had a voice in choosing a commander of the American fleet. Arbuthnot was too old for a post that required long stretches on a ship in turbulent Atlantic waters. Nor did he overflow with imagination or a craving to bring the Americans to battle. Fatigue may have shaped his attitudes toward battle as much as indolence, but whatever the case, Clinton encountered resistance to almost all of his proposals for combined operations. Not long before the capture of Charleston, he was fretting at his difficulty in getting Arbuthnot to act with him, and soon after, when he recognized that his hands were tied by his unreliable navy colleague, fretting gave way to rage. Of Arbuthnot, Clinton wrote in his journal, he "will LIE—NAY, I KNOW HE WILL IN A THOUSAND INSTANCES." Shortly after this entry he wrote, "In appearance we were the best of friends, but I am sure he is FALSE AS HELL."[13]

British tempers and judgment at home and in America did not improve. Although Clinton complained bitterly in these months after Charleston, he seemed incapable of exerting the force he had in New York. Not surprisingly, the senior officers around him felt thwarted and even useless, and they began to go home to Britain. If they found it difficult to persuade the ministry to recall them, they agitated for orders to return.

Washington knew none of this, but watched the British with surprise and concern. Why didn't they make a major attack on him? he wondered. In June, General Knyphausen led a large force into New Jersey while Clinton was returning from Charleston. But this was an expedition for forage, and Washington eluded what might have become a serious battle. He was not happy about the tactics he used to stay out of Knyphausen's way, but, given his own weak forces, he could not attack.[14]

While studying his enemy's actions, Washington also thought about the coming of his friends in the French army and navy. D'Estaing no longer figured in American plans; he had disappeared into the West Indies and then returned to France. The French had promised more than they had delivered so far, but in June it seemed that they were about ready to make a second attempt at it.

As the time drew near for their arrival, Washington's concern grew that his forces would not be strong enough for combined operations with them. He had observed a number of the soldiers d'Estaing had brought in 1779, and he knew of the reputation of the French army as a smart and effective fighting machine. What did he have to offer in an effort to act with them? The prospect of showing off his troops to the well-turned-out fighting machine that was the French army troubled him. He told Congress, "We have no Shirts." His men lacked more than shirts and other items of clothing; they also lacked powder and lead. More than appearance, comfort, and gunpowder was involved in the deplorable state of the army, for it was still badly undermanned. "Not a single draft has yet joined the army," he told Congress, "and here we are in the middle of June."[15]

Washington made a part of his appeal to Congress through a committee on cooperation, a body of delegates intended to cut through the usual bureaucratic delays. The best intentions underlying this group remained intentions, not much more than hopes. A few weeks later Washington wrote Joseph Reed, the president of the Pennsylvania Council, asking for 250 wagons. He considered Reed an old friend and a reliable official who would recognize the army's need for transportation. Wagons remained in short supply, but Reed provided words, not wagons.[16]

Then the Comte de Rochambeau, Jean-Baptiste de Vimeur, with 5,500 soldiers, arrived on July 10, 1780. With him were Admiral Louis d'Arsac de Ternay and six ships of the line. This contingent of ships and men seems to have stirred some action among Americans, and soon after their arrival small numbers of troops came to Washington from Pennsylvania and New Jersey. New Jersey's came burdened with restrictions that limited their potential, for the New Jersey legislature insisted that only officers from New Jersey should command these men—all militia—rather than allow them to be incorporated into states' Continental battalions. Although Washington predicted "ill consequences" from this arrangement, he had no choice but to accept it.[17]

Such requirements were not confined to New Jersey's troops. At least New Jersey sent men to Washington; not all of the states responded to his appeal. A common practice among the states, he noted in a letter to his brother-in-law, Fielding Lewis, was to delay sending any until they discovered what other states did. There was no eagerness to fill the allotments he requested anywhere, and Congress was engaged not in exerting itself to compel action by the states but rather in ceding powers to them. His opinion of Congress, expressed a number of times throughout 1780, was that it was losing its best men. Effective leaders in the states did not wish to take themselves away from provincial precincts, and it followed that men of inferior quality attended Congress, if any men at all showed up.[18]

Congress's ceding of its power to the states was not a subject that he discussed with the French. Yet he did not disguise his weakness in responding to Rochambeau's request for a meeting. Rochambeau wanted to form his own impression of his American ally; he had heard the admiring statements made by his French colleagues. Most of these officers who had come to America were aristocrats, but Rochambeau's origins were in a midlevel family, not a great one. Whatever his beginnings, he had mastered the vocabulary of admiration favored by French aristocrats in their greetings to Washington. He had come "with all the submission, all the zeal, and all the veneration I have for your person and for the distinguished talents which you reveal in sustaining a war forever memorable." There were still other compliments in Rochambeau's letter, though his effusions never attained the extravagance of d'Estaing's. They also included a request for a meeting.[19]

In what he said and what he wanted, Rochambeau was typical of French visitors to the Continental Army, who were all curious about Washington. By this time the war had lasted more than five years, and Washington had led the Continental Army throughout the entire period. Knowledge of his service, his refusal to profit from command, and his steadfast determination not to yield, even though his army was already overmatched by imperial forces, gradually began to contribute to a widespread impression of him as a man not just of courage, but of character. Lafayette helped spread this impression, and there were others who began to see Washington as a perfect representative of a nation created in the name of liberty and equality.

Rochambeau, now on the scene in America, gained a fresh sense of Washington's fame and was determined to see him as soon as possible after his arrival. He had crossed the Atlantic with his naval counterpart, the Chevalier de Ternay, who had come under orders from his superiors not to take chances with his ships. Only a few weeks after Rochambeau arrived, the British admiral Thomas Graves sailed into New York, an event that assured British naval superiority by adding his ships to those of Admiral Arbuthnot. Even before the reinforcement by Graves, de Ternay had rejected any notion that he would seek out the British naval force in New York waters. His refusal to challenge the British dampened Washington's spirits; Washington's desire for a decisive battle for New York had reached a high level before the French arrived. He saw immediately that with the coming of Graves, the balance of strength on the sea had again shifted back to the British. He could not know that de Ternay had come to America under orders not to take chances with the French fleet. De Ternay was out of sorts anyway and lived with a frayed temper, intensified by a wish to be elsewhere. America was not for him—he preferred taking on the British in European waters.[20]

Though Washington knew nothing of de Ternay's orders, he realized that he needed French help, and that no need surpassed that which the French navy could provide. But he delayed leaving his camp to meet his allies because, as he explained, the condition of his army threatened dissolution. He did not conceal its fragile character and in early September even wrote the Comte de Guichen, the admiral who commanded the French fleet in the West Indies, about the depletion of American strength. There was no point in hiding such conditions—the army was losing men, the Congress could raise little money, and, he might have added, the people's faith that victory was likely no longer existed. The American and French causes were inseparable, he told de Guichen, an assessment the French might have wanted to deny at this time, so enervated their American ally seemed. Washington asked de Guichen to sail the French fleet to the aid of the American army in the southern states, a request de Guichen ignored.[21]

Had the year been younger, Washington would have made his plea on behalf of his own army, with New York and General Clinton providing the target for attack. There was no possibility that Rochambeau would agree to such a venture late in the year, especially with an ally whose army was shrinking to the point of extinction. By mid-September, despite the miserable condition of his prospects, Washington saw that he could no longer delay a meeting with Rochambeau. The site chosen for the gathering was Hartford, roughly halfway between the two principals, and on September 7 he set off on horseback to meet his French ally. Though the autumn colors were still weeks away, much of the countryside was lovely. Washington found the villages he rode through on his way to Hartford handsome, and the countryside in the Connecticut Valley probably proved of even greater beauty.

He did not reveal his first impressions of Rochambeau and de Ternay, but it is clear that nothing they said charmed him. He, on the other hand, impressed the French officers who met him—his was a quiet yet powerful presence, marked by "a simplicity of manners, and mild gravity," Comte Mathieu de Dumas wrote, that "surpassed our expectation and won every heart."[22] These impressions did not change French attitudes toward American capacities. Washington had not expected to find a willingness in the French to join the Americans in attacking Clinton in New York. He knew he was not ready for a major operation with the French, and by this time he probably did not think much would come of the meeting.

Not much that bore on immediate action did; there were no plans for attack, no details about such a thing. Yet the military principles that would shape combined operations did emerge. The two sides agreed that naval superiority would have to be clear in any major operation. Washington did not have to be persuaded to adopt this principle, as he had long held it, had in fact thought much about the military and naval character of the war that he was fighting. For a creature grown up on the land, he possessed a remarkable sensitivity to the sea.[23]

If the allies were to carry the offensive to the British, they would have to control the sea around New York, and it was New York that provided the key objective of their war. This was Washington's idea, conceived because New York was "the centre and focus of all the British forces."[24] He had an outline of a plan for such an operation. The navy, taking station at Sandy Hook, would blockade the city, cutting off British supplies of men and matériel. The combined army—American and French—would number thirty thousand men, a number not actually in existence in September. Washington asked the French to build up their forces to fifteen thousand men, and he would approach Congress for a much larger army of his own.

Washington wanted more than the agreement embodied. He suggested that the French divide their forces, de Ternay taking his ships to Boston, where they would be more easily protected, and Rochambeau moving his troops to New York, where they would take positions near Washington's. Neither proposal moved the French to accommodate their American superior. That Washington was in command of the two forces was, of course, a polite fiction. Politeness carried the day, and Washington did not argue that if he was in command he should be obeyed. Rather, he listened as the French explained that their orders from the court were to hold the army and the navy together and to maintain a position on an island, not the mainland.[25]

The weakness of Washington's army compelled him to accept these conclusions, but it is doubtful that he would have insisted that the French should yield even if he had an army of first-rate strength and ability. His assessments in these circumstances were founded on a recognition of the likely consequences: He wanted to maintain French support, for it would be crucial to what he hoped to achieve. He had little chance of defeating the British with only his own army in the fight. To keep the French at his side, he did not have to follow their orders, and Rochambeau issued none for the Americans. The implications embedded in this situation in September could be read in several ways. One was that the French were useless, a latent power that would not awake; Washington dismissed this notion easily. A second understanding was simply that the French had much wisdom to offer, and if it seemed coated with caution at this time, the American course should be to wait until circumstances that seemed favorable to the French emerged, and then seize the opportunities that combined operations offered and seek action against the British.

Washington bade Rochambeau farewell shortly after the conference ended in one day's discussion, and on September 23 set off for Fishkill. On the way he met Luzerne, the French ambassador, and he dined with him that evening. Early the next morning, September 25, he was on the road again, bound for West Point, where he intended to breakfast with Benedict Arnold, the newly appointed commander of the fort. The distance between Fishkill and West Point is not long, and there were small posts along the Hudson that he felt obliged to inspect, thinking perhaps that visits by the commanding general could raise the morale of the men manning them.

Arnold's headquarters was in the house of Beverly Robinson, on the east side of the river; West Point jutted out into the river on the west side. Washington had planned to have his breakfast before looking at the defenses of West Point, but on arrival at the house, he was told that Mrs. Arnold had not yet risen from her bed and that the general was across the Hudson at the fort.

Washington could not have been pleased by Arnold's absence, but he expected that he would receive a formal greeting on the other side of the river at West Point. Such ceremonies were not to be ignored in the army, for they reinforced the importance of command and discipline of the troops. No one was more aware than Washington of the effects of such observances. But before he climbed into a barge to be ferried across the river, he ate breakfast and talked with Alexander Hamilton and other officers.

Once across the river, he was given another surprise: Arnold was not there. Nor did anyone at the fort know where he was, including its immediate commander, Colonel John Lamb. Concerned, but not deeply alarmed, Washington proceeded to inspect the variety of posts, redoubts, gun emplacements, blockhouses, and trenches that made up the fortress. What he found dismayed him: The works of the fort were in bad repair or, in the case of many sites where emplacements might have been established, did not even exist. Building materials lay around, evidence of carelessness and a lack of planning and construction. Now in a state of confusion and distress, Washington recrossed the river and entered the Robinson house once more. There he was met by Hamilton, who gave him a handful of papers that went a long way toward explaining the mysteries of the morning.

The papers included letters written by Arnold to Major John André, the acting adjutant general of the British army in New York, who in this correspondence acted as General Clinton's representative. The letters revealed a sensational story: Benedict Arnold was a traitor who was attempting to betray—indeed, in a sense to sell—West Point to the British army. The plot now uncovered had begun in May 1779, when Arnold wrote Clinton a letter that more than hinted that he was prepared to join the British. At the time, Arnold was the military commander of Philadelphia, an assignment made by Washington shortly after the British army evacuated the city. Arnold had not been happy in this command, though he made a good thing out of it, selling supplies left behind by both the departing British and their loyalist allies. The proceeds from these sales properly belonged to public authority but instead went into the pockets of Arnold and his friends. Citizens of Philadelphia complained to the local council about this conduct, and in time Arnold stood trial, but the charges against him were of minor import, and he had escaped any real penalty.

Arnold came into command of West Point about a year after he first wrote to Clinton. His messages were in code and in fact concealed his identity. Clinton turned them over to André almost from the beginning of negotiations, and those negotiations had assumed serious importance when Washington appointed Arnold to West Point. He had offered Arnold the command of a division in the army and was surprised when Arnold turned it down. But this time, in August 1780, Arnold hoped to increase his value by offering something besides himself to Clinton. His assignment to West Point met this purpose in every way. For his new command comprised more than the post itself—it included the forts at Stony Point and Verplanck's Point, stations on both sides of the river, and ground on the east side of the river from King's Ferry to Fishkill. The troops in the entire area were his, as well as those holding positions extending to the enemy's lines and down to North Castle. It was an area critical to the defense of the Highlands, an area that Washington had always wished to hold.

Clinton shared Washington's perception that the fort stood as a key point of control of the corridor to Canada and a vital opening to the New England states. His interest in a seizure of the area through a betrayal by an American increased when he learned of Arnold's appointment to the West Point command.

Arnold and André had agreed to meet to make firm the conditions for the betrayal while Washington was at Hartford. The British interest had risen as Clinton, fearing French strength, gave up plans for striking the French in Newport, a venture that had been stimulated by the arrival of Admiral George Rodney on September 14 with an additional ten ships of the line. With Arbuthnot's fleet, Rodney's ships gave the British local naval supremacy. Rodney would have the responsibility of protecting New York; Arbuthnot's squadrons would carry the army up the Hudson, take West Point, betrayed by its commander, and thereby gain access to the Highlands.

Clinton recognized that he was dealing with an unscrupulous man in Arnold, and to ascertain his price and his ability to give over the fort, he sent André to establish plans for its seizure. André went up the Hudson on the *Vulture,* a British sloop, and debarked the vessel near Haverstraw. Two days of difficulty followed, which included a meeting with Arnold, discovery and attack on the *Vulture* by Americans, and a failed effort by André to evade American militia on land. Captured just above Tarrytown, André, in civilian dress, was discovered to have papers revealing that he was on a mission involving the security of West Point.

Arnold learned of André's capture and the exposure of his plan in the hour of Washington's arrival at Robinson's house. Washington's inspection of West Point had given Arnold several hours more to make his escape to the *Vulture,* still waiting nearby. It took only a few minutes for Washington to make his way through the letters that exposed Arnold's treachery, and he immediately ordered Hamilton and John Laurens to capture him. His anger was complicated by the larger question of what Arnold's defection meant for the army: Whom could he and the army trust now? Arnold, a brilliant fighter, had demonstrated his bravery in service of the American cause—and now showed himself guilty, as Hamilton said, of "the blackest treason."[26]

As far as Washington could see, the treason evident in Arnold's conduct did not extend to his wife, Margaret (called Peggy), who had joined him in Robinson's house when he took command of West Point. Not that Washington or any of his officers there coolly examined the question. Washington had hardly finished reading the letters telling of Arnold's betrayal when he was summoned to Peggy Arnold's bedroom by Lieutenant Colonel Richard Varick, who told him that Mrs. Arnold seemed out of her mind, "frantic with distress," as Hamilton described her a few hours later. Washington went to her room immediately with Varick, who was afflicted with a high fever and who had left his own bed when the sensation created by Arnold ran through the house. When Washington arrived to see Mrs. Arnold, a scene followed with tears and ravings by Mrs. Arnold that he was there to kill her child, followed by bewildered and sympathetic reassurance from Washington. He was clearly astounded by her charge that he intended to kill her child, a baby she clutched in one of the most curious scenes in the entire affair. The historians of these events in Robinson's house have concluded that Mrs. Arnold's talents extended to high drama. Her temporary madness was a part of her performance to persuade onlookers—most certainly General Washington—that she had not been aware of her husband's plot, and knew nothing of it until he told her just before he abandoned her to go to the British army. On seeing Washington enter her room, she denied at first that he was Washington, but rather "the man who was going to assist Colonel Varick in killing my child." Finally convinced that he was the man who was attempting to soothe her spirit, she nevertheless again accused him of plotting to murder her child. Amid the shouts she issued in making this claim, and while writhing on the bed, she allowed her nightdress to fall open, exposing a beautiful body and thereby producing even more confusion in the officers standing in the room. All of this took place in a scene marked by Mrs. Arnold's shouts, tears, partial sentences, and thrashings around on the bed, involving blankets and, undoubtedly, the baby as well.[27]

Whether it was all a grand act or temporary hysteria, it moved Washington and, as far as one can tell, all or most of his aides in the house. Peggy Arnold had not finished her performance, or her agony, when, after a few minutes of trying to reassure her that he meant her no harm, Washington left the room. He carried with him an impression he would never lose: She was innocent of the guilt her husband bore, and had not known of or been a part of his plot.

Washington may have given too much thought to Mrs. Arnold's wild behavior, including the accusation that he intended to murder her child, for he failed to do something a commander in his situation might have done: alert his troops along the river to get into position to defend its most important fortress, at West Point. Hamilton did not wait for such an order but sent off a dispatch to Nathanael Greene, who was at Orangetown, New York. By the time the warning went off to Greene, Hamilton knew that Arnold had escaped and was with Clinton's army or soon would be. At this point Washington had not acted, and in fact he did nothing until early evening, sometime between six and seven o'clock, when he ordered that West Point receive reinforcements and that commanders at key points in its maze of defenses be replaced. For all he knew, Arnold had placed officers who were a part of the plot at these sites, and they were prepared to turn them over to the British.[28]

Arnold had not done any such thing. He was a skillful fighter on the battlefield, but a neglectful plotter, who was much more interested in collecting his sale price than in the details of what the British buyers would obtain. The British, in fact, were surprised when he appeared on the deck of the *Vulture* to make his way to Clinton's headquarters. Clinton had watched the negotiations conducted by Major André but he, no more than anyone on the American side, expected things to come to a climax on September 25. The capture of André had propelled Arnold's flight, exposing the betrayal as the defection of an important American general who offered himself, but nothing more.

For the American army, the question asked in the last few days of September concerned what should be done with André. He, his captors soon discovered, behaved just as an ideal gentleman should. He stood accused of being a spy, a charge he refused to agree to, but he remained calm and, in his conversations with the American officers in Washington's family, revealed that he was a man of honor, simple eloquence, and great charm. He soon had these officers on his side: They did not doubt his guilt as a spy, but they admired his presence and his style. More than anything, they saw in him a manifestation of character and courage.

Washington shared much of this feeling, but he could not bring himself to allow it to soften what had to be done. He convened a board of general officers to review the case—to try André—and to recommend punishment. Nathanael Greene served as president of the group, which included five other major generals and eight brigadiers. The trial confirmed that André had come ashore "in a private and secret manner," that he had not stayed in uniform but had worn a disguise, and that he had carried papers when captured that would have been of value to the enemy.[29]

André did not claim that he had come under the sanction of a flag, a claim made for him by Henry Clinton and Arnold shortly after they learned of his capture. If he made no such defense, neither did he concede that he was a spy. Rather, he had been sent out by Clinton apparently as a kind of agent to deal with Arnold. He did not explain exactly what his dealings were to be. He might have argued that his status as a representative of General Clinton was inherent in Clinton's order that he wear his uniform, not civilian dress, on this mission, but he made no such statement. However, he clearly did not consider himself a spy—a role much beneath a gentleman. His self-defense rested on the assumption or hope that his captors would consider him a prisoner of war.

The board's verdict was that André had come as a spy, and, in keeping with the usual punishment, decided that he should be executed. It was a decision that Washington upheld, but with regret. André had written him after his capture, identifying himself and explaining that he had come ashore to "meet a person who was to give me intelligence." The "person" was not identified in this letter. André, without giving any details, stated that he had been "betrayed . . . into the vile condition of an enemy in disguise within your posts." He also asked that he be "branded with nothing dishonourable, as no motive could be mine but the service of my king, and as I was involuntarily an impostor."[30]

André's defense, as Carl Van Doren would write, rested on the contention that he should be judged by his "intentions" rather than his "outward actions." Though his conduct while being held impressed the officers around Washington, none seemed to have been moved by such an argument. His sentence mandated that he be hanged, a requirement that many of these officers despised. Washington knew of this feeling and probably shared it. But he did not hesitate to see that it was carried out, and André went to his fate on October 2, a week after his capture.

Arnold's betrayal shook Washington, but it did not lead him to a fresh understanding of the Revolution or the war. He had thought deeply about the nature of the conflict with Britain in the years leading to independence. After the colonies declared themselves an independent nation and proved capable of a sustained effort, a circumstance well established by late 1776, his mind turned to the character of the war itself. But even as he plunged into all the complexities of making war, even the bloodletting itself, he could not divorce the war from the Revolution. Nor did he even attempt to make such a separation. While it was going on, the war *was* the Revolution for him.

This equation did not please him, for in the autumn of 1780 the war was going badly. Much the same could have been said about it from 1776 on. His own analysis led him to this conclusion as the campaign of 1779 gave way to that of 1780. At that time the army found itself in familiar straits: It was undermanned, poorly fed, usually inadequately clothed, and often short of gunpowder, muskets, tents—indeed, of equipment of all sorts, including wagons, picks, and shovels. It also lacked horses and the forage to sustain them.

The shortage of men headed Washington's list of deficiencies throughout the war. Most of his analysis of this problem led him to conclude that short enlistments were at its root. The army consisted of "comers and goers," he often noted, men who served in the militia from six weeks to six months at the most, or regulars who came in for a year. It took time to train such men, periods, in the case of militias, that often included the time taken between leaving home and arriving in camp. Once there, soldiers might find their training impaired by shortages of weapons and other equipment, and the lack of availability of experienced officers. The army from any perspective was an inefficient organization. That it often did not fight well hardly surprised anyone, and Washington, a professional of high standards, felt its failures with pain.

What made the pain even worse was the knowledge that the army's many flaws cost money. By itself, failure was a terrible matter, with ramifications extending to the economy. The army, he knew, would drain the productive power of the country in a variety of ways; indeed, an army in the process of almost constant formation and dissolution could be almost more than the economy could stand. Washington pointed to the depreciation of Continental currency as one of the most severe effects of maintaining such a wasteful institution.

The flaws exposed in the army could be traced to Congress. Washington reported to this body, of course, and he took care in protecting its reputation. He cast his letters to its president in a form that conveyed his belief that the Congress embodied the sovereignty of the new republic. He knew that this conception of the relationship of Congress to the states embraced a fiction, for the reality of politics in America was that the states were independent bodies and that sovereignty lay with them. Yet these states had created a Congress to act for them in matters relating to the war, and in this situation the Congress exercised a power that seemed to define a genuine sovereignty. Washington wrote to this body as if it were the final authority in the war; yet he also wrote to the states, to governors, and sometimes to legislatures as well. But in these instances he managed not to undercut his master, the Congress of the United States.

That the Congress was his master was in some sense ultimately untrue. The real masters in the new nation were the states, and everyone knew it. Congress in early 1780 had in effect confessed to its impotence by shifting the responsibility and costs of maintaining troops directly to each state, without an intermediate stage provided by the Congress. Though several states and the Continental Army's quartermaster department strove mightily to make this new system work, in reality it was as hit-or-miss as what it attempted to supersede. Washington was thinking of the American side of the entire war when he summed it all up as "a history of false hopes and temporary devices."[31]

While Washington only occasionally criticized Congress, by 1780 he had shed his inhibitions about the states. In most of his ruminations on the war—an almost desperate attempt to understand it—Washington returned to his dissatisfaction with the thirteen states. When they were asked for the means to maintain the army, he pointed out, their response was to delay. The purpose of this inaction was to do as little as possible. And even in the midst of a war for freedom, they rarely rose to the needs of the occasion, but remained mired "in local views and politics."[32]

Washington had assumed command of the army in 1775 convinced that only unity of effort and organization of the individual states could bring success. Five years later, that conviction had grown into something approaching an obsession. But he believed that unity of this kind had eluded all efforts to seize it, and he confessed his disillusionment to Fielding Lewis that, as things stood, "we shall become" and perhaps already have become "a many headed Monster, a heterogeneous mass that never will or can steer to the same point."[33] This was a statement made by a weary man rarely given to extravagance in expression, tired indeed of the problems that had bedeviled him since 1775.

He did not look for rescue from these problems to emerge from the people, though he wrote John Cadwalader that the Revolution would survive if there were "virtue" among the people and "wisdom" among its leaders. But the people would have to send a full representation to Congress before anything would be done, and they would have to disabuse themselves of the hope they entertained that the war would soon end. This hope was a fantasy, but every winter, Washington noted, the American people somehow came to believe that the war would end soon.[34]

Washington himself held no such belief; he also deplored the people's distrust of a standing army. He had remarked on this attitude early in the war, and may have detected it first in Pennsylvania, when he felt the opposition of the Quakers and other religious radicals to the fighting. By the time the army was settling into its positions around New York City, he found—or projected—such animus in Americans everywhere. And, of course, in the years leading up to the war and after its beginning, a rich pamphlet literature had emerged in America that pointed to the connection between standing or professional armies and tyrannies throughout human history. This belief that power in the form of the standing army oppressed liberty was widespread in America and, he failed to note, in Britain, too.

These assumptions about the failure of Congress, the states, and the people in America depressed his spirits when the campaign of 1780–81 began. These failures seemed to define the nation and the way it organized its political life, and seemingly offered little hope. Early in the campaign, he had interpreted another set of circumstances that boded well for American victory: the French entry into the war, troubles for the British Crown at home and on the Continent, and the apparent disposition of the European powers to give some support to the American cause.

By late 1778, the trust invested in the French had begun to fade. When Spain joined the war the next year, some confidence in the glorious cause returned, but the long slog through the bitter days of these years, with little accomplished, undermined his spirit. Though he hardly gave up belief that the French would make a decisive difference, his confidence in them seeped out at a rapid rate. D'Estaing's departure for the West Indies took some of the shine off the French, and their delay in a major resupply of troops hastened his sense of loss. The Spanish entry into the war seemed to make little difference, and that country did not recognize the new United States. Washington felt suspicious not only of them as the war proceeded—he questioned the reliability of all monarchs. George III had set this process of doubt in motion in the 1760s, when the American crisis began. Americans, not just Washington, had taken a hard look then.

By 1780, realism in American attitudes toward the European powers was clear and firm. Washington never believed the British would simply give up their attempts to conquer the colonies, unless they suffered massive defeat. His darkest assumptions held that for the British, the bankruptcy of their government would be "less terrible to the King than giving up the contest"; and if they succeeded in winning the war, the Crown might emerge with even "greater influence and power, a purpose that he suggested might be "the object of the present reign."[35]

The evidence in Washington's letters shows that he read the English newspapers whenever he could get them and that he sought information about the British enemy from traitors and indeed from any source coming into his hands. He did not always have the most exact information about the enemy, but he strained to understand their intentions and speculated when he lacked precise knowledge. He read desperation into the British ministry's "concessions" to the Irish people, seeing them as an effort to hold those patriots down while the government proceeded with the business of breaking the American Revolution. With triumph in the Revolution, he wrote, the next British Parliament would be as "obsequious as the last." The North ministry, he seemed to say, would endure.

As for the rest of Europe, its favorable disposition toward America promised "no security that it will remain so." It was this transitory character that impressed him, and he saw that the "change" or "caprice" of a single ministry could "alter the whole system of Europe." Nor could the sovereigns of the Continent guarantee steadiness in policy. The death of a king could turn things upside down, and he confessed that he expected that, given the advanced ages of the three most powerful monarchs on the Continent, the chances were greater that "one will die in the course of a year" than that all three will survive it. The three he presumably had in mind were Charles III of Spain (age 64), Frederick the Great of Prussia (68), and Catherine the Great of Russia (51).[36]

To some extent, throughout the year 1780 and into 1781, he was flailing, though not in responsibility as commander of the Continental Army. He performed in that great assignment with skill. On the military side, he held the army together and held the British at bay, even though he faced an army consistently more powerful than his own. He had moved his force in and out of danger, giving ground at times but still mounting a threat that compelled his enemy to keep a significant and sizable army in New York. Washington also met his administrative responsibilities as fully as possible, though his troops remained almost at all times on short rations, sometimes having no rations, were badly clothed, sometimes nearly naked, dreadfully housed, and, when they fell sick or wounded, ineffectively treated. He had worked with an unworkable system since the war's beginning. No one else could have done as well.

To all of these problems he brought an inflexible will, and a refusal to break under strain. His flailing was not concealed, and yet it was not recognized. It came in his moods: his sense, in 1780 and early 1781, that the crisis emanating from the army's problems would destroy the cause for which he fought. Yet ironically, his ability to surmount each problem, to go on no matter how desperate the army's condition, undercut his appeals to Congress for men and supplies. To the Congress he was the General, different from all other men—in fact, of another order of men. His presence and the strength he embodied seemed to suggest that he was incapable of failure.

Washington's inner turmoil stood in contrast to this reputation. For he felt he was on the edge of disaster—chaos threatened, he said repeatedly, unless the army received men under a reliable system. Current operations fluctuated with the "two army" system—one army coming and one going—and though Providence had seen the army through the worst of times before, the nation should not depend on it much longer.

As early as the middle of 1780, Washington had a surer means in mind for winning the war than dependence on Providence. The experience of war in America had made him an American who thought about his country as an arrangement of men attached to a union. What was needed, he wrote Fielding Lewis, was a Congress of "absolute powers in all matters relative to the great purposes of War, and of general concern." To the states and smaller units of government, he would leave matters of local and internal polity for the regulation of order and good government. But war and problems of general concern belonged in a congress, a body made up of "a full and well chosen representation." There was a bite in this part of his formula—he had commented before on the loss of talent in Congress as the war went along. That he was angry with Congress seems clear in this statement calling for converting it to a body of "absolute powers."[37] It was a proposal he had made privately before. No formal suggestion along these lines went to the president of the Congress. He would restrain himself and honor Congress while chaos thrived around him and the army. But he knew that the army and the Revolution were near a terrible death, whatever men thought and whatever he did.

Mutiny and Rallying the French

Washington often wondered at the patience and hardihood of soldiers who had served in what might have been considered squalor. What, he asked, had kept them under arms for years during which they were hungry and often naked or near it? Small numbers had protested, to be sure, in small upheavals, and many more had deserted—almost always going home, not to the enemy. But though the circumstances of their lives never seemed to improve, they held true to the oaths they had sworn when they entered the army, and they fought remarkably well when they had nothing but themselves for support.

Observing these men, Washington feared the worst, and on January 1, 1781, he got it—a mutiny of the Pennsylvania Line, some ten regiments in winter quarters at Mount Kemble, a camp near Morristown. At around nine in the evening, they burst from their tents carrying muskets with bayonets, and after two hours of wildness, in which they killed two officers and wounded others, they set off for Philadelphia, where Congress sat. By this time they had at least four fieldpieces and the skill to use them. A graphic description of the first hours of the affair came to Washington's headquarters in New Windsor, about six miles above West Point, on January 3.

Anthony Wayne, then a brigadier general and popular with his troops, commanded the Pennsylvania Line, but was now shoved aside by men determined to either go home or improve the conditions of life in the army. Many hoped to leave the army entirely, with honorable discharges and back pay in hand. They had engaged themselves in a riot in leaving Mount Kemble, but they soon proved that they were disciplined soldiers, for after they had forced their officers to get out of the way, they organized themselves into platoons and marched off in military fashion, not as a riotous mob.

No officer sided with them; their leaders were the sergeants who had always fought at their head. Wayne, with several colonels, followed along, fearing that the mutineers would take the road to Elizabeth Town and join the enemy. The troops soon proved otherwise and the next day settled themselves into a rough camp at Princeton.

When word of the affair reached Washington, he thought immediately of riding southward to take charge of dealing with the mutiny. He did not consider the crisis in conventional terms—that is, of only crushing and punishing the disaffected. His reactions were far more complicated: He wanted the mutiny put down, but he also wanted to treat the men involved with fairness, indeed with sympathy, and if that meant recognizing and responding to their grievances, he had long done that in his pleas to Congress. Now, with the failures of the past in mind, he knew that he would have to do far more.

Confronting the men in person was an idea, or impulse, that occurred to him almost simultaneously with the arrival of the dispatch from Wayne. Washington explained later to Rochambeau, among others, that he resisted this inclination in recognition of the likelihood that if he left Morristown, where most of the army was in garrison, an echoing revolt might explode in his absence, as those soldiers had grievances identical to those of the Pennsylvania Line.

At Princeton, Joseph Reed, a former aide of Washington and now president of the Pennsylvania Council, assumed the task of negotiating with the mutineers. By Sunday, a week after the affair began, the negotiations had fallen into place. The Board of Sergeants, representing the men, had demanded that veterans of three years be discharged at once; in case the length of enlistment was disputed, three soldiers should sit with three commissioners on a committee to resolve such disagreements. There was also an expectation by the soldiers' board that the men would be paid off and properly clothed at the time of discharge. The pay must be in specie or undepreciated currency, a demand that confirmed the loss of faith in Congress's monetary policy.

Joseph Reed did not yield to most of these requirements but he and the commission did give way to the veterans' insistence that the army live up to several of the promises it had made when the soldiers were recruited. Wayne's remaining with the army during the talks between Reed and the Board of Sergeants undoubtedly steadied everyone. The troops trusted him—they had promised to fight under his command if the British attacked in the midst of the upheaval—and so Reed and his Pennsylvania colleagues received a quiet and peaceful greeting. The agreement that Reed persuaded the sergeants to accept went partway toward the desire of the veterans to be discharged, but such action would be forthcoming only after a committee of Pennsylvania commissioners reviewed each case. No soldier was invited to sit with this body, a circumstance that kept their suspicions high. The agreement was not firm on a commitment to make good earlier promises of back pay and clothing. A general pardon for offenses committed during the mutiny was clear, however, and eased fears of reprisals. And fear there was among the men and the Board of Sergeants, fear they announced by keeping possession of the British spies they held. In a few days they gave up these three men, who after a short trial in a military court went to the gallows. Their bodies were left hanging in the open for the better part of a week.

When the men agreed to stop their mutiny, they extracted important concessions from the army: pay that the army did not have, furloughs for two months for almost half the Pennsylvania Line, and outright discharges for several hundred men. They also left behind an impression that mutiny worked, that it might indeed provide the way to elementary justice in a life filled with harshness, cruelty, and broken promises.

The mutiny confirmed several of Washington's deepest worries about his army, but it also reassured him that, though his soldiers endured abysmal circumstances in their lines, they remained fundamentally loyal. Near starvation and nakedness made them think of leaving the army; it did not send them into the arms of the enemy, where they would find food, pay, and clothing. This knowledge made it easier for him to maintain his focus on smashing the British.[1]

That focus had never really left him: He remained steady in his conviction that nothing short of recapturing New York City would end the Revolution. There were moments when he thought the British might, in exhaustion, lose heart and give up the war. He recognized such a feeling in his countrymen; every year, he said, when campaigning slacked off in winter weather, Americans looked to the new year or the next campaign as the final effort. It was a hope that was even shared by Washington's staff—Alexander Hamilton, for example, though in Hamilton's case the feeling was at times one of desperation, not hope.

The possibility of taking New York rested on realities that he could not control or even change. The British unwittingly opened themselves to attack with every detachment of troops they sent from New York to the South. General Clinton hated the process, though he himself had contributed to it in the spring of 1780, when he began the operation that led to the capture of Charleston. After the city fell, he returned to New York, leaving Cornwallis behind with four thousand soldiers. Soon Clinton received requests by Cornwallis for more troops, plus suggestions on how to conduct the war. He considered these appeals carefully and responded, though in so doing he weakened his own force by sending troops to South Carolina.

Had Clinton clung to his New York army, he could have justifiably claimed that he acted from need. He was in a sense very much alone with his problems. The colonial secretary, Lord George Germain, running the war from Whitehall, gave advice on strategy freely, though not much in the way of troops and supplies in support. Clinton's backing in Britain was firm, but he, like Washington, worried over the logistics of feeding and supplying his army. He also felt hampered by Germain's schemes for action, all of which were unrealistic and, Clinton thought, almost fantastical.

Washington did not know that his counterpart suffered under the burden of meddlers three thousand miles away. Nor did he realize that Clinton sometimes felt neglected as provisions and the materials of war dwindled in his camp. For the British army did not sustain itself by drawing on local sources. To be sure, Clinton bought what he could from nearby farms and merchants, but his soldiers could not have survived without the supplies carried in by merchantmen and transports from Britain. The British did have the advantage of hard currency at hand, but the basic allotments of food, weapons, ammunition, and equipment had to be brought in from across the Atlantic.[2]

When Washington learned that his enemy had to cope with shortages of provisions and men, he yearned to take advantage of such circumstances. He was hampered by the reluctance of the French, long considered an indispensable ally, to commit their forces to a large-scale campaign. That they were reluctant was not surprising—and not surprising to Washington. He had not hidden his problems from them; far from it, he had, from motives of honesty, told them ever since d'Estaing had arrived that he was leading an army in transit. The French really needed no reports from him on the condition of the troops he commanded if they trusted their own eyes. There were always French officers with the Americans in camp and Congress, where a great deal of truth was spoken about the Continental Army. Washington himself knew of the talk and simply followed his instincts in dealing with the French. These instincts were informed by a knowledge of the politics necessary in dealing with friends and foes. He had, from an early age, come to the conclusion that men were moved by their interests and passions.

The French government was filled with such men, as was its army and navy. He respected those he dealt with, and in the early months of their coming he trusted what they said, including promises and statements of intention, though when their statements seemed to diverge from his understanding of their interests, his skepticism took over. The French, he discovered early on, studied the political environment before they declared themselves and before they acted. They were cautious above all else. Their officers in America never seemed to feel that they were independent of the home authorities, and indeed seemed always inclined to emphasize their connections to the French court and their king.[3]

Some undoubtedly were shocked at the form and appearance of the Americans. French officers and men were well turned out, with clean uniforms, buttons polished, and muskets and swords in obvious working order. Others must have been amused at the American shabbiness, and as for the Americans on the parade ground, the less said the better.

They exempted Washington from the common scorn that the rustics-in-arms evoked. In their eyes he was different. Lafayette's affection for him approached idolatry, but Lafayette was very young when they met and was prepared to embrace him as a father. The Comte de Chastellux, only two years younger than Washington and born into a distinguished family, was far more sophisticated than Lafayette and far more learned. He was a veteran of the Seven Years' War, having fought in Germany, and brought high intelligence as well as courage to his wartime service. Like most French officers, he looked forward to meeting Washington, and may have expected that he would encounter a remote, even standoffish man. Their meeting, which occurred in

1780, disabused him of any such thoughts, as he noted of Washington's greeting that "his kindly dispositions toward me were not feigned." His impressions of Washington, formed during extended meetings, were that Washington was "the idea of a perfect whole: Brave without temerity, laborious without ambition, generous without prodigality, noble without pride, virtuous without severity, he seems always to have confined himself within those limits, where the virtues, by clothing themselves in more lively, but more changeable and doubtful colors, may be mistaken for faults." Chastellux also found Washington impressive physically, noting that his "stature is noble and lofty; he is well built and exactly proportioned," with a "fine face . . . neither a grave nor a familiar air, his brow is sometimes marked with thought but never with worry." Like many others who met Washington, Chastellux remarked that he was an "excellent and bold horseman, leaping the highest fences and going extremely quick without standing upon his stirrups, bearing on the bridle, or letting his horse run wild."[4]

The two men became friends on their visit. Washington had met Chastellux with ease, yet not with familiarity. Chastellux was an aristocratic savant accomplished in the arts and in war, and Washington dealt with him with respect, as he did most men. He kept his distance by not revealing too much of himself—or perhaps by simply being himself. A part of that self concealed a mild wit, shown only to friends. A few months after Chastellux visited Washington in his headquarters, the two were on terms that encouraged its expression. A sample could be seen when, in thanking Chastellux for sending a cask of claret, Washington wrote saying that he would not refuse the gift, which would "bring my patriotism under question, and incur a suspicion of want of attachment to the French nation."[5]

There was not much lighthearted banter in Washington's life—nor did he yearn for it. He had to take care in his manner in dealing with the French in any case, and Rochambeau, with whom his relations mattered in more important ways, did not invite teasing. Rochambeau had a grand title and the rank of lieutenant general, but he had not been born into the aristocracy. He was a plainspoken man, a professional soldier, seemingly interested only in his calling. Fortunately, he was a soldier of genuine quality and, though the Americans did not know it, a thoughtful and patient man. He possessed his own distinction, won on the battlefields of Europe, but in America he faced responsibilities that included fighting alongside an ally of doubtful strength led by a man who had made his mark in an earlier war against the French. The alliance on the American continent put Rochambeau's army at a disadvantage on several scores: The British enemy outnumbered them, and most of the time they controlled the sea, where supremacy meant control of logistics and reinforcements from Europe. The assignment to lead the French effort in America was complicated by these facts, to say nothing about the responsibility of coordinating his operations with another set of forces in the West Indies.[6]

In Rochambeau's American assignment, he served under Washington. He acknowledged his subordination, but he and Washington both knew that his status was more ambiguous than his orders from his king indicated. France was the more powerful member of the alliance, and it had interests in Europe and the West Indies that complicated the relations with the new American nation. Rochambeau arrived in Rhode Island with a small but strong army and a navy clearly inferior to British naval forces everywhere. He was to cooperate with the Americans, take orders from their commander—a formidable man to be sure, but a colonial, and in most senses an unknown quantity.

Rochambeau spoke no English; Washington, no French. But Washington had Lafayette at hand and made him his translator and often sent him to the French headquarters. There were several officers usually present there who had a knowledge of English. Chastellux was one, and he was happy to serve his commander, though the blunt-speaking Rochambeau may not always have been delighted by his highborn colleague.

Washington did not know about tensions within the French command in Rhode Island. News of Commodore de Ternay's death in December came to him in due course, as did the appointment of Destouches to head the French fleet in North America. Such changes were of interest, but the one he craved to hear—movement of the French to New York positions—did not come until May. The French in Rhode Island had always explained that they could not move without authorization from Paris. Referring to the far-distant authority forestalled pressure from the Americans, who were in the position of supplicants, an inconvenient but familiar posture, since they had already received money and weapons from the French.

The weakness of Washington's standing with the French was never clearer than it seemed to be in early February 1781, when he urged Rochambeau to send his naval force, with a heavy contingent of soldiers, against the British in the Chesapeake. The southern theater of operations had demanded attention since Gates's disaster at Camden, in August 1780. Washington had indeed shipped troops off to General Greene, who had replaced Gates in October. Now, in the new year, Virginia was threatened by a detachment of about fifteen hundred troops sent there by Clinton and led by Benedict Arnold. The thought of Arnold operating in Virginia, destroying American militia and ravaging the land, was hard to bear. It is doubtful that Washington would have proposed shifting even more troops to the South or called upon the French to make an attack on the British there had a storm off New York not damaged and scattered Admiral Arbuthnot's ships, stationed in Gardiner's Bay, on the Long Island coast. The storm achieved something neither the Americans nor the French could do—it gave the French temporary naval superiority. Washington now argued for a major attack by the entire French fleet in Rhode Island and several thousand French and American soldiers. Because he recognized that their advantage would not last long, Washington delivered his message with urgency—and then, fully aware that his French ally did not ordinarily respond quickly to such appeals, he rode to Newport on March 5, hoping to quicken French blood.[7]

The ride to Newport was not leisurely. Washington rarely walked a horse at any time; reports during the Revolution describe his riding almost always at a gallop. Newport lay about two hundred miles from New Windsor, headquarters of the American army, and he covered the ground in three days. On the way, his horse broke through a wooden bridge. Washington, who was fond of horses, knew them well, and rode them almost every day, may have been troubled by the death of this horse, but it produced only a short interruption in his journey. Mounting another horse, he was on his way again.

He arrived in Newport to discover the pleasing sight of the French troops on board their ships and prepared to sail southward. The pleasure departed immediately; the ships did not. The French had other ideas, among them a review of soldiers not yet aboard, a grand dinner, and a ball. Washington did not feel like dancing, but he made his way through the formalities the next day, saying nothing that angered his hosts. The next evening, March 8, the French set sail.[8]

By this time, the British—both Henry Clinton and Marriot Arbuthnot—had learned that the French planned to send ships and men to Virginia. Arbuthnot, from the British station at Gardiner's Bay, responded almost immediately, sending eight ships in pursuit of Admiral Destouches, who led a squadron of about the same size. The French reached the Chesapeake before the British, and though the two forces encountered one another and a certain amount of shooting ensued, neither of them delivered or received much damage. Each returned to its base in the North, and little was said about their encounter.

Washington refrained from commenting publicly on the affair, but privately he complained about the sluggish conduct of his allies in Newport. He managed to contain himself until he returned to New Windsor, but once he was back with the army, his disappointment and annoyance poured out. To Philip Schuyler he confessed his disappointment that the French had not sent their whole fleet and the full detachment of troops he had requested and thereby missed destroying Arnold during a time when the British fleet was in a "debilitated" condition. The delay in sailing was particularly "unaccountable." "But," he concluded, "it is our true policy to make the most of their assistance without censuring their mistakes, therefore it is I [who] communicate this in confidence." He wrote in similar terms to the president of the Congress and two of his colleagues in Philadelphia, and he did not hide his feelings from senior commanders in the army. He hoped that news of his disenchantment would not find its way to the French, but inevitably it did. Several days later, evidently repenting of his candor, he wrote Luzerne, the French envoy to Congress, with no hint of the failure of the French expedition, but instead praise for the "good conduct and bravery" of the French officers and sailors involved. A similar letter went to Rochambeau on the same day. These efforts clearly pleased Luzerne and Rochambeau.[9]

The rumbles with the French never reached the level of real thunder and lightning and soon gave way to more serious problems. They occurred at a moment in Washington's life in which a variety of things were going wrong. Three weeks before he rode off to Rhode Island, he had endured a break with Alexander Hamilton, one of the key aides in his military "family." He valued this group—his designation of them as a family expressed his feeling of close personal regard, indeed affection, as well as a determination to use the conventional language of European armies. He was fonder of Lafayette than of any of these young men, but he was also closely attached to Hamilton, whose character and personality combined the genteel ideals of American aristocrats with the hard realism of men determined to rise in the world. Washington recognized his great ability and respected and trusted him. It was Hamilton he sent to the northern army and its chief, Horatio Gates, after Saratoga, to remind that esteemed general that, though he had won a splendid victory at Saratoga, he and his army remained under Washington's command. Hamilton, a young officer with little experience compared with the veteran Gates, carried out this assignment with zest while managing, barely, to remain within the bounds of civility. There was an edge to Hamilton on occasions when decisiveness was required, as the joust with Gates revealed. There was also a set of attitudes in him that owed much to the code of an eighteenth-century gentleman, a side to him much in evidence in his dealings with Arnold's wife, Peggy, and Clinton's spy, Major John André.[10] The sentimentality exposed in the André affair assumed an almost silly form in his letters to Elizabeth Schuyler. These letters, in their extravagant appeals to the language of love, probably would have yielded both laughter and admiration among several of his brother officers in Washington's family.

Washington probably never knew just how complicated a creature Hamilton was. In February, just before the troubles with the French in Newport, his regard for Hamilton received a sharp blow. The two men were in the army's headquarters, a house of several stories. They met by chance on the stairs leading to an upper floor, where Washington stated that he wished to speak to him. Hamilton, on his way to deliver a letter to Colonel Tench Tilghman, replied that he would come to Washington immediately after he delivered a letter, and then proceeded down the stairs. This done, he encountered Lafayette on his way back up the stairs and stopped for a short time to talk. When he reached the top of the stairs, he met a Washington now angry at the wait. Washington, obviously upset, reproached him for keeping him waiting for "ten minutes," adding, "I must tell you Sir you treat me with disrespect." Hamilton's account of his response, "given without petulancy," he said, was a quick "I am not conscious of it Sir, but since you have thought it necessary to tell me so we must part." Washington responded, in "effect," Hamilton reported, "Very well Sir if it be your choice," and the interview ended. Not for long, however. Washington, evidently shocked and distressed by this explosion, sent Tilghman to Hamilton with a message telling of his "great confidence" in Hamilton's "abilities, integrity, (and) usefulness" and of his desire to "heal a difference which could not have happened but in a moment of passion." Hamilton responded to Tilghman that he was unwilling to discuss the incident—a conversation about it could not serve any purpose other "than to produce explanations mutually disagreeable"—but he would come to Washington if he "desired it." Tilghman evidently conveyed to Washington a sense of Hamilton's feeling that further talk was useless, and the break was clear. To Hamilton's credit, he offered to remain in service on the staff until other members temporarily away from headquarters returned. Washington accepted Hamilton's refusal to discuss the blowup further and thanked him for his offer to remain until others were once more in place. Thus, this sad affair ended with both men wounded but determined to maintain a working relationship for the time being.[11]

Hamilton was twenty-six years old when he broke with Washington, who was forty-nine. Not only was he young; he was young for his age—brilliant, proud, and extraordinarily sure of himself, but not a man who had mastered his vanities, nor would he during the war. Whether Washington recognized all of his aide's weaknesses is not clear, but he dealt with them with sensitivity and generosity.[12]

Perhaps he acted so thoughtfully because he recognized something of himself in Hamilton. While he lacked Hamilton's intellectual talents, and his own judgment of men and their actions far surpassed Hamilton's, in other ways the resemblance is striking. He had begun his military career when he was twenty, Hamilton when he was twenty-two; like Hamilton he was hot-blooded, impatient, and ambitious, hoping for a commission in the British army. Washington had also found a great family—the Fairfaxes—to attach himself to, though his connection occurred naturally and took on the character of an adoption. The Fairfaxes liked him and obviously received satisfaction from assisting his rise. There is little evidence, if any, of Washington's conscious cultivation of this great family—he was only a boy when he came to know William Fairfax, and a naive boy at that. Hamilton had cultivated the Schuylers, a wealthy Dutch family of New York. He became a favorite of Philip Schuyler, whose daughter Elizabeth would marry Hamilton later in the war. Washington seems not to have written witty and extravagant letters to young women like those that flowed from Hamilton's pen to Kitty Livingston and Elizabeth Schuyler, though he was fond of Sally Fairfax and wrote her affectionate letters. His most romantic effusion came in his praise of the charming sound musket balls made in battles.

Another young man was giving him heartburn at about the time Hamilton uncovered his own resentment. The young man was John (Jack) Parke Custis, Martha's son and Washington's stepson. As we have seen, Washington felt fond of this young man and in a sense responsible for him. He had, when Custis was a boy, spoken directly to him of conduct that was not acceptable. In the background of his relationship with his stepson was Martha, who loved her son deeply; Washington might have exercised more discipline on Jack had he not recognized that doing so would have hurt Martha. Now, presumably, Jack Parke was grown up, an adult who sat in the Virginia legislature, though without attending its meetings. His reasons for staying away from the legislature were not clear, but Washington expressed his annoyance at Jack's failure to attend its sessions. "So young a Senator as you are," he wrote Jack, "little versed in political disquisitions, can yet have much influence in a populous assembly; composed of Gentlemen of various talents and of different views." Moreover, as he reminded Jack, it was his duty. Washington left unsaid his feelings about the honor and responsibility of a gentleman to serve his country.[13]

As if to remove the sting Jack might find in his stepfather's reproaches, Washington then stated his own ideas of what the present Congress was doing and how it should be reformed. What he had to say was what he had told others, some in the Congress, others in the army: Because the Congress was weak, it should be reformed, with "a controuling power in Congress to regulate and direct all matters of general concern." The Congress could not fashion policy for managing such concerns; its powers were only to recommend actions to the states, yielding a situation in which one state gives "obedience" and another "refuses it," and a third state "mutilates" and "adopts" only a part of the recommended policy, and all "vary in time and manner."

Washington, in delivering this analysis of the workings of power, was taking John into his confidence—to what effect is not clear.[14]

Jack Parke Custis was a familiar problem, and so was Washington's mother, Mary Ball Washington, a lady, in the parlance of Virginia society, who expected deference apparently at all times and under all circumstances. Her expectations sometimes surprised her son and made him uncomfortable when they did not distress him. In February 1781, a time when the war seemed to be going badly and Alexander Hamilton had temporarily, at least, overturned the balance that usually marked Washington's staff, Mary Ball Washington publicly embarrassed the family. She had long been a person who craved attention, and when she did not get it, she complained. At this time she pled poverty, a doubtful ploy perhaps, to get her taxes reduced. She made her discontent known to members of Virginia's government, including the legislature. Few of these men knew her, but they knew her son and idolized him. Not surprisingly, they acted before thinking the matter through. The product of their thought was a proposal to provide her with a pension funded by the state.

In March, Washington's friend Benjamin Harrison responded to this proposal by his legislative colleagues with strong disapproval. Washington, he told them, would be "displeased" by such an "application." Harrison knew his friend well—Washington immediately asked Harrison to pass along his opposition to the idea, saying that he thought the entire family would not wish that a pension be granted as long as they were able to support her. To drive home his belief that his mother needed no public aid, he ran down the subsistence he had provided her several years before he was called into the army: He had bought her a house and lots near Fredericksburg, a location he chose for its proximity to his sister, Betty Lewis. He had also given her money, and while in the army he had instructed Lund Washington, the manager left in charge at Mount Vernon, to provide her with additional sums when she asked for them. Ask she did, though not often, confining many of her requests to a particular slave or some piece of household furnishing.[15]

She and her son rarely wrote one another, and he could not visit her during the war. Lund Washington sometimes mentioned her in his letters, and Washington received word of her health occasionally from others. Brigadier General George Weedon, a Virginian on a visit home, learned of her refusal to be inoculated for smallpox in 1778, reporting that she apparently feared that the procedure would bring on the disease, not prevent it. Betty Lewis caught it in the natural way, and Weedon said, "It was in almost every House in Town and Country."[16] Washington had ordered that virtually every soldier who had not had the disease should receive inoculation, but he did not attempt to persuade his mother. Her concern about money presented a problem he could deal with or ignore; smallpox inoculation, he knew, was not something he could force on her. And now, in 1781, beyond getting word to the family to look after her, ignoring her surprising demands was about all that he could do.

The incomprehensible behavior of Mary Ball Washington, the irresponsibility of John Parke Custis, and the break with Hamilton all irritated Washington in different ways, but, if his correspondence in these weeks can be trusted, none of these tempests blew him off course. The course he wished to follow would see him leading a combined operation with the French in an attack to capture New York; he thought this might end the war with the British, convincing them that their efforts to put down the Revolution were futile. Such a hope at this time seemed a fantasy, yet he held it while at the same time confessing in a letter written in April to Colonel John Laurens that "we are at the end of our tether," an admission that sounded as if he were prepared for final defeat. He was not, of course—what he was prepared for, personally, was combat.[17]

But he could not have his wish. Instead, as he explained to Henry Laurens, he had to find food for hungry soldiers, clothes for the naked, and medicine for the sick. These were familiar tasks, and he went about them with his customary vigor. For several weeks, nothing worked, his troops suffered even more, and civilians in Connecticut and New Jersey complained more than usual about the "calls" on them for meat and flour. The "calls" were actually impressments, and though Washington almost always ordered that warrants for payment for these provisions be given (though almost always the payment was to be made in the future), he knew that the process of acquisition irritated those providing the supplies.

No one was more irritated than his troops, who, in the winter, had resorted to plundering people near their camps. Washington feared another mutiny and hated, though he understood, the plundering. To forestall open mutiny, he took action in May that violated his respect for propriety and law: He ordered that funds sent by the Massachusetts government as pay for its soldiers should not be used for that purpose but instead spent on provisions for the entire army. Washington had complained openly to Congress for years about support for the army, but his pronouncement that the army was at the end of its tether was new in its bleakness.[18]

The French failure in Virginia in March introduced its own sort of bleakness and reinforced Washington's feeling that the game might be up. Once greeted as indispensable allies, the French seemed frozen in their position. This appearance may have had its origins in French perceptions of American weakness; whatever the case, Washington, in early May, though not willing to give up on the French, regarded them with little confidence.

As Washington was musing over impending disaster, Rochambeau wrote on May 11 asking for a meeting and, to Washington's surprise, indicated that he was now willing to join his army to the American one for an attack on New York. Rochambeau's change of mind owed much to the reports his son, the Vicomte de Rochambeau, had recently brought him from Paris. His superiors may have found wisdom in Washington's designs on New York, but more likely they had come to favor a movement against the British in the southern states. Their preferences, shared by Rochambeau, continued to be based on the value of the West Indies, and they had decided to strengthen their navy there. Admiral François Joseph Paul de Grasse, the Comte de Grasse, would soon sail with a major force to the French islands, intending to make at least a short foray to Chesapeake Bay. Rochambeau did not reveal his own or de Grasse's preferences in his first letter to Washington about the new strategy.[19]

Washington set out on May 18 for Wethersfield, Connecticut, where the meeting was to be held. He took with him Henry Knox, who commanded the artillery for the army, and the brilliant French engineer Brigadier General Louis Lebègue Duportail, who had come to America four years earlier and who had more than proved his worth. The American group arrived at Wethersfield a day later to discover that Rochambeau and his party had not yet made their appearance. Rochambeau rode in with Chastellux two days later; Admiral Barras, now the commander of the French squadron in Rhode Island, did not attend.

Washington's summary of his discussions with Rochambeau is not deeply revealing except on one point: he was committed to a New York operation—"our object is New York"—and opposed to a shift of French and American forces to the South. Rochambeau agreed to the strategy and declared his intention of marching his army to the North River. Privately, however, he disagreed and wrote to de Grasse in the West Indies, recommending that the French fleet make its weight felt in the Chesapeake—not in New York waters.[20]

The reasoning behind an attack on New York was entirely Washington's: The British in recent months had weakened their defenses around New York through successive detachments to the South. Of course, if they successfully conquered the rebels in the Chesapeake, they could return these troops to the city. Moving American troops to the South had by this time little appeal to Washington, who commented on the wastefulness of such action, which wore out the troops and was costly in money and supplies. Besides, as he noted in his diary, northern soldiers were disinclined to make the move—the march would be long, and when they arrived they would find a climate not to their liking.[21]

Rochambeau, in his uneasiness about an attack on New York, had also raised questions about abandoning the base in Rhode Island; on this score, Barras echoed his colleague's doubts. The navy had built up a store of supplies in Newport, and both army and navy had weapons, including heavy guns, there. Guns and supplies would be cumbersome to move, but they could not be abandoned. Rochambeau proposed that at least five hundred troops be left there when the march to New York was undertaken. Washington agreed, and over the next few weeks the number to hold in Rhode Island was settled.[22]

Three days after the conference ended, a letter from John Laurens, still in Paris, arrived that reassured Washington that Admiral de Grasse would be coming to America. Laurens also reported that the French would provide six million livres but did not say whether this sum would be a loan or a gift. Reassurance was not certainty: In early June, Washington heard from Rochambeau that he had suggested to de Grasse that after the navy delivered a "great stroke" against the British in the Chesapeake, it should come to New York with five to six thousand men for the long-desired attack there, but this statement to de Grasse was not thunderous endorsement of the New York operation that assumed first place in Washington's plans, and in fact Rochambeau did not report all that he had written to de Grasse. The substance of his communication made clear his doubts about the New York operation and indicated that his own study of strategy at this point led him to think that the Chesapeake should be the place to strike.[23]

Washington seems early on to have caught the hints that the French favored a shift southward and, with Rochambeau's unenthusiastic letter in hand, noted in response that perhaps it would be best if the decision about the target of de Grasse's effort were made after more was known of the strength of the British fleet in American waters. From the time of the French entry into the war, Washington had insisted that their military force should not be ventured unless it had naval supremacy. This belief—a strategic principle for him—defined his recommendations now, and he made his argument without reminding the French that, two months before, they had such superiority on the sea and failed to use it.[24]

His eyes remained fixed on New York even as he forced himself to think of the Chesapeake. The French army marched in from Newport to a staging ground at Dobbs Ferry on July 6, with the American army nearby. They looked like professional soldiers dressed in clean uniforms, carrying weapons they obviously knew how to use. The Americans, shabby and sometimes bare naked, were impressed. Two weeks later, on July 19, at a conference at Dobbs Ferry, Rochambeau pressed Washington for a clear understanding of where his combined force would be used. The answer he received did not please him: Washington's response was that it was not possible to "fix a definitive plan" for the campaign. Where the combined force would fight depended upon the number of troops and ships de Grasse brought with him— their strength and that of the enemy. If de Grasse could remain along the coast of the mainland and force his way into New York Harbor, and provided that the British were in a divided condition, New York should be "our primary objective." But if he brought no troops, a limited operation in Virginia would have to do.[25]

Two days after the conference at Dobbs Ferry, Washington wrote de Grasse telling him of his eagerness to see the French fleet off the coast. His hope for the arrival of the French fleet could not have surprised de Grasse, but Washington explained it by reporting that Rochambeau's army was now tied in with the Americans, with the joint force stretching down the Hudson River to the Bronx. Facing them, the British had about five thousand regulars (English and German) and perhaps three thousand loyalist militia. There were only six British ships of the line in the harbor. Their dispositions, he implied, were not strong, and this led him to believe that there should be no change in the plan to take New York—unless the British recognized the danger and returned troops from Virginia.[26]

At this time, late July and early August 1781, Washington struggled to anticipate not only British intentions but those of the French as well. His desire to strike at the enemy's weakest point was undercut by his ignorance of what his ally intended to do. In fact, he did not even know where de Grasse was, and where de Grasse would use his fleet was equally unclear. Washington knew that Barras still sat in Rhode Island and seemed determined to remain there, despite the agreement reached at Wethersfield that he should sail his ships to Boston. Of course, it was obvious that if Barras should join his squadron to de Grasse's, French naval superiority in American waters might be attained.

The French had to be dealt with carefully, because of tension between its two naval commanders in America. Barras was senior to de Grasse in service, but de Grasse had recently received promotion, making him higher in rank. As one who had not served as long as Barras, he hesitated to order him to bring his Rhode Island fleet southward. Barras, in any case, did not want to serve under his former junior colleague and made his distaste for such a position clear by declaring that he was considering sailing not to New York or the Chesapeake or the West Indies, but in an opposite direction—to Newfoundland.

Watching conditions that threatened turmoil, Washington attempted to calm them and to keep his strategy responsive to changing circumstances. In mid-August he suggested to Barras that he add his ships to de Grasse's. The British seemed to have sent Admiral Robert Digby and a squadron of ships to reinforce commanders—he mentioned Graves and Rodney—in America. At the time he wrote Barras, he expected that Henry Clinton would be reinforced by troops sent up the coast from Virginia, and he had learned that transports had just arrived in New York from Europe with several thousand Hessian soldiers.[27]

Lafayette at this time led a small American army in Virginia. Washington had attempted to advise him during the year on how to defend the state against the British army there, led by Major General William Phillips until his death, in May 1781. In the months since Benedict Arnold's arrival at the beginning of the year with around two thousand troops, Virginia had seen much campaigning, with the Americans on the run and seeking a way to stop a British rampage. Lafayette, aided by Baron Steuben, who was sent by Washington to infuse the Virginia militia with discipline, had held Arnold's force off in places, but most of the time he had to yield ground in the face of superior numbers. Those numbers grew in May when Cornwallis arrived. In mid-August, Washington wrote Lafayette with instructions to "prevent" the British from retreating into North Carolina, and to concert measures with de Grasse, who was on his way. By this time, though Washington did not say so to Lafayette, the American effort against New York had been abandoned. The Chesapeake would provide the ground for the combined Franco-American operation he had so badly wanted. New York would have to wait.

On August 17, Washington wrote Admiral de Grasse about the change in strategy, a change, he explained, that owed much to his reading of the balance of forces north and south. The arrival of three thousand Hessian troops gave the enemy an impressive force in New York, and he feared that British troops in the southern states might be on their way to New York. Without a doubt, the French refusal to attempt to take ships across the bar in New York Harbor also played a part in the decision.[28]

Washington was known for his measured judgment, and he rarely if ever acted impulsively. But he could move quickly, and he now demonstrated a capacity for rapid judgment. He wanted to anticipate British strategy as quickly as possible in order to bring French naval power to bear. He might have thought, given his earlier experience with the Comte d'Estaing, that he should get the French into action before they disappeared. Whatever his feelings, he asked de Grasse to think about what the allies should do if they found that the British had the greater part of their army in the Chesapeake, or only a detachment of troops there, or if the British had totally withdrawn their troops. Washington made his own preferences clear: The allies should lose no time in attacking with their "United Force" if the British were there in full strength; and if the British had withdrawn to New York or strengthened Charleston, the allies should send a sizable force southward to confine them to Charleston and prevent them from expanding their ground in South Carolina and Georgia. Whatever the British did, Washington recommended that the allies establish a base for the French fleet at Portsmouth, Virginia. He wanted a permanent station in the Chesapeake.[29]

This last recommendation of a permanent station was made before Washington met de Grasse. He had not yet fully realized that de Grasse intended to remain in the Chesapeake for the shortest possible time. A few weeks later, when Washington met him, his hopes for combined operations were quickly dashed, though de Grasse promised to stay until the end of October.

While wishing for more, Washington settled for less, but he had to make use of his ally almost immediately. The first task was to get the French and his own troops on the road to Virginia. How to do so without revealing to Henry Clinton what they were doing was a question of importance. The march of the two armies from the Hudson could not fail to be observed, but their destination could be concealed for a time. Washington thought that Clinton would suspect that his force on Staten Island might soon be under attack; a few months earlier Washington had planned such an attack, issuing orders to a large number of his commanders to prepare for such a venture.

Clinton's agents had learned of what was planned at that earlier date, and he expected that something similar was afoot now that his enemies had brought their armies together along the Hudson. Another possibility forecast the Americans setting up in New Jersey, close enough to Virginia to give Lafayette support, but Clinton discounted the likelihood that Washington and Rochambeau would continue on to Virginia, where food supplies were low. Besides, if the British controlled Chesapeake Bay, as Clinton thought they would, the Americans and the French could not depend upon supply from the sea. Thus, during these late-summer months, Clinton seemed without fear that his enemy might move to attack Cornwallis. For a few days at least, he may have been fooled by the sight of thirty boats mounted on carriages pulled along by American troops. The natural inference was that no army would encumber itself in this fashion unless it intended to sail them. And where would they sail? A likely answer was from the New Jersey shore across the water to Staten Island. The French added their own note of deception by building large ovens at Chatham, New Jersey, an indication that they were preparing for a long stay there.[30]

Clinton's own state of mind did not permit him to linger long over the question of what Washington and his French allies were up to. He had been convinced for months that his army in New York was in danger, and throughout much of the summer he fretted over how much the navy could do to protect him against attack from the sea. Arbuthnot gave up his command in early July, and though Clinton was happy to see him go, he was no clearer than before about how much naval support he would have.[31]

The march to the Chesapeake began on August 19. Washington wrote de Grasse asking him to send ships up the bay to Head of Elk to meet a portion of the army there for transport to Virginia. He did not expect all to be accommodated, but having several thousand exempted from a march sure to be fatiguing would protect his force. De Grasse obligingly provided ships, as did a number of American ship owners; those soldiers who could not be fitted in simply marched, an action American troops were accustomed to.

Marching troops to the South remained on Washington's mind even as he worried over the seagoing voyages of both de Grasse and the British enemy. Rochambeau literally did not know the way from New York to Virginia, and it was up to Washington to give him information about the best of the roads. This he did, just as earlier he had laid out the easiest routes from Rhode Island to New York.[32]

Logistics, as always, also demanded attention. Feeding troops on the move was more difficult than when they were in garrison—and finding means of carrying supplies was hard wherever the soldiers happened to be. This was no time for constitutional scruples, and Washington, feeling urgency, now authorized the quartermaster general to use force in impressing horses and oxen needed to pull wagons filled with supplies essential to the move. As for the provisions themselves, he depended, with doubts, on Barras to carry at least fifteen hundred barrels of salted meat when he came to the Chesapeake. He had not met Barras and was beginning to wonder if he ever would, a feeling that might have turned to anger had he known that Barras was at this time considering sailing to Halifax, apparently with the idea of an attack all his own. This was a passing fancy and never had a chance of becoming an embarrassing reality.[33]

Rochambeau, always a solid and reliable commander, at last felt he could act under his orders and put his troops in motion on schedule. On September 8, they began to march into Head of Elk. Washington, who had been there for two days, was delighted and greeted his colleague with a warmth and enthusiasm that surprised a French staff officer who was present. Rochambeau soon gave him additional reasons for delight. Washington expected that the American troops, all from northern or eastern states, might bring little spirit to the enterprise in the South, given how they had suffered in the service of their country. To soften their anger at their treatment, he asked Robert Morris, who, as the financial official for Congress, was responsible for providing money, to find specie to give a month's pay to each soldier. Morris tried but failed to come up with the full amount. Rochambeau then came to the rescue again and made up the difference from money he had with him. There is no way to measure the importance of this generosity, but it is clear that the French action contributed strongly to American morale.[34]

For a few days in early September, Washington felt unshackled from the bonds of command. Ships had appeared from the Chesapeake to ferry troops down the bay; other soldiers were well on the march; the French had committed themselves to the operation; de Grasse had arrived; and Cornwallis, who he had feared might turn his army around to attack the Carolinas, once more seemed to be isolating himself—this time on the York River.

Washington's account of these days in his diary does not express either optimism or pessimism; rather, it is, as he almost always was, measured and matter-of-fact. There was an exemption to his usual behavior, however. De Grasse's appearance in the bay on September 5 gave him such delight that he waved his hat and white handkerchief to Rochambeau, who was on board a ship approaching Chester, where Washington had received the news of the French arrival. He did not tell others of this incident, nor did he write of it; but others did, and it explains why he felt it safe now to go home to Mount Vernon for a short visit. He set out on horseback and reached Baltimore on September 8; most of a day was spent there, and then he was soon on horseback again, riding with only a couple of aides to Mount Vernon. This was his first visit since he had ridden to Boston in May 1775 to assume command of what became the Continental Army. Martha Washington had gone to his camp several times in the intervening years, but these few days at home were different, and though Washington said little of them, they strengthened his spirit.[35]

His stay was a short three days, and on September 14 he rode to Williamsburg to supervise the preparation of the combined army. The next day he wrote de Grasse "to block up Lord Cornwallis in York River," a wish—certainly not an order—given his uncertainty about where the French fleet was. While wondering about de Grasse's position, he found Lafayette in Williamsburg; the two men met as a father and son might greet each other after a long separation. Lafayette's arms embraced Washington as his affection flooded out, and Washington, we may be certain, took more than ordinary comfort in the gesture. That evening, another French aristocrat, the Marquis de Saint-Simon, the commander of the French soldiers carried by de Grasse, gave a "rich supper" for Washington. The company included several of the important leaders of both armies, and Washington received the plaudits of all.[36]

De Grasse had vanished for a good reason: to fight the British for control of the waters of the bay. The results of the shooting were affected by bad weather—a minor storm, in fact—and neither the British, led by Admiral Thomas Graves, who had come down from New York, nor the French enjoyed a triumph in their brief clash in open waters. But the French retained control of the bay, a point driven home when Admiral Barras, untouched by the battle between de Grasse and Graves, slipped into the Chesapeake after the naval battle had ended with a cargo of heavy artillery and provisions. His arrival also added eight ships of the line to the twenty-eight under de Grasse.

On returning to the bay, de Grasse wrote Washington that he wanted a meeting with his American and French colleagues. Washington did not resist this request—he himself had requested it earlier—and on September 17, he, Rochambeau, Henry Knox, and Louis Duportail, plus many staff officers, set sail from Williamsburg for Lynnhaven Bay, sixty miles away, where de Grasse awaited them on the *Ville de Paris,* his flagship, which was at anchor along with thirty-one ships of the line. De Grasse provided their transportation, a handsome launch that had been captured from the British. The voyage took them down the James River and across the bay: They did not arrive in quiet, as de Grasse put on a great ceremony and naval parade in their honor.[37]

The conference itself did not last long: De Grasse seemed most concerned that the Americans understood that he could not loiter in the Chesapeake, though when pressed by Washington to remain until the British surrendered, he reported that his orders were to leave no later than mid-October. Washington's concern was that the French keep their naval power and army contingent at Yorktown long enough for a conventional siege to be mounted. A siege was preferable to an all-out assault, because it would be less costly in bloodshed. The deadline before November for de Grasse's departure seemed to promise time for such siege operations. Reassured on this score, Washington asked that French frigates sail up the York to cut off British escape and to deny them access to foodstuffs if they stayed put. De Grasse refused, saying that his ships would be in great danger from British guns along the river. He also would not make his ships available for operation against the British in the Carolinas if the siege was of short duration. Washington also pushed for help in taking back Charleston. De Grasse's refusal proved easier to accept when he offered the use of two thousand seamen and a supply of powder should the Virginia siege fail and a major assault prove necessary.

Throughout the meeting, Washington's impression of de Grasse gradually seemed to improve. The French admiral's style was far more demonstrative than Rochambeau's, but tact, or courtesy, found only restricted space in it. He did not hide his belief that he had, in coming to the Chesapeake, already done "more than could be expected."

Whatever the impression created by de Grasse's attitude, Washington and Rochambeau could not have been less than pleased at the farewell the sailors in the fleet gave them. First, the officers of the *Ville de Paris* made their way into the launch by the dozens to bid Washington goodbye. Sunset approached before they cleared the coast, and as the launch moved through the fleet on course for home, several hundred sailors clung to masts and yards and, holding muskets, fired them in tribute to the visitors—most particularly, it is likely, to General Washington. It was an astonishing sight to Washington, and its flash and thunder found an echo in the ships' cannon, shot off in a recognition that roared.

That demonstration was the best part of the return trip. For the weather shared no admiration of the occupants of the launch. A storm discovered the boat and pounded it with wind and rain. At times it faced a headwind and at other times no wind; some release was found in an inlet along the shore, but the winds relented only occasionally. Three days later the party went ashore at Williamsburg.

Washington remained buoyant, a feeling he almost never experienced, when he reflected on the conference and the strength de Grasse added to the armies arriving from New York. His army had made the journey largely intact, though he had feared that desertions and sickness would rob it of its power. In fact the Continental Army seemed prepared to fight its way into Yorktown. The prospects for success, he wrote, are "as favorable as could possibly have been expected."[38]

Then came a letter written September 23 by de Grasse, who apparently was not the brave seaman Washington thought he was. The letter informed Washington that the French would be sailing their fleet out of the bay; it seems that they had learned that the British squadron in New York had been reinforced, perhaps by as many as ten ships of the line. De Grasse now reported that he would clear out from the Chesapeake and seek maneuvering room on the open sea. Two ships would be left at the mouth of the York River.

De Grasse had lost his bearings; his mind seemed disordered; he imagined the British squadron in New York roaring down on his fleet. Seeking maneuvering room from which to fight a British fleet sitting in New York was one course of action. In a battle that he imagined, the fighting might drive us "leeward and put it beyond our power to return." In such a case he would reclaim the troops he had brought and had promised Washington he could use. In still another unmoored speculation, he considered sailing to New York to block the enemy's fleet in New York Harbor.

This message reeked of indecision and perhaps panic, hardly the stuff that made heroes. Washington, appalled at the exposure of intellectual and moral weakness in de Grasse's letter, wrote back immediately, pointing out the strategic value of the French squadron in the Yorktown operation. What Washington wrote constituted a short but telling lesson in strategic thinking. He reminded de Grasse of what the presence of the fleet meant to the campaign. The fleet was central to the allies' efforts, even if it did not have to fight. Stationed in the bay, it limited the British effort to deny food and other supplies to the American army. It held the British in place and prevented them from reinforcing their strongpoints. Left unsaid was an analysis of the importance of the French troops carried in de Grasse's ships.[39]

What Washington left no doubt about was the importance of French naval power to the campaign for Yorktown and the strategic place the Chesapeake held for the progress of the war. In the end, this linkage in his argument for holding the de Grasse fleet in place may have been decisive. De Grasse's departure from the bay, he wrote, "would be not only the disgrace and loss of renouncing an enterprise," but it might lead to the disbanding of the army. And success in the enterprise "must necessarily go a great way towards terminating the war." Put another way, what Washington said about the context of the move on Yorktown was that if "the present opportunity should be missed . . . no future day can restore us a similar occasion for striking a decisive blow . . . [and] an honorable peace will be more remote than ever."

Lafayette carried this letter to de Grasse. Two days later, on September 27, Washington, on receiving a letter from de Grasse promising to stay, wrote that de Grasse's resolution "proves a great Mind knows how to make personal Sacrifices to secure an important general Good."[40]

De Grasse did not deserve such praise, but he had, with assistance, overcome his near panic. There was no guarantee that he would not change his mind. In any case, Washington was determined to use the opportunity that Cornwallis's immobility gave him. The next step was clear: Move the Franco-American force into position and strike the enemy.

11

Yorktown

The British sat nearby, apparently satisfied and even complacent, after raiding Virginia. But Cornwallis, who had arrived in Virginia on May 20 with a much-depleted army, was anything but satisfied. He had marched through the Carolinas seeking battle with Nathanael Greene, and when in mid-March 1781 he got his wish at Guilford Courthouse, he won the battle, or at least controlled the ground on which it was fought, with Greene in retreat. But he had almost lost his army. He went into the battle with around two thousand men and came out with fewer than fifteen hundred. Earlier combat with Greene had also killed many of his troops, who were near exhaustion when Guilford Courthouse ended. His soldiers were also hungry and in tatters after slogging hundreds of miles through the rough country that made up the Carolinas.

Sometime in these days of bleakness, Cornwallis had decided that the key to ending the war lay in Virginia. So off he and his men went, marching to join the army already there, which he believed was commanded by his old friend William Phillips. When he arrived on May 20, he was told that Phillips had died five days earlier.

Cornwallis now commanded the entire army in Virginia. He seemed confused for a short time by his situation: Phillips's death was a hard blow for him, and though in Virginia his military situation seemed both better—he now headed an army of around seven thousand—and worse, for his military chief, Henry Clinton, remained the same. Years before, he had shared Phillips's delight at being paired with Clinton: When the three officers were younger, Phillips had written of their friendship in these terms: "How we should agree, how act, how triumph, how love one another!" Now Phillips was dead, and Cornwallis and Clinton did not love one another. They were so estranged that

Cornwallis did not even keep his superior informed of his movements in the Carolinas, and he did not tell Clinton of his march to Virginia until late May.[1]

Clinton had his own problems. The most immediate continued to be Admiral Arbuthnot. He and Arbuthnot had long since passed the point where they could plan, let alone carry out, joint operations. Theirs remained an ugly relationship—and the one Clinton had with his own superior, Lord George Germain, the colonial secretary, had even less beauty.

The Atlantic Ocean imposed part of the difficulty Clinton and Germain had with one another. The distance made communication treacherous—a letter sent to Germain based on information at hand often became irrelevant, because the information, reliable when it left Virginia for Germain in England, no longer described reality in Clinton's America. Clinton did not always tell Germain of the conditions he faced in fighting Washington. Germain had little skill in making his wishes clear and little tact in expressing them, and Clinton's tender spirit led him to resent almost any opinion Germain offered about the war in America; the resentment soon attained a heat that made him incapable of understanding what lay behind Germain's efforts to exercise his authority. Two years earlier, in 1779, he had protested to Germain with a directness not ordinarily found in a general's communications with his superiors. The heart of his complaint was that he was expected to act in impossible ways, given his limited strength. Such expectations carried the assumption that he would be blamed if "I should adopt other measures and fail; and, should I follow that system with success, I appear to have no merit." He was on American ground, he reminded Germain—"I am on the spot. The earliest and most exact intelligence on every point ought naturally, from my situation, to reach me." Was Germain, he asked, not prone to "adopt the ill digested or interested suggestions of people who cannot be competent judges of the subject, and puzzle me by hinting wishes with which I cannot agree yet am loath to disregard?" The conclusion to this blunt analysis was explosive: "For God's sake, my Lord, if you wish me to do anything, leave me to myself and let me adapt my effects to the hourly change of circumstances. If not, tie me down to a certain point and take the risk of my want of success."[2]

Germain obviously did not have great confidence in Clinton, and he served in a cabinet that shared his doubts about the American war and its commander. Most did not understand the situation, but those who thought they did often failed to see the linkages between campaigns in the West Indies and those on the American continent. In 1781, Britain faced political problems at home, a growing threat on the European continent, and in the English colonies in America an opposition that refused to give up, no matter how depleted its army became.

In spring, Germain gradually came to see that the French were about to increase their efforts in the West Indies and on the American continent. When he received word that de Grasse had sailed in strength for America, his concern increased. But concern did not become alarm, and his report to Clinton in April that he thought de Grasse's intentions included an appearance at Newport was put in a way best described as "casual." In May, he speculated in a letter to Clinton that the French intended to attack Halifax or, perhaps, Penobscot, in Maine. In his April dispatch he had offered the reassurance that Admiral Rodney would follow de Grasse, implying that Clinton should not worry about the French navy.[3]

Clinton's nerves and his judgment were unsteady at best during the spring and summer, and he so distrusted Admiral Arbuthnot, still the navy chief in America, that he seemed incapable of acting. He had known that Arbuthnot would be recalled, but nothing seemed possible to him until a replacement took over the navy in America.

Cornwallis was not exactly the victim of the disagreements between Germain and Clinton, but the failure of these two to work through their differences about strategy did not help him formulate his own plans. When he arrived in Virginia in May, he understood that he must operate according to the orders that had been given to Phillips. Those orders were to establish a naval base and to unsettle American forces by raiding the countryside. There was a good deal of inventiveness and confusion in such instructions, and they soon underwent frequent revisions because of Clinton's demands that Cornwallis return troops to New York. Clinton did not disguise his dismay at Cornwallis's movement into Virginia, but at the same time he insisted that he exploit the Chesapeake.[4]

The order to find a place for a naval station proved difficult to satisfy, because the naval officers rejected suggestions that they use Portsmouth after it was strengthened and then had to answer claims that

Old Point Comfort was a better spot. While discussions were taking place, the army pursued American units under Lafayette and Steuben and tried to satisfy Clinton's requests that its troops, or some of them, be sent back to New York.

Near the middle of summer, amid a flurry of orders and actions, Cornwallis decided to keep his army intact, pull out units still remaining at Portsmouth, and dig in at Yorktown and at Gloucester Point, across the York River. These sites, he knew, were far from ideal. British generals always preferred the high ground; Yorktown was on low ground. The lay of the land left no choice but to fortify fields exposed to enemy artillery. Nor did the land lend itself to the protection of big ships. Cornwallis had his doubts about his orders, but he resolved to make the best of things, and put his men to digging in as August began.

Washington may have at first resisted the campaign in Virginia, but once he accepted the fact that in order to retain French support he would have to yield to their plan to strike in the Chesapeake, he gave it all the strength of will that he had. He also worked in his usual extraordinary way to make the change in plans effective. He never forgot that the objective of his army was the defeat of the British enemy.

As commander in chief of the French and American armies, he assumed the lead in the great effort to bring on the action that would destroy the enemy. He organized the effort: he told the French how to move their troops from Rhode Island to the South; he saw to it that they took the proper routes; and he helped to deceive Clinton for as long as possible that he and Rochambeau were not going to lead their armies away from New York. When de Grasse threatened to sail his ships out of Chesapeake Bay, he forced him to see that such action would be catastrophic, that it could even mean the loss of the war.

At the end of September, when the siege of Yorktown began, Washington ceded the intellectual leadership of the effort to Rochambeau. The French knew much more about how to conduct a siege than he; Rochambeau had led, or at least participated in, fourteen sieges in Europe, as he and his staff did not hesitate to point out. Washington's pride was not involved, and he did not have to be persuaded to yield to the French prescriptions on how to go about squeezing Cornwallis into surrendering. The Americans needed help, and they followed French instructions about laying out the trenches and redoubts that made up the parallels used to encircle the British.[5]

Rochambeau and his staff felt confident in their knowledge, but most of the senior French officers were not blinded by their own brilliance and recognized that the ragged and apparently undisciplined Americans could fight. The previous six years attested to that. And then there was George Washington, for whom most of the French had developed high regard; he may not have known the intricacies of siege warfare, but he understood war, and he embodied along with that understanding the constituents of greatness. Going into battle with him was for many of the French more than an opportunity to inflict revenge on an old enemy—it was an honor.

To attack Cornwallis's army, Washington had first to move his Franco-American force into position—close quarters with the enemy—from which an assault could be launched. He had expected that once the move to Virginia was completed, there would ensue a short siege followed by an all-out assault by virtually all his infantry. He did not expect the enemy to give up without a great battle.

The final march to Yorktown began at 4:00 A.M. on September 28, what would be a warm, sunny day. The French marched at the head of the columns and the Americans followed—both formations on foot, as was the custom. What was different was Washington's decision to place cannon in several places in the column. Ordinarily, horses pulled it along at the rear. There was little chance of the British bringing off a surprise if infantry and artillery were arranged in this fashion.[6]

The column proceeded unmolested and, after a march that saw more than a few men fall out from the oppressive sun, arrived at positions abut two miles from where the British were still digging trenches, redoubts, and emplacements. Cornwallis had not driven his men hard, with the result that his lines were not complete. He half-expected Clinton to reinforce him by bringing much of the army in New York to Virginia on ships; or, if that expectation failed, he nursed a belief that escape beckoned across the river at Gloucester Point, where he had placed Colonel Thomas Dundas's brigade.[7]

Yorktown did not look worth defending. It was a small town—no more than sixty privately occupied houses and several public buildings—located about twelve miles from the mouth of the York

River. The river was a half-mile wide there. Yorktown was on the south side; Gloucester sat across from it. The builders of Yorktown had located the town on a low bluff, and the immediate surface around it was open. The town drew its military importance from its location; though it faced the river, it was vulnerable all the way around, from the land as well as from the water.[8]

Because the ground was not covered by woods or other obstacles, it could not be crossed by infantry without severe losses. A siege, however, could protect men on foot, provided that they advanced through trenches dug in parallels zigzagging toward the enemy. The British were in the process of finishing two lines of trenches and redoubts when the siege began. Their artillery was placed along these fortifications— the farthest about twelve hundred yards from the town. Several hundred yards farther out from the town, the allies—the French on the left, Americans on the right—swung their parallel, soon a semicircle, pressing on their enemy.

The evening after, September 29, Cornwallis received a dispatch by packet boat from Clinton, reporting that by October 5 he would send a force of five thousand men to come to Cornwallis's aid. That information helped Cornwallis to decide to consolidate his forces in order to preserve them for a joint attack with the reinforcing army apparently promised by Clinton. He therefore ordered the outer line abandoned and the troops to pull back closer to the town. Only two heavily fortified positions on the outer line would be held: two redoubts near its east end and the so-called Fusiliers' Redoubt on the west.[9]

For Washington, the beginning of the move to Yorktown on September 28 must have seemed like just another day. Before the march stepped out, he wrote letters and undoubtedly read even more that he had received. The most important of those he wrote was to the Board of War, in Philadelphia, in which he enclosed an appeal from Dr. James Craik for blankets to cover wounded soldiers in the army's hospital. Washington's sympathy for these men is evident—"poor fellows," he called them, and added that if the blankets were not provided, "their lives will be Sported with in the most Distressing Manner."[10]

He slept under a tree that night, several hundred yards from the British, and the next day, after meeting with Rochambeau, he issued orders for organizing a large working party to construct a fortified line for the Americans. The French handled their part in establishing fortifications for themselves, but in a fashion agreeable to American colleagues.

Although Washington deferred to Rochambeau's judgment on the placement of the allies' lines, he did not relinquish his command or his control. Rather, he acted much as usual, giving orders and forcing the action. The opening week of the siege did not find him ordering his commanders to attack across the front. He made certain, however, that men digging the trenches and throwing up the emplacements were protected. As a result, there were firefights here and there along the lines as both sides patrolled in front of the works that were taking form.[11]

Washington's skill in preparation for the battles to come was much in evidence. He issued the "Regulations for the Service of the Siege," a set of prescriptions for the making of emplacements and trenches, the dimensions of gabions, fascines, and hurdles, the manning of trenches, their relief, including the assignment of officers—and much more.[12] The procedure for the relief of units in the trenches required the relieving unit to march in with "Drums beating [and] Colours flying," an obvious concession to the code of gallantry favored by gentlemen who had not been shot at much. This procedure of relief proved more complicated than the simple instruction implied—it was dangerous because it aroused the interest of British artillerymen only a few hundred yards away. These soldiers fired their cannon at these attractive stretches of the American trenches, and they inflicted casualties on troops, both those being relieved and those assuming their places.[13]

Several of the Americans seemed not to care about safety. One, a militiaman, climbed onto the parapet, a fortification recently built, and shouted that he would not "dodge for the buggers," that is, the British gun crews firing at him. He "damned his soul" if he would, and stood and attempted to strike with his spade every cannon ball that came his way. He did not last long in this action, as one of the projectiles hit him and, as an American officer who stood watching said, "put an end to his capers."[14]

Such behavior did not discourage others. Alexander Hamilton, a lieutenant colonel now commanding his own brigade, ordered Captain James, a company commander, to take a chance that risked the lives of an entire unit. Captain Duncan described the action in his diary:

His company arrived at the relief point and planted their colors. The next movement, he said, "was rather extraordinary. We were ordered to mount the bank, front the enemy, and there by word of command go through all the ceremony of soldiery, ordering and grounding our arms; and although the enemy had been firing a little before, they did not now give us a single shot." Captain Duncan, a little astonished himself, remarked that the British silence at this display probably grew from astonishment at the spectacle. Perhaps so, though more likely the British officers watching the American performance did not dismiss it as insanity but admired it, and may even have wished that they had ordered something like it themselves. Duncan was not so kind, but remarked that Hamilton, "one of the first officers in the American army," in this instance "wantonly exposed the lives of his men." Perhaps Hamilton, who surely enjoyed this performance, later thought more about the recklessness of what he had ordered. His letters to Elizabeth and others about the campaign do not mention it, for according to the code he and others of his status lived by, telling of such an exploit might sully the glory of it. Rochambeau, who soon learned that the regulation calling for the display of drums and flags when one unit relieved another endangered lives, repudiated the practice— "vainglory," his aide Baron Ludwig von Closen called it—and ordered that "from now on the trench would be relieved in absolute silence; even the hour was changed."[15]

Washington wrote nothing that survives about it, but that he quietly enforced a practice similar to Rochambeau's is likely. He could not allow such excesses to distract him (and he doubtless realized that he should not have approved the original procedure of relief of working parties). He had other examples of extravagant behavior to deal with in these early days of the campaign, at least one of which involved a court-martial. A Captain Duffy was charged with attempting to stab a fellow officer, Captain Ballard, with a sword. Failing in the attempt, he fired a pistol at him. The pistol, according to the records of the case, belonged not to Duffy but to a third officer, Captain Brewer, who had been asked by Ballard to find an "amicable settlement" to the Duffy-Ballard "quarrel." Brewer obviously did not succeed, whereupon Duffy "snapped"—that is, pulled the trigger—at him. This time the pistol did not fire, and Duffy was brought to a court-martial (presumably his fate whether the pistol had discharged or not). He was thrown out of the service for his trouble, with all concerned, we might assume, feeling great satisfaction. There is little chance that Washington attended the legal proceedings, and no doubt that he approved the sentence with ease.[16]

The main purpose of the siege proceeded without great notice of such conduct. Cornwallis's army did not really trouble the work of the besiegers, and the full opening of the first parallel occurred on October 6. A week later, on October 11, the second parallel was completed, only three hundred yards from British emplacements. The allied artillery had by this time been fixed in firing positions and was blasting the British and German enemy in theirs. Getting the heavy artillery into firing positions had been slowed by a shortage of horses to move them, but once emplaced, it proved devastating. In a sense the British troops paid with their lives for Cornwallis's lack of judgment in establishing shallow trenches.[17]

But the British did strike back, with "a galling Fire," as Washington described it to Nathanael Greene, and inflicted "a more considerable loss" than expected on the allied army. The British lacked the heavy siege artillery that the Americans used to such effect, and soon lost the *Charon,* a frigate with forty-four guns, just off the town, where it had lurked in the river. The sinking of British ships in the river relieved Washington of a major concern: the possibility that Cornwallis would call on them to ferry his army to Gloucester, from which he might escape to march northward in an attempt to join Clinton. (Presumably Clinton would move at least a part of his New York force down to link up with Cornwallis.) Washington, who thought ahead and in anticipation of what his enemy might do, had for some days attempted to persuade de Grasse to station ships from his fleet close off Yorktown to prevent such a British move. He also explained that a naval bombardment by de Grasse's ships would help the French troops on land. De Grasse, however, had refused, saying he feared British fireships. His preference for a few days at least was to sail his ships upriver, far from Yorktown, a desire he did not explain to his American allies.[18]

Washington followed up on the heavy fire on British lines with an order for assaults on two redoubts near the river on the east side of the town. Taking these two fortifications was necessary, as they blocked the full extension of the second parallel. The French in Baron Viomenal's command, though led by Colonel de Deaux, were assigned responsibility for the redoubt on the left; the Americans, under the general command of Lafayette and headed by Lieutenant Colonel Alexander Hamilton, had responsibility for the second redoubt, about a quarter-mile to the right, near the river. Each corps, French and American, was composed of about four hundred men, with several hundred others in reserve.

At about 8:00 P.M., the two assaults began. The Americans faced a smaller force, about seventy men. Carrying unloaded muskets with fixed bayonets, they smashed through the abatis fronting the redoubt and in about ten minutes captured it. Their losses were light—nine dead, thirty-one wounded—in part because John Laurens, leading a small detachment, slipped around the face of the redoubt and entered it from the rear. The British put up a good fight but surrendered fairly quickly. The French at number 9, as the redoubt was called, ran up against a better-prepared fortification. It had not been as badly damaged as number 10 in the days preceding the attack, and the obstructions covering it at the front seem to have been deeper. The French artificers, however, cleared the tangle of trees, brush, and fascines covering the place, and their troops went over the top in a grand rush. There was more musket fire from both sides, but the defenders surrendered almost as soon as the French infantry entered their works.[19]

Both assaults had succeeded with light casualties, even considering the fierceness of the fight. Washington expected a response, and Cornwallis delivered it the next day, a raid of his own that was thrown back with little difficulty. The shelling of British positions resumed immediately, and the next night, desperate to escape, Cornwallis began loading boats with his troops for a crossing to Gloucester Point. In darkness he had landed about a thousand men when the weather turned foul, and further crossing proved even more dangerous. Cornwallis was not a fool, and in the rain and wind he ordered the detachment back to Yorktown. The allies continued to batter his lines that day, with a promise of even more death and suffering.[20]

On October 17, after twenty days of siege and with no help from Clinton imminent, Cornwallis sent an officer to Washington to conduct negotiations for surrender. At the beginning of the discussions, Cornwallis hoped that Washington might grant parole to his soldiers. Washington disabused him of any such notion, insisting that surrender meant that the British and German soldiers would be prisoners of war.

After a day of talk, Washington's terms were accepted, and on October 19 the formal ceremony of surrender was held.[21]

Washington undoubtedly took satisfaction at this transaction that saw a British army surrender—and on his terms. Yet though he was pleased, he made no demonstration of it—no vainglorious sentiments left his lips, and no prideful letters came from his pen. Nor did he attempt to humiliate British officers and men. He had always respected his enemy in the Revolution, with the possible exception of the German commanders at Trenton and British ministers and their king in England.

The British commander and his soldiers nevertheless felt humiliation at whatever Washington intended on October 19. The ceremony took place at 2:00 P.M., with the British soldiers, aside from the incapacitated wounded, marched from their positions in Yorktown, muskets on their shoulders, between two detachments of French and American troops. The two lines were spaced to permit the passage of several files, but even with this separation, it must have felt like a gauntlet. A British band played a dirge, probably "The World Turned Upside Down," music matched by sad and angry British faces, though the Hessian and Anspach regiments were probably largely impassive. The French line on the British right showed off clean and crisp infantry, dressed in white uniforms, well turned out in every respect. The Americans, the poor country cousins, badly dressed and not always of disciplined bearing, waited in a second line across from the French. Washington, Rochambeau, Admiral Barras (de Grasse did not leave his ship), General Benjamin Lincoln, who had given up Charleston the year before, and assorted staff officers sat quietly on their horses. They had expected Cornwallis to lead his army out, but—under what Baron von Closen called "the pretext of an indisposition" he excused himself from this sad ceremony, and Brigadier General Charles O'Hara served in his stead.

When General O'Hara arrived where Washington and his colleagues sat astride their horses, he attempted first to present his sword to Rochambeau, who refused it and pointed to Washington as the allies' commander. Washington, probably miffed at Cornwallis's absence, pointed to Lincoln, who took the sword, only to return it immediately. The British soldiers were then ordered to leave their weapons in a pile nearby, an action they performed with ill grace, attempting to break their muskets by forcefully throwing them to the ground. American officers soon stopped this petulance and the surrender was completed.[22]

Washington gave a dinner for Cornwallis that night, with Rochambeau and senior French and American general officers present. Brigadier General O'Hara again filled in for his commander. The occasion, though more comfortable, apparently never gave way to the type of warm exchange of sentiments so common to gatherings of European officers. The restraint in such a gathering was not present elsewhere in the weeks following.

Washington dispatched Colonel Tench Tilghman, one of his favorite aides, to Philadelphia the next day with the news of the surrender. It was greeted with joy there, and almost everywhere in America there were grand celebrations. The reactions in Britain were understandably quite different: Lord North's exclamation at hearing the news—"O' God, it is all over"—described his administration more accurately than it did the war. Washington was concerned that Americans would assume that Yorktown ended the need for full support of an army; that assumption was indeed to plague the effort Washington and others were to make in the next two years.[23]

12

The War's End

Despite its greatness, Washington's victory at Yorktown set off conflicting impulses within him. One was a sense of caution, almost a distrust of the event itself. Most Americans around him on his staff and in the army, as well as civilians all over the country, assumed that Cornwallis's surrender meant that the war was over. Such a feeling also existed across the Atlantic in British governing circles, with at least one powerful exception: George III dissented from claims of its importance immediately after the news arrived. For different reasons, Washington agreed with the king that the war would go on.

The sense of caution that so often shaped Washington's attitudes ran up against his hope—a feeling that Yorktown had created promising possibilities leading to peace, if only others could see them. The others in this case were the French, to whom he felt immensely grateful, from Louis XVI on down. He had always respected Rochambeau and had often made his appreciation clear; de Grasse was more difficult to deal with, but Washington's recognition of the necessity of naval supremacy compelled him to thank him for his support in the capture of Yorktown. Gratitude might have been expressed in various ways: Washington threw to the winds his own sense of balance and, with it, his moderate, matter-of-fact style of expression, in favor of the extravagant. It was to de Grasse, he said, that victory at Yorktown should be ascribed. This judgment appeared in a letter Washington wrote to de Grasse on October 28, in which he also praised de Grasse's "mastery of the American Seas" and "the Glory of the French Flag." This characterization was a warm-up to his ultimate accolade: "de Grasse is the Arbiter of the War." He also assured de Grasse of his "attachment to your Glory." These effusions were an example of laying on the flattery with a trowel—and perhaps were necessary. They did not bring out the modesty in de Grasse, nor did they evoke a willingness to undertake an expedition with the Americans against Charleston, Savannah, or New York—all places Washington wished to attack.[1]

The ceremony on the field of surrender was hardly over when Washington began asking that the French provide the naval cover for an attack on Charleston. The French under de Grasse had no desire for such an effort and, putting aside Washington's requests, praise and solid reasoning notwithstanding, sailed off in early November for the West Indies. For a few days before sailing, they made a tentative offer to transport two thousand American soldiers to Wilmington, but soon explained that the French court had ordered the shift of naval forces to the West Indies without further delay. The Americans feared that should the French navy clear out of the Chesapeake too soon, a British squadron rumored to be coming from the south would destroy troops and supplies still near the edges of the bay. This concern failed to move the French, and in early November de Grasse took his ships to the French islands.[2]

That the French navy would remain in North American waters was never more than a faint possibility. For the French, clearing the American states of the British army never assumed the importance that the Americans accorded it. Had Washington commanded without restrictions all the allied forces in North America, including the French fleet, he would have forced the British out of not just Charleston and Savannah, but New York as well. In the plans he announced to the French, Charleston assumed the highest priority. There were several reasons for this ranking: He knew that with Rochambeau's army in Virginia, where it would remain throughout the winter, and de Grasse seemingly committed to the West Indies, the only conceivable chance he had of involving the French lay in persuading them that a southern campaign might be managed within their larger plans. To be sure, a southern campaign had other attractions for Washington. It would please delegates to Congress from the Carolinas, and it would give relief to Nathanael Greene, whose army had fought well at Guilford Courthouse and who now wished to reclaim the southern states for the nation, a design that Washington also believed in. But Washington's deepest desire remained recapturing New York City.[3]

Several historians have commented unfavorably on Washington's attempt to bring about a major move against New York. His judgment, they say, may have been founded on a desire to revenge himself on an enemy that in 1776 drove him from the city in a most humiliating manner. He was caught asleep on Brooklyn Heights, according to this interpretation, and then put to flight up New York Island, his army disorganized and running for its life. The running did not end until he crossed the Delaware River, the remains of his force in tatters. Apparently, if this theory of his defeat is to be believed, he never recovered emotionally and would not until he recaptured New York City.

There is little doubt that Washington felt anger at the British or that his feelings rose to hatred. He had commanded men in New York who suffered and died following his orders, for a cause he believed in without reservation. He knew that he had acted against one of the great powers of the world and that it had acted in ways that would destroy the liberties of a people who asked little of the empire but gave it much. They fought and he fought at their head to protect a liberty that had a long existence in America.

These feelings did not, however, form his understanding of how New York related to American strategy. He had clear ideas about how the war should be fought if it was to bring victory to his country. New York's importance seemed obvious to him, and the British agreed with him. New York had been since 1776 the key to their efforts. Holding it strengthened the ties that connected New England to the Mid-Atlantic states, not just New York State but Pennsylvania and New Jersey, as well as the Chesapeake, including both Virginia and Maryland. The British testified to its importance through much of what they did and how they used its harbor and rivers. Most British troops entered the United States through New York; the major part of the army made its home there and conducted operations through its port. The commander in chief of all British forces made his headquarters in the city. The city also contained the highest number of loyalists. Washington decided early on that he must defeat the British there if independence was to be won. This understanding of the war can be explained in various ways, but the major element in his comprehension rested on judgment—on military realities—not an obsessive desire for revenge.[4]

British intentions concerning the war in 1781 remained unknown to him—and to the British themselves. This uncertainty underlay virtually all that occurred in the next year. As far as danger to their national power was involved, the British government had to calculate how continuing the war with the colonies (as they still referred to the American states) would affect their effort to hold off the French and the Spanish in the West Indies. With the failure, in 1779, of the French and Spanish fleets to bring off an invasion of Britain, that sort of threat faded. They also had to contend with the Dutch, now an important challenger in overseas trade. The war on the North American continent, now entering its seventh year, appeared to have no end—two large armies had surrendered to the rebels, and only two major ports were firmly in imperial hands. Generals Gage, Howe, Clinton, Cornwallis, and Burgoyne had all given their best, only to see their efforts yield to near collapse, and two of their number captured. A similar list of failed admirals could also be drawn up—Lord Richard Howe, Marriot Arbuthnot, and Thomas Graves, for example. They had fought well at times (when they fought), but none had been able to bring Britain's full naval power to bear. Perhaps accidents, bad luck, and the weather had undone their fleets more than the French navy had, but even when their ships had the weather gage in a strategic sense, they somehow allowed their superiority to fade away. The ragtag American army, often dismissed by the regulars as amateurs, seems to have grown in skill even as its troops suffered from a lack of supplies. By 1782, several British leaders were coming to see that leadership was something the Continental Army did not lack. George Washington's toughness, his endurance, impressed more and more of the enemy.[5]

The circumstances shaping the war were grim enough, but at the beginning of 1782, the British had also to face the fact that the French had begun to exert themselves both on the North American continent and on the sea. Taken together, these realities and recent history offered a bleak future for Britain at war. It was not only Lord North who believed it was all over—and, as the realists in Britain recognized, there was little reason not to accept the American claim to independence, no matter how that admission soured the mouth.

Washington expected the worst from the British as he pondered a future that now seemed simpler, lacking, as it did, a large enemy force in the Chesapeake. The British, he thought, might trick the Americans in a peace treaty with terms that allowed them to renege on a recognition of independence; or they might mount a new military campaign while supposedly they negotiated peace. For a few weeks after Yorktown, he had smaller matters to deal with. The easiest to face was presented by General Horatio Gates, still in disgrace and wanting something to do in the war. He might be ignored, but Congress could not, and it wanted Washington to do something with Gates. The difficulty in satisfying both Gates and Congress lay in the history of the Battle of Camden. There, Gates had run, not stopping for about sixty miles. What Congress might have in mind was not clear, though as Gates wrote in a letter to Washington, Congress intended that he should be "employed in service" as Washington "should direct." But Gates also told his old commander in this letter that he would not serve until the "Stigma" under which he "laboured" was "removed." How Washington might fetch a stain-free reputation out of the catastrophe of Camden, Gates did not say, and Washington simply replied that Gates's "circumstances" were "distressing," but he could not direct Congress to provide "relief" to Gates. There the problem sat, with Gates fuming and Washington probably thinking, "You brought this mess on yourself."[6]

Congress's request concerning Gates was a small part of the war, and he had to turn to more immediate problems almost as soon as he saw the troops captured at Yorktown marched off to their camps in Virginia. The French would also stay in Virginia for the winter, and they were under a command that knew how to cope with it. Some duties were pleasant and fulfilled with satisfaction, such as replies to the congratulations on the Yorktown victory sent by government officials in Alexandria and the General Assembly of Maryland. Washington would soon become practiced in accepting with modesty the praise that came to him. (The happy comments occasioned by Yorktown grew into a chorus with the end of the war.)[7]

Bad news soon intruded, though Washington was not deeply affected. It came as a surprise: the death of John Parke Custis, Martha's son. He had fallen ill a short time before Yorktown, though he had been thought to be in good health. George Washington did not care for Jack Custis, but Martha loved the boy, and his death saddened her deeply. Without any false display of grief, Washington gave her as much comfort as possible during their week together.

The new year beckoned—so did Congress—and he and Martha

soon traveled to Philadelphia. He was to remain there throughout the winter, from late November to April 1782, when he made his way back to the army in Newburgh, New York.

Little had been settled in Philadelphia. Congress had established three major committees or boards to act as executive authorities, and Washington as commander in chief was expected to meet with their leaders. The most important of them was the superintendent of finance, Robert Morris, a fascinating figure of great ability but little luck who, after the war, ended his days in a debtors' prison. Morris and a small number of Philadelphia merchants had founded the Bank of Pennsylvania the year before, with the intention of creating an institution that would supply a currency of reliability. Depreciation of congressional and state notes had deprived the army of almost all that it required—weapons, food, and supplies of virtually every kind—and it had made sustaining troops and officers extraordinarily difficult.[8]

Whatever the day brought—whether problems of replacing departing troops, supplying those in camp, dealing with Congress, maintaining the discipline of the army while attempting to keep its morale as high as possible, or performing the other seemingly endless tasks facing a commander—Washington attempted to fathom the future. Quite specifically he considered first whether peace was in the offing and, if it came, what problems it would bring for the army and the new nation.

Washington had also to think of the next campaign while everyone else, including the Congress and the people, thought of a world without the war. De Grasse's departure for the West Indies destroyed the plans Washington had for clearing the southern states of the enemy. Little could be done on any grand scale without naval supremacy—Yorktown had driven that fact home—and Washington was left to think about small-scale operations, which, if nothing else, would serve to keep his troops fresh.[9]

High and dry, he found himself trying to anticipate his enemy's moves. His survey of British strength on land in North America reassured him that his enemy could not mount a major campaign without reinforcement. There was no intelligence from any source that suggested that the British were on the move. Nevertheless, he ordered a review of British strength, with particular attention to the number of soldiers available to them in America, from Halifax to the southern states. New York received a careful look. The conclusion, in May

1782, was that the British forces, including loyalist militia and regulars, numbered thirteen thousand. It was, though "careful," an estimate that could not be relied on with certainty. On the bright side, the loyalist militia had shrunk in size throughout the early months of 1782, and the regulars, nine thousand altogether, seemed to be subject to drainage to the West Indies.[10]

More attention was paid in the review to possible operations than to the size of the enemy. Given the intelligence available to American planners in Washington's military family, the review took on the cast of an exercise in a near vacuum. The memorandum recording possibilities assumed that perhaps a successful siege of New York City could be conducted with twenty-five thousand troops. The Continental Army outside the city had nothing like that figure and lost men as the year went on. The part to be played by Rochambeau's army could not be charted, though in the spring the French had marched and sailed from Virginia to New York. Rochambeau returned to France, and his successor gave no indication of a desire to join Washington in an attack on New York.

Given the number of troops available to him and to the British in New York, Washington concluded that he could not attempt to take the city. Peace was in the air in any case, and the British on New York Island seemed somnolent. He did not trust the British, even when their new commander in America, Sir Guy Carleton, began assuring him that he had no intention of mounting an aggressive campaign. Carleton had arrived in America on May 5, 1782, and a week later Washington's old adversary, Henry Clinton, sailed for home. The communications coming out of the headquarters of the new commander in chief from that point on had a different tone, with no threat discernible.[11]

Washington's primary reaction to this change was one of suspicion laced with dislike, though he knew that he would have to take Carleton seriously on a multitude of matters. But peace, if it was coming, would be decided in Europe, not in the headquarters of the British commander. The war, in a quiet phase in America, he knew, continued in Europe. The issues in play there were complex, and sorting them out could not be done fully from the evidence available to him. To understand them, he relied on friends such as Lafayette and on travelers, newspapers, and occasionally officials in the American Commission in Paris. Congress, too, sometimes passed along information that had come to it, largely from the same European sources.

Washington followed English politics as closely as possible. He could not discover the details of cabinet and parliamentary strife, but his overall grasp was usually accurate. The attitude of the king seemed especially crucial in any decision the government might make, he thought, and he awaited news of the king's speech at the opening of Parliament in 1782. In February, a frigate arrived with a copy.

The speech did not reassure him. The king preferred war to peace, and for several months hence he took comfort from the idea that the colonies in America might agree to independence and yet assume a subordinate status in the empire. How exactly an arrangement of this sort might be devised was not clear, and in any case most British leaders at this time wished to cut their country's losses by giving up the colonies altogether. North resigned his office on March 20, with great relief that at last he could be free of problems that seemed always to defy solutions. The king did not want him to go but finally agreed, and then faced the difficulty of finding a replacement he could stomach. For a short period the solution was Lord Rockingham, a man whom the king despised. But Rockingham died soon after taking office. Then came the customary maneuvers, and the Earl of Shelburne replaced him. Shelburne was widely distrusted by English politicians, known almost as much for his lies as for his ability, but despite his reputation, he knew how to read his king. He seems to have held hopes for a constitutional arrangement that satisfied both Englishmen and Americans, but whatever his hopes and beliefs, he moved so as to satisfy his royal master and Parliament.[12]

After a suggestion by Benjamin Franklin, now one of the members of the peace commission appointed by Congress, both sides agreed to negotiations. Talks were not conducted easily, but by November 30 a preliminary agreement on ending the war had been reached, with plenty of problems left to be decided. The Americans insisted that before they would agree to talk, the British must recognize their independence. Once the British gave in to this requirement, hard bargaining about a whole series of questions got under way. These included the location of boundaries, the Newfoundland and St. Lawrence fisheries, loyalist property, and prewar debts owed "on either side." There were other demands by the Americans, of great interest to Washington, among them that the British withdraw their forces from the United States "with all convenient speed," a requirement that brought all sorts of trouble in the months ahead. Resolution of all these matters came in January 1783, when a final agreement was signed by the negotiators. France and Spain, the two major continental powers at war with Britain, made peace shortly thereafter. Final approval by all sides had been reached by the end of 1783, the American ratification by Congress coming on September 3.[13]

In August 1782, Washington confessed that his revulsion for the enemy continued, a feeling that he could not banish for years afterwards: "From the former infatuation, duplicity, and perverse system of British Policy; I confess I am induced to doubt everything & to suspect everything." Carleton offered reassurance as the talks went on in Paris, but he too suffered from a lack of knowledge of what was being said. No doubt he did not tell Washington everything he knew, but he did report that the king had instructed his ministers to concede independence at the opening of the negotiations. At other points, he claimed to know nothing fresh about the Paris proceedings. During most of the year, this assertion of ignorance rang true. The British in America were not the last to know what was going on in Europe—they were the next to last.

What Washington felt about the British was undoubtedly shared by the officers and men of the Continental Army. These men also harbored suspicions of the Congress in Philadelphia. The uncertainty about the negotiations for peace fed their uncertainty about money owed them by the United States. The Articles of Confederation provided that "All charges of war, and all expenses that shall be incurred for the common defense or general welfare, and allowed by the united states in congress assembled, shall be defrayed out of a common treasury." In practice, this meant that Congress was expected to pay all officers, not including those of the militia, from funds contributed by the states. The states in the Congress had laid out this system but had failed to send money to Congress for the common treasury. Their failure was quite typical of their conduct by 1780, even though it was considered a scandal by the officers and bitterly resented. In that year, Congress gave in to demands that it do something—perhaps without conviction—and resolved to grant pensions for life to officers who remained in service until the end of the war. Such officers would receive pensions of half their regular pay. Where the money would come from for such payments was not clear, and the promise to pay did not bring unanimous agreement—or agreement of any sort from several of the states. Delegates from all the New England states opposed this arrangement, arguing that it forecast the creation of a caste.[14]

Army officers themselves probably held no such fear. Certainly, after the battle of Yorktown, the promise made in 1780 had lost its attractiveness, and in fact seemed by many not to be believed. Those officers who had volunteered their services for the duration of the war had long considered themselves badly treated and even betrayed, and quite naturally began questioning whether pensions promised them when the war ended, as well as pay, would be honored.

Congress had begun making plans for reducing the size of the army and cutting down the officer corps even before peace seemed to be in the offing. When it became known in 1782 that negotiations for peace had begun, sensitivities throbbed, and requests—soon to be demands—were made that Congress pay the soldiers who had served it.

Washington had always worried over what he thought was owed to his officers, but he did not give sustained attention to the matter until Yorktown. The end of the war as a remote possibility now gave way to a feeling that it was coming. He had watched the development of his officers since 1775 with great interest: These men, a varied lot, came from all over the republic, and they were not all of genteel status. But Washington treated them all as if they were gentlemen, and wanted them paid as if they were. Basic fairness required that they receive the pay their rank called for and that they conduct themselves as men of quality. In the army, such a style of conduct imposed standards of dress and rations as well as of leadership. Many officers found that in the army they could not live like gentlemen; they could not even support their families. It was not that they led lives of extravagance in the army, but that they were not paid, on occasion for many months at a time.

After Yorktown, Washington felt forced to complain to Congress about the conditions of life they endured. He had sensed the damage to morale and pride before his officers said anything explicit about such matters. He expected that the chain of command would be respected by everyone in the army, but on these problems of pay and later of pensions, he did not insist that it be observed. He usually communicated his dissatisfactions to Congress, and in the case of matters of such importance, he almost always confined his communication to its president. But increasingly as the war went along, he also wrote members, especially those he knew personally. He avoided language that might embarrass the president of Congress and never sought to undercut his authority.[15]

After Congress created institutions with executive authority, Washington often wrote their secretaries, as they were called. Sometimes his letters carried an angry tone. The secretary of war, Benjamin Lincoln, received the harshest of Washington's protests on behalf of officers in 1782 and 1783. A blast from Washington must have stung, because Lincoln had served under him and had also been recommended to Congress for the secretaryship by him. In August 1782, Washington questioned a newly established policy regarding the issue of rations to continental officers. Rank established the number of such rations an officer might draw, a standard no one protested against. What angered Washington was the slashing of any rations an officer might claim. It was a change that drew deep anger, because officers were badly fed in the best of times, and now the old grievance about quality was expanded to include a reduction of rations authorized. As Washington remarked, this cutting came at a time of deplorable circumstances. "Is it policy," he asked, "is it Justice, to keep a Sore, Constantly gangreened, when no good End is, or possibly can be answered by it?" Six weeks later, he listed the consequences of the new policy for his officers—"want of money" for day-to-day life, debts, loss of credit, distress of families, "bare rations" when civil officers have more. He also noted the loss of pride that congressional action brought in American officers who, faced with the hospitality of their French peers, could not reciprocate and felt humiliated by their plight. And always lurking in the background of these discussions of pay for the officers was the vexing matter of back pay. All such matters seemed especially pressing as the coming of peace appeared more imminent.[16]

Late in the year, as rumors of a peace treaty increased, discontent in the army rose so high that Washington, who had thought of going home to Mount Vernon for the winter, decided to remain with his troops. The soldiers in huts at Newburgh and in camp at West Point were not exactly enjoying their winter quarters but apparently were reconciled to them. Many of their officers were not, among them a number who had requested leave or resigned from the army altogether. The largest number, however, stayed with their soldiers and worried over their pay, which was largely missing, and apparently talked over their chances of obtaining pensions when they left the service.

The most widely shared fear among these officers was that with peace, Congress would order their return to civilian life but not with their back pay in their pockets, and not with any assurance that they would ever receive pensions. The full extent of their response to this fear is not known, but some evidently resolved not to accept the dissolution of the army.

The discussions in Congress at this time about the army's future did not include plans, or even suggestions, for its dissolution. Most members of Congress, in fact, had not thought through what should be done regarding most questions raised by the approaching end of the war. Uncertainty about the negotiations in Paris was prevalent in Congress, which probably had no more information than Washington about what was going on. A very different sort of negotiations had bedeviled Congress for many months—the impost on imports had preoccupied almost everyone. State finances could not be ignored; nor could the difficulty of simply keeping members in Philadelphia as the war seemingly ground down after Yorktown.[17]

A small number of delegates had given thought to the army—not in any narrow sense, but rather as offering a means of strengthening the financial condition of the national government. They pointed out that in dealing with the army, the national government would have to be strengthened. This entailed giving much more power to the Congress, a shift of sovereignty from the states to Congress, in other words. The delegates included Robert Morris, the superintendent of finance; Gouverneur Morris; and Alexander Hamilton. James Madison shared many of their beliefs but was not part of the inner circle. Other delegates did not consider themselves a part of any combination or faction, and the three most active, the two Morrises and Hamilton, differed among themselves on some matters—the need to make peace, for example. Robert Morris had a secretive side, Hamilton was always an independent creature, and Gouverneur Morris could be erratic, even extravagant, in thought and action. All admired Washington and in different ways were his friends.[18]

Hamilton knew more than any of his colleagues in Congress about what went on in the army—for the most part knowledge gained through friends still in the service. He also understood the Congress, a body he appealed to in debates with fellow members to find support for the army. He thought at this time in terms larger than those concerning the morale of its soldiers; a favored focus found him examining circumstances affecting taxation. After much thought and study of how land and "numbers" (population) figured into the levying of taxes, he concluded that the problem was too large and complicated to yield the immediate answer required for doing justice to the army. He did not share this conclusion with Washington, but he did give him a review of the problem he thought his old commander faced.

The problems—Hamilton characterized them as "matters of delicacy and importance"—threatened to become "an embarrassing scene" and might occur "whether we have peace or a continuance of the war." If the war continued, the army, he argued, would have to submit itself to "*defend*" the country; if peace were made, the army would have to "submit itself to *procure justice* to itself," an oblique reference to back pay and pensions. This second option frightened Hamilton more than the first, but both possibilities led him, in this letter to Washington, to insist that nothing promising could happen to the American union without a change in the way the central government was funded. He, like his old commander, wanted a shift in power from the states to the Congress, or to whatever institutions were developed to finance the national government. In this letter of February 13, 1783, he phrased his ideas in language made familiar in the Articles of Confederation and in current discussions of national policy regarding relations between center and periphery. The real problem, apparently concealed by concern about the threat of an angry army, resided in a Congress that could not tax. Washington had made this assumption for years, had stated it in letters to delegates in Congress and to his friends outside of Congress. But he did not do more than adjure his congressional superiors to act; he did not look for more power as commander in chief, nor did he want it, though he suggested that perhaps at times he should have taken part in discussion in Congress. All his instincts, however, were for an army that remained remote from politics. He refused indeed to seize power, as one of his officers urged him to do.[19]

Washington's moral and political instincts are clear in his response to Hamilton's February letter. In his letter of March 4, he drew a clear line between civilian and military authority. His letter also revealed a resolve not to use the army to seize directly the subsistence to keep itself intact. It had been "in one or two instances its own proveditors," an oblique reference to the history of the Republic of Venice—an action he said "would be productive of Civil commotions and end in blood." Washington was almost never shaken in his beliefs or conduct, and he now felt that Hamilton's "apprehensions in case of Peace are greater than there is cause for." But he admitted that he might be mistaken and that "the old leven" is "again beginning to work, under the mask of the most perfect dissimulation & apparent cordiallity." The choice of words in this sentence indicates that he thought that Horatio Gates, who was in camp at this time, probably had given encouragement to whatever unhappiness now existed in the army. As for his own actions, he would follow a moderate course. He told Hamilton that states "cannot, surely, be so devoid of common sense, common honesty, & common policy as to refuse their aid on a full, clear, & candid representation of fact from Congress." Though he did not say so openly, he thought Congress would profit from an "Adjournment" for a few months in order to convey to the states the need for renewed support of national purposes.[20]

Washington, for all his intensity in calling every year of the war for renewed support for the army, seemed curiously uninformed of the feelings of a large number of officers. He also was uninformed about one aspect of money available to keep the revolutionary effort intact. He had apparently been told "from some source or another" that another loan from the Dutch was in prospect, and when it came the army would be able "to rub along." His reactions to Hamilton's letter, with its dire forecast, left him unmoved, perhaps because he had learned from experience that Hamilton sometimes gave way to impulse and emotion. Still, without telling Hamilton, he began to consider the possibility that officers might use violence to obtain "justice" from Congress.[21]

A week later, the possibility seemed more than a prospect. On March 10, Colonel Walter Stewart rode in from Philadelphia, sent by a combination of nonmilitary men—perhaps delegates—to organize army officers for action. Stewart carried a call for a meeting of officers on March 11, at which presumably the group would organize itself into a force avowedly committed to compel Congress to a settlement. The call, later labeled the "First Newburgh Address," offered no specific plan other than the gathering of the officers the next day to make a "last remonstrance." Stewart was housed by General Gates's command, an arrangement that made his appearance even more curious. He had not written the notification of the meeting on March 11; that action had been taken by Major John Anderson, undoubtedly a member of a combination of army officers and others in Philadelphia. The number and names of this group have never been discovered.[22]

Washington read the message brought by Stewart and immediately issued orders prohibiting the meeting scheduled for March 11. To say that he was "horrified" would be to put the matter accurately. He had awakened, if he had been asleep, to the danger that the army was on the verge of becoming a political subversive. No one outside of the instigators of the plan to mobilize the officers believed that the army or the Congress would be served by such a transformation.

But something more than heading off the March 11 meeting seemed required, Washington thought, and he now called a second meeting for March 15, in place of the first, which had not come off. This postponement would give officers time to cool off and to think things through. Ostensibly to give the meeting discipline and substance, he appointed Horatio Gates as moderator. Every line would send at least one officer as its representative.

On the day Washington issued the order convening the meeting on March 15, a second "address" appeared, this one written in camp and carrying a message that informed everyone that General Washington agreed with the critics of Congress and hence had called for the meeting in which grievances could be stated. This second address was a clever and cynical pronouncement, again written by Anderson and intended to trap Washington in a position he never held. By this time, Washington had come to understand the key elements of what he faced. That Stewart had distributed the call for an officers' meeting indicated that he and other officers believed that the army was available for action against Congress.[23]

The meeting was held in a building, one hundred by thirty feet, recently constructed and called the Temple of Virtue. It sat on the west side of the camp, a favorable location, for it faced the camp and was marked near its entrance by a long flagstaff. Its roof was ridged and carried a long gable; its walls and ceiling were plastered, an unusual feature in the cantonments of the Continental Army. The large room, which made up most of the building, was cut by large sash windows. At either end were two smaller rooms, used for several purposes, including sitting courts-martial.

Officers crowded into the main room with an air of expectancy created by the addresses as well as the curious events since their distribution. There had been talk about the army's fate in the months since Yorktown, and the intensity of feeling had grown with Washington's simultaneous actions of canceling one meeting and convening another.

Few, if any, officers expected that he would appear at the meeting. But he had intended to come from the moment he summoned the officers to attend. When the officers had found seats and were awaiting the beginning of the meeting, a door to the room where they sat opened and General Washington strode in. Without any preliminary explanation, he asked Horatio Gates, who was presiding, if he could speak. Gates could not have been pleased to see his commander, nor did he wish to listen to him, but he could not refuse his request. Washington's opening was an angry exclamation: "Gentlemen: By an anonymous summons, an attempt has been made to convene you together—how inconsistent with the rules of propriety!—how unmilitary!—and how subversive of all order and discipline—let the good sence of the Army decide." According to Major J. A. Wright, who was present, Washington appeared "sensibly agitated" as he spoke these words. The agitation did not disappear as he continued, though the passion that accompanied it now focused on the army and the nation it served. Not that officers who were outside of any combination or conspiracy were not afflicted with legitimate fears, he thought; indeed, they might take dangerous action unless Congress acted to provide back pay and pensions. These officers—presumably a majority—feared that when peace came, they would be ordered to disband without any settlement of their accounts. They then would be forced to apply as individuals to authorities set up in Philadelphia by Congress or sent off to audit-

294 · *Washington's Revolution*

ing offices in the states, where they would be sent from board to board "drawing attendance at all, and finally perhaps be postponed until we lose the substance in pursuit of the shadow."[24]

Long concerned about what was being done to the army by the Congress and the states, Washington now thought of what the army might do to the Revolution. There had been suggestions that it simply refuse to continue as the fighting army of the United States or that it withdraw its troops and take up station in the wilderness. The shadowy group in Philadelphia, as well as the one in camp, whispered these ideas. Washington, initially skeptical of the existence of such combinations or at least doubtful of their strength, had continued to assume that, through its suffering and despite its officers' profound uneasiness, it would remain apart from political action. He had thought that Congress would eventually meet its responsibilities, but in March, with Hamilton's warnings and those of others, plus the Newburgh addresses, he confronted an altered political reality.

Washington simply dismissed as unworthy the author responsible for the attempt to persuade the officers to form a conspiracy. He branded "the secret mover" of this scheme, "in which candor and liberality of Sentiment, regard to justice, and love of Country have no part," as guilty of "the blackest designs."

Hamilton had written Washington in February that "An idea is propagated in the army that delicacy carried to an extreme prevents your espousing its interests with sufficient warmth." Washington, always sensitive to any aspersions on his reputation, had not responded to Hamilton then, but now, in this meeting with the officers, he met the charge head-on. His purpose was not primarily to defend himself, but to remind his listeners with forcefulness that he had always acted in the service of the army's well-being and, more than that, he was among the first "embarked in the cause of our common Country." Nor had he ever "left your side one moment, but when called from you, on public duty," had in fact been "the constant companion and witness of your Distresses, and not among the last to feel, and acknowledge your merits—As I have ever considered my own Military reputation as inseperably [*sic*] connected with that of the army." He was saying in these powerful sentences that he was one of them and insisted, as he came to the climax of this part of his appeal, that "it can *scarcely be supposed,* at this late stage of the war, that I am indifferent to its interests."

He then asked, "How are [these interests] to be promoted?" The address of the anonymous group behind the initial call for a meeting had proposed two possibilities to the officers: "remove into the unsettled Country—there establish yourselves, and leave an ungrateful Country to defend itself." Or, if peace comes, "never sheath your Swords, says he, until you have obtained full and ample Justice." Washington took these suggestions apart, exposing their fatuousness and finally, in exasperation, dismissing them as "impracticable in their Nature." Along the way he nearly exploded with fury, saying "My God! What can this writer have in view by recommending such measures?—Can he be a friend to the Army?—Can he be a friend to this Country?—Rather is he not an insidious Foe?—Some Emissary, perhaps, from New York, plotting the ruin of both, by sowing the seeds of discord & seperation between the Civil and Military powers of the Continent?"

By this point in Washington's address it had become clear that he believed that the army held the fate of the Revolution and the United States in its hands, and he feared that if the army moved against the Congress, the Revolution and the new nation might be lost. To prevent such an outcome, he then confessed that he could not "conclude this Address" without giving his "decided opinion" that Congress "entertain exalted sentiments of the Services of the Army;—and from a full conviction of its Merits & sufferings, will do it compleat Justice: That their endeavors, to discover & establish funds for this purpose, have been unwearied, and will not cease, till they have succeeded."

The address to the officers then explained the slowness of congressional action on back pay and pensions. Congress, "like all other large bodies representing a variety of different interests to reconcile," deliberated slowly. Why should the army distrust them? he asked, and in their distrust "adopt measures" that "may cast a shade over the glory which has been justly acquired; and tarnish the reputation of an Army which is celebrated thro' all Europe, for its fortitude and Patriotism?" Such action, he said, would not "bring the object we seek nearer— No!—most certainly in my opinion, it will cast it at a greater distance."

Lest anyone doubt his commitment to the army, Washington then declared it—simply and directly: He was grateful, he said, for the confidence his troops had placed in him, and he confessed "the sincere affection I feel for an Army I have so long had the honor to command." This feeling obliged him to declare his determination to strive for "compleat justice for all your toils & dangers," and, he reassured them, "you may freely command my services to the utmost of my abilities."

Reminding the officers of what he had done in the Revolution and would continue to do, he ended the major part of his address by calling on them to refrain from repudiating their own enormous sacrifices and instead to "express your utmost horror & detestation of the Man who wishes, under any specious pretences, to overturn the liberties of our Country & who wickedly attempts to open the flood Gates of Civil discord, & deluge our rising Empire in Blood."

This plea was a challenge to the officers to match not only his standards of conduct but their own during the entire course of the war. The Revolution was at stake, and so was their "own sacred honor," the "rights of humanity" and the "National character of America." Should they do so, he insisted, "you will give one more distinguished proof of unexampled patriotism & patient virtue." And "you will, by the dignity of your conduct, afford occasion for Posterity to say, when speaking of the glorious example you have exhibited to Mankind, 'had this day been wanting, the world had never seen the last stage of perfection to which human nature is capable of attaining.'"

This final declaration of the importance of the officers' conduct was brilliantly phrased in Washington's taut and tension-filled prose. Ending on such an emotional note seemed, somehow, to leave the crisis unresolved. What then? What can a speaker—in this case a great commander, known for his restraint and his apparent remoteness—do? Washington stood silently for a few moments, looking at his audience, and they, seated, at him. He felt dissatisfied with what he had said, felt that he might not have persuaded these officers that Congress could be trusted to give them—in the parlance of these tense days—"justice," and in his uncertainty he pulled a letter from his pocket written by a member of Congress. The letter, really a pledge, contained a promise that Congress would fulfill its obligations to the army, obligations as the officers defined them. Washington began to read the letter to the officers, or tried to read it—he stumbled over the words, apparently in difficulty seeing the text. He then stopped and pulled his spectacles from his pocket, saying as he did so, "Gentlemen, you will permit me to put on my spectacles, for I have not only grown gray but almost blind in the service of my country."

The response to this statement, by the officers sitting before him, has been described as evoking their tears. The man standing before them had long commanded their respect and even their affection. They probably had brought to the meeting an animosity toward Congress; they were tired of sacrifice, and weary of excuses and delays in getting paid. Washington had surprised them when, unannounced, he walked into the meeting. Most surely were moved by his talk of sacrifices they had made and by evocation of the glorious cause. They also knew that they could believe his promises that he would stand with them. They indeed were willing to wait on Congress, knowing that the greatest man in America was with them.

Some undoubtedly *were* in tears; all listened as he finished reading the letter. He spoke no dramatic farewell. He simply stopped when he finished reading the letter and left the room. He did not know it then, but he had smashed an enormous threat to the Revolution.

While the struggle at Newburgh was being resolved, other mundane problems still festered. Washington fretted over peace, as well he might, for the negotiations that Franklin had incited almost exactly a year before, in March 1782, seemed endless. The armies on both sides had heard rumors soon after that agreement was near, and then, at the end of November, that the preliminary articles had been signed. Washington's pessimism regarding British willingness to accept independence lingered even after he was told that the king had come to accept the loss of his colonies. Through all of the uncertainty and the speculation about the king and Parliament, his hope for the end of the war ran up against his profound fears and hatred of the British. Banishing his conviction of British "duplicity"—the mildest of the words he used to describe the enemy—was almost impossible for him. A few days after the affair at Newburgh, he was informed by Congress and General Carleton, the British army commander, that both sides were in full agreement and that formal approval would follow soon, as it did on September 3.[25]

Planning for demobilization in America was already under way. Washington wanted to know when the British would give up the posts they still held. The principal one was New York, and Carleton promised to evacuate his army by late December, a promise he would keep. But British units would remain in the Northwest long after this date. Washington also looked forward to recovering American property in British hands. Slaveholders everywhere in America began clamoring for the return of their slaves, men and women who had fled to New York, enticed by British offers of protection and freedom. Well before the British departed America, Carleton and Washington had met in Orangetown, New York, to discuss methods and procedures for the evacuation. Carleton was sick that day, and the meeting was short, but arrangements both before and after were worked out fairly easily.[26]

Only one problem could not be resolved: the American claim to the black slaves who had found refuge in the city. Washington provided Carleton with the names of some but could not give a full list. Before the matter of the slaves could be discussed, several thousand had already sailed off on British ships—most, apparently, to Nova Scotia. When Washington and Carleton met, six thousand loyalists and slaves had already been taken away. The seventh article of the Treaty of Paris promised that in their withdrawal from the United States, the British would not carry "away any Negroes or other Property of the American Inhabitants," a provision Washington apparently did not notice when he first read the text of the treaty.[27] In the May meeting, Carleton explained that "it could not have been the intention" of the British government to violate their "Faith to the Negroes" who had come to their jurisdiction under the terms offered earlier. Carleton also pointed out that sending the slaves back to the Americans would be sending some to their executions and others to less severe punishments.[28]

Washington did not argue the case, though several of his slaves, he said, were among those who had fled to the British. He had come to the conclusion earlier in the arrangements for British withdrawal that there was little chance the slaves would be returned. He sent this conclusion to several of the claimants, including his friend and fellow planter Benjamin Harrison. He seems not to have felt surprise or disappointment at the British decision. He was neither an abolitionist nor a rabid slave owner, and he did not give much time to thinking over the plight of slaves, in or out of American hands.[29]

Unlike American slaves, American Indians found no place in the peace treaty—not that they would have welcomed any mention of themselves as unfair as that accorded slaves. They did not attend the conference in Paris held by the treaty-making powers, and would not have been served well by being there. The British at this meeting took the easiest course for themselves, as if to say that since there was nothing more that the Iroquois or any other tribe could do for them, they saw no reason to defend Indian rights in western lands, and it is likely that many Americans wanted to face the Indians—and perhaps subdue or destroy them—unencumbered by the advice or action of others.

The American attitudes were not exactly Washington's. He shared the general dislike, perhaps hatred, of Indians by many Americans. From an early age, when he was the colonel of the Virginia Regiment, he felt the common revulsion. The Indians for him were "wild beasts," "wolves," "savages"—dangerous and treacherous, the enemies of the stability and order prized by the whites. But, to be sure, they possessed attributes that he admired, especially their fighting skills which he felt were common to savages and wild animals. He also had reason to praise their aptitude for bushfighting and their helpfulness in fighting the French when their interests were involved.[30]

Now that the British had been repulsed and the West was an open preserve, Washington could see that the violence marking life there would increase. The root cause could not be ascribed to the Indians, however. In the absence of the British, settlers would pour in, and with them speculators and monopolizers of land indifferent and hostile to Indian claims of use and ownership.

The result would be bloodshed and war. He did not spare the intruders from responsibility, calling them "avaricious men" and a "parcel of banditti." He did not include honest American farmers under these designations, but the implication in what he wrote was that by their presence they might spur the Indians to violence. The grim prophecy was made in letters to James Deane, a leading member of a congressional committee charged to look into the West.[31]

Understandably, Congress looked to him for advice on Indian affairs. The policy he recommended reached back to the British attempt in 1763 to bar settlement west of the Appalachian Mountains by a proclamation line. Washington proposed that such a line be drawn, beyond which no settlement or intrusion would be allowed. In the areas where the Indians lived inside or beyond the line and in which settlement was proposed, the whites should purchase the land, not seize it by force.

Such a possibility existed, for the Iroquois still lived in northern and western New York. Their expulsion would evoke a violent reaction leading to war, an expectation shared by both Philip Schuyler of New York and Washington.[32]

Washington's ideas were recommendations, and in 1783 he could only announce them, not put them in place. What seems most impressive in them was his manifest desire to deal justly with the Indians and his proposal that whites enter into contracts with them. His arguments were clearly put, emphasizing the likelihood of bloodshed if old methods of aggressive seizure by whites were continued. He had seen too many of these blatant attempts—the most recent being the armed expedition into the West in 1779 that had destroyed Iroquois villages and tribesmen, a foray that he had opposed, though Congress backed it. Finding a way of settling the West that avoided such destruction, thus saving the lives of settlers as well as of Indians, had to be done quickly, he believed, or the new United States, with a border hundreds of miles away on the Mississippi, would plunge into a new, terrible war.[33]

After much effort, the British, their ships loaded with troops, loyalists, and blacks, sailed from New York in late December. Washington said nothing to them at the moment of their leaving. He was thinking of his own departure from the American army, a happy series of ruminations on the previous eight years dampened by worry over the men he had led—officers and enlisted soldiers. Of equal concern was the American nation, its condition and future.

Saying farewell to the officers and men of the army was necessary—for him and for them. Before he spoke to them, he urged Congress to give its thanks to the army for its service and suggested that the delegates send a committee to Newburgh, carrying formal appreciation for the sacrifices that ordinary men had made for their country. By this time—the second half of the year 1783—it was increasingly clear that Congress would not meet the army's demands that officers who had served until the end of the war receive pensions. Congress, which had twisted and turned during the last years of the war, now approved action calling for an accounting of what was owed enlisted men. Officers, who had been counting on half pay for life, were now to receive notes worth five years of pay—pensions, in effect, that would earn 6 percent interest per year. Washington declared his satisfaction at this promise but, concerned that money owed the officers would be slow in coming, proposed that at least three months of pay be given each officer leaving the service. Without such an advance in pay, officers would go home as paupers, and suffer the humiliation such men usually received.[34]

Congress ignored this request for money to enable officers to reenter civilian life with at least some ease. It also failed to make good on its promise of pensions by not establishing the institutions and procedures to make its promise reality. But whatever it resolved to do, or hoped to do, ran up against a disabling fact: Congress could not tax, and action to give it such power through a tariff on imported goods failed. Even Virginia failed to approve giving such power to Congress.

Whatever the financial circumstances of officers and men, it was necessary to bid them farewell as he left the army. In November, almost two months before he delivered his resignation to Congress, he marked his own departure with a "Farewell Address to the Armies of the United States."[35] The emotional power of this statement arises from the history of the Revolution, reconstructed by Washington in terms that recognize the sacrifices made by the officers and men. He does not mention Trenton or Yorktown, or the glory of the victories there; his admiration is for the courage of his troops and their long-standing devotion, despite the pain and suffering they endured, including "the extremes of hunger and nakedness." Who, he asks, "could imagine that the most violent local prejudices [held initially by these soldiers] would cease so soon, and that Men who came from the different parts of the Continent, strongly disposed, by the habits of education, to despise and quarrel with each other, would instantly become but one patriotic band of Brothers."

There was little doubt that Washington loved his soldiers, and wished the best for them; nor was there doubt that he felt uncertain about their conduct when they reentered the world of civilians, that point, as he said, when they exchanged "military character" for "that of a citizen." The transition, he knew, would not be eased greatly by a generous Congress, but he still hoped that the states would enable it to pay its debts, "so that the Officers and Soldiers may expect considerable assistance in recommencing their civil occupations from the sums due to them from the public, which must and will most inevitably be paid." There was no promise in these words and no certainty, but there was honesty and hope for social stability in a time of great uncertainty.[36]

Early in his address to the army, Washington had invoked the "interpositions of Providence" as the underlying circumstance that led to success in the Revolution. At the end he offered "his prayers to the God of Armies" on behalf of his soldiers. Whatever he could do for his men "has been done," and as he retired from service, he appealed for "heaven's favours" on their behalf. It was a complicated farewell—one part gratitude, another part forecast of a cloudy future, but a future that might yield its "blessings" to men rightfully disposed. Washington's hope was that these soldiers would remember the past eight years, which had brought them honor—and the commitment to keep the nation free and to make it great. It was a gracious farewell, and in places an expression of hope qualified by doubts.

Only a parting from Congress remained to be done as the year came to a close. Washington, a quiet and modest man, was one who knew the value of ceremony. To leave his command, he had only to write Congress with his resignation. Such a course, he recognized, would serve neither his needs nor the nation's. To discover what Congress wanted, he wrote Thomas Mifflin, its president, and received an answer indicating that Congress wished to receive his resignation on December 23. Washington had arrived on December 19 in Annapolis, where Congress was meeting. In the next two or three days, preparations were made for his appearance before Congress. The preparations fell to a committee led by Thomas Jefferson and rounded out by Elbridge Gerry of Massachusetts and James McHenry of Maryland. Washington's appearance before Congress was the great event of the occasion, but it was not the only one he made. On Monday, December 22, Congress gave a public dinner in his honor, an event that, according to attendee Dr. James Tilton, drew some two to three hundred gentlemen. Tilton described it in a private letter as happy and satisfying, saying that the "usual number of 13 toasts [were] drank, besides one given afterwards by the general . . . 'Competent powers to congress for general purposes.'" His forthcoming retirement had not dulled Washington's sense of the important. He also proved his thoughtfulness in the ball that followed, organized by the governor of Maryland, by "dancing every set that all the ladies might have the pleasure of dancing with him, or as it has since been handsomely expressed, *get a touch of him.*"[37]

The proceedings the next day replaced the high spirits of the ball with high seriousness in Washington's speech and President Mifflin's response. At noon, Washington entered the room where Congress sat, the galleries packed with Annapolis gentry. He was seated and then invited by Mifflin to speak. This proved difficult for him; Washington's feeling as he spoke almost stopped his voice. The hand in which he held his speech shook as he forced out the words, and when he began the praise of his aides, his military family, he had to hold it with both hands. His deepest feeling, however, emerged as he commended "the Interests of our dearest Country to the protection of Almighty God, and those who have the superintendence of them, to his holy keeping." At this point he seems to have been almost unable to continue, but then he ended with "an Affectionate farewell to this August body under whose orders I have so long acted, I here offer my Commission, and take my leave of all the employments of public life."

Jefferson had read Washington's speech before it was delivered and wrote a response for President Mifflin that included a sentence that indicated clearly that Congress recognized the general's high regard for civilian supremacy in a republic. "You have," he told Washington, "conducted the great military contest with wisdom and fortitude invariably regarding the rights of civil power through all disasters and changes."[38]

Jefferson, who wrote Mifflin's statement, understood Washington far better than did this president of Congress. Washington had demonstrated throughout the war his commitment to civilian supremacy in the American republic. His convictions about the relationship of the army to Congress remained firm and clear, never wavering in the face of appeals that he take matters into his own hands and, in effect, exercise the powers of a king or dictator. Such action on his part, or the army's, would be giving up the meaning of the Revolution, a surrender he would not accede to, as he explained to his officers at Newburgh. He made his belief in civilian control even clearer virtually every day, in the way he dealt with Congress. There was no question of yielding power to them—he had never claimed such power; he was the servant of the American people and of Congress, nothing less and nothing more.

All the time that he served as commander of the Continental Army, he was in fact also the leader of the Revolution. His unspoken and undefined responsibilities in this role transcended those of his assignment as commander in chief, and he became, as the war developed, a symbol of the freedom the young republic embodied. He was the political leader of the Revolution, though he drafted no legislation and signed no laws. But if he failed, it was widely understood, the Revolution failed.

For Washington, more than any American leader in or out of Congress, by his actions and example, held together the political structure that constituted the United States. Several of his officers came to proclaim this fact through their insistence that the army was the Revolution and Washington its leader. It was the institution—despite its failures and, at times, its weakness—that held together, demonstrating to the enemy that American independence possessed a reality that could not be crushed. Had Washington not persevered in the service of the cause he called "glorious," the Revolution would have given way to slow collapse. None of the Americans around him in the army, the Congress, or the states commanded the moral force he embodied. Success in maintaining the American effort would not have been achieved without him.

He succeeded in large part because he understood that the Revolution represented a rare opportunity—something quite new, in fact—to lead a people in defense of principles long honored in conceptions of liberty, stifled or suppressed elsewhere in the world. He did not fully sense the possibilities, or the range, of political liberty when the war began in 1775; nor did anyone else in or out of Congress. The war itself called out his best efforts and stiffened his resolve to honor the ideals proclaimed in the great state papers issued in the early years of resistance, culminating in the Declaration of Independence.

In assessing his performance in conventional military terms—his thought on strategy, his tactical capabilities and action, and his administrative record throughout the war—the basic comparison has to be with his British enemy. Washington's strategic sense proved to be of a very high order. He saw early on that, because of the disparity in military strength, the wisest course for his army lay in fighting a war of attrition. Such a war would not yield outright military defeat of the British, but, pursued with care, it held promise of wearing them out until they were willing to accept American independence. If the likelihood of defeating the British army on the battlefield was slim, or nonexistent, the Americans still had to fight—attrition did not mean avoidance of the enemy.

Washington knew much about the British army: It was not large, but its level of competence had been high for many years. Its leaders in the 1770s and after were not brilliant, but Gage, the Howe brothers, Clinton, and Cornwallis were able professionals. British regiments were better than competent; their men and field-grade officers were skillful. Perhaps the greatest advantage the British had was their navy. Washington assumed from the beginning of the war that naval power—not just the weight of shipboard guns, but the capacity for moving and supplying troops—was of great importance. He faced a European country of surpassing naval experience and power.

In contrast to the British military, the Americans had to summon an army from nothing, and putting it together had to be done repeatedly. Had knowledge existed of how to create an army from nothing, the American task still would have been daunting, for the will to give up old allegiances to provinces and to adopt fresh ways of dealing with the world as it existed was not strong. Washington supplied much that was missing in political will and in insight. But the underlying circumstances of the new nation, divided and uncertain of how to proceed, and fearful of a standing or professional army, dogged his action throughout the entire war. He, with the unreliable assistance of the states, created an army, only to see it dissolve, many times. He responded by pulling it together again and again, including not just its regiments of infantry but its logistical services as well. He began as commander with an army outside Boston that was little more than a collection of town and county militias. There were virtually no structure, procedures, regulations, or army-wide logistical and other organizations in support. A body of officers experienced in military organization and in combat was also lacking. The creation of an army while conducting military operations had few precedents and had to be done during a siege and, later, under the most pressing kinds of fighting.

Despite the persistence of the underlying circumstances of a weak

306 · *Washington's Revolution*

central authority, he fought his way through using what was available to hold off superior forces in almost every battle. Only at Yorktown did he go into battle with a favorable hand. When his army's prospects were at their bleakest, as in December 1776, he seized control at Trenton and Princeton—not because his army was stronger, but because he had imagination and daring. He also demonstrated that he knew how to run a battle and in the process to inspire an army and a nation. His and his army's fortunes had desperate moments after these brilliant attacks, but they sustained Washington's vision and his hold on the Revolution. Whatever the course of the military conflict, he insisted on a policy of attrition, and his strategy under all sorts of circumstances remained steady.

That the American conception of civil supremacy remained firm even when the army seemed the only reliable institution in the war—and its commander the center of authority—owed more to Washington, a general, than to anything else. War, he knew, could dissolve the claims of the civilian world to ultimate authority. Such claims in America were hardly more than a wish in the dark days of the war. Washington made the claims a reality. His thought indeed amounted to a form of constitutionalism. Here, on this matter of the people and the army, he insisted that the people's voice should be loudest.

Washington's imagination—his conception of what freedom meant in a free nation—is sometimes overlooked in the certitude of his physical bravery. He was a general, after all; he fought and he overcame enormous obstacles. But he also possessed a grand imagination, a vision of his new country. That vision, often a daring instrument, set him apart and made him the great leader of the Revolution.

Epilogue

Return to Virginia

Washington had not been home a month when he described himself to Chastellux as "a private citizen of America, on the banks of the Potowmac; where under my own Vine & my own Fig Tree—free from the bustle of a camp & the intrigues of a Court, I shall view the busy world, 'in the calm lights of mild philosophy.' " The quotation was from Addison's *Cato,* long a favorite and an understandable choice for a literary expression that, he hoped, would characterize the substance of his retirement. This comment to Chastellux followed a formula he had devised to explain his private thought to friends who were not intimates—he had few intimates—and, though revealing, did not expose much of what he really felt. More of his innerness took form in his letters to Lafayette at the beginning of February, but even in these letters, he did not wander far from the stoic stance he almost always assumed in explaining himself. To Lafayette he evoked the soldier-statesman-courtier he claimed not to be. Such men, he said, acted roles in life far from the one he aspired to, one in which he had renounced "public employments" in favor of "retireing within myself." He was now a man who envied no one, but was determined to be "pleased with all" and moving "gently down the stream of life, until I sleep with my Fathers."[1]

What he hoped for was a quiet life. But he must have known he would not find such a life—he was too well known, and bore the burdens of the unrestrained admiration of America and much of Europe. He also had plans to carry out and responsibilities that denied the tranquillity he craved. They were, of course, of a different order than he had grown accustomed to in the army, and included getting Mount Vernon, the house and plantation, and his holdings in the West in order. And there was also the matter of his place in the world—how he might help shore up the new republic. That the republic was weak and part of a world made up largely of monarchies promised extraordinary problems.

Homecoming presented uncertainties in a variety of realms, but it also offered the affection of family and friends, all eager to see him and to express their love for him. Martha Washington, not surprisingly, was at the top of the list, a woman who had waited for him with patience and without complaints. She had seen something of him during the war, usually in uncomfortable circumstances featuring cramped houses and a spartan diet, and had endured the possibility of the loss of her husband to death in combat. Martha Washington bore it all well and free of self-pity. When Washington arrived home at Christmas, she was still in mourning for her son Jacky, who had died two years before. She never fully recovered from his death, but having her husband home transformed her moods. To those individuals she met at this time, she seemed happy or at least content, and to have kept to herself her deepest feelings about her family. Yet it was clear that she loved her husband, whose return had made her happy. It was a feeling he gave back in full measure.

Washington's affection for his family seems to have grown during the war, a time when he could do little for his brothers and their children. He had looked after his mother when he could during the war, and in peace he continued to serve her whenever possible, though without enthusiasm. By contrast, his nephews—the sons of his brothers John Augustine Washington and Charles Washington—captured his attention without trying. The favorite nephews were George Augustine Washington (1763–93), son of Charles, and Bushrod Washington (1762–1829), son of John Augustine Washington, of whom George was especially fond.

The nephews had chosen different sorts of careers and do not seem to have come to Washington's close attention until they were around twenty years old. George Augustine became a focus of attention early on—he served as an aide to Lafayette during several years of the Revolution, an association that inevitably quickened his uncle's interest. But he suffered from tuberculosis and sought relief by taking passage to the West Indies, the same course of treatment Lawrence Washington had followed, accompanied by his brother George, more than thirty years earlier. Lawrence had died shortly after his attempt at a cure, but George Augustine lived ten years beyond his voyage. His uncle clearly felt concern about him and paid for the West Indies experiment, commenting at the time that his nephew "looks very thin" and was "troubled with the pain in his Breast." Martha Washington felt a similar concern, which she expressed to her nephew, who clearly was moved by it.[2]

Bushrod Washington, the oldest of three sons of John Augustine Washington, endured no severe physical problems, and probably came to his uncle's attention because he was the firstborn of George Washington's favorite brother. He had a quick mind and found a place with James Wilson, the distinguished Philadelphia attorney. Washington played a part in this arrangement by recommending Bushrod to Wilson. A recommendation of this kind from Washington was difficult to reject, but there is no reason to suspect that Wilson acted against his own wishes in taking Bushrod into his firm.[3]

Although Washington did not know John Augustine's youngest son, Corbin (1765–1799), well, he recommended him to Tench Tilghman as being a young man capable of learning the mercantile business. John Augustine had asked his brother to do so and also urged him to request that Tilghman allow the boy to live with the Tilghman family rather than in a boardinghouse. Corbin was nineteen and, as far as Washington could tell, "had good natural abilities—an amiable disposition, & an uncommon share of prudence & circumspection." When Washington received his brother's letter asking him for help in prying open the doors of business for Corbin, his first step was to ask Robert Morris to accept the boy. Morris replied that he was leaving business, and recommended others to assume the task. Washington chose Tilghman, encouraged by John Augustine, who thought Tilghman was preferable to all others and reminded George that "Colonel Tilghmans regard and respect for you may induce him to take more pains in instructing my son than could other wise be reasonably expected." Washington did not respond to this comment, but he did recommend Corbin, whatever he thought about his brother's willingness to use his reputation.[4]

One nephew, Fielding Lewis Jr. (1751–1803), son of Washington's sister Betty and Fielding Lewis, received little sympathy and no financial help, though he requested it while sitting in the Frederick County jail, imprisoned for not paying his debts. Young Lewis admitted that his plight had arisen from "youthful Folley" but avoided giving any additional explanation. This excuse met a cold response. His own "circumstances," Washington explained, left him in no condition to advance money. His estate made no money during his nine years' absence, he reported; he brought no money home from the army, and his debtors "took advantage of the depreciation & paid me off with Six pence in the pound." He himself owed money that, if his creditors demanded payment immediately, he would be able to pay off only by selling part of his estate.[5]

This explanation of his refusal to come to Fielding Jr.'s assistance made up the body of his letter. He followed it with a postscript in which he remarked on Fielding's failure several years before to respond to his father's request for a list of his debts. Fielding Sr. had written Washington in 1769 that his son seemed certain in a year or two to have spent every "shilling" of his young wife's fortune, "as I cannot perceive the least amendment since his Marriage, nor has he the least regard to any advice I give him." Young Fielding's request to Washington came in midstream of an unhappy life, and (to give this account fullness), eight years after the appeal to his uncle, even his mother, Betty Washington Lewis, seemed prepared to give up on him, writing her brother George that "Fielding is so distrest that his Children would go naked if it was not for the assistance I give him."[6]

The happiness Washington felt in his family outweighed the distress he received from the conduct of Fielding Lewis Jr. and the complaints from his mother. These matters did not enter his life of retirement every day, but came after his return and the deluge of praise, honors, and celebration. He had expected that approval of his performance in the Revolution would be sounded for a short time after he left the army, but what appeared was massive and continuous. Its most common expression came through the mail as strangers of every sort as well as old colleagues wrote him. He especially welcomed hearing from officers who had served under his command—and they did not hesitate to write.

Henry Knox, who had led the artillery division, was among the first. Knox had been an admirer of Washington during the war and did not now conceal his feelings, saying that "I should do violence to the dictates of my heart were I to suppress entirely its sensations of affection & gratitude to you for the innumerable instances of your kindness and attention to me, and although I can find no words equal to their warmth I may venture to assure you that they will remain indelibly fixed." Washington had more than thought well of Knox, and the year before his own retirement assigned him to the task of disbanding the army. Knox was still fulfilling that charge when he wrote Washington with this declaration of affection, but he also wanted something: a recommendation to Congress that Knox receive another command, preferably as secretary of war. Congress complied the next year.[7]

David Humphreys, an aide who had served with distinction, also wrote in January. Like Knox, he wanted an appointment in the government and suggested to Washington that he had the competence to carry out the duties of the secretary of foreign affairs, a regimental commander, or a secretary to one of the commissions Congress was sending abroad. Washington, ever loyal to his military family, recommended that Congress make Humphreys secretary of foreign affairs. Congress responded with an offer of appointment as secretary of the commission negotiating commercial treaties in France.[8]

Throughout 1784, many such letters passed between Washington and his former officers. All conveyed feelings of respect and admiration for him, and he in turn revealed his own high regard for these men, as well as his willingness—indeed, eagerness—to give them all aid possible. This flood of letters that began with his return did not lessen, and though he did not know many of those who wrote, he responded to virtually every one.

The variety of correspondents and the subjects they chose to air must have surprised him. He probably knew Walter Stewart, who had been a colonel in the 2nd Pennsylvania Regiment and inspector of the Northern Army and was a Philadelphia merchant when he wrote. Stewart wanted a letter of introduction to the governor of Cuba, an instrument, he said, that would help collect a debt owed his firm. Ever polite, Washington wrote the letter that did in fact enable Stewart to collect what was owed him, some twelve thousand dollars.[9]

Though many wanted something from him—money in the form of a gift or loan, help in getting a job, or recognition of some kind—many more wrote simply to convey their gratitude for his leadership in the Revolution. These writers lived all over Europe and the United States and included with their appreciation gifts of all sorts. Admiral d'Estaing, along with "all the French sailors," sent a gold medal studded with diamonds to convey to Washington their "most profound admiration and attachment which you inspire." Over the next few months, John Jones, a former commissary to the old Virginia Regiment led by Washington in 1755, sent "a fine fat turtle" from Curaçao, and Reuben Harvey, an Irish merchant, sent "Cork Mess Beef" and "a firkin of Ox tongues with Roots."[10]

Such gifts could have been smothered by the poems and addresses written in Washington's honor, many published and all wrapped in praise, apparently in fear that simple statement was inadequate to the task. Had Washington attended all the dinners in his honor, drunk the toasts to his fame, and danced at all the balls that frequently accompanied such affairs, he would have either died from gluttony or collapsed from exhaustion. As it was, he answered the letters with humility and professed to find the poetry moving, and nowhere did he confess to fatigue at all the celebration.

There is much in the praise heaped on him that is revealing. Most of the writers of letters and organizers of public tributes had never written him before. He was unknown to them, and they to him. The achievement of the Revolution, the independence and liberty it brought to America, impressed these correspondents more than anything else. But they also wondered about its leader, George Washington, and concluded that the Revolution's triumph was his. Besides the fact of his leadership of an army lacking in experience and just about everything else, he had, as an admirer put it, "in obedience to your Country's call, [undertaken] the Arduous task, and nobly embarked in the sacred cause of Liberty, rejecting every emolument which you might in justice have claimed for such signal & important services."[11]

Letters came from his old French colleagues. Admiral d'Estaing wrote, as did the Comte de Grasse, Rochambeau, and of course Chastellux and Lafayette. Congratulations on his success in the war and his act disavowing any claim to power in the young republic constituted more than routine recognition. The writers of these letters liked him, and said so. In fact, the standing Washington assumed in popular appreciations often revealed an almost mystical attitude. He remained for them a creature apart, a man set above all others, a unique being— not a god, but at the least a chosen instrument of Providence.

Washington did not seek such a status and bore, without complaint, the celebration of his honor and his virtue. All he wanted, he said as he left the army, was a quiet life. But as he must have realized in 1784, quiet was not to be his. As great as the Revolution was, there was more to be done if the United States was to survive. A part of the task, he knew, would fall to him. But for the moment, he would dream under his own vine and fig tree.

Acknowledgments

Much of my research for this book was done in the rooms of the Mark Twain Project, in the Bancroft Library at the University of California, Berkeley. It should not be assumed that I confused George Washington with Mark Twain, or that I did not know where I was when working on this book. It is true that Peter Hanff, deputy director of the Bancroft, and Robert Hirst, editor of the Mark Twain Project, made the arrangements for my work, including extracting volumes of Washington papers from storage elsewhere for my use. I am deeply in their debt, and in Neda Salem's for her help in the Bancroft. Andrew Miller, my editor at Knopf, has been a perceptive and thoughtful commentator with high standards. He does his work with great skill and intelligence, and I wish to thank him. I wish also to thank his colleague, Will Heyward, for much help in a variety of ways, and for giving it so thoughtfully and tactfully

My debt to Edmund S. Morgan is enormous. He talked with me frequently over the years about my work on Washington, encouraged me to persist in it, and was in all ways a source of insight and inspiration right up to his death. Others who read what I wrote, gave insightful criticism, or provided valuable encouragement include Irv Scheiner, Bill Youngs, Amy Greenberg, Terry Carroll, and Ruma Chopra. I'm especially indebted to Caroline Cox, a superb scholar, who, before her death, put her own work aside to give mine an especially searching reading.

My daughter Holly's support of this book and all of my scholarly life has meant more to me than I can say. My son, Sam, to whom this book is dedicated, has been an important presence in many ways. Beverly, my wife, has been the key person in my life in a long marriage, and also a wonderful critic in the making of this book. I cannot describe adequately all that I owe her.

Notes

ABBREVIATIONS

PGW: Col. Ser. W. W. Abbot and Dorothy Twohig, eds., *Papers of George Washington: Colonial Series* (Charlottesville: University of Virginia Press, 1983–1995, 10 vols.)

PGW: Rev. War Ser. W. W. Abbot and Dorothy Twohig, eds., *Papers of George Washington: Revolutionary War Series* (Charlottesville: University of Virginia Press, 1985– , 21 vols. to date)

PGW: Conf. Ser. W. W. Abbot and Dorothy Twohig, eds., *Papers of George Washington: Confederation Series* (Charlottesville: University of Virginia Press, 1992–1997, 6 vols.)

Fitzpatrick, ed., *Writings* John C. Fitzpatrick, ed., *The Writings of George Washington from the Original Manuscript Sources* (Washington, D.C.: Government Printing Office, 1931–1939, 39 vols.)

Freeman Douglas Southall Freeman, *George Washington: A Biography* (New York: Charles Scribner's Sons, 1948–1957, 7 vols.). Volume 7 completed by John A. Carroll and Mary W. Ashworth.

Flexner James Thomas Flexner, *George Washington* (Boston: Little, Brown, 1965–1972, 4 vols.)

PROLOGUE: VIRGINIAN

1. To describe the Virginia of Washington's youth is a daunting assignment, and this Prologue covers only a small part of the ground. I have listed here some of the scholarship that I have found most useful in writing this general introduction. The list here touches on only two aspects of Virginia's culture: politics and slavery. Bernard Bailyn's *The Origins of American Politics* (New York: Alfred A. Knopf, 1968) provides an insightful interpretation of the political lives of all the thirteen colonies. His account of Virginia is, of course, necessarily brief, but his perceptions are searching. Almost as useful is Leonard Labaree's *Royal Government in America* (New Haven, Conn.: Yale University Press, 1930; repr., New York: Frederick Ungar Publishing Co., 1958). Jack Greene's *The Quest for Power* (Chapel Hill: University of North Carolina Press, 1963) is equally fine in its treatment of the assemblies of Virginia and the southern colonies. Charles S.

Sydnor's *Gentlemen Freeholders: Political Practices in Washington's Virginia* (Chapel Hill: University of North Carolina Press, 1952) is a work of great value.

Slavery in Virginia has received penetrating study in many books and articles. The following have been extraordinarily useful: Philip D. Morgan, *Slave Counterpoint: Black Culture in the Eighteenth-Century Chesapeake and Low-country* (Chapel Hill: University of North Carolina Press, 1998), a monumental study; Lorena S. Walsh, *Motives of Honor, Pleasure and Profit: Plantation Management in the Colonial Chesapeake, 1607–1763* (Chapel Hill: University of North Carolina Press, 2010); T. H. Breen, *Tobacco Culture: The Mentality of the Great Tidewater Planters on the Eve of the Revolution* (Princeton, N.J.: Princeton University Press, 1985); and Edmund S. Morgan, *American Slavery, American Freedom* (New York: W. W. Norton, 1975).

I YOUNG WASHINGTON

1. For the history of Washington's family, see Freeman, 1:15–47, 527–34; Flexner, 1:9–12.
2. The documents of George Washington's education are sparse. See *PGW: Col. Ser.,* 1:1–4. Freeman and Flexner give useful accounts; see vol. 1 in both biographies.
3. Charles Moore, ed., *George Washington's Rules of Civility and Decent Behavior* (Boston and New York: Houghton Mifflin, 1926). A modern reprint can be found in John H. Rhodehamel, ed., *George Washington: Writings* (New York: Library of America, 1997), 3–10.
4. *PGW: Col. Ser.,* 1:10. For "A Journal of My Journey over the Mountains Began the 11th of March 1747/8," see *PGW: Col. Ser.,* 1:6–23; quotation 10. "Quotation" refers to the cited work.
5. Ibid., 1:13
6. For the trip to Barbados, see Donald Jackson, ed., *The Diaries of George Washington* (Charlottesville: University of Virginia Press, 1976–1979, 6 vols.), 1:24–117. Much of this material is in facsimile and not useful.
7. *PGW: Col. Ser.,* 1:56–61.
8. For Washington's account of his "Journey to the French Commandant," see Jackson, ed., *Diaries,* 1:118–61, which includes helpful editorial comment as well as his account.
9. Ibid., 1:162–210, for Washington's report and editorial interpretation.
10. Ibid. and *PGW: Col. Ser.,* 1:118 quotation.
11. Washington's and Dinwiddie's letters back and forth in late May and early June are helpful in understanding the events of the days covered. See *PGW: Col. Ser.,* 1:87–140. See also, for the governor, John Richard Alden, *Robert Dinwiddie: Servant of the Crown* (Charlottesville: University of Virginia Press, 1973).
12. Dinwiddie to Washington, May 25, 1754; Washington's reply, May 29, 1754. *PGW: Col. Ser.,* 1:102, 107.
13. Ibid., 1:107–115; quotation 109.
14. For the beginnings of the campaign at Great Meadows, see ibid., 1:122–57.
15. For the dimensions of Fort Necessity, ibid., 1:126n12; the quotation is from a letter to Governor Dinwiddie, June 3, 1754, ibid., 1:123.
16. Negotiations with the Indians can be followed in Jackson, ed., *Diaries,* 1:202–10.

17. *PGW: Col. Ser.,* 1:159–73.
18. On responses to the defeat at Fort Necessity, see ibid., 1:177–78; W. Fairfax's words were "Marlbro's Campaigns"; and "rout," 1:201; 1:209 (John Robinson and House of Burgesses for Robinson's comments).
19. The quotations are from a letter to William Fairfax, ibid., 1:186 ("naked") and 189 ("if not more than ten men").
20. Ibid., 1:206–7; 208n9, on winter weather.
21. Dinwiddie's decision to divide the Virginia Regiment into independent companies is discussed in ibid., 1:224n1. See this note for quotation.
22. The events discussed in this paragraph and the preceding one can be followed in ibid., 1:224–35; for the lease of Mount Vernon, 1:232–34.

2 THE MAKING OF A SOLDIER

1. For Braddock's background, see Paul E. Kopperman, *Braddock at the Monongahela* (Pittsburgh: University of Pittsburgh Press, 1977), 7–8, 135–36; and Lee McCardell, *Ill-Starred General: Braddock of the Coldstream Guards* (Pittsburgh: University of Pittsburgh Press, 1958), 124–28.
2. Robert Orme to Washington, Mar. 2, 1755, *PGW: Col. Ser.,* 1:241-245.
3. Leonard W. Labaree et al., eds., *The Papers of Benjamin Franklin* (New Haven, Conn.: Yale University Press, 1959– , 41 vols. to date), for his assistance to Braddock, 6:13–27. Franklin tells the story in his autobiography; see the edition edited by Labaree, 216–221.
4. Kopperman, *Braddock,* 3–18.
5. Ibid., 19–30.
6. Washington's account of the battle appears in several of his letters. For the quotations, see Washington to Mary Ball Washington, *PGW: Col. Ser.,* 1:336 ("four Bullets"); to Dinwiddie, 1:340 ("in the shoulder"); to Dinwiddie, 1:339–340 ("English soldiers," "broke & run").
7. Ibid., 1:351–54; "scandalous," 1:353.
8. To Robert Jackson ("wondrous works"); Dinwiddie to Halifax: ibid., 1:349, 351n2. Among excellent accounts by modern historians, see Kopperman, *Braddock,* 31–121; and Fred Anderson, *Crucible of War: The Seven Years' War and the Fate of Empire in British North America, 1754–1766* (New York: Alfred A. Knopf, 2000), 94–107.
9. Washington to Robert Orme, July 28, 1755, *PGW: Col. Ser.,* 1:347; Orme to Washington, Aug. 25, 1755, 2:9–11; Orme to Washington, Nov. 10, 1755, 2:165–66.
10. Washington to Dinwiddie, July 18, 1755, ibid., 1:339–40, quotations.
11. Washington to Warner Lewis, Aug. 14, 1755, ibid., 1:360–64.
12. There have been many attempts to explain the meaning of honor in the American Revolution and at other times. One of the most helpful is in Caroline Cox, *A Proper Sense of Honor: Service and Sacrifice in George Washington's Army* (Chapel Hill: University of North Carolina Press, 2004). See also Kwame Anthony Appiah, *The Honor Code* (New York: Norton, 2010), a stimulating modern perspective, and Joanne B. Freeman, *Affairs of Honor: National Politics in the New Republic* (New Haven, Conn.: Yale University Press, 2001), a suggestive and instructive interpretation.

13. *PGW: Col. Ser.*, 2:13–54. Washington's own commission and instructions from Governor Dinwiddie are in ibid., 2:1–8.

14. Washington to Andrew Lewis, Sept. 6, 1755, and to Adam Stephen, Sept. 11, 1755, ibid., 2:23, 27.

15. Washington to Dinwiddie, Oct. 11, 1755, ibid., 2:101–7; quotation 102.

16. On Dagworthy, see ibid., 2:63n4, 74n6.

17. William Shirley to Washington, Mar. 5, 1756, ibid., 2:323.

18. Washington to Dinwiddie, Apr. 7, 1756, ibid., 2:333, quotations.

19. Washington's reports to Dinwiddie and John Robinson, Speaker of the House, are filled with accounts of depredations by the Indians in these years.

20. For Washington's skepticism regarding the chain of forts built along the frontier, see, for example, his letter of Apr. 7, 1756, to Dinwiddie, ibid., 2:332–35, especially 334.

21. Washington to Adam Stephen, Nov. 28, 1755, ibid., 2:184, 186n4.

22. Ibid., 4:1 quotations. The entire letter is in ibid., 4:1–10 with notes.

23. Ibid., 4:2; 4:3 for the quotations in this paragraph and the next.

24. Ibid., 4:25 for Dinwiddie's angry response.

25. Ibid., 4:26 for the order to Washington.

26. Washington's answer on Nov. 24, 1756, contains an effective apology for remarks the governor had found "unmannerly," but sustains what he had written on Nov. 9. See ibid., 4:30.

27. For the Virginia Council's statement, as reported by the governor, see ibid., 4:54–55. The governor's citation of Lord Loudoun's judgment is suspect, as the editors of vol. 4 of the *PGW: Col. Ser.* point out on page 53n4.

28. Washington wrote the governor on Dec. 2, 4, and 10, 1756. Ibid., 4:34–37; 40–41; 48–49.

29. For Washington's letter of Jan. 10, 1757, to Lord Loudoun, see ibid., 4:79–93; quotations 4:81, 89.

30. Ibid., 4:79–80, 136–38.

31. To Dinwiddie, July 11, 1757, ibid., 4:295–96.

32. To Dinwiddie, May 30, 1757, ibid., 4:171–73.

33. To John Robinson, May 30, June 10, 1757, ibid., 4:174–75, 199; quotations 174, 199.

34. To John Robinson, May 30, 1757, ibid., 4:175; and to Dinwiddie, Oct. 24, 1757, ibid., 5:25.

35. Robinson to Washington, Nov. 3, 1757, ibid., 5:43–44. For Robinson, see ibid., 1:113n4. He was Speaker of the House of Burgesses in the years 1738–65.

36. Ibid., 5:44–46; quotation 45.

37. Ibid., 5:46–47; quotations 46.

38. Ibid., 5:115n3.

39. Ibid., 5:117; quotations 117 and 126.

40. Ibid., 5:138–139n1, 344–45; quotations 344.

41. Washington to Francis Halkett, Aug. 2, 1758, ibid., 5:361; John Forbes to Col. Henry Bouquet, Sept. 23, 1758, ibid., 6:24n3.

42. Washington to Francis Fauquier, Aug. 5 and Sept. 2, 1758, ibid., 5:369–71, 439–43.

43. These arguments appear in letters to Col. Bouquet, Acting Governor John Blair, Governor Francis Fauquier, and others.

44. *PGW: Col. Ser.*, 6:45

45. The orderly books from Sept. 21 through Nov. 24, 1758, provide most of the information needed to follow Washington's part in the advance to Fort Duquesne. They are scattered throughout *PGW: Col. Ser.,* 6.
46. *PGW: Col. Ser.,* 6:98–100; quotation 99. For the letter to Bouquet, Nov. 6, 1758, see 6:115–16.
47. For the skirmish of Nov. 12, see 6:120–21n1. *The Pennsylvania Gazette,* Nov. 30, 1758, described the incident.
48. *PGW: Col. Ser.,* 6:116 quotation.

3 FROM PLANTER TO PATRIOT

1. Much about Washington's relationship with Sally Fairfax has been written, though in fact not much is known about it. Their letters are scattered throughout his papers.
2. Mount Vernon, the house, is discussed with great insight in Robert Dalzell Jr. and Lee Baldwin Dalzell, *Mount Vernon: At Home in Revolutionary America* (New York and Oxford: Oxford University Press, 1998). The Dalzells' book is broadly conceived and offers much on the people who lived on the plantation.
3. For the Custis estate, see *PGW: Col. Ser.,* 6:201–312.
4. Information on the work of Washington's slaves is scattered throughout his diaries and letters. See Donald Jackson, ed., *The Diaries of George Washington* (Charlottesville: University of Virginia Press, 1976–1979, 6 vols.), vols. 1 and 2.
5. Ibid., 1:261, 266–67, 275; quotations 261, 267, 275.
6. Ibid., vol. 1; see note "Grains of Wheat," 1:267–68 and passim. For fishing and slaves, 1:261, 266 ("Negroes askd the let of the Sein today.").
7. Ibid., 1:250, 263, 265. There are excellent studies of tobacco planting in Virginia and Maryland. The process of planting and harvesting can be followed in G. Melvin Herndon, *Tobacco in Colonial Virginia: "The Sovereign Remedy"* (Williamsburg: Virginia 350th Anniversary Celebration Corp., 1957). T. H. Breen, *Tobacco Culture: The Mentality of the Great Tidewater Planters on the Eve of the Revolution* (Princeton, N.J.: Princeton University Press, 1985) discusses its broader implications insightfully.
8. There are several lists of books owned by Washington or held by him for Martha Washington's son, John Parke Custis. The inventory made of books held before the Revolution is in *PGW: Col. Ser.,* 7:343–50. This inventory is of books at Mount Vernon.
9. For the background of these changes in agricultural practices, see John J. McCusker and Russell R. Menard, *The Economy of British America, 1607–1789* (Chapel Hill: University of North Carolina Press, 1985), especially 117–43. Lorena S. Walsh, *Motives of Honor, Pleasure and Profit* (Chapel Hill: University of North Carolina Press, 2010), on plantation management, provides a broad but deep account of the plantation system in the Chesapeake.
10. Walsh, *Motives of Honor* provides several examples: 612–14.
11. See Philip D. Morgan, *Slave Counterpoint: Black Culture in the Eighteenth-Century Chesapeake and Lowcountry* (Chapel Hill: University of North Carolina Press, 1998) for a superb account of slavery in the plantation system.
12. This account of the linking of British firms and tobacco planters is based on Washington's letters and Jacob M. Price, "The Rise of Glasgow in the Chesa-

peake Tobacco Trade, 1707–1775," *William and Mary Quarterly*, 3rd Ser., 11 (April 1954): 179–99.

13. The relationship with Robert Cary and Company lasted until the Revolution.
14. *PGW: Col. Ser.*, 7:153–55; quotation 154.
15. Washington's dealings with Robert Cary and Company in the early years of his raising tobacco may be followed in ibid., 7.
16. Jonathan Boucher came from England in 1759 as a tutor; he returned to England soon after to be ordained by the Bishop of London.
17. Washington to Boucher, May 30, 1768, ibid., 8:89–90 (Washington's appraisal); Boucher to Washington, Aug. 2, 1768, ibid., 8:122, 123.
18. For all the quotations in this paragraph, Washington to Boucher, Dec. 16, 1770, ibid., 8:411–12.
19. Boucher to Washington, Dec. 18, 1770, ibid., 8:414.
20. Boucher to Washington, May 9, 1770, ibid., 8:332–33. See especially 333n1.
21. John Parke Custis to Martha Washington, July 5, 1773, ibid., 9:266n2.
22. For the history of the beginnings of the revolutionary crisis, see Edmund S. and Helen M. Morgan, *The Stamp Act Crisis: Prologue to Revolution* (Chapel Hill: University of North Carolina Press, 1953) 3–39.
23. Ibid., quotations, 91.
24. Washington to Francis Dandridge, Sept. 20, 1765, *PGW: Col. Ser.*, 7:395.
25. Washington to Robert Cary & Co., Sept. 20, 1765, ibid., 7:398–402, quotation on 401–2.
26. Morgan and Morgan, *Stamp Act Crisis*, 261–81.
27. For the Massachusetts Circular Letter to the Colonial Legislatures, Feb. 11, 1768, see Merrill Jensen, ed., *English Historical Documents: American Colonial Documents to 1776* (New York: Oxford University Press, 1969), 714–16.
28. For this paragraph and the two preceding it, see Washington to George Mason, Apr. 15, 1769, and Mason's reply of the same day, *PGW: Col. Ser.*, 8:177–84 and 180n. For George Mason, see the splendid biography by Jeff Broadwater, *George Mason: Forgotten Founder* (Chapel Hill: University of North Carolina Press, 2006), 47–53.
29. Morgan and Morgan, *Stamp Act Crisis*, 155.
30. Washington activities listed here are recorded in *PGW: Col. Ser.*, 8.
31. For the resolutions and Washington's action, see ibid., 8:187–90; Broadwater, *George Mason*, 51–53.
32. *PGW: Col. Ser.*, 8:353–54, especially note 2.
33. Merrill Jensen, *The Founding of a Nation* (New York: Oxford University Press, 1968), 354–72.
34. For the continuing use of the word "oppression" in reference to the Stamp Act, see Washington's letter to the British firm Capel and Osgood Hanbury on July 25, 1767, *PGW: Col. Ser.*, 8:14–15.
35. William Waller Hening, *The Statutes at Large: Being a Collection of All the Laws of Virginia from the First Session of the Legislature, in the Year 1619*. Richmond, Va., 1905–1915, 13 vols. The quotation in *PGW: Col. Ser.*, 8:352, is from the records of the House of Burgesses, 8 Hening, 570–79. On George William Fairfax's trip to England, see ibid., 9:153, 159–60, 298–99 and notes 1 and 2, 386–87. Washington's report on the land grant of 1754, "To the Officers and Soldiers of the Virginia Regiment of 1754," is in ibid., 9:143–48. For the trouble over shipping flour to the West Indies, see Washington to Daniel J. Adams, July 20, 1772,

and Jan. 12, 1773; to Robert McMickan, Feb. 12, 1773, ibid., 9:69–72, 157–59, 174–76.

36. On the death of Patsy Custis, see Washington to Burwell Bassett, June 20, 1773, ibid., 9:243–44. On Jack Custis's decision to marry, see Washington to Benedict Calvert, Apr. 3, 1773, ibid., 9:209–11.
37. For the Intolerable Acts, see Jensen, ed., *English Historical Documents*, 780–85.
38. *PGW: Col. Ser.*, 10:94–101.
39. Ibid., 10:99n10; Broadwater, *George Mason*, 64–65.
40. Broadwater, *George Mason*, 65–67; *PGW: Col. Ser.*, 10:119–27, Fairfax County Resolves.
41. For the quotations in the preceding paragraph, see *PGW: Col. Ser.*, 10:119; resolutions 2 and 3 on 120.
42. Washington to Bryan Fairfax, July 4, 1774, ibid., 10:109–10; Fairfax to Washington, July 17, 1774, 10:114–18; Washington's response to Fairfax, July 20, 1774, 10:128–31.
43. Paul Smith et al., eds., *Letters of Delegates to Congress, 1774–1789* (Washington, D.C.: Library of Congress, 1976–2000, 26 vols.), 1:61–62.
44. Ibid., 302.

4 BOSTON

1. *PGW: Rev. War Ser.*, 1:27–28n, 56n3; Freeman, 3:460–82, for an account of his travel to Boston. For a fine introduction to the city, see Jacqueline Barbara Carr, *After the Siege: A Social History of Boston, 1775–1800* (Boston: Northeastern University Press, 2005).
2. Address from the New York Provincial Congress, *PGW: Rev. War Ser.*, 1:40.
3. The estimates of American strength varied in these early days of his command; those of the British in Boston varied even more. See ibid., 1:79–80. On July 10, 1775, Washington wrote Richard Henry Lee that he had an army of sixteen thousand "effective men" but only fourteen thousand fit for duty, 1:98–100.
4. Washington to John Hancock, July 10 and 11, 1775, ibid., 1:85, and passim.
5. Washington's impressions of the soldiers he found surrounding Boston are scattered throughout his letters written in his first months as commander. See ibid., 1:85–92, 113, 336; for the Callendar case, 71, 74n1.
6. Ibid., 1:318, 325, 338n8, 375n3.
7. Cases noted under General Orders, ibid., vols. 1 and 2.
8. George Washington to Lund Washington, Aug. 20, 1775, ibid., 1:335–36.
9. Nathanael Greene to Washington, Sept. 10, 1775, ibid., 1:445–46; quotation 445.
10. Ibid., 1:446n1. The fine the men paid was reported in General Orders, Cambridge, in ibid., 1:454–55.
11. Washington to John Hancock, Sept. 21, 1775, ibid., 2:29 quotations.
12. Ibid., 2:5, 16–17, 50, 279–84. See also Robert K. Wright Jr., *The Continental Army* (Washington, D.C.: Center of Military History, U.S. Army, 1983), chap. 1 and passim.
13. James Warren and Joseph Hawley to Washington, July 4, 1775, *PGW: Rev. War Ser.*, 1:61–62n1.
14. E. Wayne Carp's *To Starve the Army at Pleasure* (Chapel Hill and London: University of North Carolina Press, 1984) provides an excellent opening for the

study of administration and supply of the army. Every volume of *PGW: Rev. War Ser.* contains letters on the problems of supplying the army.

15. Washington to John Hancock, Aug. 4–5, 1775, *PGW: Rev. War Ser.*, 1:227. The full letter is valuable: 1:223–30.

16. Washington to Hancock, July 10, 14, 21, 27, 1775, ibid., 1:83–92, 115–18, 136–44, 180–81.

17. Wright, *Continental Army*, 45–56.

18. Washington to Hancock, July 21, 1775, *PGW: Rev. War Ser.*, 1:139–40 quotations.

19. The growth of American resistance is traced in many studies. See, for example, Edmund S. and Helen M. Morgan, *The Stamp Act Crisis: Prologue to Revolution* (Chapel Hill: University of North Carolina Press, 1953).

20. Washington to Hancock, July 10, 1775, *PGW: Rev. War Ser.*, 1:73 quotations; 1:85–86 ("riding the lines").

21. On Gage, see John Shy, "Thomas Gage: Weak Link of Empire," in George Anthan Billias, ed., *George Washington's Generals and Opponents: Their Exploits and Leadership* (New York: De Capo Press, 1994, 2 vols.), 2:3–38; on William Howe, see Ira D. Gruber, *The Howe Brothers and the American Revolution* (New York: Atheneum, 1972), a superb book.

22. Generals Gage and Howe were often puzzled; their superiors in England sometimes gave in to panic.

23. On Benjamin Church, see Carl Van Doren, *Secret History of the American Revolution* (New York: Viking Press, 1951), 19–23.

24. Of Washington's most helpful observers, Joseph Leach, who reported through Lieutenant Colonel Loammi Baldwin, stands out. See *PGW: Rev. War Ser.*, 1:157–58 and passim.

25. Questions of this sort were most commonly raised in the councils of war, held with general officers.

26. For this paragraph and the one preceding it, see *PGW: Rev. War Ser.*, 1:432–34; quotations 433.

27. Ibid., 1:450–51. This was the generals' reply to his proposal.

28. Ibid., 2:29.

29. The best way to understand the attitudes and policies of Congress is to read the letters of delegates in Paul H. Smith et al., eds., *Letters of Delegates to Congress, 1774–1789* (Washington, D.C.: Library of Congress, 1976–2000, 26 vols.). See also Jack N. Rakove, *The Beginnings of National Politics: An Interpretive History of the Continental Congress* (New York: Random House, 1979).

30. *PGW: Rev. War Ser.*, 2:71–72. See also L. H. Butterfield, ed., *Diary and Autobiography of John Adams* (Cambridge, Mass.: Harvard University Press, 1961, 4 vols.), 2:117 (on Lynch); 120 (on Harrison).

31. For the "Proceedings of the Committee of Conference," see *PGW: Rev. War Ser.*, 2:185–203; and Leonard W. Labaree et al., eds., *The Papers of Benjamin Franklin* (New Haven, Conn.: Yale University Press, 1959– , 41 vols. to date), 22:225–41. Franklin wrote Richard Bache on Oct. 24, "Here is a fine healthy Army, wanting nothing but some Improvement in its Officers, which is daily making," 22:242. The letters of Christopher French on Sept. 18, Oct. 9, and Nov. 13, 1775, *PGW: Rev. War Ser.*, 2:9–10, 130–32, 362–63, provided the moment of humor mentioned in the paragraph above.

32. Washington to Brigadier General Joseph Spencer, Sept. 26, 1775, *PGW: Rev. War Ser.*, 2:55–56 for "subordination" and "discipline."
33. Lynch's letter and quotations, ibid., 2:366–67, for this paragraph and the one above.
34. For the Articles of War, see *PGW: Rev. War Ser.*, 1:44–46n3 and passim. The Articles in full appear in Worthington Chauncey Ford et al., eds., *Journals of the Continental Congress, 1774–1779* (Washington, D.C.: United States Government Printing Office, 1904–37), 2:90, 111–23.
35. *PGW: Rev. War Ser.*, 2:235–36 quotations.
36. Ibid., 2:236 quotation.
37. Ibid., 2:247, 261, 268–70.
38. Washington to Joseph Reed, Jan. 14, 1776; to Nicholas Cooke, Jan. 16. 1776; and Council of War, Feb. 16, 1776; ibid., 3:87–89, 104–5, 320–22.
39. Washington to John Hancock, Feb. 9, 1776, ibid., 3:274–77; quotation 274. The opinions of Washington's generals were expressed in "Council of War, 16 Feb. 1776." See ibid., 3:320–24.
40. Ibid., 3:335, 336 for both quotations.
41. Washington to Reed, Jan. 14, Feb. 10, and Feb. 26, 1776, ibid., 3:90, 288–89, 370, quotations. The letters in full, ibid., 3:87–91, 286–90, 369–76.
42. *PGW: Rev. War Ser.*, 3:370 quotation.
43. Christopher Ward, *War of the Revolution* (New York: Macmillan, 1952, 2 vols.), 1:117–26 offers a helpful review of the run-up to the end of the siege.
44. *PGW: Rev. War Ser.*, 3:372.
45. Ward, *War of the Revolution*, 1:126–27.
46. For this paragraph and the five above it, see ibid. and *PGW: Rev. War Ser.*, 3:369–76, Washington's account of Feb. 26–Mar. 9, 1776, to Lt. Col. Joseph Reed. His General Orders, Feb. 27, 1776, ibid., 3:379–80, are also informative.
47. Washington notified President John Hancock of the sailing of the British fleet on Mar. 27, 1776. Ibid., 3:548–49.

5 NEW YORK

1. William H. Guthman, ed., *The Correspondence of Captain Nathan and Lois Peters, April 25, 1775–February 5, 1777* (Hartford: Connecticut Historical Society, 1980), 36.
2. Washington to Joseph Reed, Apr. 1, 1776, and to Charles Lee, May 9, 1776, quotations, *PGW: Rev. War Ser.*, 4:10 (on Frye), 4:245 (on Ward).
3. The bitterness in Washington's comments on Frye and Ward was unusual; he ordinarily displayed a great deal of patience in his assessments of his generals.
4. For Charles Lee, see John Shy's essay in George Anthan Billias, ed., *George Washington's Generals and Opponents: Their Exploits and Leadership* (New York: De Capo Press, 1994, 2 vols.), 1:22–53.
5. For Washington's first plans for Arnold's Canadian campaign, see Washington to Schuyler, Aug. 20, 1775, *PGW: Rev. War Ser.*, 1:332, 333n6, and 406.
6. Pauline Maier, *American Scripture: Making the Declaration of Independence* (New York: Alfred A. Knopf, 1997), 155–56.
7. Ira Gruber, *The Howe Brothers and the American Revolution* (New York: Norton, 1972), 91–105.

8. Henry Steele Commager and Richard B. Morris, eds., *The Spirit of 'Seventy Six: The Story of the American Revolution as Told by Participants* (New York: Harper and Row, 1975), 132, 134.

9. Christopher Ward, *War of the Revolution* (New York: Macmillan, 1952, 2 vols.), 1:211–12.

10. Ibid., 1:212–13.

11. *PGW: Rev. War Ser.,* 6:126–27.

12. Ward, *War of the Revolution,* 1:216–18.

13. Freeman, 4:153–75; Robert Harrison to John Hancock, Aug. 27, 1776, *PGW: Rev. War Ser.,* 6:140–44, 155–56; Ward, *War of the Revolution,* 1:225–26.

14. Ward, *War of the Revolution,* 1:231–32.

15. *PGW: Rev. War Ser.,* 6:153–54.

16. Washington to John Hancock, Sept. 2, 1776, ibid., 6:199–201, quotation 199.

17. Ibid., 6:199.

18. Ibid., 6:394, 396 quotations. The entire letter reveals Washington's convictions about militia and ordinary enlisted men as clearly as anything he ever wrote. He makes a powerful argument for a standing army. See 6:393–400.

19. Ibid., 6:396.

20. Ibid., 6:398–400 and note 2 on 400–1.

21. See General Orders, Sept. 3, 4, 5, 6, 8, 11, ibid., 6:204–5, 212–13, 221, 229, 244, 277, for Washington's concern about plundering and unit discipline.

22. Washington to John Hancock, Sept. 16, 1776, ibid., 6:313. Quotation appears in Washington's account of the British landing at Kips Bay. See also the notes to the letter and quotations from other sources there.

23. Ward, *War of the Revolution,* 1:238–45.

24. Ibid., 1:246–52. See Allen French, ed., *Diary of Frederick Mackenzie: Giving a Daily Narrative of His Military Service . . .* (Cambridge, Mass.: Harvard University Press, 1930, 2 vols.), 1:47–48.

25. Ward, *War of the Revolution,* 1:253–59; Robert Harrison to John Hancock, Oct. 20, 1776, *PGW: Rev. War Ser.,* 6:592–94.

26. Ward, *War of the Revolution,* 1:260–66, for this paragraph and the one preceding.

27. Washington to Nathanael Greene, Nov. 8, 1776, *PGW: Rev. War Ser.,* 7:116; the whole letter, 7:115–17, is valuable for discovering Washington's thought. General Nathanael Greene's correspondence with Col. Magaw sheds some light on the loss of the fort. Richard Showman, ed., *The Papers of Nathanael Greene* (Chapel Hill: University of North Carolina Press, 1976–2005, 12 vols.).

28. Ward, *War of the Revolution,* 1:267–74; *PGW: Rev. War Ser.,* 7:162–69 and notes 1–9. Greene's biographer, Terry Golway, in his *Washington's General: Nathanael Greene and the Triumph of the American Revolution* (New York: Henry Holt, 2005), 102, writes that the defeat "was, to a large extent, Nathanael Greene's fault."

29. Washington's retreat to Trenton, where he crossed the Delaware into Pennsylvania, can be followed in his and others' letters, *PGW: Rev. War Ser.,* 7:193–275, and in Ward, *War of the Revolution,* 1:275–90.

30. Charles Lee to Washington, Nov. 19, 1776, *PGW: Rev. War Ser.,* 7:187.

31. Lee to Washington, Nov. 30, 1776, ibid., 7:235.

32. Washington to Joseph Reed, Nov. 30, 1776, ibid., 7:237n1.

33. Ibid., 7:238n1, a continuation of Reed's letter found in note 1.

34. George Washington to Samuel Washington, Dec. 18, 1776, ibid., 7:370–71.
35. Ward, *War of the Revolution,* 1:285–90.
36. George Washington to Samuel Washington, Dec. 18, 1776, *PGW: Rev. War Ser.,* 7:369–72.
37. David Hackett Fischer, *Washington's Crossing* (New York: Oxford University Press, 2004), 182–203, an especially astute account.
38. Ibid., 206–33.
39. Ibid., 234–345.

6 THE PHILADELPHIA CAMPAIGN

1. Robert J. Taylor, ed., *Papers of John Adams* (Cambridge, Mass.: Harvard University Press, 1963– , 17 vols. to date), 5:95.
2. Marcus Cunliffe, *George Washington: Man and Monument* (New York: Little, Brown, 1958), 81–82.
3. Bartholomew Dandridge to Washington, Jan. 16, 1777, *PGW: Rev. War Ser.,* 8:79–80 quotations.
4. Washington to Jonathan Trumbull Sr., Jan. 10, 1777; to Philip Schuyler, Jan. 18, 1777; to John Parke Custis, Jan. 22, 1777; ibid., 8:38, 99, 123 quotations.
5. Joseph Reed to Washington, Dec. 22, 1776, ibid., 7:414–16.
6. Washington to Jonathan Trumbull Sr., Dec. 12, 1776; to John Hancock, Dec. 13, 1776; ibid., 7:321–22, 324–25.
7. Washington to John Hancock, Jan. 22, 1777, ibid., 8:125–26; David Hackett Fischer, *Washington's Crossing* (New York: Oxford University Press, 2004), 346–62.
8. For an example of Washington's willingness to add certain benefits for service in both regular and militia units, see *PGW: Rev. War Ser.,* 8:57 and note 1.
9. Washington also advised recruiters (always officers) to pay only a part of a bonus promised to new soldiers, with the remaining part withheld until the recruit was in camp.
10. For the new regiments authorized by Congress in December 1776, see *PGW: Rev. War Ser.,* 8:39n; for recruiting instructions with information on inducements, Jan. 12[–27], 1777, see 8:44–45.
11. Ibid., 8:44 ("free from Lameness or other bodily Infirmity"). For the complete instructions, 8:44–45n2.
12. This paragraph and the one immediately above: for quotations, Samuel Webb to Washington ("over & above"), Jan. 22, 1777, ibid., 8:132; Washington to Jonathan Trumbull Sr. ("most extravagantly"), Mar. 3, 1777, 8:505; William Heath to Washington ("Uneasy"), Mar. 16, 1777, 8:587.
13. Washington to William Shippen Jr., Jan. 28, 1777; to Horatio Gates, Feb. 5–6, 1777; to Nicholas Cooke, Feb. 10, 1777, ibid., 8:174, 248, 296–97, passim. See also Elizabeth A. Fenn, *Pox Americana: The Great Smallpox Epidemic of 1775–82* (New York: Hill and Wang, 2001).
14. The complications and problems of recruiting are revealed in many of the letters to and from Washington. See, e.g., Washington to Mass. Council, Feb. 1, 1777; to Jonathan Trumbull Sr., Feb. 1, 1777; to Henry Knox, Feb. 11, 1777, *PGW: Rev. War Ser.,* 8:218–19, 220–21, 307–8.
15. Washington to William Livingston, Apr. 1, 1777; to Nicholas Cooke, Apr. 3,

1777; to John Hancock, Apr. 12, 1777; Brig. Gen. Samuel H. Parsons to Washington, Apr. 15, 1777, ibid., 9:40–43, 52–53, 128–29 (especially important), 172–75. Washington to Continental Congress Committee . . . State of the Army, July 19, 1777, 10:332–36.

16. On the creation of departments, Robert K. Wright Jr., *The Continental Army* (Washington, D.C.: Center of Military History, U.S. Army, 1983), 26, 29–32, 36; Taylor, ed., *Papers of John Adams,* 3:100.

17. Washington to William Heath, Apr. 10, 1777; Samuel H. Parsons to Washington, Feb. 23, 1777; *PGW: Rev. War Ser.,* 9:116–17, 8:430-431 and note 1.

18. Ibid., 7:404n3

19. These conclusions are based on many letters of the leaders and the books by Willcox, Mackesy, Ward, and Gruber cited in these notes.

20. Ira D. Gruber, *The Howe Brothers and the American Revolution* (New York: Atheneum, 1972), 193.

21. Ibid., 187–88, 233–40, for this paragraph and the one following.

22. Washington to James Warren, May 23, 1777, *PGW: Rev. War Ser.,* 9:512, for quotation ("wretched policy").

23. Ibid., 9:571. For Howe's movements of his army, ibid., 10:11–12, 149–50.

24. Washington to John Augustine Washington, June 29, 1777, ibid., 10:149–50.

25. Ibid., 10:150.

26. Anthony Wayne to Washington, Sept. 2, 1777, ibid., 11:131–32.

27. This account of the battle at Brandywine is based on ibid., 11:187–95. See also Christopher Ward, *War of the Revolution* (New York: Macmillan, 1952, 2 vols.), 1:341–55.

28. Washington to John Hancock, Sept. 11, 1777, *PGW: Rev. War Ser.,* 11:200–1 quotations.

29. Ibid., 11:248–49n2.

30. General Orders, Sept. 16, 1777, ibid., 11:243n–44, 253.

31. For this paragraph and the one preceding it, Washington to John Hancock, Sept. 18, 1777; Council of War, Sept. 23, 1777; ibid., 11:262–63, 294–98, passim.

32. General Orders, Oct. 3, 1777, ibid., 11:373.

33. Ibid.

34. For the Battle of Germantown, ibid., 11:373–402.

35. Ward, *War of the Revolution,* 1:365.

36. Ibid., 1:369. For the operations in Pennsylvania, see also Thomas J. McGuire, *The Philadelphia Campaign: Germantown and the Roads to Valley Forge* (Mechanicsburg, Pa.: Stackpolebooks, 2007) and Stephen R. Tauffe, *The Philadelphia Campaign, 1777–1778* (Lawrence: University Press of Kansas, 2003), both fine books.

7 VALLEY FORGE

1. *PGW: Rev. War Ser.,* 11:592n2. See also Johann Ewald, *Diary of the American War: A Hessian Journal,* trans. and ed. Joseph P. Tustin (New Haven, Conn., and London: Yale University Press, 1979), 97–102.

2. *PGW: Rev. War Ser.,* 11:585n2.

3. Hazelwood to Washington, Nov. 15, 1777; James Varnum to Washington, Nov. 16, 1777; Washington to New Jersey Militias, Nov. 20, 1777; ibid., 12:268–69,

283–84 (Fort Mifflin); 333–34 (Fort Mercer). See also Christopher Ward, *War of the Revolution* (New York: Macmillan, 1952, 2 vols.), 1:372–77.

4. Anthony Wayne to Washington, Nov. 25, 1777, *PGW: Rev. War Ser.,* 12:380; 403 quotations. See also 12:371–73, 391–403 for the recommendations of other generals.

5. Washington to Richard Henry Lee, Oct. 28, 1777, ibid., 12:41–42 and note 5. Mifflin's resignation as quartermaster general was accepted by Congress on Nov. 7, 1777.

6. Joseph Trumbull to Washington, June 15, July 19, Aug. 12, 1777, ibid., 10:46–47, 342–43, 594–95; Washington to John Hancock, July 2, 1777, 10:169. See also E. Wayne Carp's *To Starve the Army at Pleasure* (Chapel Hill and London: University of North Carolina Press, 1984), 42–43.

7. Henry Laurens to Washington, Nov. 13, 1777, *PGW: Rev. War Ser.,* 12:244–47.

8. Henry Laurens to Washington, Dec. 12, 1777, ibid., 12:599–600n1.

9. Ibid., 12:599n1 quotations.

10. Ibid., 12:606 quotations.

11. Ibid.

12. Ibid., 12:606.

13. Henry Laurens wrote Washington Dec. 20, 1777, on the remonstrance of the Pennsylvania Council and Assembly about the winter quarters of the army. See ibid., 12:651–52.

14. Ibid., 12:21; 27 quotation.

15. Washington to Horatio Gates, Oct. 30, 1777, ibid., 12:59–60.

16. Alexander Hamilton to Washington, Nov. 6, 1777, ibid., 12:141 quotation; Horatio Gates to Washington, Nov. 7, 1777, 12:155n8 quotation.

17. Major General Stirling to Washington, Nov. 3, 1777, *PGW: Rev. War Ser.,* 12:111n4.

18. Conway, born in Ireland in 1733. Educated in France, he began serving in the French army when he was fourteen. By 1772 he was a colonel. He crossed the Atlantic in spring 1777, recommended by the American diplomat Silas Deane. Congress took Deane's recommendation seriously and made Conway a brigadier general.

19. Thomas Conway to Washington, Dec. 31, 1777, and Jan. 10 and 27, 1778, *PGW: Rev. War Ser.,* 13:78, 195–96, 359–60.

20. Henry Laurens wrote Washington on April 28, 1778, of Conway's resignation. See ibid., 14:669.

21. Ibid., 12:470n3, 588. This committee, consisting of Robert Morris, Elbridge Gerry, and Joseph Jones, visited the army on Dec. 3, 1777; the next day its work was interrupted by Howe's army, which seemed ready to attack. The committee reported its findings to Washington on Dec. 10, a report primarily for Congress that declared against an attack on Philadelphia by Washington. In January 1778, a second camp committee of Congress began its work on the reorganization of the army; it continued its study in March.

22. For the background of the decision to move the army to Valley Forge, see Wayne Bodle, *The Valley Forge Winter: Civilians and Soldiers in War* (University Park, Pa.: Penn State University Press, 2002), 15–71. For the "Order of March" to Valley Forge, Dec. 10, 1777, see *PGW: Rev. War Ser.,* 12:585–87.

23. Washington to Anthony Wayne, Dec. 27, 1777; General Orders, Jan. 6, 1778; *PGW: Rev. War Ser.,* 13:26, 158–59.

24. Ibid., 13:435n1–436, on Martha Washington's visit to Valley Forge.
25. Bodle, *Valley Forge,* provides an assessment of life at that winter camp. See also the section given to it in Henry Steele Commager and Richard B. Morris, eds., *The Spirit of 'Seventy Six: The Story of the American Revolution as Told by Participants* (New York: Harper and Row, 1975), 637–50.
26. Proclamation on Threshing Grain, Dec. 20, 1777, *PGW: Rev. War Ser.,* 12:655; see 12:655 note.
27. Washington to Henry Laurens, Dec. 23, 1777, ibid., 12:683–87 and notes.
28. Circular to the States, ibid., 13:36–39.
29. Nathanael Greene to Washington ("like Pharoh"), Feb. 15, 1778, ibid., 13:546.
30. Henry Lee to Washington ("drain"), Feb. 19, 1778; Greene to Washington ("gleaned"), Feb. 20, 1778; ibid., 13:599, 607.
31. Washington to Laurens, Dec. 23, 1777, ibid., 12:683 quotation.
32. Washington to Laurens, Mar. 24, 1778, ibid., 14:293 quotation.
33. Bodle, *Valley Forge,* 57.
34. For the plan of reorganization, Jan. 29, 1778, see *PGW: Rev. War Ser.,* 13:376–409. The discussion below is based on this plan.
35. Washington to Brig. Gen. John Thomas, July 23, 1775, *PGW: Rev. War Ser.,* 1:160 quotation.
36. Ibid., 1:160 quotation. For the entire letter, 1:159–62.
37. Washington to Continental Congress Camp Committee, Jan. 29, 1778, ibid., 13:377 quotations.
38. Ibid., 13:377, an argument about human nature and officers, which he repeated to John Bannister, Apr. 21, 1778, 14:573–79.
39. For all these matters of policy, see William B. Willcox, *Portrait of a General: Sir Henry Clinton in the War of Independence* (New York: Alfred A. Knopf, 1964), 169–231; Piers Mackesy, *The War for America, 1775–1783* (Cambridge, Mass.: Harvard University Press, 1964), 180–86.
40. For the background of the Battle of Monmouth Court House and its course, see Willcox, *Portrait,* 233–37; or Franklin and Mary Wickwire, *Cornwallis: The American Adventure* (Boston: Houghton Mifflin, 1970), 109–13. The best American account is in *PGW: Rev. War Ser.,* 15:531–601. These pages include the movement of American units before and after the battle. The heart of the fighting is explained best in pages 573–76. General Charles Lee's performance can be followed in the account of the battle. Lee's conflict with Washington and his later career are on display in *The Lee Papers* (New York: 1872–1875, 4 vols.).

8 CITIZEN OF THE WORLD

1. My analysis of Sir Henry Clinton owes much to the brilliant biography by William B. Willcox, *Portrait of a General: Sir Henry Clinton in the War of Independence* (New York: Alfred A. Knopf, 1964). There are shrewd appraisals of Clinton throughout. See especially the final chapter, 492–524.
2. Ibid., 211–25.
3. Ibid., especially 213–23. See also Piers Mackesy, *The War for America, 1775–1783* (Cambridge, Mass.: Harvard University Press, 1964), 225–32.
4. Willcox, *Portrait,* 225–32; *PGW: Rev. War Ser.,* 16:38 quotation.
5. Alexander Hamilton to Washington, July 20, 1778, *PGW: Rev. War Ser.,* 16:109;

Washington to John Sullivan, July 22, 1778, 16:133; Washington to Lafayette, Aug. 19, 1778, 16:329–30; Washington to Nathanael Greene, Aug. 21, 1778, 16:343–44; John Sullivan to Washington, Aug. 23, 1778, 16:358–59 notes; John Sullivan to Washington, Aug. 29, 1778, 16:418–19 notes. These letters contain information about the French inability to cross the bar into New York Harbor, the planning for the Rhode Island expedition and its failure, including the disputes concerning responsibility. See also Christopher Ward, *War of the Revolution* (New York: Macmillan, 1952, 2 vols.), 2:587–95. Greene's praise of Col. John Laurens appears in Washington to Henry Laurence, *PGW: Rev. War Ser.*, 16:555 (quoting from Green's letter of Aug. 28–31). For d'Estaing, see Jonathan R. Dull, *The French Navy and American Independence: A Study of Arms and Diplomacy, 1774–1787* (Princeton, N.J.: Princeton University Press, 1975).

6. *PGW: Rev. War Ser.*, 16:360n2–361 quotation.
7. To Washington, Sept. 5, 1778, ibid., 16:523.
8. To d'Estaing, Sept. 11–12, 1778, ibid., 16:570.
9. Ibid., 16:571–73.
10. Washington to Nathanael Greene, Sept. 1, 1778, ibid., 16:459 quotation.
11. Ibid., 16:461 quotations.
12. To John Sullivan, Sept. 1, 1778, ibid., 16:464–65, all quotations in this paragraph.
13. Ibid., 16:154 quotation. Washington's concerns about the flood of foreign officers, recommended and often appointed by Congress, are clear in his letters to Henry Laurens, July 24, 1778, and to Gouverneur Morris, same date, ibid., 16:150–53, 153–55. See Laurens's reply to Washington, July 31, 1778, ibid., 16:208–12 and notes.
14. Washington to Gouverneur Morris, July 24, 1778, ibid., 16:154 quotations and the La Neuville case.
15. To Gouverneur Morris, July 24, 1778, ibid., 16:155 quotation, one of the uncommon instances of rhetorical extravagance from Washington's pen.
16. Ibid., 16:151.
17. *PGW: Col. Ser.*, 10:125.
18. Ibid., 10:155.
19. Robert K. Wright Jr., *The Continental Army* (Washington, D.C.: Center of Military History, U.S. Army, 1983), 149, 227.
20. For a sample of recruiting woes, see John Banister to Washington, Apr. 16, 1778, *PGW: Rev. War Ser.*, 14:531–32. For similar accounts, ibid., 16:445–46, 517–18, 558.
21. Washington was not primarily concerned with his own personal finances during the Revolution, though his letters to Lund were increasingly sharp. His sympathy for his army—officers and men—who were hit hard by the depreciation of currency was constant. He wrote Gouverneur Morris, Oct. 4, 1778, "what officer can bear the weight of prices, that every necessary article is now got to? A Rat, in the shape of a Horse, is not to be bought at this time for less than £200,—A saddle under Thirty or forty—Boots twenty—and Shoes and other articles in like proportion!" He cautioned John Parke Custis on Oct. 12, 1778, not "to turn Lands etc into Cash" at this time, likening such action to a "Lottery." Ibid., 17:253, 351–54; quotation 353.
22. *PGW: Rev. War Ser.*, 17:47–48, Washington wrote Admiral d'Estaing on Sept. 19 that the British in New York were taking the linings out of "soldiers coats," evidence that they would send a body of troops to the West Indies. There was further evidence coming to Washington in October and November, ibid., 17:591–

95. Washington believed by October that the British would remain in New York. For additional accounts, see Willcox, *Portrait.*
23. John Sullivan to Washington, Sept. 4, 1778, *PGW: Rev. War Ser.,* 16:520–21. See ibid., 17:254–55, note 4, for the memo sent to Congress.
24. To Gouverneur Morris, Oct. 4, 1778, ibid., 17:253–55, and passim.
25. Mackesy, *War for America,* 159–61, 186–89; Willcox, *Portrait,* 220–23, 229–30, 241–42, 255.
26. Willcox, *Portrait,* 253.
27. Circular to Seven General Officers, Feb. 14, 1778; Council of War, Oct. 16, 1778; *PGW: Rev. War Ser.,* 17:373, 399–402.
28. Ibid., 17:626–27, for an example of Washington's response to Nathanael Greene's advice.
29. Willcox, *Portrait,* 216–18.
30. To John Sullivan ("mysterious"), Sept. 12, 1778, *PGW: Rev. War Ser.,* 16:592 quotation.
31. Willcox, *Portrait,* 271–75.
32. Ibid., 277–78.
33. Ibid., 278–79; Ward, *War of the Revolution,* 2:596–603; *PGW: Rev. War Ser.,* 19:692–693n3.
34. Ward, *War of the Revolution,* 2:604–10.
35. On Charles Lee, see *The Lee Papers* (New York: 1872–1875, 4 vols.). The account most favorable to Lee is John Shy's essay in George Anthan Billias, ed., *George Washington's Generals and Opponents: Their Exploits and Leadership* (New York: De Capo Press, 1994, 2 vols.), 1:22–53.
36. Don Higginbotham, *The War of American Independence: Military Attitudes, Policies, and Practice, 1763–1789* (Bloomington, Ind., and London: Macmillan, 1971), 328–29. See also Washington to John Sullivan, May 4, 8, 11, 13, 19, 24, and 31, 1779, *PGW: Rev. War Ser.,* 20:325–26, 399–400, 444, 476, 543–44, 589–91, 606–7, 716–23.
37. Ward, *War of the Revolution,* 2:638–45.

9 WEARY BUT RESOLUTE

1. To Benjamin Harrison, Oct. 25, 1779; to Jack Custis, Nov. 10, 1779; to Edmund Pendleton, Nov. 1, 1779; John C. Fitzpatrick, ed., *The Writings of George Washington from the Original Manuscript Sources* (Charlottesville: University of Virginia Press, 1931–1944, 39 vols.), 17:20, 91, 52.
2. Order of Troop Cantonment, ibid., 17:210–11.
3. Ibid., 17:423 quotation. There is an excellent account of the difficulties of living with Mrs. Ford in Flexner, 2:358.
4. Not much is known about Captain Gibbs, who joined the headquarters officers group in 1777. He was a New Englander.
5. For concern about recruitment and specific problems in states, see Washington to President of Congress, Mar. 18, 1780; Fitzpatrick, ed., *Writings,* 17:169–71.
6. To William Heath, Feb. 1, 1780, ibid., 17:474 quotation and substance of the three paragraphs above.
7. To William Irvine, Jan. 9, 1780, ibid., 17:368–69 quotation.

8. To President of Congress, Jan. 27, 1780, ibid., 17:449 quotation and substance.

9. To Robert Howe, Mar. 11, 1780, ibid., 18:105. For the number of British troops, see William B. Willcox, *Portrait of a General: Sir Henry Clinton in the War of Independence* (New York: Alfred A. Knopf, 1964), 301.

10. For the study of British secret and spying operations, the starting point is Carl Van Doren, *Secret History of the American Revolution* (New York: Viking Press, 1951). Washington's efforts are revealed in letters scattered throughout *PGW: Rev. War Ser.*

11. Washington reviewed the British campaign in a letter to Benjamin Harrison, Oct. 25, 1779, Fitzpatrick, ed., *Writings,* 17:21. He drew information from a broad array of sources, including the *Pennsylvania Gazette,* travelers' accounts, and the reports of a variety of observers. His conclusion about frequent British movements up and down the Hudson River: "There is something unaccountable in all this that cannot be reconciled with 'any principle of common sense.'" The reports of spies dealt with smaller matters—the size of enemy units, their health, ship movements, and enemy plans for action.

12. Willcox, *Portrait,* 260–78.

13. Ibid., 311.

14. To President of Congress, June 18, 1780, Fitzpatrick, ed., *Writings,* 19:26.

15. Ibid., 19:27.

16. To Joseph Reed, June 19, 1780, ibid., 19:32–33. (Washington wrote the Committee on Cooperation the same day.)

17. To Gov. William Livingston, June 18, 1780, ibid., 19:28.

18. To Fielding Lewis, May 5 [–July 6], 1780, ibid., 19:130–33.

19. Quoted in Flexner, 2:365.

20. Washington expressed his dismay at Ternay's refusal to enter New York Harbor in a letter to Lafayette, July 22, 1780, Fitzpatrick, ed., *Writings,* 19:236.

21. To de Guichen, Sept. 20, 1780, ibid., 20:39–41.

22. Quoted in Flexner, 2:371.

23. Conference at Hartford, Sept. 22, 1780, Fitzpatrick, ed., *Writings,* 20:76.

24. Ibid.

25. The minutes of the meeting are short; Washington's hopes are clear in these brief records, ibid., 20:76–80.

26. For the Arnold-André conspiracy and its details, see ibid., 20, as the facts of the case are scattered. There are two excellent books on the entire affair: Van Doren, *Secret History,* 140–422, with an appendix that includes at least a part of the correspondence of Arnold and André, 439–81, and a narrative by General Clinton that also contains letters by Washington, André, Arnold, and others. A more recent book, James Thomas Flexner, *The Traitor and the Spy* (Boston: Little, Brown, 1953) is based on an even larger number of documents. Hamilton's comment that the episode was of the "blackest treason" is in Harold C. Syrett, ed., *Papers of Alexander Hamilton* (New York: Columbia University Press, 1961–1979, 26 vols.), 2:440.

27. The fullest account of the scene in which Washington and other officers visited Peggy Arnold in her bedroom is in Van Doren, *Secret History,* 346–49. Hamilton's letter of the same day to Elizabeth Schuyler is also valuable; Syrett, ed., *Papers of Alexander Hamilton,* 2:441–42.

28. Hamilton to Greene, Sept. 25, 1780, Syrett, ed., *Papers of Alexander Hamilton,* 2:440–41.

29. No full record of André's trial was kept, but for what is known of the trial and his final days, see Van Doren, *Secret History,* 355–71.
30. The basis of this paragraph and indeed of my account of André's action is Van Doren's *Secret History;* quotations 342; quotation in the paragraph following, ibid., 360.
31. To John Cadwalader, Oct. 5, 1780, Fitzpartrick, ed., *Writings,* 20:122.
32. Washington to Fielding Lewis, May 5 [–July 6], 1780, ibid., 19:132.
33. Ibid.
34. To John Cadwalader, Oct. 5, 1780, ibid., 20:122 quotations; full letter, 20:121–23.
35. Ibid., 20:122. (Washington found the expectations of some that the British would give up the American war "delusionary.") He made this point to others; for example, in a letter to Fielding Lewis on July 6, 1780, 19:133; and in a letter to the President of Congress, 19:403–9; quotations 19:406–7. Washington also made most of these comments around this time to a committee of Congress.
36. Writing to Henry Laurens on Aug. 20, 1780, Washington commented on Ireland. Quotation in preceding paragraph, ibid., 19:406–7; entire letter, 19:403–9. His account of European politics, with comments on monarchy, appears in several letters at this time. For the analysis of the kings of European countries, see Washington to President of Congress, Aug. 20, 1780, 20:407 and notes.
37. Washington to Fielding Lewis, ibid., 19:132. He expressed the same ideas elsewhere, e.g., to John Augustine Lewis, 19:134–37.

IO MUTINY AND RALLYING THE FRENCH

1. The story of the January mutiny can be reconstructed in part from Washington's correspondence, *PGW: Rev. War Ser.,* 21:55–68. But the best account, based on multiple sources, is Carl Van Doren, *Mutiny in January* (New York: Viking Press, 1943).
2. Clinton's problems with the navy and Germain over the Charleston campaign are discussed with much insight by William B. Willcox, *Portrait of a General: Sir Henry Clinton in the War of Independence* (New York: Alfred A. Knopf, 1964), 293–320. For the British logistical problems, see R. Arthur Bowler, *Logistics and the Failure of the British Army in America, 1775–1783* (Princeton, N.J.: Princeton University Press, 1975), especially chapters 3 and 4.
3. The French officers Washington dealt with most often in the war—the Comte d'Estaing, who held the ranks of both lieutenant general and vice admiral; the Comte de Rochambeau, a lieutenant general; and the Comte de Grasse—all cited their superiors in Paris as placing restrictions on them, always preventing them from operations favored by the Americans.
4. Howard C. Rice Jr., ed., *Travels in North America in the Years 1780, 1781, and 1782 by the Marquis de Chastellux* (Chapel Hill: University of North Carolina Press, 1963, 2 vols.), 1:105, 111, 113.
5. To Chastellux, July 19, 1781, Fitzpatrick, ed., *Writings,* 22:395.
6. For Rochambeau, see Arnold Whitridge, *Rochambeau* (New York: Macmillan, 1965).
7. Around Mar. 1, 1781, Washington received letters from Rochambeau and Admiral Destouches, who had replaced de Ternay, saying that they intended to send eleven hundred men to the Chesapeake, accompanied by the entire French fleet

at Newport. See George Washington to Lafayette, Mar. 1, 1781, Fitzpatrick, ed., *Writings*, 21:322.

8. There is an excellent account of the entertainment that vexed Washington in Flexner, 2:415–16.

9. Washington to Schuyler, Mar. 21, 1778; to Henry Laurens, Mar. 11, 1781; to Joseph Jones, Mar. 24, 1781; to William Fitzhugh, Mar. 25, 1781; to Lauzun and Rochambeau, Mar. 31, 1781; Fitzpatrick, ed., *Writings*, 21:361, 333, 373, 376, 396, 397.

10. Hamilton's earlier dealings with Horatio Gates can be followed in Washington to Hamilton, Oct. 30, 1777, and Hamilton to Washington, Nov. 10, 1777, *PGW: Rev. War Ser.*, 12:60–62, 191–94, and Harold C. Syrett, ed., *Papers of Alexander Hamilton* (New York: Columbia University Press, 1961–1979, 26 vols.), vol. 1.

11. Syrett, ed., *Papers of Alexander Hamilton*, 2:563–68, for the encounter and quotations. Ron Chernow, *Alexander Hamilton* (New York: Penguin, 2004), 151–53, provides a thoughtful account of this clash, and emphasizes Hamilton's willingness for a break.

12. Chernow's *Hamilton* is generally excellent on Washington's relations with his staff.

13. Washington to John Parke Custis, Feb. 28, 1781, Fitzpatrick, ed., *Writings*, 21:318 quotation.

14. Ibid., 21:320.

15. George Washington to Benjamin Harrison, Mar. 21, 1781, ibid., 21:341–42.

16. George Weedon to George Washington, Mar. 30, 1778, *PGW: Rev. War Ser.*, 14:362 quotation.

17. To John Laurens, Apr. 19, 1781, Fitzpatrick, ed., *Writings*, 21:439 quotation.

18. George Washington to Henry Laurens, May 1, 1781, ibid., 22:21. See also Washington to Major General Heath, Apr. 30, 1781, ibid., 22:58–59.

19. George Washington to Lauzun, May 23, 1781, ibid., 22:104–5.

20. Ibid., 22:103 quotation ("our object is New York").

21. Donald Jackson, ed., *The Diaries of George Washington* (Charlottesville: University of Virginia Press, 1976–1979, 6 vols.), 3:369–70.

22. Conference with the Comte de Rochambeau, Weathersfield, May 23, 1781, Fitzpatrick, ed., *Writings*, 22:105.

23. John Laurens to Washington, May 26, 1781, ibid., 22:116n76.

24. Conference with Rochambeau at Dobbs Ferry, July 19, 1781, ibid., 22:395. See also Jackson, ed., *Diaries*, 3:396–97, and his earlier letter to Rochambeau, June 13, ibid., 22:208.

25. Conference at Dobbs Ferry, July 19, 1781, Fitzpatrick, ed., *Writings*, 22:396n1.

26. Washington to de Grasse, July 21, 1781, ibid., 22:400–2.

27. Washington to the Comte de Barras, Aug., 15, 1781, ibid., 22:499.

28. Washington to Lafayette, Aug. 15, 1781, ibid., 22:501–2.

29. Washington to de Grasse, Aug. 17, 1781, ibid., 23:8–9.

30. Willcox, *Portrait*, 417–20; Jackson, ed., *Diaries*, 3:413n2.

31. Willcox, *Portrait*, 402.

32. Washington to Rochambeau, Aug. 19, 1781, Fitzpatrick, ed., *Writings*, 23:35–37, 82–83.

33. Washington to Lafayette, Sept. 2, 1781, ibid., 23:76–77.

34. Washington to Robert Morris, Aug. 17, 1781, ibid., 23:12, 89, 95; Baron Ludwig von Closen wrote in his journal that American troops from New York, New Jer-

sey, and Pennsylvania at Head of Elk "did not wish to continue their march or embark unless they received part of their backpay." When Rochambeau was told of this, he gave Washington fifty thousand livres. Evelyn M. Acomb, trans. and ed., *The Revolutionary Journal of Baron Ludwig von Closen, 1780–1783* (Chapel Hill: University of North Carolina Press, 1958).

35. Jackson, ed., *Diaries*, 3:419 and note 1.
36. Washington to de Grasse, Fitzpatrick, ed., *Writings*, 23:93 quotation. Flexner gives a short account of the supper, 2:448.
37. Washington remarks briefly in his diary on his visit to de Grasse on the *Ville de Paris* off Cape Henry: "to my satisfaction except not obtaining an assurance of sending Ships above York and one that he could not continue his fleet on this Station longer than the first of November." Jackson, ed., *Diaries*, 3:420.
38. Fitzpatrick, ed., *Writings*, 23:132–33. The story of Washington's departure from the *Ville de Paris* is well told in Flexner, 2:449–50.
39. Washington to de Grasse, Sept. 25, 1781, Fitzpatrick, ed., *Writings*, 21:361, 333, 373, 376, 396, 397; 21:136–37. For de Grasse's letter of Sept. 23 to Washington and the reply to it, Fitpatrick, ed., *Writings*, 23:136n21.
40. For the quotations in the paragraph above, ibid., 23:137; for Washington's letter of Sept. 27, 1781, to de Grasse, praising him for promising to remain in Virginia, 23:143.

11 YORKTOWN

1. William B. Willcox, *Portrait of a General: Sir Henry Clinton in the War of Independence* (New York: Alfred A. Knopf, 1964), 386. An excellent account of Cornwallis and Guilford Courthouse is Franklin and Mary Wickwire, *Cornwallis: The American Adventure* (Boston: Houghton Mifflin, 1970), 274–310.
2. Willcox, *Portrait*, 268–69.
3. Ibid., 394 and note 8.
4. Ibid., 392–408.
5. Wickwire and Wickwire, *Cornwallis*, 354–64; Washington, General Orders, Sept. 30, 1781, Fitzpatrick, ed., *Writings*, 23:153–54.
6. Washington wrote accounts of the move of the Franco-American army to Yorktown from Williamsburg to Congress and general officers of the army. See Washington to Major General William Heath, Oct. 1, 1781, and to the President of Congress, Oct. 1, 1781, Fitzpatrick, ed., *Writings*, 23:157, 158–59. See also Edward G. Lengel, *General George Washington: A Military Life* (New York: Random House, 2005), 337–38.
7. Willcox, *Portrait*, 421–27. Wickwire and Wickwire, *Cornwallis*, 369–70.
8. For a valuable description of Yorktown and its setting, see Evelyn M. Acomb, trans. and ed., *The Revolutionary Journal of Baron Ludwig von Closen, 1780–1783* (Chapel Hill: University of North Carolina Press, 1958), 140–41.
9. Wickwire and Wickwire, *Cornwallis*, 369–70.
10. Washington to Board of War, Sept. 28, 1781, Fitzpatrick, ed., *Writings*, 23:151.
11. General Orders, Sept. 29, 30, 1781, ibid., 23:153–54.
12. "Regulations for the Service of the Siege," ibid., 23:179–85.
13. Ascomb, trans. and ed., *von Closen*, 143–46.

14. "Diary of Captain James Duncan," in William H. Egle, ed., *Pennsylvania Archives,* 2nd Ser. 15 (Harrisburg, Pa., 1890), 748.
15. Acomb, trans. and ed., *von Closen,* 146.
16. General Orders, October 11, 1781, Fitpatrick, ed., *Writings,* 23:206–7; Court-martial held on Oct. 2, 1781, reported in these General Orders.
17. Washington reported the opening of the first parallel to the President of Congress on Oct. 6 as the work began. Fitzpatrick, ed., *Writings,* 23:188.
18. Washington also kept de Grasse informed about the siege, writing him Oct. 11 and 16 of the opening of the second parallel and other progress. Fitzpatrick, ed., *Writings,* 23:209.
19. There are several accounts of the assaults on the redoubts. Fitzpatrick, ed., *Writings,* 23:227–28 to the President of Congress and de Grasse. See also Acomb, trans. and ed., *von Closen,* 148–49, and Hamilton to Lafayette, Oct. 15, 1781, Harold C. Syrett, ed., *Papers of Alexander Hamilton* (New York: Columbia University Press, 1961–1979, 26 vols.), 2:679-80. An old and excellent account by Henry B. Carrington, *Battles of the American Revolution* (New York: n.p., 1876), is reprinted in Syrett, ed., *Papers of Alexander Hamilton,* with Hamilton's letter.
20. Washington wrote Greene of the British attack in response to the raids of Oct. 14. See his letter of Oct. 16, 1781, Fitzpatrick, ed., *Writings,* 23:231.
21. On the negotiations for surrender of Cornwallis's army, see Washington to Cornwallis, Oct. 17 and 18, 1781, and to the President of Congress, Oct. 19, 1781, Fitzpatrick, ed., *Writings,* 23:236–38, 242. See also Acomb, trans. and ed., *von Closen,* 152–53; Wickwire and Wickwire, *Cornwallis,* 384–86; and Freeman, 5:378–91.
22. The ceremony has been described many times. Washington's note in his diary is less than a page. See Jackson, ed., *Diaries,* 430–31, and editor's account, 432n1.
23. North's despairing exclamation has been widely noted. See Andrew Jackson O'Shaughnessy, *The Men Who Lost America: British Leadership, the American Revolution, and the Fate of the Empire* (New Haven, Conn.: Yale University Press, 2013), 3.

12 THE WAR'S END

1. Fitzpatrick, ed., *Writings,* 23:284–85. Washington states his hopes for future actions against the British before he lays on the praise in these quotations.
2. Washington to de Grasse, Oct. 20, 1781, and de Grasse's reply of Oct. 23, 1781, ibid., 23:249, 250n59. Washington wrote again, Oct. 28, 1781, recommending operations against New York the following summer, ibid., 23:284–85, 286–87.
3. Even Ron Chernow, in his *Washington: A Life* (New York: Penguin, 2010), seems to suggest Washington may have had settling old scores in mind. Chernow's discussion of the New York "campaign" is far more subtle and thorough than this phrase hints.
4. It is only fair to say that most writers—military historians and biographers—believe that Washington was mistaken in his emphasis on taking New York.
5. Admiral Howe is a special case—his "failure" was as a commissioner charged with persuading the Americans to remain in the empire. Ira Gruber's fine biog-

raphy of Howe and his brother William gives a full account of his American experience. See *The Howe Brothers and the American Revolution* (New York: Athaneum, 1972).

6. Washington to Horatio Gates, Nov. 1, 1781, Fitzpatrick, ed., *Writings,* 23:315–16 quotations.

7. Washington to William Ramsey, John Fitzgerald . . . and Other Inhabitants of Alexandria, Nov. 19, 1781, ibid., 23:355–56; Washington to General Assembly of Maryland, Nov. 23, 1781, 23:358–59.

8. For Robert Morris, see Clarence L. Ver Steeg, *Robert Morris: Revolutionary Financier* (Philadelphia: University of Pennsylvania Press, 1954) and E. James Ferguson, *The Power of the Purse: A History of American Public Finance, 1776–1790* (Chapel Hill: University of North Carolina Press, 1961).

9. Washington wrote Lafayette Nov. 15, 1781, that if de Grasse, who had departed, could have stayed two months longer, "the allies could have achieved the total extirpation of the British force in the Carolinas and Georgia." Fitzpatrick, ed., *Writings,* 23:341.

10. Memorandum, Newburgh, May 1, 1782, ibid., 24:194–215. For the numerical estimates, 24:195.

11. Though Carleton's tone in his communications with Washington was different, Washington noted in a letter to Nathanael Greene that the "terms of conciliation that Carleton brings resembles those of 1780." Ibid., 24:276.

12. William Fowler Jr., *American Crisis: George Washington and the Dangerous Two Years After Yorktown, 1781–1783* (New York: Walker & Co., 2011), 48–52. John Brooke, *King George III* (New York: McGraw Hill, 1972), 219–22.

13. Jonathan R. Dull, *A Diplomatic History of the American Revolution* (New Haven, Conn.: Yale University Press, 1985), 137–63. See also Leonard W. Labaree et al., eds., *The Papers of Benjamin Franklin* (New Haven, Conn.: Yale University Press, 1959– , 40 vols. to date), 38:263–75, 382–88.

14. Articles of Confederation, Article 8. Fowler, *American Crisis,* 138–39.

15. See Washington to Joseph Jones, Dec. 14, 1782, in which he warns Jones of a letter from line officers stationed along the Hudson who express their grievances. Washington notes their hardships. Fitzpatrick, ed., *Writings,* 25:289.

16. Washington to Secretary at War, Benjamin Lincoln, Aug. 21, 1782, ibid., 25:50. See also letter of Oct. 2, 1782, 27:226–29.

17. Jack N. Rakove, *The Beginnings of National Politics* (New York: Alfred A. Knopf, 1979), 337–42.

18. Robert Morris is probably the least well known of this group. He was made superintendent of finance on June 27, 1781. The son of an English merchant who lived in Maryland, he was authorized to use five million dollars from French and Dutch loans and smaller sums from Pennsylvania. He persuaded Congress to charter the Bank of the United States in 1781. He was wealthy, having made money through his firm, Willing and Morris. He voted against the Declaration of Independence, but signed it.

19. Hamilton to Washington, Feb. 13, 1783, Harold C. Syrett, ed., *Papers of Alexander Hamilton* (New York: Columbia University Press, 1961–1979, 26 vols.), 3:253–54. Washington to Colonel Lewis Nicola, May 22, 1783, in answer to a document sent by Nicola in which he proposed that Washington should be given—or take—powers of government that only a monarch or dictator could

exercise. Washington replied in "great surprise and astonishment" and, after declaring his abhorrence of the proposal, forbade any repetition of it. Fitzpatrick, ed., *Writings*, 24:272–73.

20. Washington to Hamilton, Mar. 4, 1783, Syrett, ed., *Papers of Alexander Hamilton*, 3:277–79.

21. Ibid., 3:277.

22. Ibid., 3:286–88 and notes 1–9. For a solid account of the Newburgh affair, see Richard H. Kohn, *Eagle and Sword: The Federalists and the Creation of the Military Establishment in America, 1783–1802* (New York: Free Press, 1975), 17–39, and Fowler, *American Crisis*, 174–88.

23. Washington's thoughts in the crisis, as well as his actions at the critical moments of the affair, can best be followed in his letters to Joseph Jones of Mar. 12, 1783; to the President of Congress, Mar. 12, 1783; to Hamilton, Mar. 12, 1783; and to Benjamin Harrison, Mar. 19, 1783; and in his speech of Mar. 15, 1783; ibid., 26:213–16, 229–32, 216–17, 239–41.

24. The complete address to the officers, Mar. 15, 1783, is in Fitzpatrick, ed., *Writings*, 26:222–27. All quotations are from his speech. The report on Mar. 18 in the speech by Major J. A. Wright that Washington appeared "sensibly agitated" when he began is in ibid., 26:229–32n40. There are other letters in Syrett, ed., *Papers of Alexander Hamilton*, vols. 2 and 3, that are helpful.

25. Fowler, *American Crisis*, 129–30.

26. For the meeting with Carleton, May 6, 1783, Fitzpatrick, ed., *Writings*, 26:402–6.

27. The reference to Negroes in the Treaty of Peace is in Article 7. Washington wrote Theodorick Bland on Mar. 31, 1783, that he had not noticed the treaty article on blacks, and that he had not attempted to recover his own slaves who had run away to the British, ibid., 26:274.

28. Carleton's quotations, ibid., 26:404.

29. Washington to Benjamin Harrison, May 6, 1783, ibid., 26:401. See also Fowler, *American Crisis, 199–201*.

30. In a sample of Washington's attitudes in 1783, see his letter to James Duane, Sept. 7, 1783, Fitzpatrick, ed, *Writings*, 27:134–40; quotations 136–37, 140.

31. For these characterizations of whites, ibid., 27:133, 136–37.

32. Ibid., 27:137.

33. For a short account of the expedition against the Iroquois in 1779, led by General John Sullivan, see the essay by Charles P. Whittemore on Sullivan in George Anthan Billias, ed., *George Washington's Generals and Opponents: Their Exploits and Leadership* (New York: De Capo Press, 1994, 2 vols.), 1:137–62. Washington's letter of appointment of Sullivan, *PGW: Rev. War Ser.,* 19:388–89.

34. Washington wrote to members of Congress about pay and pensions for officers. A representative example is his letter to Theodorick Bland, Apr. 4, 1783, Fitzpatrick, ed., *Writings*, 26:285–91. This letter also contains his suggestion that Congress write an address of gratitude.

35. For this address in full, ibid., 27:222–27; quotation 223–24.

36. Ibid., 27:225–26, quotations this paragraph and the following one.

37. The account by Dr. Tilton of the public dinner (Dec. 23, 1783) in Washington's honor, ibid., 27:285n86. The ceremony at which he resigned receives fine treatment in Freeman, 5:472. There is a splendid short monograph on the entire

affair in Julian Boyd et al., eds., *The Papers of Thomas Jefferson* (Princeton, N.J.: Princeton University Press, 1950–, 40 vols. to date), 6:402–14, with the speeches by Washington and Mifflin.

38. Quotations from Washington's speech, ibid., 6:412; Mifflin's, 6:413.

EPILOGUE: RETURN TO VIRGINIA

1. Washington to Chastellux, Feb. 1, 1784, *PGW: Conf. Ser.*, 1:85; to Lafayette, Feb. 1, 1784, 1:87–88.
2. George Washington to Charles Washington, Feb. 28, 1784, ibid., 1:163.
3. George Washington to Bushrod Washington, Jan. 15, 1784, ibid., 1:48–49. See also note on 49.
4. For Corbin Washington, see ibid., 1:262; his placement with Tench Tilghman took a little more effort than Washington wished to make. See his letter to Robert Morris, June 2, 1784, 1:420–21, and Robert Morris to Washington, 1:450–52. John Augustine wrote George Washington July 8, 1784, 490–91. Washington eventually placed Corbin with Tench Tilghman. See G. Washington to Tilghman, July 14, 1784, 1:503–4.
5. Fielding Lewis Jr. wrote Washington on Feb. 22, 1784, who responded Feb. 27, 1784. See ibid., 1:145–46, 1:161–62.
6. Fielding Lewis's parents' comments are in ibid., 1:62n2.
7. Henry Knox to Washington, Jan., 3, 1784, ibid., 1:5–8, including notes. Quotations at 6.
8. For Humphries, see his letters of Jan. 6 and May 18, 1784, ibid., 1:13–15, 397–98. Washington's replies of Jan. 14 and Jun. 2, 1784, are on 1:40–41 and 1:416–18.
9. Walter Stewart to Washington, Jan. 26, 1784, ibid., 1:81–82. Washington's reply with the letter of recommendation Stewart requested, Feb. 5, 1784, 1:105–106n2. Stewart had been a colonel of the 2nd Pennsylvania Regiment in the war. In the final two years of the war, he was inspector of the Northern District and reported to Washington. Washington's letter to Stewart includes lighthearted joking that indicates that George and Martha Washington were on good terms with the Stewarts.
10. D'Estaing to Washington, Feb. 26, 1784, ibid., 1:158–60 and notes, quotations at 158, 159. For John Jones's letter of May 12, 1784, 1:379; Reuben Harvey's of May 25, 1784, 1:408–9.
11. John Davidson to Washington, Jan. 20, 1784, ibid., 1:61–63, quotation at 62n2.

A Note on the Sources

The principal source for this book is the modern edition of the *Papers of George Washington,* edited in Charlottsville, Virginia, and published by the University of Virginia Press. The two series most useful for me were the *Colonial Series,* containing ten volumes, and the *Revolutionary War Series,* which has reached twenty-one volumes as I write. These volumes contain Washington's correspondence, all the surviving letters written and received by him, and a great variety of other documents, including the army's general orders, reports, circulars of various sorts, and letters by and to others that bear on Washington's activities, and some financial passages, among others. The notes are extraordinarily full and help make the *Papers* a magnificent source.

The *Papers* are now at a midpoint of the Revolutionary War, and until they are finished scholars will have to consult John C. Fitzpatrick, ed., *Writings of George Washington* (Washington, D.C.: Government Printing Office, 1931–1939, 39 vols.). This collection offers a selected collection of Washington's correspondence but does not include (with some exceptions) letters to him. It is a fine work, and represents the Revolution, especially its second half, helpfully.

Washington's diaries have also been printed in a modern edition: Donald Jackson and Dorothy Twohig, eds., *The Diaries of George Washington* (Charlottesville: University of Virginia Press, 1976–1979, 6 vols.). Washington apparently stopped keeping a diary in the war, from the beginning of 1776 to the beginning of 1781. Though he did not reveal all that he thought and did in the years of diary keeping, he did record much that is useful to the study of his life.

I have found the modern editions of the papers of the other founders helpful in the study of Washington, though I have not cited them often in this book. Thomas Jefferson, John Adams, Benjamin Franklin, and Alexander Hamilton have all been served well in the modern editions. The collections of their works are still in progress, with the exception of Hamilton's.

SCHOLARSHIP

Books and essays on Washington and the Revolution are abundant. I cannot begin to mention them all, but I will list several that I especially admire for the insights and inspiration they provide.

BIOGRAPHIES: Douglas Southall Freeman, *George Washington: A Biography* (New York: Charles Scribner's Sons, 1948–1954, 6 vols.); James Thomas Flexner,

George Washington (Boston: Little, Brown, 1965–1972, 4 vols.); John Ferling, *The First of Men: A Life of George Washington* (Knoxville: University of Tennessee Press, 1988); Ron Chernow, *Washington: A Life* (New York: Penguin Press, 2010).

SPECIALIZED STUDIES AND ESSAYS: Joseph J. Ellis, *His Excellency: George Washington* (New York: Alfred A. Knopf, 2004); Edward C. Lengel, *General George Washington: A Military Life* (New York: Random House, 2005); Paul Longmore, *The Invention of George Washington* (Berkeley: University of California Press, 1988); Don Higgenbotham, *George Washington Reconsidered* (Charlottsville: University of Virginia Press, 2001). There are many essays of great merit, especially those by Higgenbotham, Bruce Ragsdale, Dorothy Twohig, W. W. Abbot, E. S. Morgan, and Gordon Wood. E. S. Morgan, ed., *The Meaning of Independence: John Adams, George Washington, and Thomas Jefferson* (Charlottesville: University of Virginia Press, 1976) expresses the judgments and insight of a great American historian.

Index

Page numbers beginning with 317 refer to endnotes.

ILLUSTRATION CREDITS

Surrender of Lord Cornwallis at Yorktown, Va. Oct. 19th, 1781: Courtesy of the
Library of Congress
Detail of Continental soldier in the background of a *Portrait of George Washington:*
Courtesy of the Colonial Williamsburg Foundation. Gift of John D. Rockefeller, Jr.
General Thomas Gage: Courtesy of Yale Center for British Art, Paul Mellon
Collection
Washington Rallying the Troops at Monmouth: Courtesy of University of California,
Berkeley Art Museum. Gift of Mrs. Mark Hopkins.
Portrait of Sir Henry Clinton: Courtesy of William L. Clements Library, University
of Michigan
John Laurens: Courtesy of Independence National Park
Friedrich Wilhelm Augustus, Baron von Steuben: Courtesy of Independence National
Park
General Nathanael Greene: Courtesy of Independence National Park
Jean-Baptiste Donatien de Vimeur, Comte de Rochambeau: Courtesy of Indepen-
dence National Park
George Washington Following the Battle of Princeton: Bequest of Jane J. Boudinot,
1927. Courtesy of Mount Vernon Ladies' Association.
General Sir William Howe: Courtesy of Anne S. K. Brown Military Collection,
Brown University Library
George Washington at Princeton: Courtesy of Pennsylvania Academy of Fine Arts.
Gift of Maria McKean Allen and Phebe Warren Downes through bequest of their
mother, Elizabeth Wharton McKean.

A NOTE ABOUT THE AUTHOR

Robert L. Middlekauff is Preston Hotchkis Professor of American History, Emeritus, at the University of California, Berkeley.

A NOTE ON THE TYPE

This book was set in Old Style No. 7, a font originally cut by the Edinburgh typefounders Miller & Richard in 1860.

Composed by North Market Street Graphics, Lancaster, Pennsylvania

Printed and bound by Berryville Graphics, Berryville, Virginia

Designed by M. Kristen Bearse